THE GUGGENHEIM MUSEUM COLLECTION: PAINTINGS 1880-1945

THE GUGGENHEIM MUSEUM COLLECTION

PAINTINGS 1880-1945

Volume II

by Angelica Zander Rudenstine

The Solomon R. Guggenheim Museum, New York

Published by
The Solomon R. Guggenheim Foundation
New York, 1976

International Standard Book Numbers
Complete Set—ISBN 0-89207-002-1
Volume I   ISBN 0-89207-003-x
Volume II   ISBN 0-89207-004-8

Library of Congress
Card Catalogue Number 75-37356

Published with the partial assistance of a
grant from The Ford Foundation, and supported by a grant from the National En-
dowment for the Arts in Washington, D.C.,
a Federal Agency.

CATALOGUE: NUMBERS 145-252

Dmitri Nikolaevich Kardovsky

Born 1866, Pereslavl'- Zalesskij (Vladimir Province, NW of Moscow).
Died 1943.

145   Portrait of Marya Anastasievna
        Chroustchova. 1900.

50.1289

Oil on canvas, 59¼ x 37⅜ (150.4 x 94.9)

Signed with monogram and dated l.r.: *DK / 1900*; inscribed on stretcher, not in the artist's hand (photographed before replacement of stretcher, but barely visible): *Herr F. Kardofsy—Elizabethplatz ¼.*

PROVENANCE:

Alexander de Chroustchoff, Munich, and Harrow-on-the-Hill, England, 1901-08;[1] purchased from Otto Stangl, Munich, 1950.[2]

CONDITION:

In 1957 the work was lined with wax resin and cleaned; some minor losses along the edges, a 1 x 4 in. area 5 in. from the left and 33 in. from the bottom, and some tiny losses in the face were inpainted with PBM; the work was surfaced with PBM and placed on a new stretcher. In 1961 a 4 in. damage 2½ in. from the bottom was repaired and inpainted.

There is slight wear at the edges, and some ground cracks (closed through the lining process) are visible in places, but the condition is otherwise excellent. (Aug. 1974.)

Biographical information about the sitter and her husband is fragmentary. According to their son, the late Boris Chroustchoff, who was in correspondence with J. J. Sweeney in 1959-60, his parents owned a large estate in southern Russia as well as a house in Munich and one in St. Prex near Geneva. Corroborating evidence for the existence of the latter is provided by Jawlensky, who in his memoirs speaks of going to St. Prex at the outbreak of the First World War precisely because his friend "de Chrustchoff" had an estate there, and he adds that *"Frau Chrustchoff half uns, in St. Prex ein kleines Häuschen zu mieten"* (A. Jawlensky, "Lebenserinnerungen," in C. Weiler, *Jawlensky, Köpfe, Gesichte, Meditationen,* Hanau, 1970, p. 116, trans., London, 1971, p. 101).

Boris Chroustchoff adds that his father was "a very great friend of Kandinsky and other members of the Blaue Reiter school (especially Javlensky). . . . Both Kandinsky and Javlensky often used to stay with us in the Ukraine, and were constant visitors when we lived in Munich. . . . Our house was always full of painters, who found a very good subject in my mother. In fact Javlensky painted a very fine portrait of her in a red dress which has now disappeared" (letters of December 27, 1959, and January 10, 1960).

Marya Anastasievna and Alexander were separated in 1901. She returned to Russia with her daughter, who died soon afterwards, and Marya herself apparently perished during the Revolution. Alexander remained in Western Europe with his son and they moved to England. Boris completed his educa-

1. According to Boris Chroustchoff, son of the sitter, his father and mother, who had been living in Munich, were separated in 1901, and his father, Alexander, took the portrait with him to England, where it hung in their house in Harrow-on-the-Hill until 1908, when it apparently "disappeared" (correspondence with the Museum, 1960). Whether it was actually stolen, or whether it was sold remains to be established. Boris Chroustchoff has since died, and further information has not hitherto been discovered.

2. It has hitherto not been possible to establish where or when Stangl acquired the picture.

tion at Harrow and subsequently served as a volunteer for the British Air Force in World War I. He later settled in Oxford (information contained in part in the de Chroustchoff letters, in part supplied by Isaiah Berlin in correspondence with the author, 1974).

The painting was acquired in 1950 as a Kandinsky, an attribution that was accepted both by Eichner and by Grohmann (see below REFERENCES). In August 1961, E. Steneberg of Frankfurt presented the Museum with convincing evidence for an attribution to Kardovsky. He noted in particular that the monogram *DK* (as opposed to *WK)* was that of Kardovsky and that his particular form of it, reminiscent of a Japanese printmaker's mark, was used only during Kardovsky's Munich period. Further research into the attribution initiated by D. Robbins and carried out by L. Berryman, both in the Soviet Union and in New York, confirmed Steneberg's findings, and the change in attribution was formally accepted and recorded in 1967.

The earliest source for the attribution of the portrait to Kandinsky is as yet unclear, although it appears to have originated with Grohmann. According to Stangl, L. Grote and Grohmann were both consulted about the work in 1950 and both concurred that it was the work of Kandinsky (correspondence with the author, 1974). Whether the work had been so attributed earlier is not known. Boris Chroustchoff speaks of the painting as a Kandinsky, but this may merely reflect his acceptance of Grohmann's attribution rather than any prior association of the picture on his own (or his father's) part with Kandinsky's name. In 1959 he had received a letter from Grohmann asking whether he were related in any way to the "Marie de Chroustchoff whose famous portrait by Kandinsky is in the Guggenheim Museum." Chroustchoff, who had not seen or heard of his mother's portrait since it had "disappeared" (as he put it) from his father's Harrow-on-the-Hill house in about 1908,[1] was "staggered" to discover that the painting was in the Museum (correspondence with Sweeney, 1960). His failure to mention Kardovsky's name in relation to it is understandable both in view of the number of years that had elapsed since he had last seen it and of Grohmann's clear conviction that the attribution to Kandinsky was not in question. Moreover, Chroustchoff's attribution of a portrait of his father (fig. a) to Kandinsky (when he wrote to Sweeney about it) would

fig. a.
Kardovsky, *Alexander de Chroustchoff Hunting Hares on his Estate,* oil on canvas, 25⅝ x 28 in., 65 x 71 cm., present whereabouts unknown.

seem to have been based in part at least upon the identical monograms and dates borne by the two works, rather than upon any more compelling stylistic or documentary factors, thus suggesting that he possibly lacked such additional evidence. ("I am enclosing a photograph of another painting by Kandinsky which he painted in the same year, and which bears the same signature as my mother's portrait. This is a painting of my father, shooting hares on his Estate in southern Russia on an autumnal day" [letter to Sweeney, January 1960].)

Whether the Guggenheim portrait was painted in Munich or in Russia is unclear. Kardovsky's movements during the year 1900 are well documented and would have allowed him to paint the picture in either place. Having begun his studies at the St. Petersburg Academy of Art in 1892 under Pavel Chistiakov and Ilia Repin, he had in 1896, together with his fellow-students Jawlensky, Werefkin, and Grabar, decided to go abroad. They departed in the summer of that year, spent some time in Paris and elsewhere, and arrived in November in Munich, where they spent the next four years studying in the school of Anton Ažbè *(Dmitri Nikolaevich Kardovsky: ob iskusstve,* ed. E. D. Kardovskaia, Iz. Akademi Khodozhestv USSR Moscow, 1960, p. 66. See also Weiler, London, 1971, p. 95. For extensive information on the Ažbè school and its influence on Kandinsky and his circle see Weiss, 1973, chapter 1, et passim). Early in April of 1899 Jawlensky reports that he, Werefkin, Kardovsky, Grabar, and Ažbè went to Venice together (Weiler, 1971, p. 96). By April 25, 1899, Kardovsky was back in Russia for his wedding to Olga Della-Vos, a pupil of Repin to whom he had been engaged for less than one year. The young couple set out on a protracted wedding trip visiting many cities, and they finally settled in Munich (at an unrecorded date), remaining there until the spring of 1900. They then returned to St. Petersburg, where Kardovsky continued his studies at the Academy. He was, however, ill with pleurisy for most of the summer of 1900 and spent the first part of the following winter in the Crimea recuperating (Kardovskaia, 1960, pp. 69, 76).

Thus, Kardovsky was in Munich in the early months of 1900 and in Russia for the remainder of that year and could have painted the portrait of Marya Anastasievna in either place.

The movements of the de Chroustchoff family are much more difficult to trace. Boris Chroustchoff's letters seem to imply that the family was living in Munich in the period immediately preceding the break-up of his parents' marriage, but this would presumably not have prevented them from spending some months annually on their Russian estate, and indeed it would have been remarkable if they did not. The presence on the original stretcher of a Munich address for Kardovsky establishes only that if painted in Russia, the picture was brought back to Munich by the time of the de Chroustchoff's 1901 separation. The portrait of Alexander (fig. a), which Boris Chroustchoff described as having been painted on his father's estate in Russia on an autumn day, would—if the description is accurate—have been painted in the fall of 1900, and since this work was definitely brought back to Munich in 1901 (and thence to England) it is certainly plausible to imagine that the Guggenheim painting had a similar history. There is, however, no compelling evidence on this point and the question remains for the time being unsolved.

EXHIBITIONS:

New York, SRGM 74, 118, 132 (checklists; as Kandinsky).

REFERENCES:

F. P.[orter], "Evolution in Art," *Art News,* vol. 51, summer 1952, repr. p. 99 ("*Baroness X,* by Kandinsky"); Eichner [1957], p. 77, pl. 39 ("*Kandinsky, Frau von Kruschtschoff,* 1900"); Grohmann, 1959, p. 46, repr. p. 257 ("Kandinsky, Maria Krushchov, 1900"); J. Hahl, "Kandinsky und Kardovskij," *Pantheon,* vol. xxxii, Oct./Nov./Dec. 1974, pp. 382-390, repr. color, p. 383.

Paul Klee

Born December 1879, Münchenbuchsee, Bern.
Died June 1940, Muralto-Locarno.

NOTE: Klee kept a detailed record of his work in an Oeuvre Catalogue (here-after OC), which he began in the spring of 1911 and continued until his death. It is not totally complete, and omissions are especially frequent in the pre-1911 years. The document is preserved in the Klee Stiftung, Bern. It covers the years 1883-1940 and records seven hundred and thirty-three paintings, three thousand, one hundred and fifty-nine so called "colored sheets," fifty-one glass paintings, fifteen sculptures, and one collage; the numbers inscribed upon the works themselves coincide in almost all cases with the numbers in the OC, al-though there are exceptions.

The entries in the OC include date, number, title, and description of medium; the latter category is not always complete nor in every case totally accurate, and an effort has been made, therefore, to analyze the medium and technique in-dependently of, as well as in relationship to, the OC entry. The entries in the present catalogue include Klee's OC entry verbatim; any discrepancy between this and the actual medium of the work is noted.

M. Poser of the Guggenheim Museum made the transcriptions from the Klee manuscript in Bern. J. Glaesemer of the Klee Stiftung examined the Guggen-heim Museum's Klee collection with the author in April 1973 and made many invaluable suggestions, especially concerning the artist's often complex me-dium and technique; these are gratefully incorporated in the entries which follow.

146   Flowerbed. 1913.
       (Blumenbeet; Flower garden).

OC *1913, 193, Blumenbeet Öl, auf Pappe A.*[1]

48.1172 X109

Oil on board, 11⅛ x 13¼ (28.2 x 33.7)

Signed and dated u.l.: *Klee / 1913 193.*

PROVENANCE:
Early history unknown; Karl Nierendorf, New York, by 1948; acquired with the Es-tate of Karl Nierendorf, 1948.

CONDITION:
At an unrecorded date filling and inpainting of 3 damages (½ in., 2⅛ in., and 2¼ in.) near the top center were performed. The surface was then coated with natural varnish.

There are some losses along the edges, down to the dark underpainting in some places, down to the board in others. Traction cracks are present in most areas, both in the upper paint layer and in the white layer be-neath. A very slight rabbet mark ca. ¼ in. wide is visible only in a raking light. The board has a slight convex warp. The overall condition is good. (Apr. 1973.)

1. The "A" notation in the OC stands for *"ohne Natur"* and indicates that the work was done from imagination or fantasy rather than from nature.

There is a layer of dark underpainting over which is a layer of white oil paint. The com-position was drawn onto the white paint in pencil, and penciled outlines are visible in places. Both the white base and the pencil underdrawing are common practice in Klee's early oils (see *The Diaries of Paul Klee,* Berkeley and Los Angeles, 1964, pp. 231, 243, 244).

Jordan suggests that the use of segmented, triangular forms in this, and a closely related oil entitled *Flower Path,* 1912, 124 (present whereabouts unknown, *Cahiers d'Art,* vol. 20-21, 1945/46, repr. p. 17), probably reflects the influence of Cubist paintings. He cites Le Fauconnier's *Abundance* and Gleizes' *Landscape with Figures,* both of which were reproduced in the *Blaue Reiter Almanach,* as possible sources of this influence, but also emphasizes that the relationship of one plane to the next, and the compositional structure in the Klee paintings are even more reminiscent of Fauve models than they are of Cubist ones.

The segmented and triangular shapes of these two paintings occur in many of the watercolor landscapes of Bern and its surroundings which Klee painted during 1913. (See, for example, *In the Quarry,* 1913, 135, where they are used to define the trees and bushes along the side of the quarry.) However, whereas in the watercolors these forms are integrated into a clear landscape composition, in *Flower Path* and *Flowerbed* they become an all-over pattern which is the composition itself. In this respect they are more closely related to the abstract compositions of the following year such as *Colored Circles Linked by Bands of Color,* 1914, 218 (Paul Klee Stiftung, Kunstmuseum Bern).

EXHIBITIONS:

Munich, *Muenchener Neue Secession IV Ausstellung,* 1918, no. 69 *(Blumenbeet);* New York, SRGM 74, no. 109; 192, *Paul Klee,* no. 14, repr.; 276 (no cat.).

REFERENCE:

J. M. Jordan, *Paul Klee and Cubism, 1912-1926,* unpublished Ph.D. dissertation, Institute of Fine Arts, New York University, Feb. 1974, pp. 265-268, repr.

147 Dance You Monster to My Soft
Song! 1922.
*(Tanze Du Ungeheuer zu meinem sanften
Lied!)*.

OC 1922, A[1] 54, *Tanze Du Ungeheuer zu
meinem sanften Lied! Aquarell u. Ölfarbezeichnung. Gaze gipsgrundiert.*

38.508

Watercolor and oil transfer drawing on
plaster-grounded gauze mounted on
gouache-painted paper. Approximate dimensions of unevenly cut gauze support:
13¾ x 11½ (35 x 29.2); approximate height
of gauze plus painted borders: 15¾ (40);
dimensions of paper mount: 17⅝ x 12⅞
(44.9 x 32.7)

Not signed; inscribed by the artist across
lower edge of gauze support: *Tanze Du
Ungeheuer! Zu meinem sanften Lied*; across
lower edge of paper mount: *1922/54 Tanze
Du Ungeheüer zu meinem sanften Lied!*

PROVENANCE:

St. Annen-Museum, Lübeck, Germany,
1927-37 (information supplied by Max
Hasse, St. Annen-Museum, correspondence
with the author, August 1974; he is not sure
whether the work was purchased directly
from the artist or from an intermediary);
banned by the German government as de-
generate art, 1937; purchased from Rudolf
Bauer by Solomon R. Guggenheim, 1938;
Gift of Solomon R. Guggenheim, 1938.

CONDITION:

The work has received no treatment.

There are a considerable number of losses
both of pigment and of plaster. These are
scattered over the entire surface and readily
visible to the naked eye. Although there is
no apparent incipient cleavage at present,
the surface is clearly vulnerable to flaking
and the condition in general is fragile. (Feb.
1974.)

Klee's oil transfer technique, first used in 1919, has been analyzed and documented by Glaesemer (*Paul Klee, Handzeichnungen I,* Bern, 1973, pp. 258-260).
The artist first brushed Japan paper with black oil color or printer's ink to
create a kind of carbon paper; when it was almost dry, he placed it face down

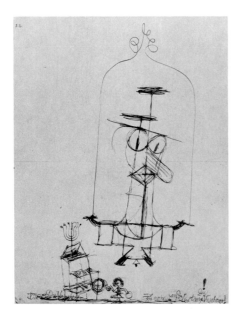

fig. a.
Klee, *Dance You Monster to My Soft Song!,*
blue ink on paper, 13½ x 10¼ in., 34.3 x 26
cm., Galerie Rosengart, Lucerne.

1. The *"A"* in this case was added by Lily Klee to indicate that the medium was watercolor
   (Aquarell). Information supplied by J. Glaesemer (Apr. 1973).

147

on a clean sheet of paper or cloth and laid a preparatory drawing (face up) on top of it. He then traced over the drawing with a stylus, thus transferring its outlines in soft black to the lower sheet. Drawings which have been used for oil transfer are easily identified by the stylus marks which are clearly visible on them. The oil transfers in turn are identified by the residual black smudge marks of the oil color. Klee's earliest experiments in this technique were left as black and white transfer drawings. (See, for example, Glaesemer, nos. 646 and 647.) Only later did he begin to add watercolor and to use the technique in the creation of paintings.

The preparatory drawing used to transfer the composition to the present painting is in the collection of the Galerie Rosengart, Lucerne (fig. a). Although the dimensions of the drawing sheet are slightly smaller than those of the gauze mount of the painting, the internal dimensions of the actual figure are identical in the two works. The identifying stylus marks are plainly visible on the drawing sheet and, although these marks do not in every detail follow the lines of the drawing itself, they do correspond precisely to the outlines of the forms in the Guggenheim painting. Thus, Klee's alterations were made with the stylus during the actual transfer process. This is the case, for example, of the written inscription along the lower edge of the work, which has been considerably changed in the painted version. It is also true of the top of the central figure's head; Klee's placement of this figure slightly higher in the field of the painted version forced him to reduce the curly top of the head he had used in the drawing to a more formalized and slightly squashed scroll. Had he included the freer curls of the original drawing, they would have run into the top edge of the field.

The apparently mechanical demands of the transfer technique were often modified in this way by Klee at the stylus stage of the process.

EXHIBITIONS:

Munich, Galerie Hans Goltz, *Zehn Jahre neue Kunst in München,* Nov.-Dec. 1922, no. 151, repr.; Lübeck, Behnhaus, *Impressionismus, Expressionismus, Neue Sachlichkeit,* 1927 (no cat.);[2] New York, Buchholz Gallery and Willard Gallery, *Paul Klee,* Oct. 9-Nov. 2, 1940, no. 28; New York, SRGM 74, no. 103; 78, 83, 95, 118 (checklists); Philadelphia, SRGM 134-T, no. 74, repr.; The Arts Club of Chicago, *Wit and Humor,* Feb. 28-Mar. 31, 1962, no. 11, repr.; New York, SRGM 173, no. 51, repr.; 192, *Paul Klee,* no. 51, repr. color; 195 (no cat.); 196 (checklist); 202, p. 43, repr. color; 205, *Rousseau, Redon, and Fantasy* (checklist); 220, p. 43, repr.; 227 (no cat.); 232, 241, p. 225, repr.; 266, 276 (no cats.).

REFERENCES:

Art of Tomorrow, 1939, no. 508; C. Giedion-Welcker, *Paul Klee,* New York, 1952, p. 68, pl. 55; W. Grohmann, *Paul Klee Drawings,* New York, 1960, pp. 26-27; M. Huggler, *Paul Klee: Die Malerei als Blick in den Kosmos,* Frauenfeld-Stuttgart, 1969, p. 78, repr. pl. 5.

2. Information supplied by Hasse (Aug. 1974).

148   Contact of Two Musicians.   1922.
      (Kontakt zweier Musiker).

*OC 1922, A 93, Kontakt zweier Musiker
Ölfarbezeichnung und Aquarell Nesselstoff,
kreidegrundiert.*

48.1172 x527

Watercolor and oil transfer drawing on
chalk-primed linen gauze, mounted on
gouache-painted board. Approximate dimensions of unevenly cut gauze support: left
and right sides, 17⅞ (45.4); top, 11½ (29.2);
bottom, 12 (30.5); dimensions of painted
surround: left side, 17¾ (45.1); top, 11⅞
(30.2); dimensions of entire board, 25¼ x
18⅞ (64.2 x 47.9)

Signed u.r.: *Klee*; inscribed by the artist
across lower edge of mount: *1922 x 93
Kontakt zweier Musiker*; in pencil l.l.
corner of mount: *Sond.Cl. (Sonder Classe*
was Klee's designation for works he considered to be particularly successful, and
these were generally not for sale.); in pencil
on reverse of mount: *"Samlg K Privatbesitz"*
(possibly referring to the artist's own
collection).

PROVENANCE:
Probably remained in the artist's collection
until his death in 1940 (*Klee,* exhibition
catalogue, Nierendorf Gallery, New York,
October 1947, specifies that the work came
from the artist's Estate; see also above
inscriptions); acquired with the Estate of
Karl Nierendorf, 1948.

CONDITION:
The work has received no treatment.

There are numerous cracks in the chalk
priming, but these are minor. The condition
in general is good. (Feb. 1974.)

Klee's musicians are attached to one another by means of a wire-like con-
traption reminiscent of that which activates his *Automaton,* 1922, 228, of the
same year. In both works, Klee is expressing the fascination for E. T. A. Hoffmann's view of the world which characterized not only his own work of the
early 1920's but also that of Schlemmer and the Bauhaus theater. Schlemmer
produced a Hoffmann ballet, *The Figural Cabinet,* in the spring of 1922, and as
C. Geelhaar has pointed out, Klee's works of this period are filled with Hoff-
mannesque characters (*Paul Klee and the Bauhaus,* Greenwich, Connecticut,
1973, pp. 66-72). The puppet-like automata of Klee's "concert," appearing on
a curtained stage, seem to be almost a direct illustration of Schlemmer's statement: "The endeavor to free man from his physical bondage and to heighten
his freedom of movement beyond his native potential resulted in substituting
for the organism the mechanical human figure *(Kunstfigur): the automaton and
the marionette. . . .* the Russian Brjusov demands that we 'replace actors with
mechanized dolls, into each of which a phonograph shall be built' " (*The
Theater of the Bauhaus,* ed. W. Gropius, Middletown, Connecticut, 1961,
p. 28).

For a discussion of the oil transfer technique, see above cat. no. 147.

EXHIBITIONS:
Munich, Galerie Hans Goltz, *Paul Klee, 2. Gesamtausstellung,* May-June 1925, no. 11
(*"Privatbesitz"*); New York, SRGM 78, 83, 95, 118, 129 (checklists); 192, *Paul Klee,* no. 55,
repr.; 195 (no cat.); 196 (checklist); 202, p. 114, repr.; 205, *Rousseau, Redon, and Fantasy*
(checklist); 227 (no cat.); 232, 241, p. 230, repr.; 266, 276 (no cats.).

REFERENCES:

W. Grohmann, *Paul Klee Handzeichnungen, 1921-1930*, Berlin, 1934, no. 19, p. 18; Idem, "L'humour goethéen de Paul Klee," *XXe Siècle*, nouv. sér., no. 8, Jan. 1957, p. 34; SRGM *Handbook*, 1970, p. 230, repr.

---

149   Red Balloon. 1922.
(Roter Ballon).

OC *1922, 179, Roter Ballon Ölbild klein-eres Format Nesselstoff auf Pappe geklebt, kreidegrundiert.*

48.1172 x524

Oil (and oil transfer drawing?) on chalk-primed linen gauze, mounted on board,[1] 12½ x 12¼ (31.7 x 31.1)

Signed and dated l.l.: *Klee / 1922 / 179* (now invisible to the naked eye but clear under UV); inscribed by the artist on reverse: *1922 /// 179*[2] */ Roter Ballon / Klee. / breiter Rahmen. / nicht zu flach / glasen. nicht zu flacher Rahmen / glasen.*[3]

PROVENANCE:

Hermann Lange, Krefeld, by 1931 (Kunst-verein exhibition catalogue; Lange's name appears twice on the reverse of the work); Karl Nierendorf, New York, by 1948; acquired with the Estate of Karl Nierendorf, 1948.

CONDITION:

There are numerous abrasions in the upper right quarter of the painting which have been partially retouched; the date of these repairs is unknown. In 1953 surface dirt was removed with benzine and inpainting performed in tiny scattered areas at the upper left and lower right corners. The board was mounted on tempered Masonite.

Some cleavage has occurred between the gauze and the board; it is difficult to determine whether this condition is developing, but it seems to be stable. There is some minor cleavage between the board and the Masonite along the top edge. The overall condition is good. (Apr. 1973.)

The motif of the balloon, both as a mode of travel and as decorative free form, recurs periodically in Klee's oeuvre. (See, for example, *The Balloon*, 1926; *Balloon over Town*, 1928; *The Balloon at the Window*, 1929.)

The structural characteristics of *Red Balloon* bring it into close relationship with *Little Fir-Tree Painting*, also of 1922 (Kunstmuseum Basel, Öffentliche

---

1. In consultation with J. Glaesemer, it was tentatively concluded that Klee may have used an oil transfer drawing at a certain stage in his work on this picture. Traces of black in the background and the particular quality of some of the black outlines gave rise to this hypothesis, but further research is necessary before it can be definitely proved. It has also not been finally established whether the chalk priming was applied to the gauze, the board mount, or to both. For a discussion of the oil transfer technique, see above cat. no. 147.

2. This inscription has hitherto been published as *1922 VI 179*.

3. Glaesemer suggested that Klee's framing instructions were probably for Goltz. The label attached to the lower edge of the reverse has been identified by J. Kornfeld as a label of Hans Goltz's gallery with which Klee had a contract at that time.

149

Kunstsammlung); both works illustrate Klee's January 30, 1922, notes on rhythmic structure. In the lecture notes, Klee describes a rhythmic construction in which "the structured plane and the structureless plane face one another in such a way that the two types of plane alternate both horizontally and vertically" *(The Thinking Eye,* ed. J. Spiller, New York, 1961, p. 308). The linear contrasts depicted in Klee's accompanying diagram are translated in both of the paintings into contrasts of color and tone.

Klee's strict concentration on pictorial problems and his exclusion of all discussion of thematic content is characteristic. As R. Verdi has pointed out, Klee insisted that pictures are not born from ideas, but rather from the desire to solve pictorial problems: *"Die bildende Kunst beginnt niemals bei einer poetischen Stimmung oder Idee, sondern beim Bau einer oder mehrerer Figuren, bei der Zusammenstimmung einiger Farben und Tonwerte oder bei der Abwägung von Raumverhältnissen. . . . "* ("Plastic art never begins with a poetic mood or idea, but with the construction of one or several figures; the harmonization of a few colours and tonal values or in the relative proportion of spaces. . . ." *Paul Klee: Dokumente und Bilder aus den Jahren 1896-1930,* ed. Klee Gesellschaft, Bern, 1949, p. 5, trans. R. Verdi, "Paul Klee's 'Fish-Magic:' An Interpretation," *Burlington Magazine,* vol. cxvi, March 1974, p. 153.) As Verdi suggests, Klee was not prepared to discuss the thematic content of his works; his theoretical writings must thus be seen as a source of elucidation of the formal rather than the philosophical and iconographical aspects of his work.

EXHIBITIONS:

Dusseldorf, Kunstverein für die Rheinlande und Westfalen, *Paul Klee,* June 14-July 6, 1931, no. 17 *("Bes.Hermann Lange, Krefeld")*; New York, SRGM 79, 81, 83 (checklists); Vancouver, SRGM 88-T, no. 34; Montreal, SRGM 93-T, no. 24; New York, SRGM 97 (checklist); London, SRGM 104-T, no. 35; New York, SRGM 112, 118 (checklists); 129 (repr.); Philadelphia, SRGM 134-T, no. 72; New York, SRGM 144 (checklist); Worcester, Mass., SRGM 148-T, no. 19, repr.; New York, SRGM 151, 153 (checklists); Boston, Museum of Fine Arts, *Surrealist & Fantastic Art from the Collections of the Museum of Modern Art and the Guggenheim Museum,* Feb. 14-Mar. 15, 1964, no. 34; New York, SRGM 173, no. 52, repr. color; 192, *Paul Klee,* no. 58, repr. color; 198-T (no cat.); 202, p. 112, repr. color; 205, *Rousseau, Redon and Fantasy* (checklist); 227, 228 (no cats.); 232, 241, pp. 228-229, repr. color; 276 (no cat.).

REFERENCES:

SRGM *Handbook,* 1959, p. 91, repr. p. 90; T. M. Messer, *Elements of Modern Painting,* commentary, SRGM 132, 1961, repr. color, n.p.; H. H. Arnason, *History of Modern Art,* New York, 1968, p. 258, color pl. 106; SRGM *Handbook,* 1970, pp. 228-229, repr. color.

150   Curtain. 1924.
(Vorhang; Untitled).

OC 1924, 129, *Vorhang kl. aquarell Nessel-*
stoff aufgeklebt Krapplack Kleistergrund.
Ausserdem 129 a, b, c, d. (The final phrase
["*Ausserdem . . .*"] is included as a footnote
at the bottom of the page.)

71.1936R 115

Watercolor on chalk-primed linen mounted
on paper, mounted on board, varnished with
madder. Linen support: 7⅛ x 3⅝ (18.1 x
9.2); paper mount: 8 x 3⅞ (20.2 x 9.9);
board mount: 11⅛ x 6¾ (28.2 x 17.2)
Inscribed by the artist across lower edge of
board mount: *1924. 129. b. Klee*; l.r. below
signature: *für Fräulein Grunow.*[1]

PROVENANCE:

Gertrud Grunow, Weimar;[1] Hilla Rebay,
Greens Farms, Connecticut;[2] Estate of Hilla
Rebay, 1967-71; acquired from the Estate
of Hilla Rebay, 1971.

CONDITION:

The work has received no treatment.
The linen support is slightly cracked at the
top edge and there are 3 pinpoint losses in
the paint layer. The painted border shows
some slight chipping at the upper right, and
the board mount is somewhat discolored.
The condition in general is good. (Feb.
1974.)

The format of the OC entry, with its a-d footnoted addition, is unique and suggests that the original picture 129 was cut into four (thus creating 129 a-d) or
five (thus creating 129, and 129 a-d). Only two of the other works in the series
have hitherto come to light: *Curtain,* 129a (fig. a), formerly Saidenberg Gallery,
New York, and an untitled work, 129c, in the collection of Angela Rosengart,
Lucerne (fig. b, hitherto unpublished; the relationship of this work to the others
in the series was first pointed out by J. Glaesemer, in conversation with M.
Poser, 1974). The medium, colors, and scale of the motifs in 129a and 129c are
identical to those of the Guggenheim example, and it is extremely likely that
they originally formed part of a single whole.

    Glaesemer, in conversation with the author, April 1973, has offered yet
another possible explanation for the OC entry and for the almost identical nature of the works involved. All of the works listed under 129 might, he suggests,
have been cut from 128, *Mural* (fig. c). Once again the medium, colors, and
scale of motifs are identical. If Glaesemer's theory is correct, the single work
must have been divided into two very soon after its completion since the 1925
Goltz catalogue contains an entry for each: "*Wandbild,* 1924, 128" and "*Vor-*
hang, 1924, 129." (See below EXHIBITIONS and fn. 3.)

1. Fräulein Grunow, who taught a class at the Bauhaus, was in her 60's in 1924, and was a
   friend and supporter of many of the Bauhaus artists. See Felix Klee, *Paul Klee,* New York,
     1962, pp. 53-54, 184.

2. No records have hitherto come to light to indicate where or when Hilla Rebay acquired the
   work.

The repetitive, serial nature of these compositions made them especially suitable for cutting, and Klee is known to have subdivided several compositions in this way. The most explicit example of the practice is represented by the three works *Pirla, Pal,* and *Between Pirla and Pal.* As C. Geelhaar has pointed out, the last of these was cut from the center of the composition originally formed by all three, and the title makes witty reference to this earlier relationship (*Paul Klee and the Bauhaus,* Greenwich, Connecticut, 1973, p. 89).

The titles *Mural* and *Curtain* may in one sense be intended metaphorically since the works are so diminutive. The images themselves, however, which have so often been compared to the abstract signs of a hieroglyphic language, are somewhat reminiscent of the ornamental style and serial patterns of Islamic wall decoration or of Coptic textiles, and something of this implicit relationship may be suggested in the titles. The division of the field into rectangles and bands of tightly juxtaposed small-scale motifs is characteristic of a large group of works produced by Klee between 1924 and 1927. (For other examples see *Coolness in a Garden of the Torrid Zone,* 1924, 186, Geelhaar, 1973, repr. p. 92; *Pastorale,* 1927, 20, W. Grohmann, *Paul Klee,* New York, 1954, repr. cc 82.)

Geelhaar has also suggested that the structures of these paintings were "composed by the artist like a text or musical score," and he sees their free-flowing irregularities as an illustration of Klee's own dictum that spontaneity and vivacity of form are essential ingredients in an abstract, structured composition (1973, p. 94). Klee's advice to his students on this subject is revealing: "What I saw by way of your theoretical exercises in the field of structures was not very rewarding in terms of spontaneity. A certain trend towards rigidity predominated, often resulting in chillingly symmetrical ornamentation . . . it is hard to retain life in such abstractions. One tends to ignore altogether the bridge that leads from natural and inherently coherent rhythm to its precise representation" (lecture of November 27, 1923, in *The Nature of Nature,* ed. J. Spiller, New York, 1973, p. 43).

It is also possible that Klee's 1924 pictures were influenced to some extent by ancient Mediterranean scripts such as those reproduced in K. Weule's *Vom Kerbholz zum Alphabet,* Stuttgart, 1915, a book which Klee apparently owned (*The Thinking Eye,* ed. J. Spiller, New York, 1961, p. 516).

EXHIBITIONS:

Munich, Galerie Hans Goltz, *Paul Klee, 2. Gesamtausstellung,* May-June 1925, no. 145 ("*Vorhang.* 1924, 129")?;[3] New York, SRGM 241 (addenda); 276 (no cat.).

---

3. It is possible that the entry refers to the entire work (including the Guggenheim fragment) prior to cutting. (See above.)

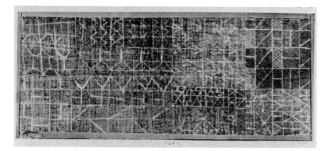

fig. a.
Klee, *Curtain*, 1924, 129a, 3⅝ x 9¼ in., 9.2 x 23.5 cm.,
formerly Saidenberg Gallery, New York.

fig. b.
Klee, *Untitled*, 1924, 129c, canvas only, 9¼ x 1⅝ in.,
23.4 x 4 cm., Collection Angela Rosengart, Lucerne.

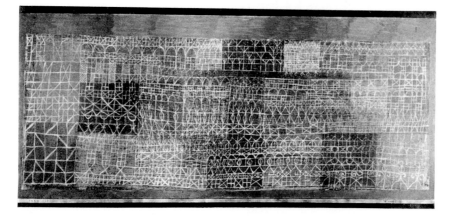

fig. c.
Klee, *Mural*, 1924, 128, 9⅞ x 21⅝ in., 25.2 x 54.9 cm.,
Paul Klee Stiftung, Kunstmuseum Bern. Copyright Cosmo-
press, Geneva.

151   In the Current Six Thresholds. 1929.
      (In der Strömung Sechs Schwellen).

OC *1929, 92 S.2, in der Strömung sechs Schwellen. Tempera = und Ölfarben 43 x 43 Leinw. auf Keil.*

67.1842

Oil and tempera on canvas, 17⅛ x 17⅛ (43.5 x 43.5)

Signed and dated l.r.: *Klee 1929*; inscribed by the artist on stretcher (barely visible): *in der Strömung Sechs Schwellen / Klee / 1929.*

PROVENANCE:

Purchased from the artist by D. H. Kahn-weiler, 1936 or 1937;[1] purchased from Kahnweiler by Curt Valentin, New York, 1954; G. David Thompson, Pittsburgh, by 1960 (date and source of acquisition unknown);[2] purchased from Thompson by Galerie Beyeler, Basel, 1960; purchased from Beyeler by Heinz Berggruen, Paris, 1963; purchased from Berggruen, 1967.

CONDITION:

Some losses in the 4 corners were inpainted at an unrecorded date.

Apart from some tiny scattered paint losses the condition is excellent. (Sept. 1972.)

The relationship between Klee's horizontal band paintings and his month-long Egyptian journey of the winter 1928-29 has been widely accepted in the literature and is based in part upon Klee's own explicit references to the relationship in his choice of titles for many of these works (*B.e.H. [Upper Egypt]; Evening in Egypt; Place near the Canal, Necropolis,* etc.). Moreover, in a letter to Lily written on April 17, 1929, he even offers some insights into the way in which one of these paintings, *Monument on the Edge of Fertile Country,* 1929, 40, is expressive of his Egyptian experience: "I am painting a landscape somewhat like the view of the fertile country from the distant mountains of the Valley of the Kings. The polyphonic interplay between earth and atmosphere has been kept as fluid as possible" (W. Grohmann, *Paul Klee,* New York [1954?], p. 273).

The statement raises important questions about the content of *Monument on the Edge of Fertile Country,* which consists of a series of horizontal bands intersected at irregular intervals by verticals and diagonals; at every intersection, moving from right to left, the individual horizontals are divided into two, and according to the number of intersections the original horizontal band is thus divided into halves, quarters, eighths, or sixteenths by the time it reaches the left margin. The colors on the right are pale beige, ochre, gray, and pink; moving towards the left, browns and some blues are gradually introduced, and the ochres and pinks become slightly darker. (For an interesting analysis of the effects of this use of color see Geelhaar, p. 120; also Klee, *The Nature of Nature,* ed. J. Spiller, New York, 1973, p. 142 [not 235 as stated in Geelhaar, fn. 1].)

1. Information supplied by M. Jardot, in correspondence with the author, Sept. 1972. Although the picture was exhibited at Galerie Simon in 1934, it seems not to have been purchased by Kahnweiler until about 2 years later. The Kahnweiler records show that Curt Valentin purchased the picture in May 1954.

2. A J. B. Neumann label on the reverse, hitherto unidentified with any exhibition, might indicate that he owned the picture before Thompson.

Even with Klee's own explicit description of this work as "somewhat like the view of the fertile country," or perhaps precisely because of it, the question of how closely the image itself may be said to reflect an actual landscape setting remains unresolved. Geelhaar's detailed and poetic reading of the picture is evocative: he sees the pale tones as "the shimmering quality of blinding sunlight and hot desert sand." The desert is on the right, the Monument in the middle zone, and on the left the "fertile country, where blue irrigation channels cut across the dark brown of the cultivated earth" (p. 120). He sees the work as an illustration of Klee's 1922 discussion of the relationship between abstraction and reality: "It is interesting to observe how real the object remains in spite of all abstractions. . . . There are times when something almost seems to be painted after nature, from a model so to speak . . ." (*The Thinking Eye*, p. 463).

While it is possible that Klee had such an image in mind as he created the painting, and while the analysis is undoubtedly suggestive, it makes assumptions about the iconography of Klee's horizontal band paintings which are problematic and require further study. Geelhaar's explicit reading of the image contrasts strongly with W. Haftmann's much more general interpretation of the closely related *Highway and Byways*, which he sees "not [as] a landscape . . . but rather [as] a kind of pictorial metaphor, a formal simile for an existing emotion, which suddenly revealed itself as a dreamy recollection of Egypt" (*The Mind and Work of Paul Klee*, New York, 1954, pp. 148-149). The differences in these two approaches to the content in Klee's 1929 paintings characterizes to some extent the nature of the problems which remain unresolved.

In the Current Six Thresholds poses these problems even more pointedly since the actual linguistic meaning of its title (quite apart from the relationship of that title to the image) is also unclear. The strictly mathematical structure, similar in kind to that of *Monument on the Edge of Fertile Country* but lacking the diagonal intersections of that painting, is characteristic of many of the works in this 1929-30 series. Following his own technical notes on the Golden Section (*The Nature of Nature*, pp. 295-296), Klee has divided the horizontals into halves, quarters, eighths, and sixteenths as they are intersected by verticals on their path from right to left. In its dark palette, and in its suppression both of space and light, this picture is clearly an even more austere example of Klee's constructive principles. Geelhaar (1973) has pointed to the relationship that exists between *In the Current Six Thresholds*, *Movements in Sluices*, 1929, 289 (pen drawing), and *Moving Thresholds*, 1929, 236 (watercolor), suggesting that in all three the subject is that of water or currents in motion. In the drawing and the watercolor (which, he says, followed the painting), Geelhaar sees the static austerity of the Guggenheim painting opening up into a dynamic "character-style"—a much more expressive depiction of the actual movement of rippling water. He implies a progression from a static, earthbound form to a freer mobile one, and in support of this notion he quotes Klee's discussion of the comparative qualities of the static and the dynamic in art ("Ways of Studying Nature," *The Thinking Eye*, p. 67, first published 1923).

Spiller presents the issues in an even more problematic form. He juxtaposes *Movement in Locks,* 1929, UE9, and *Floods,* 1929, UE7, with Klee's November 27, 1923, notes on structural rhythmics, implying a direct connection between these works and the ideas on straight and vibrating lines expressed in the notes, a connection which is difficult to sustain *(The Nature of Nature,* pp. 43-51). Furthermore, his use of *In the Current Six Thresholds* to illustrate ideas on the horizontal, vertical, and diagonal which were written in 1921 in the context of a discussion of the problem of balance presents similar problems of context and applicability. The implied relationship of the painting to the two marginal sketches (which do come from the notes for the December 12, 1921, lecture) complicates the issue still further *(The Thinking Eye,* p. 212).

Geelhaar's reading of the three works is both illuminating and evocative, but once again it raises the problems posed by Klee's iconography, the problem of relationship between title and picture, and the problems posed both by Klee's theoretical writings themselves and by their applicability to his own paintings. The iconographical relationship of *In the Current Six Thresholds* to its own title, to the other horizontal band paintings, to the Egyptian experience, and to the theoretical notion of the static and the dynamic, are questions that require further investigation. (For illuminating discussion of some of these problems see Büchner, pp. 365-370; Geelhaar, op. cit., passim; Ch. Kröll, *Die Bildtitel Paul Klees,* Inaugural Dissertation, Bonn, 1968, passim; Haftmann, *The Mind and Work of Paul Klee,* New York, 1954, passim.)

EXHIBITIONS:

Dusseldorf, Kunstverein für die Rheinlande und Westfalen, *Paul Klee,* June 14-July 6, 1931, no. 69; Berlin, Galerie Alfred Flechtheim, *Paul Klee, neue Bilder und Aquarelle,* Nov. 5-Dec. 10, 1931, no. 2 ("*In der Strömung Sieben Schwellen,* 1929"); Paris, Galerie Simon, *Paul Klee,* June 12-25, 1934 (no cat.; the picture is mentioned in H. Schiess's review); Kunsthaus Zürich, *G. David Thompson Collection,* Oct. 15-Nov. 27, 1960, no. 83, traveled to Kunstmuseum Düsseldorf, Dec. 14, 1960-Jan. 29, 1961, The Hague, Haags Gemeentemuseum, Feb. 17-Apr. 9, 1961, Turin, Museo Civico di Torino, Galleria d'Arte Moderna, Oct.-Nov. 1961; Basel, Galerie Beyeler, *Klee,* Mar.-June 15, 1963, no. 34, repr.; New York, SRGM 192, *Paul Klee,* no. 102, repr. color; New York, SRGM 198-T, 204, 227, 228 (no cats.); 232, 241, p. 232, repr. p. 233; Cleveland, SRGM 258-T, pl. 24; New York, SRGM 276 (no cat.).

REFERENCES:

H. Schiess, "Notes sur Klee à propos de son exposition à la Galerie Simon," *Cahiers d'Art,* vol. 9, no. 5-8, 1934, pp. 179-180; J. Spiller, ed., *P. Klee, The Thinking Eye,* London, 1961, p. 212; J. Büchner, "Zu den Gemälden u. Aquarellen von Paul Klee im Wallraf-Richartz Museum," *Wallraf-Richartz Jahrbuch,* Band xxiv, 1962, p. 366; T. M. Messer, *Paul Klee Exhibition at the Guggenheim: A Postscriptum,* New York, 1968, repr. color, p. iv; H. H. Arnason, *History of Modern Art,* New York, 1968, color pl. 107; C. Geelhaar, *Paul Klee and the Bauhaus,* Greenwich, Conn., 1973, pp. 126-127, repr. p. 122.

152 Open Book. 1930.
(Offenes Buch).

OC *1930, 206 E6, Offenes Buch Wasser-*
farben gefirnist Leinwand (Keilrahmen)
Weisslack grundiert orig.leisten[1] *0.45 0.42.*

48.1172 x526

Gouache over white lacquer on canvas.
Dimensions inside tape: 17⅝ x 16⅜ (44.8 x
41.7); entire support: 18 x 16¾ (45.7 x 42.5)

Signed l.l.: *Klee*; inscribed by the artist on
stretcher (barely visible): *1930. E6 "Offenes*
Buch" Klee.

PROVENANCE:

Rolf de Maré, Paris, by 1931 (C. Einstein,
Die Kunst des 20.Jahrhunderts, 3rd ed.,
Berlin, 1931, repr. p. 553); Karl Nierendorf,
New York, before 1948;[2] acquired with the
Estate of Karl Nierendorf, 1948.

CONDITION:

At an unrecorded date brown paper tape
was applied to the edges, apparently to hold
down the narrow tacking margins; it covers
approximately 3/16-¼ in. of the painted surface. In 1967 cleavage in the upper left
corner was set down with parchment size,
and some other cleaving areas had previously been set down with wax. Neither
treatment has proved effective.

Areas of cracking and active cleavage in the
white lacquer, notably along the lower margin, around the upper left corner of the
book, and at the center of the right margin,
pose considerable dangers and have hitherto
not been successfully counteracted. There is
an extensive overall crackle pattern in the 2
solid colors, and almost invisible cracks
throughout the areas of crosshatching. Some
minimal flaking of the pale brown wash has
exposed the white lacquer in places. (Apr.
1973.)

EXHIBITIONS:

New York, SRGM 78, 87, 95, 97 (checklists); London, SRGM 104-T, no. 36, pl. 4; New York,
SRGM 118, 129, 151 (checklists); 153 (checklist; commentary, repr. color); 173, no. 60, repr.
color; Pasadena, SRGM 193-T, *Paul Klee,* no. 113, repr. color; New York, SRGM 202, p. 113,
repr. color; Columbus, Ohio, SRGM 207-T, p. 32, repr. color; New York, SRGM 227, 228
(no cats.); 232, 241, p. 234, repr. p. 235; 266, 276 (no cats.).

REFERENCES:

W. Grohmann, *Paul Klee,* New York, 1967, p. 118, repr. color p. 119; D. Robbins, *Painting*
between the Wars, New York, 1966, no. 24, repr. color slide.

1. Possibly refers to a frame made by Klee. The white lacquer mentioned in Klee's OC description was applied over sizing which contained granules, as well as some blue and red
   underpainting. This was then followed by the light brown wash which covers the entire
   surface. The composition was then outlined, in part colored, and the crosshatching added;
   the darker brown substance, concentrated in the margin areas, probably came last, before
   the varnishing of the entire surface. The blue and red underpainting shows through in
   certain places; it is unclear whether this was Klee's original intention, or whether this has
   emerged as the lacquer film has shrunk and lost its opacity. Some intersecting horizontal
   and vertical impressions in the white lacquer are visible near each of the 4 corners of the
   book; it is unclear whether these too have become visible only as the lacquer has aged.

2. A Galerie Flechtheim label on the stretcher may indicate Nierendorf's source. Alternatively,
   it may date from a hitherto unidentified exhibition in which the picture appeared.

153   Rolling Landscape. 1938.
        (Wogende Landschaft).

OC *1938, 409 Y9, Wogende Landschaft
Aquarellfarben Segelleinen mit gestaltetem
Kreide = Kleistergrund.*

48.1172 x529

Gouache on chalk-and-glue-primed sailcloth, mounted on tempera-painted board.
Sailcloth support: 15⅞ x 21¼ (40.2 x 54.2);
board mount: 18½ x 24⅜ (47.1 x 61.9)

Formerly signed u.l.: *Klee.* (The signature
has been lost through flaking [see below
CONDITION]. Although the signature is recorded in the Guggenheim's 1948 and subsequent records, no photograph of it exists.);
inscribed on reverse, not in the artist's hand
(transcribed but not photographed before
mounting): *Wogende Landschaft / 1938.
No. 682.* (No. 682 is the Nierendorf inventory number, suggesting that this entire
inscription dates from his ownership.) Not
dated.

PROVENANCE:

Karl Nierendorf, New York, by 1942 (Nierendorf Gallery Inventory of September 9,
1942, No. 682); acquired with the Estate of
Karl Nierendorf, 1948.

CONDITION:

In 1954 the picture was mounted on Masonite with PVA emulsion and a rigid frame
support added to the reverse. Edges of the
board, especially the left, were filled and
inpainted. In 1955 the center and some of
the margin areas were set down with PVA.

The board is extensively chipped along all
edges. The gray border area has an overall
fine crackle pattern with some incipient
cleavage, and there are some water stains
in this area. Extensive flaking and cleavage
in the colored areas, especially at the upper
left, the left and right edges, and the left
half of the lower edge, has proved impossible to prevent. The overall condition of
the paint layer is fragile. (Feb. 1974.)

EXHIBITIONS:

Toronto, SRGM 85-T, no. 44; New York, SRGM 107 (checklist); 118 (checklist; *Rolling
Landscape* substituted for *Severing of the Snake,* Apr. 20); 129 (checklist); Philadelphia,
SRGM 134-T, no. 89; New York, SRGM 144 (checklist); 173, no. 65, repr.; 192, *Paul Klee,*
no. 162, repr. color; 195 (no cat.); 196 (checklist); 202, p. 115, repr.; 227 (no cat.); 232, 241,
p. 240, repr. p. 241; 266, 276 (no cats.).

REFERENCE:

SRGM *Handbook,* 1959, p. 92, repr. p. 93.

154   Severing of the Snake. 1938.
(Zerteilung der Schlange).

OC *1938, 262 R2, Zerteilung der Schlange
Aquarellfarben auf gestaltetem Kreide—
Kleistergrund jute.*

48.1172 x57

Gouache on burlap mounted on built up
chalk and gesso-primed burlap, mounted on
Masonite board. Unevenly cut burlap support: left side, 20½ (52.1); right side, 19⅞
(50.6); top and bottom, 15½ (39.4); gesso-primed mount: 28¼ x 23 (72.0 x 58.4)

Signed u.r.: *Klee.* Not dated.

PROVENANCE:
Karl Nierendorf, New York, by February
1940 (exhibition catalogue); Mrs. Horatio
Gates Lloyd, Haverford, Pennsylvania, ca.
1944-46?;[1] returned to Nierendorf, ca. 1946;
acquired with the Estate of Karl Nierendorf,
1948.

CONDITION:
In 1974 the chipped and fragile edges of the
work were consolidated, filled, and in-painted with PVA.

The gessoed mount is extremely fragile,
with extensive chipping and flaking at all
edges; there is an overall irregular crackle,
and considerable loss of gesso. There is also
some minor flaking of the paint film. In the
painted area of the composition, there is
some minor abrasion with paint loss. The
overall condition is fair but fragile. (Feb.
1974.)

The metaphorical significance of the snake in Klee's oeuvre is variously seen as
a premonition of death, a symbol of rebirth, a reminiscence of ancient Egyptian
religion, a symbol of time, of eternity, or of the irreversible course of fate. As a
central element in *Insula Dulcamara,* also of 1938, the snake is interpreted by
M. Huggler as a symbol of the eternal flux of the universe, the birth of the
World and the Soul out of Chaos (*Paul Klee: Die Malerei als Blick in den
Kosmos,* Frauenfeld, 1969, pp. 188-191, 221-222). C. Geelhaar's comprehensive analysis of the same painting sees the snake as a symbol rather of time and
eternity ("Et in Arcadia Ego . . . ," *Berner Kunstmuseum Mitteilungen,* no.
118, May-June 1973, pp. 1-4).

Iconographic precedents for the severing of a snake with a knife have hitherto
not been found, and the particular meaning which Klee may have attributed to
the image is not clear.

1. Mrs. Gates Lloyd was the lender to the 1944 Philadelphia exhibition. She remembers buying
the work from Nierendorf at approximately the time of the exhibition and returning it to
him about 2 years later in exchange for another work by Klee, but she is not sure of the
exact dates of these transactions (correspondence with the author, Feb.-Mar. 1972).

A label on the reverse bears the inscription "collection J. B. Neumann." It has hitherto not
been possible to establish when Neumann owned the work.

EXHIBITIONS:

New York, Nierendorf Gallery, *Paul Klee,* Feb. 1940, no. 8; New York, Buchholz Gallery and Willard Gallery, *Paul Klee,* Oct. 9-Nov. 2, 1940, no. 96; New York, The Museum of Modern Art, *Paul Klee Memorial Exhibition,* June 30-July 27, 1941, no. 62, traveling exhibition; Cincinnati Art Museum, *Paul Klee and Alexander Calder,* Apr. 7-May 3, 1942, n.p.; The Philadelphia Art Alliance, *Paul Klee,* Mar. 14-Apr. 9, 1944, no. 31; New York, SRGM 106 (checklist); 118 (checklist; withdrawn Apr. 20); 129 (checklist); Boston, *Surrealist & Fantastic Art from the Collections of The Museum of Modern Art and the Guggenheim Museum,* Feb. 14-Mar. 15, 1964, no. 37, repr.; New York, SRGM 173, no. 66, repr.; 202, p. 107, repr. p. 106; 227 (no cat.); 232, 241, p. 238, repr. p. 239.

REFERENCES:

K. Nierendorf, *Paul Klee, Paintings, Watercolors, 1913-1939,* New York, 1941, pl. 56; SRGM *Handbook,* 1959, p. 92, repr. p. 93.

Franz Kline

Born May 1910, Wilkes-Barre, Pennsylvania.
Died May 1962, New York.

155   Elizabeth. 1944.

62.1613

Oil on canvas, 20 x 16 (50.9 x 40.6)

Signed and dated u.l.: *Franz Kline* / 44;
with monogram on reverse: *FK 44*.

PROVENANCE:

Gift of Mr. and Mrs. Leon A. Mnuchin,
1962.

CONDITION:

The work has received no treatment.

The edges and corners are in good condition. Some scattered pigment cracks show signs of incipient cleavage, and some small losses have occurred. This is especially true of an area 4 in. long running vertically to 9 in. from the bottom and 6 in. from the right. There is a heavy coat of discolored varnish. The condition in general is fair to good. (Feb. 1974.)

fig. a.
Kline, study for *Elizabeth*, 1944, sepia on paper,
9 x 8 in., 22.9 x 20.3 cm., Collection Mr. and
Mrs. I. David Orr.

Several existing paintings of the artist's wife Elizabeth suggest that the present work (hitherto known as *Untitled*) does indeed represent her. Three paintings in the collection of Mr. and Mrs. I. David Orr depict a similar head. (Two of these, painted in the mid 1940's, are reproduced in *Franz Kline,* exhibition catalogue, Whitney Museum of American Art, New York, 1968, figs. 15 and 16; the third, dated 1941, is reproduced in E. de Kooning, "Kline," *Art News Annual,* vol. 27, part II, November 1957 [1958 no.], p. 90, center left.) While the first two show Elizabeth with her long hair loose and the Guggenheim and *Art News* versions show her with her hair up, the structure of the face is extremely close in all four works. David Orr, who was a close friend of the artist, confirms that Elizabeth is represented in all four works (in conversation with the author, May 1974). (For a discussion of this period in Kline's work and of some of the other paintings of Elizabeth, see H. Gaugh, "Kline's Transitional Abstractions, 1946-50," *Art in America,* vol. 62, July-August 1974, p. 44.)

Even more striking is the relationship between the Guggenheim painting and a sepia drawing of Elizabeth which must have served as the preliminary study for the painting (fig. a). The features of the figure are delicately indicated in the drawing, and her right hand holds a spoon—elements which have been eliminated in the painted version—but the layout of the forms upon the canvas and the structural basis of the composition is directly traceable to the drawing.

Elizabeth was born in England and became a dancer. She met Kline in London in 1937 and they were married in New York in December 1938.

EXHIBITIONS:

New York, SRGM 144 (checklist); 177 (no cat.); Washington, D.C., Smithsonian Institution, National Collection of Fine Arts, International Art Program traveling exhibition, *The Disappearance and Reappearance of the Image: Painting in the United States Since 1945,* Bucharest, Sala Dalles, Jan. 17-Feb. 2, 1969, traveled to Timisoara, Rumania, Muzeul Banatuliu, Feb. 14-Mar. 1, 1969, Cluj, Rumania, Galeria de Arta, Mar. 14-Apr. 2, 1969, Bratislava, Slovenska Národná Galéria, Apr. 14-June 15, 1969, Prague, Národni Galerie v Praze, July 1-Aug. 15, 1969, Palais des Beaux-Arts de Bruxelles, Oct. 21-Nov. 16, 1969.

156 Self-Portrait. ca. 1945.

62.1612

Oil on canvas, 10¾ x 7 (27.3 x 17.9)

Signed l.r.: *Franz Kline*. Not dated.

PROVENANCE:

Gift of Mr. and Mrs. Leon A. Mnuchin, 1962.

CONDITION:

At some point prior to its acquisition by the Museum, the canvas was inpainted in 2 areas: a 3 x 3 in. area at the center of the sitter's chest; scattered spots ca. ½ in. from the top edge.

The edges and corners, with the exception of the lower edge and lower right corner, are in good condition; there is some chipping and paint loss in these 2 locations. There are 2 curved areas of pigment cracks with some possible incipient cleavage: an 8 in. crack along the left side of the work, and a 2 in. crack 3 in. from the left side and 2½ in. from the bottom. There are some other areas of minor pigment crackle, especially along the top edge. The heavy natural varnish is discolored, but the condition in general is good. (Feb. 1974.)

Although undated, this painting is closely related in style to a self-portrait which is signed and dated 1945 (Collection Mr. and Mrs. I. David Orr, *Franz Kline,* exhibition catalogue, Whitney Museum of American Art, New York, 1968, fig. 5). A pencil study for the Orr self-portrait (fig. a) is also clearly related to the Guggenheim painting.

Although there are 1946 pictures to which the present work is comparable (such as the dated self-portrait in the collection of Mr. George W. Staempfli, New York), its 1945 date is corroborated by David Orr, who clearly remembers that both his own portrait and the Guggenheim work were painted and hung in Kline's apartment at 150 West 4th Street. The artist had moved out of this apartment by the end of 1945 (David Orr in conversation with the author, October 1974).

fig. a.
Kline, study for a self-portrait, pencil on paper, 6 x 5 in., 15.3 x 12.7 cm., Collection Mr. and Mrs. I. David Orr.

EXHIBITIONS:

See above cat. no. 155.

REFERENCE:

"Editorial," *Art News,* vol. 61, summer 1962, repr. p. 23.

Oskar Kokoschka

Born March 1886, Pöchlarn, Austria.
Lives in Villeneuve, Switzerland.

157   Knight Errant. 1915.
       (Der Irrende Ritter).

48.1172 x380

Oil on canvas, 35¼ x 70⅛ (89.5 x 180.1)

Signed l.r.: *OK*; on reverse: *OKOXOK*. Not dated.

PROVENANCE:
Purchased from the artist by Oskar Reichel, Vienna, before March 1916;[1] purchased from Reichel by Otto Kallir (-Nirenstein), Paris and New York, 1934; purchased from Kallir by Karl Nierendorf, New York, ca. 1946?; acquired with the Estate of Karl Nierendorf, 1948.

CONDITION:
In 1953 acute cleavage between the paint and priming layers was treated by infusion of wax; some losses were filled with gesso and inpainted. In 1955 the canvas was lined with wax resin, the surface cleaned, and some losses filled and retouched with PBM. The inpainted areas are as follows: the entire top edge up to ½ in. in width; the lower half of the right edge up to ½ in. in width; an area approximately 1½ x 4 in. near the top right corner where heavy impasto apparently flaked off; 2 small areas above the signature, and 2 very small areas in the sky. Some additional cleavage was arrested in 1972 by further infusion of wax resin.

Cracks in the paint layer are visible in a limited number of scattered locations, and there has been some flaking. The edges and corners show considerable wear. An unidentified pale brown powdery substance, possibly a mold, is visible to varying degrees in portions of the knight's body and is particularly prominent on the left knee, the left foot, the lower portion of the jacket, and around the right armpit. Tests to define the nature of this condition have so far proved inconclusive. (Feb. 1972.)

The composition centers upon a figure in gray armor stretched out as if floating above a barren landscape bordering on the sea. In the stormy sky a small blue figure with the body, claws, and widely spread wings of a bird and the head of a man is perched on a long green branch, which extends below the knight's left arm. On the far right a nude female with long blond hair rests her head upon her left hand, as if deep in thought.

The "knight" has been almost universally accepted as a self-portrait, and was described as such by Kokoschka (*Studio International,* January 1971). Interpretations of the composition as a whole beyond this fact have been based to some extent on whether the picture was thought to have been painted before or after Kokoschka's war experience on the Russian front where, in September 1915, he was seriously wounded and abandoned on the battlefield. (His own vivid account of this experience, written in Prague in 1934, was first published by Wingler in 1956, *Oskar Kokoschka Schriften, 1907-1955,* Munich, pp. 69-76.) Among those who have dated the picture during the artist's convalescence and thus regarded it as illustrative of his personal experience at the hands of the Russians are Westheim (1917 and 1918), Einstein, and C. S. Pond (exhibition catalogue, Springfield, Massachusetts, 1945).

E. Hoffmann (p. 153) first corrected this error in chronology and established that the picture was in fact painted just before Kokoschka's departure for the front, and this has been confirmed on more than one occasion by the artist himself (Wingler, no. 105; *Studio International,* January 1971). Within this chronological context, various interpretations have been offered. The picture is seen by some as a strangely prophetic vision of the artist's own impending fate and thus an imagined depiction of himself wounded and abandoned upon the battlefield (Selz, p. 310; Wingler, no. 105; Bultmann, 1961, p. 32; Hodin, p. 58). Others have seen the knight as overcome "by the forces of war and destruction" and the artist as thereby symbolically yielding to forces beyond his control (Myers, p. 62). Still others have seen the composition as more generally symbolic of man confronted by his destiny, or as reminiscent of the Agony in the Garden (E. Hoffmann, p. 154; Wilckens, p. 46; Plaut, 1948, p. 55; W. Hoffmann, p. 60).

E. Hoffmann, Selz, and Hodin all see the bird-man in the sky as the figure of Death; E. Hoffmann first suggested (and Hodin concurred) that the white scrawled shapes to the right of this creature were the letters *"E S,"* an evoca-

---

1. On Mar. 24, 1916, Rainer Maria Rilke visited Oskar Reichel, and in response to Kokoschka's *Knight Errant* which he saw there, he wrote the following lines in the guest book: *"Rühre einer die Welt: dass sie ihm stürze ins tiefe / fassende Bild; und sein Herz wölbe sich drüber als Ruh. / Herrn Dr. Reichel dankbar unter den Eindruck dieses / Nachmittags: / Rainer Maria Rilke / (Wien am 24. März 1916)."* ("Let someone touch the world: [so] that it may fall [for him] into the profound, framing picture; and may his heart arch above it as tranquillity. To Dr. Reichel, gratefully, under the impression of this afternoon." An elegiac distich [pattern for *Duino Elegies*], trans. Theodore Ziolkowski, Professor of German Literature, Princeton University.)

When Reichel sold the painting to Kallir in 1934, he also gave him the page from the guest book specifying that it had been written in relation to the Kokoschka.

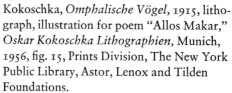

fig. a.
Kokoschka, *Omphalische Vögel*, 1915, litho-
graph, illustration for poem "Allos Makar,"
Oskar Kokoschka Lithographien, Munich,
1956, fig. 15, Prints Division, The New York
Public Library, Astor, Lenox and Tilden
Foundations.

tion of Christ's despairing cry: *"Eloi, Eloi, lama sabachthani"* ("My God, my
God, why hast thou forsaken me?" *St. Mark* 15.34, *St. Matthew* 27.46).

As in most of Kokoschka's paintings of this period, many of the individual
details are ambiguous; but it is clear that the interrelationships between the
various works of 1914-15 and their obvious connections with events in the artist's own life are crucial ingredients in the iconography and must be taken into
account in any attempt to explain it. By 1914 Kokoschka's three-year tumul-
tuous relationship with Alma Mahler was in its final phase, and all of the major
works produced during this and the preceding year reflect his preoccupation
with this intense experience. In works of 1914-15 (*Der gefesselte Kolumbus*
[*The Fettered Columbus*], the *Bach Cantata, The Tempest,* the six fans which
Kokoschka painted for Alma, "Allos Makar," and *The Burning Briarbush)* the
artist expresses, sometimes in explicitly narrative terms, sometimes in more re-
motely symbolic terms, a combination of his own direct experience with Alma
and of the more general and eternal dilemma of man's tortuous relations with
woman. It is precisely in the combination of the autobiographical and the symbolic, the actual and the imaginary, that the ambiguities of his iconographic
motifs are most apparent and their meaning most elusive, but it is nonetheless
clear that his relationship with Alma provided the material for both the writings and paintings of this period. The imagery of *Knight Errant,* though open
to a variety of interpretations, is to a considerable extent explicable within the
same context.

The nude female in the lower right of *Knight Errant* inevitably evokes the
memory of Alma, who appears throughout *Der gefesselte Kolumbus* and the
Bach Cantata similarly generalized and lacking in detailed facial characteristics

fig. b.
Kokoschka, *Der gefesselte Kolumbus*, 1913, pl. 8, lithograph, 11⅜ x 11⅛ in., 28.9 x 28.3 cm., The Museum of Modern Art, New York. Purchase.

but nonetheless unmistakable. Her identification in this instance is further supported by analogy with the final plate in the *Bach Cantata*—a direct portrait of Alma—in which she is shown thoughtfully resting her head upon her hand. The crouching pose of the "Alma" in *Knight Errant*, by itself almost undecipherable, becomes clear if compared with Kokoschka's use elsewhere of the sphinx (or other feline form with human head) in connection with the Alma theme. (See, for example, the fifth fan.) E. Hoffmann has pointed out that the sphinx had already been used by Kokoschka as the symbol of the femme fatale in the artist's play *Sphinx and Strawman* in 1907, and its significance in the fan context is no less clear.

The bird-man in the sky, so often interpreted as a figure of death, may also be symbolically linked to the sphinx-like Alma, and in turn throw light on her presence in the painting. The human features of the bird bear a remarkable resemblance to those of Kokoschka himself. (Compare, for example, the 1911 self-portrait, Wingler, repr. p. 29.) Moreover, in the 1915 illustration for his poem "Allos Makar" (an anagram for Alma-Oskar), Kokoschka portrayed himself as a comparable bird-man, this time explicitly juxtaposed with Alma as sphinx (fig. a). They are shown side by side battling over a snake or worm, and the anguished theme of the poem is the draining and futile nature of human love.

The position and meaning of the knight himself has been variously interpreted, but once again iconographical analogies within his contemporary writings and paintings can throw light on the problem. Plate 8 of *Der gefesselte Kolumbus* (fig. b) depicts the artist as Columbus, suspended in the air in a pose almost identical to that of the Knight in the Guggenheim painting. His eyes appear to be fixed in terror upon the skeleton in the lower right corner who lies, as if in wait, propped up on both elbows and staring out at the spectator. (A preparatory drawing for this lithograph, published by E. Rathenau as a drawing for *Die chinesische Mauer* [*Oskar Kokoschka Drawings 1906-1965*, Coral Gables, 1970, p. 83], shows the fearful, tormented face of Columbus even more clearly.) Nothing in the text of Kokoschka's play provides explicit sources for the iconography of the composition, but death appears as a leitmotif throughout this drama in which the cruelty of human love is the central theme; the final lines suggest that only when the body is sacrificed can the naturally painful relationship between man and woman achieve peace.

In the *Bach Cantata* and Kokoschka's illustrations for it similar preoccupations prevail. The dialogue between Hope and Fear in the text dwells alternately on the necessity of surrendering the body to achieve spiritual peace and the agonizing fear of death and the grave. Fear seems ultimately to prevail and the emotions expressed are those depicted on the face of the Columbus illustration cited above (fig. b). *("Todesangst . . . Mein letztes Lager will mich schrecken . . . Das offene Grab sieht greulich aus.")*

In *The Burning Briarbush* of 1911, written at the outset of Kokoschka's relationship with Alma, his sense of the tragic dilemma posed by man's confrontation with woman is perhaps expressed in its clearest form. The dialogue reveals the woman first wooing the man, winning him, becoming dependent upon him, and then being abandoned by him. In bitter revenge she wounds him, destroys his strength as he destroyed hers, and they are reunited only in death. Images of a shining knight (a "metal man"), the animal nature of woman, and the destructive interrelationship between them evoke many of the same themes expressed again and again in the works of the following years. The *Knight Errant,* painted as this painful liaison approached its end, may perhaps represent a final statement of the universal dilemma. In this sense the Knight, clearly suspended above the landscape (and not, as some commentators have insisted, lying prostrate and wounded upon it), evokes the notion of a being suspended between heaven and earth. Unlike the figure of Fear in the *Bach Cantata,* or its counterpart in the *Der gefesselte Kolumbus* who looks down to the grave in terror, the knight here looks up in apparent peace and evokes therefore the figure of Hope. *("Ich lege diesen Leib vor Gott zum Opfer nieder . . . Ich fahr ins Himmelshaus, Ich fahre sicher hin mit Frieden."* ["I lay this body down as an offering to God . . . I am going to the House of God, and I am going there in peace."]) Within the context of Kokoschka's immediately preceding works and the references throughout these to his relationship with Alma or to the more general issue of man's relationship with woman, the imagery of *Knight Errant* reveals itself clearly and coherently as yet another comment on this theme. Whether the picture may also be seen—as it most often has been—as a premonition of war and man's helplessness in the face of it is more difficult to establish.

EXHIBITIONS:

Kunsthaus Zürich, *Oskar Kokoschka,* June 6-July 3, 1927, no. 41 (for sale); New York, Galerie St. Etienne, *Oskar Kokoschka,* Jan. 9-Feb. 2, 1940, no. 14; The Arts Club of Chicago, *Kokoschka,* Jan. 3-27, 1941, no. 9 (lent by O. Kallir); New York, Buchholz Gallery, *Kokoschka,* Oct. 27-Nov. 15, 1941, no. 12; New York, Galerie St. Etienne, *Kokoschka,* Mar. 31-Apr. 24, 1943 (checklist); Springfield, Mass., George Walter Vincent Smith Art Museum, *Kokoschka,* Nov. 4-25, 1945, no. 5 (dated 1914, lent by O. Kallir); Oberlin, Ohio, Allen Memorial Art Museum, *Hofer, Munch, Hartley, Kokoschka, Schmidt-Rottluff,* Apr. 1946, no. 8; Boston, Institute of Contemporary Art, *Kokoschka,* Oct. 4-Nov. 14, 1948, no. 24, repr.;[2] New York, SRGM 81, 83 (no cats.); London, SRGM 104-T, no. 38; Boston, SRGM 119-T, no. 35; Lexington, Ky., SRGM 122-T, no. 15, repr.; London, Tate Gallery, *Kokoschka,* Sept. 14-Nov. 11, 1962, no. 46, repr.; Kunstverein in Hamburg, *Kokoschka,* Dec. 8, 1962-Jan. 27, 1963, no. 24, repr.; New York, SRGM 162, *Van Gogh and Expressionism* (checklist; commentary, repr. color); New York, Galerie St. Etienne, *25th Anniversary Exhibition,* Oct. 17-Nov. 14, 1964, no. 17, repr.; New York, SRGM 173, no. 40, repr.; Kunsthaus Zürich, *Kokoschka,* June 1-July 24, 1966, no. 34, repr.; Karlsruhe, Badische Kunstverein, *Kokoschka,* Aug. 21-Nov. 20, 1966, no. 27, repr.; New York, SRGM 196 (checklist); 202, p. 109, repr. color p. 108; Columbus, Ohio, SRGM 207-T, p. 14, repr. color p. 15; New York, SRGM 227 (no cat.); 232, pp. 250-251, repr. color; 236 (no cat.); 241, pp. 250-251, repr. color; Cleveland, SRGM 258-T, pl. 14.

REFERENCES:

P. Westheim, "Oskar Kokoschka," *Das Kunstblatt,* vol. 1, Oct. 1917, p. 304, repr. (dated 1916); Idem, *Oskar Kokoschka,* Potsdam [1918], pp. 14, 36, pl. 38 (dated 1915); A. Roessler, *Kritische Fragmente,* Vienna, 1918, repr. p. 111; O. Kokoschka, "Vom Bewusstsein der Gesichte," *Genius: Zeitschrift für Werdende und alte Kunst,* Munich, 1919, pp. 39-46, repr. p. 42 ("'Der Irrende Ritter' Selbstbildnis. 1916"); A. Faistauer, *Neue Malerei in Österreich,* Vienna, 1923, p. 80, pl. 34; C. Einstein, *Die Kunst des 20. Jahrhunderts,* Berlin, 1926, p. 147, repr. p. 452 (dated 1915); E. Hoffmann, *Kokoschka, Life and Work,* London, 1947, pp. 123, 153-154, repr. opp. p. 112; J. S. Plaut, "Oskar Kokoschka," *Art News,* vol. 47, Oct. 1948, pp. 40, 55; B. Myers, *The German Expressionists,* New York, 1957, p. 62; L. v. Wilckens, "Oskar Kokoschka," *Documents,* 1951, p. 46; P. Selz, *German Expressionist Painting,* Berkeley, 1957, p. 310, pl. 142b; H. M. Wingler, *Oskar Kokoschka,* Stuttgart, 1958, p. 41, no. 105, repr.; B. Bultmann, *Kokoschka,* London, 1961 (German ed. 1959), p. 32; J. P. Hodin, *Oskar Kokoschka: The Artist and His Time,* Greenwich, Conn., 1966, pp. 7, 58, 134-135, 145-147, 228, repr. opp. p. 53; W. Hofmann, "L'Espressionismo in Austria," *L'Arte Moderna,* no. 20, vol. iii, 1967, p. 60, repr. color p. 57; "Kokoschka's Early Work, A Conversation between the Artist and Wolfgang Fischer," *Studio International,* vol. 181, Jan. 1971, p. 5.

2. The picture was lent anonymously, on the instructions of Hilla Rebay; she felt that the work (recently acquired with the Nierendorf Estate) was not worthy of the Guggenheim collection (letter from Hilla Rebay to James Plaut, May 3, 1948). It was not shown again until after her retirement.

František Kupka

Born September 1871, Opočno, Bohemia.
Died June 1957, Puteaux.

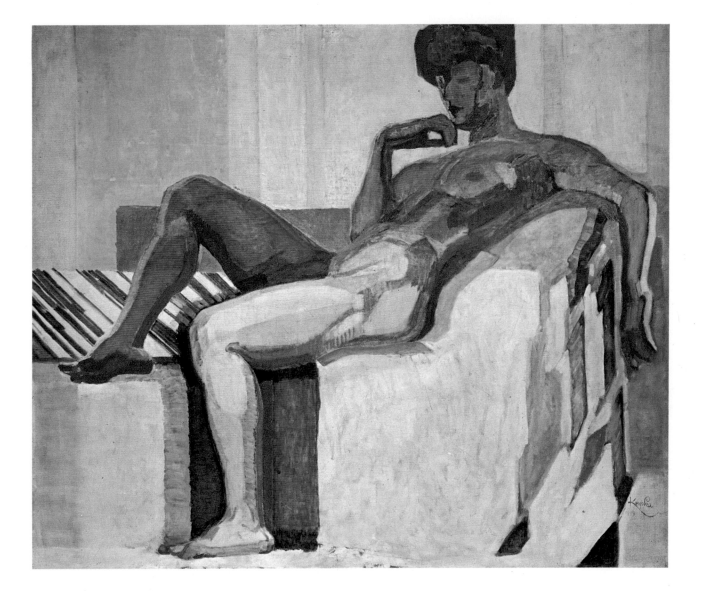

158   Planes by Colors, Large
Nude. 1909-1910.
(Plans par couleurs, grand nu).

68.1860

Oil on canvas, 59⅛ x 71⅛ (150.1 x 180.8)

Signed and dated l.r.: *Kupka / 1909*.[1]

PROVENANCE:

Madame Eugénie Kupka, 1957-58; pur-
chased from Eugénie Kupka by Richard L.
Feigen, New York, 1958; purchased from
Feigen by Mr. and Mrs. Andrew P. Fuller,
New York, 1961; Gift of Mrs. Andrew P.
Fuller, 1968.

CONDITION:

At some time prior to acquisition by the
Museum the painting was lined with wax
resin. Some minor inpainting at the upper
corners and along the top and left edges
probably dates from this time.

There is considerable wear at the edges, and
there are some scattered cracks in the paint
film, mainly in the upper half of the canvas.
The condition is otherwise good. (Dec.
1973.)

Kupka's work on the *Large Nude* extended over a period of several years
during which he produced at least eighteen studies for the picture and probably six after it. The figure represented is his wife, Eugénie (Fédit in conversation with Rowell, June 1974).

Rowell has convincingly argued that an earlier large-scale oil version of the
composition was almost certainly completed by 1906. Her hypothesis is based
upon the discovery of a photograph of the artist in his studio in which the
lower left section of this framed and hence probably completed oil is clearly
visible (fig. e). The position and treatment of the two legs in this painting
differ slightly from that of the Guggenheim version; careful examination of
the latter has uncovered no pentimenti and it is clear, therefore, that another
version is involved.

Several items in the photograph serve to establish that it was taken no later
than early in 1906. Pinned to the easel is a study for *Autumn Sun,* probably
painted in 1905-06. The lower of the two paintings standing to the artist's right
in the photograph is signed and dated 1904. (The upper work is *The Judgment
of Paris,* but its precise date is not known.) Finally, the photograph itself clearly
served as model for Kupka's *Self-Portrait,* which has hitherto been dated 1905
(Vachtova, repr. p. 104), but which Rowell dates 1906. It is clear, therefore,
that an oil version of the nude was finished by 1906. The sequence within the
large group of studies is extremely difficult to establish, but several of them
may possibly have been made in preparation for this earlier version. The problem is further complicated by Rowell's recent discovery of a slide, owned by
Lillian Lonngren Anders, of an otherwise unknown 1904 painting of the subject (Rowell, 1975, p. 132).

1. The signature and date were added in pencil over cracks in the original paint layer, thus
suggesting a considerable lapse in time between the completion of the picture and the
application of the signature.

fig. a.
Kupka, study for *Large Nude,* black and white chalk on tracing paper, 13 x 18 in., 33 x 45.7 cm., Fogg Art Museum, Harvard University, Cambridge, Massachusetts, Gift Richard Feigen Gallery, Inc.

fig. b.
Kupka, study for *Large Nude,* reverse of fig. a, black chalk on tracing paper rubbed with blue and yellow pastel, 13 x 18 in., 33 x 45.7 cm., Fogg Art Museum, Harvard University, Cambridge, Massachusetts, Gift Richard Feigen Gallery, Inc.

fig. c.
Kupka, study for *Large Nude,* pastel, 14 x 18¾ in., 35.6 x 47.6 cm., Fogg Art Museum, Harvard University, Cambridge, Massachusetts, Gift Richard Feigen Gallery, Inc.

fig. d.
Kupka, study for *Large Nude,* black chalk on tracing paper, 17½ x 12¾ in., 44.5 x 31.1 cm., Fogg Art Museum, Harvard University, Cambridge, Massachusetts, Gift Richard Feigen Gallery, Inc.

fig. e.
Photograph of Kupka
in his studio, 1905-
06 (?), Courtesy of
Madame Martinel-
Kupka, Paris.

The first study—and possibly the only one drawn after the model—may have
been that in which the figure faces from left to right (fig. a). This drawing was
until recently unknown, as it was mounted face-down and has suffered considerable damage especially at its upper edge. It is characterized by a rapid,
fluent, sketchy style, the outlines frequently reworked; the sitter's left arm is
shown in two different positions. The drawing was made on tracing paper,
and Kupka subsequently traced it through to the verso of the sheet, thereby re-
versing the image (fig. b). All of the lines of the verso figure, deliberately and
rather mechanically traced through, correspond to lines of the much more
spontaneous recto figure; only the line defining the bottom of the left foot is
omitted from the verso study; the corresponding line from the recto, faintly
visible through the tracing paper, serves in its stead. Both of these drawings
show traces of a grid drawn along at least two edges. Kupka's fascination with
the notion of figures twisting, turning, and revolving in space, figures seen from
one side and then another is documented in several other contexts (see, for
example, Rowell, 1975, pp. 62-67, 70-72); it is interesting to note, therefore,
that the innumerable studies for the *Large Nude,* all of which show the figure
facing from right to left, may have derived originally from a figure posed in
the opposite direction.

One further drawing probably belongs to the 1904-06 series (fig. c). In this
study, which is almost identical in pose to figs. a and b, the left arm is curled
around the end of the couch and bent forward at the elbow—a position which
was thus probably carried through to the first oil version. In all three studies,
the relationship between the two legs of the sitter is extremely close to that of
the early oil visible in the photograph; the heel of the right foot is placed much
closer to the left knee in these early versions than it is in the Guggenheim painting. In addition, the rather heavy-set quality of the two legs is common to all
four works. The head and torso (fig. d), in which the left arm is once again

fig. f.
Kupka, *Blue Nude,* 12½ x 19 in., 31.8 x 48.3 cm., present
whereabouts unknown.

bent forward at the elbow, may also belong to the early phase, although this is
more open to question. The *Blue Nude* (fig. f), which is known to the author
only from a black and white photograph, may perhaps be a transitional work.

Whether Kupka continued to work on the subject periodically during the
next four to five years, as seems most likely, or whether he took it up again
sometime in 1908 or 1909 is not clear. In all of the other studies, the left arm
hangs straight down behind the couch as it does in the Guggenheim painting.
The sequence is difficult to establish, but the first four studies in the new series
were probably those in which the artist appears to be experimenting with new
positions for the figure (figs. g [top and bottom], h, and i). One of these studies
(fig. i) is on the reverse of a horse and rider. These two drawings and the study
fig. h are close in style to the drawings for *Lysistrata* which Kupka may have
started as early as 1905-06. (For a discussion of the idea of sequential movement as represented in fig. h, see Rowell, 1975, pp. 49 ff.) This would suggest

fig. g.
Kupka, two studies for *Large Nude,* charcoal
on white paper, 22¾ x 18¾ in., 57.8 x 47.6
cm., Fogg Art Museum, Harvard University,
Cambridge, Massachusetts, Gift Richard
Feigen Gallery, Inc.

fig. h.
Kupka, study for *Large Nude,* pencil, 4½ x 6¾ in.,
11.4 x 17.2 cm., Private Collection.

fig. i.
Kupka, study for *Large Nude,* pencil on board, 6⅜ x 11
in., 16.2 x 27.9 cm., Private Collection.

fig. j.
Kupka, study for *Large Nude,* National Gallery, Prague.

fig. k.
Kupka, study for *Large Nude,* pastel on white paper,
19¾ x 23 in., 50.2 x 58.4 cm., Joseph H. Hazen
Collection.

fig. l.
Kupka, study for *Large Nude,* pastel on blue-gray paper,
17¾ x 22 in., 45 x 56 cm., Musée National d'Art
Moderne, Paris.

fig. m.
Kupka, study for *Large Nude,* pastel on blue-gray paper,
18⅞ x 22½ in., 48 x 57 cm., Musée National d'Art
Moderne, Paris.

fig. n.
Kupka, study for *Large Nude,* pastel on blue-gray paper,
18½ x 23⅞ in., 47.1 x 60.6 cm., National Gallery, Prague.

that Kupka was working on the studies for the second version for at least two to
three years. In the next group Kupka was concerned with general questions of
tone and atmosphere, as well as with the integration of the nude into the structured background (figs. k, l, m, n). In the final group he undertook the more

fig. o.
Kupka, study for *Large Nude,* charcoal, sketchbook
page, Collection Denise Fédit, Paris.

fig. p.
Kupka, study for *Large Nude,* charcoal, sketchbook
page, Collection Denise Fédit, Paris.

fig. q.
Kupka, study for *Large Nude,* pastel on paper,
18⅞ x 23⅝ in., 48 x 60 cm., Musée National d'Art
Moderne, Paris.

fig. r.
Kupka, study for *Large Nude,* pastel on white paper,
19¾ x 23⅝ in., 50 x 60 cm., Private Collection, Paris.

fig. s.
Kupka, study for *Large Nude,* pastel, 18⅛ x 15¾
in., 46 x 40 cm., Collection Mr. and Mrs.
Herman Elkon.

detailed delineation of the colored planes within the nude's head and body
(figs. o-s). The conception for the highly linear quality of the background
planes in the final painting may well postdate all of the studies and have been
evolved in part while Kupka was actually working on the canvas itself.

Kupka's 1909 signature and date were, as has been noted above,[1] added substantially after the completion of the work, when the artist probably no longer
remembered precisely when it was finished. A label on the reverse for the 1946
Budapest exhibition carries the date 1905-10 in Kupka's handwriting. These
dates, which would encompass Kupka's early conception of the nude and his
final painted version, are compatible with other evidence which suggests a 1910
date for the painting's completion. The division of the body into rather starkly
differentiated color zones is closely related to *Family Portrait* probably completed about the same time (Vachtova, 1968, color pl. iii; Siblík places the
Guggenheim painting shortly after the *Family Portrait*). Moreover, according
to Rowell, a pastel study for *Family Portrait* presents the head of the woman in
a series of brightly colored juxtaposed planes almost identical to those of the
Guggenheim *Large Nude.* The presence on the sketchbook page (fig. o) of a
study for one of the late *gigolettes,* similar in style to *Gallien's Taste, The
Cabaret Actress,* which dates from ca. 1909, would also tend to support the
notion that the *Large Nude*'s final studies date from late in 1909 or early the
following year.

After the painting was completed, Kupka apparently planned to develop it still further in the direction of the *Planes by Colors* (Musée National d'Art Moderne, Paris) or the *Portrait of Follot* (The Museum of Modern Art, New York). The drawings after the painting (figs. t-w) clearly represent this later phase, which was, however, apparently never realized. An extremely detailed ink and gouache version of the Guggenheim painting (fig. x) was obviously intended to serve as the basis for a woodcut—a medium which Kupka began to explore after World War I—but this too was apparently never executed.

For a brief comment on Kupka's use of the term *"plans par couleurs"* to define the element of structure in painting, see Rowell, 1975, cat. no. 42.

fig. t.
Kupka, page of sketches, pencil on ruled paper, 6⅞ x 7½ in., 17.5 x 19.1 cm., The Museum of Modern Art, New York. Gift of Mr. and Mrs. Frank Kupka.

EXHIBITIONS:

Paris, *Salon d'Automne,* Oct. 1-Nov. 8, 1911, no. 811 *(Plans par couleurs, peinture);*[2] [Paris, *Salon des Indépendants,* Mar. 20-May 16, 1912, no. 1833, 1834, or 1835 *(Plans par couleurs)?*];[3] Paris, Jeu de Paume, *Kupka-Mucha,* June 1936, no. 16, repr. ("*Plans par couleurs,* 1910"); Prague, Galerie S.V.U. Manes, *Kupka,* Nov 14-Dec. 8, 1946, no. 9 ("Plochy podle barev, 1910, 150 x 180 [*Plans par couleurs*]); Paris, *Salon des Indépendants,* Apr. 14-May 9, 1954, no. 1630 ("*Plans par couleurs,* 1909"); São Paulo, Brazil, *IV Bienal,* Sept.-Dec. 1957, no. 45 (France); Paris, Musée National d'Art Moderne, *Kupka,* May 27-July 13, 1958, no. 5; New York, SRGM 216, 221 (no cats.); 232, 241, p. 254, repr. color p. 255 (dated 1909); 260, 266 (no cats.); 289, no. 42, repr.

REFERENCES:

A. Salmon, *Paris-Journal,* Sept. 30, 1911, p. 5; G. Kahn, "Art moderne: Le Salon d'automne, peinture et sculpture," *Mercure de France,* Oct. 16, 1911, p. 872;[2] A. Warnod, *Comoedia,* Oct. 31, 1911;[4] R. Catenoy, *Fantasio,* Nov. 1, 1911, p. 231; E. Siblík, "François Kupka," *Aventinum,* 1929, p. 11; G. Turpin, "Kupka," *Dictionnaire biographique des artistes contemporains, 1910-1930,* Paris, vol. II, 1931, pp. 284-288; G. Kahn, *Kupka-Mucha,* exhibition catalogue, Paris, 1936, p. 3; L. Degand, "Kupka," *Art d'aujourd'hui,* sér. 3, Feb.-Mar. 1952, p. 55 (dated 1905-10), repr. p. 56; D. Fédit, *L'Oeuvre de Kupka,* Inventaire des collections publiques françaises, Paris, Musée National d'Art Moderne, 1966, p. 48; L. Vachtova, *Frank Kupka: Pioneer of Abstract Art,* New York, 1968, pp. 103, 299 no. 87, repr. p. 73 (dated 1909-10); [M. Rowell], SRGM *Handbook,* 1970, p. 254, repr. color p. 255 (dated 1909); Idem, *Kupka,* exhibition catalogue, New York, 1975, pp. 130-132, repr. p. 131.

2. The reviewers (see REFERENCES), with the notable exception of Kahn, reacted extremely negatively to Kupka's painting.

fig. u.
Kupka, page of sketches, charcoal on paper, National Gallery, Prague.

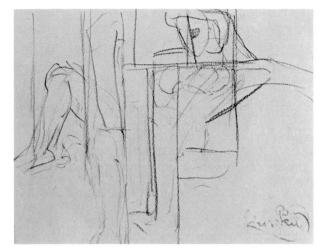

fig. v.
Kupka, sketch possibly after *Large Nude,* black chalk on paper, 5⅜ x 7¾ in., 13.8 x 19.9 cm., Fogg Art Museum, Harvard University, Cambridge, Massachusetts, Gift Richard Feigen Gallery, Inc.

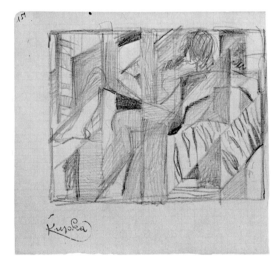

fig. w.
Kupka, sketch possibly after *Large Nude* (?), pencil on ruled paper, 6⅞ x 7½ in., 17.5 x 19.1 cm., The Museum of Modern Art, New York. Gift of Mr. and Mrs. Frank Kupka.

fig. x.
Kupka, study after *Large Nude* (?), ink and black and white gouache, 10¼ x 11⅝ in., 26 x 29.5 cm., Private Collection.

3. The *Large Nude* has often been identified with Kupka's 3 entries in the 1912 *Salon des Indépendants,* nos. 1833, 1834, 1835 (all *Plans par couleurs*). However, a set of exhibition records with identifying sketches, recently discovered by Rowell among the artist's papers, identifies two of the 1913 entries as *Planes by Colors* (Musée National d'Art Moderne, Paris, AM 3549-P) and *The Oval Mirror* (The Museum of Modern Art, New York). Although there is no sketch for the 3rd work, R. Allard's description of the series as *"fantaisies post-cubistes"* (*Revue de France,* Mar. 1912, p. 72) would suggest that the *Portrait of G. Follot* (The Museum of Modern Art, New York) is a more likely candidate than is the Guggenheim *Large Nude.*

4. I am indebted to V. Spate for bringing this reference to my attention.

159 The Colored One. ca. 1919-1920(?).
(*La Colorée*).

66.1810

Oil on canvas, 25⅝ x 21¼ (65 x 54)

Signed l.l.: *Kupka*. Not dated.

PROVENANCE:

Madame Eugénie Kupka, 1957-58; purchased from Eugénie Kupka by Richard L. Feigen, New York, 1958; purchased from Feigen by Mr. and Mrs. Andrew P. Fuller, New York, 1961; Gift of Mrs. Andrew P. Fuller, 1966.

CONDITION:

The picture has received no treatment since its acquisition, but appears to have been cleaned at an earlier date; some extremely minor losses were inpainted.

There is slight wear at the edges with some abrasion and losses. The upper center of the canvas shows scattered irregular cracks in the paint layer, but there is no evidence of cleavage. Apart from 2 minor stains, some small paint losses, and minor abrasions, the condition is good. (Sept. 1973.)

The painting represents a nude female with legs extended, as if in the act of offering her body to the brilliant golden sun which fills the upper quarter of the canvas. In a general sense it may be said, therefore, to evoke Kupka's lifelong preoccupation with the notion of man's integration with nature, or with the more cosmic interrelationship of man, the earth, and the wider universe. Whether it is more specifically interpretable as expressive of a sun-cult is much less clear. Although Kupka is said to have attributed extraordinary generative powers to the sun and to have himself indulged in some form of sun-cult, there is no specific evidence to document the point.

The painting is extremely difficult to date with any precision, since it is an unusually isolated example which is not readily related to any of Kupka's securely datable works. Both its theme and its style, however, are perhaps most suggestive of *Robust Brushstroke* and *A Tale of Pistils and Stamens I* (both in the Musée National d'Art Moderne, Paris, Inv. AM4179P and 4181P). The brilliance of color, the black outlining, and the preoccupation with cosmic and germinating themes characteristic of these works of ca. 1919-20 would suggest that the Guggenheim painting probably dates from approximately the same time.

An undated pastel study for the work is in a private collection (fig. a).

fig. a.
Kupka, study for *The Colored One,* pastel on paper, 10 x 9 in., 25.4 x 22.9 cm., signed l.l.: "*Kupka,*" Private Collection.

EXHIBITIONS:
New York, SRGM 187 (checklist, dated ca. 1919-20); 195 (no cat.); 196 (checklist, dated 1919-20); New York, Spencer Samuels, *Frank Kupka,* Mar.-Apr. 1968, no. 40, repr. (dated 1919-20); New York, SRGM 227 (no cat.); 232, 241, p. 257, repr. (dated 1919-20); 266 (no cat.); 289, no. 116, repr.

REFERENCES:
SRGM *Handbook,* 1970, p. 257, repr.; M. Rowell, *Kupka,* exhibition catalogue, New York, 1975, p. 209, repr.

Mikhail Larionov

Born May 1881, Tiraspol, Russia.
Died May 1964, Paris.

160   Glass. 1912.
(Стекло, Steklo; *Le Verre; Glasses*).

53.1362

Oil on canvas, 41 x 38¼ (104.1 x 97.1)

Signed l.r.: *M. Larionov*; signed and dated
l.l.: *1909*. М.Л.; inscribed by the artist on
reverse: *M. Larionow / „Le verre" / 1909 /
moscou* / "Стекло" / М. Ларіоновъ /
Москва / Палашевскій пр. уголь
Трехпрудный пер. # 2/7 / (Тверская ул.)
("Steklo / M. Larionov / Moskva / Pala-
shevskii pr. ugol' Trekhprudnyi per. # 2/7 /
[Tverskaia ul."]); on stretcher: *M. Larionow 43 rue de Seine Paris 6ᵉ*.

PROVENANCE:
Purchased from the artist, 1953.

CONDITION:
At some point prior to its acquisition by the
Museum the picture was restretched, presumably by the artist, so that along 13 in. of
the right edge, the frayed ends of the canvas
threads were visible, and the edge—which
is under considerable stress—was nailed to
the stretcher with tacks hammered through
the visible painted surface (see photo).

The support is generally fragile. In certain
areas, especially in those sectors where there
is some impasto, a fine crackle has developed in the pigment and there is some danger of flaking. Since the paint is in places
applied extremely thinly, and since many
areas of the canvas were left unpainted, it is
often difficult to determine exactly where
flaking has occurred. A slight indication of a
margin 2⅜ in. from the bottom edge and 2
in. from the top is due to the proximity of
the stretcher. 2 abrasions in the paint film
are visible: 1 in the lower right corner, 2¼
in. long, 1 close to the upper right corner,
6 in. long. (Mar. 1973.)

The title of this work has been the subject of considerable uncertainty. Larionov's own title, *Steklo* (glass), was later translated into French as *Le Verre*. The
painting has also been known as *Il Bicchiere* (the drinking glass), *The Glass*,
and more frequently as *Les Verres* or *Glasses* (drinking glasses).

The painting actually contains five tumblers in the foreground, a goblet on
the left, and two bottles. The title *Il Bicchiere* or *The Glass* (in the singular)
clearly applies only to the drinking glasses in the foreground and takes no account of the goblet or bottles. The fact that the singular form is used seems to
imply that these drinking glasses are to be seen in Futurist terms as a single
glass in motion. *Les Verres* or *Glasses*, on the other hand, while acknowledging
the fact that there are many glasses rather than one, fails to take into account
the additional glass objects (goblet and bottles) represented in the painting.

Larionov's own title, *Steklo* or *Le Verre,* is clearly intended as a generic noun
referring to the actual substance glass, rather than to any individual object
made of that substance, and indeed the Russian term is only applicable in this
sense. E. Eganbyuri's book on Larionov and Goncharova published in 1913
bears out this interpretation: "In his Rayonist works, Larionov renounces
painting still lifes, street movement, descriptive objects, but paints simply
'glass' as a universal condition of glass with all its manifestations and properties—fragility, ease in breaking, sharpness, transparency, brittleness, ability to
make sounds, i.e. the sum of all the sensations, obtainable from glass . . ." (pp.
38-39, trans. S. Bodine).

The chronology of Larionov's early work and of the development of Rayonism—his own major stylistic innovation—presents several problems. Few of his pictures were dated at the time of execution, and although he sometimes added dates later these were often inaccurate. (For a discussion of some of the issues involved, see *Burlington Magazine,* July, September, October, and December 1972. For a related discussion see above Goncharova, cat. no. 61.)

The earliest published date for *Glass* is 1912, a date provided in 1913 by Larionov himself for the *Target* exhibition catalogue.[1] Eganbyuri also dated the picture 1912 (p. xxi; see above Goncharova, cat. no. 61 regarding the general reliability of this publication).

In 1914, however, when *Glass* was brought to Paris for an exhibition at the Galerie Paul Guillaume, Larionov for the first time dated the picture 1909 (see below EXHIBITIONS). The 1909 date inscribed on the surface of the canvas was probably added at this time. Subsequently, Larionov apparently claimed to Seuphor and others that *Glass* had been shown at an exhibition at the Society of Free Esthetics in Moscow in 1909. However, no catalogue, review, or discussion of this event has ever come to light, and it is therefore difficult to accept the accuracy of the artist's recollection. Nonetheless his statement on the subject, presumably reinforced by the inscribed date on the canvas itself, has repeatedly led authors since 1914 to date the picture 1909 (see below EXHIBITIONS; also Seuphor, 1950 and 1955; Degand; Chamot, 1955; SRGM *Handbook,* 1959; Dorival; Carrieri; George; Daulte; Loguine).

Larionov also claimed that the picture had been shown in the one-day exhibition held at the Society of Free Esthetics on December 8, 1911. This event undoubtedly did take place—a catalogue and reviews exist—but neither *Glass* nor any other Rayonist work is mentioned, and it is therefore difficult to imagine that they were represented. Nonetheless, the appearance of *Glass* in this exhibition has become a widely accepted fact, and December 1911 has often been cited as another *terminus ante quem* for the existence of Rayonist paintings (see, for example, C. Gray, 1962 [though in her exhibition catalogue of 1961, she dates *Glass* 1912]; also Schafran; Vergo).

Since Larionov regarded *Glass* as his first fully Rayonist work (Seuphor, 1950), the origin and development of his Rayonist style as a whole is intimately bound up with the establishment of a correct date for this painting. In this connection it is important to bear in mind the artistic climate in Moscow and St. Petersburg during the years up to 1914, a climate of experimentation, innovation, and self-conscious preoccupation with the avant-garde. Larionov, Goncharova, and their associates were deeply involved with the innovative nature

---

1. This may have been a study for the present work, but more probably it was the picture itself with a more tentative title.

of this era, and the constant and rapid developments in their styles and theories were instantly reflected in the many exhibitions which they organized to bring their work to the attention of the public. In any attempt to establish a chronology for the works of this era, therefore, the exhibition catalogues and the reviews (which were often vocal responses to the appearance of a new style) must provide the essential documentary evidence.

Since the 1909 Society of Free Esthetics exhibition seems not to have taken place at all, and since neither *Glass* nor any other Rayonist work was apparently shown in the December 1911 Society of Free Esthetics show, the earliest exhibition in which explicitly Rayonist works are known to have appeared was the *World of Art,* which opened in Moscow in November 1912. This exhibition contained not only "*Glass,* rayonist method," but also *Rayonist Study.* Moreover, *Glass* is specifically referred to in Essem's review of the show in *Apollon.*

The second exhibition known to have included Rayonist works was the *Union of Youth,* which opened in Moscow in December 1912, a month after the *World of Art.* Confusion about the dates of this show—it has from time to time been erroneously cited as having opened in December 1911—has led to confusion about the origins of Rayonism itself, but the reviews of the exhibition conclusively prove that the 1912 date is correct. (For a discussion of this problem see Rudenstine.) This exhibition included two further Rayonist works —*Rayonist Sausage and Mackerel* and *Portrait of a Fool* which were reproduced, respectively, in Larionov, Лучизм (Luchizm, *Rayonism),* Moscow, 1913, n.p., and Eganbyuri, p. 61.

The third exhibition in which Rayonist works appeared was *Target,* which opened in Moscow in March 1913 and included three such works, all of which had already been exhibited within the previous five months, and all of which were dated 1912 in the *Target* catalogue. The three were *Glass, Rayonist Sausage and Mackerel,* and *Portrait of a Fool.* V. Parkin's review of the show (published in *Donkey's Tail and Target,* ed. Myunster, Moscow, 1913, pp. 67-69) not only refers specifically to *Portrait of a Fool* and *Rayonist Sausage and Mackerel,* reproducing the latter with the date 1912, but, more importantly, draws particular attention to these works as being examples of a "new style advocated by Larionov, Rayonism." The novelty of the style was in itself worthy of comment. Eganbyuri's book, which—as has already been mentioned —also appeared in 1913, lists no Rayonist works before 1912.

On the basis of this evidence, it seems likely that Rayonism emerged as a style during the course of 1912. The publication date of Larionov's own manifesto on the subject would tend to support this thesis. It appeared in two forms. One, entitled Лучизм (Luchizm, *Rayonism),* appeared as an independent pamphlet and was published in Moscow in April 1913. The essay itself is undated; the title page carries the date 1913. (I am indebted to Bowlt, University of Texas at Austin, who owns a copy of this rare document, for supplying the above information.) A revised version, Лучистая живопись (Luchistaia zhivopis, *Rayonist Painting),* was published in the anthology *Donkey's Tail and Target* of July 1913. In this latter edition, the manifesto is signed and dated "June 1912."

Whether the manifesto was in fact written as early as June 1912 cannot be definitely established. Contemporary Russian sources tend to be contradictory on the issue of when the theory was first discussed. For example, an eminent (unnamed) Soviet specialist on the period cited by Gray definitely remembers that the theory of Rayonism was already being discussed in 1911 (1961, no. 33). Eganbyuri, in an article on the Western European connections of Larionov and Goncharova published in 1922, suggests in passing that Rayonism dates from 1911 (жар птица, Zhar ptitsa, *Firebird,* no. 7, 1922, p. 39). N. Punin, on the other hand, in a 1928 article on Larionov, states that the theory of Rayonism was first presented in 1912-13 (Материалы по русскому искусству, Materialy po russkomu iskusstvu, *Materials on Russian Art,* Leningrad, 1928, pp. 287-291). It is certainly possible that Larionov's ideas for the essay were being formulated during the spring and summer of 1912, as he began to experiment with the style itself. Early signs of a movement towards Rayonism can be seen, as Gray has suggested (1961, no. 30), in works such as *Head of a Soldier* (first exhibited at the *Blaue Reiter* exhibition of March-April 1912), which probably dates from the very end of 1911 or the beginning of 1912. But it is not until well into 1912 that the style is fully established with the creation of works such as *Glass, Rayonist Sausage and Mackerel,* and *Portrait of a Fool.*

EXHIBITIONS:

Moscow, Мир искусства (Mir Iskusstva, *World of Art),* Nov. 1912, no. 155b (Стекло [прием лучизма], Steklo [priëm luchizma], *"Glass,* Rayonist method"), traveled to St. Petersburg, Jan.-Feb. 1913, no. 206; Moscow, Мишень (Mishen, *Target),* Mar. 24-Apr. 7, 1913, no. 79 (Стекло [этюдъ], 1912, Steklo [Etiud], 1912, *"Glass,* study, 1912");[1] Moscow, *No. 4,* Mar.-Apr. (?) 1914, no. 93 (Стекло, Steklo, *Glass);* Paris, Galerie Paul Guillaume, *Exposition Natalia Gontcharova et Michel Larionov,* June 17-30, 1914, no. 16 (*"Le Verre [rayonnisme] 1909");*[2] Rome, Palazzo di Belle Arti, *Seconda Biennale Romana, Espozione Internazionale di Belle Arti,* Autumn 1923, no. 23 *(Il Bicchiere);* Paris, "Galerie l'Epoque," *Larionov; peintures et dessins,* Apr. 11-25, 1931, no. 32 (*"Verrerie,* 1910");[3] Paris, Musée National d'Art Moderne, *L'Oeuvre du XXe siècle,* May-June 1952, no. 53 (*"Les Verres* 1909"); London, Tate Gallery, *Twentieth Century Masterpieces,* July-Aug. 1952, no. 45 (*"Grasses* [sic] 1909"); New York, SRGM 81, 83 (no cats.); 84, 95, 107, 144, 196 (checklists, *"Glasses,* 1909"); Los Angeles County Museum of Art, *The Cubist Epoch,* Dec. 15-1970-Feb. 21, 1971, traveled to New York, The Metropolitan Museum of Art, Apr. 9-June 8, 1971, no. 156 (*"Glasses,* 1911-12?"), color pl. 160; New York, SRGM 260 (no cat.).

REFERENCES:

Essem (pseud. S. Makovsky), *Apollon,* no. 2, Feb. 1913; E. Eganbyuri (pseud. I. M. Zdanevich), Наталия Гончарова, Михаил Ларионов *(Natalia Goncharova, Mikhail Larionov),* ed. Myunster, Moscow, 1913, pp. xxi, 38-39 (Стекло [концентрация впечатлений и лучизм], Steklo [kontsentratsiia vpechatlenii i luchizm], *Glass [concentration of impressions and rayonism];* M. Seuphor, *L'Art abstrait: ses origines, ses premiers maîtres,* Paris, 1950, p. 37; L. Degand, "Le Rayonnisme, Larionov, Gontcharova," *Art d'aujourd'hui,* sér. 2, Nov. 1950, p. 26, repr. p. 27; M. Chamot, "The Early Works of Goncharova and Larionov," *Burlington Magazine,* vol. 97, June 1955, p. 173 [attributed to The Museum of Modern Art, New York]; M. Seuphor, "Au Temps de l'avant-garde," *L'Oeil,* no. 11, Nov. 1955, p. 29; SRGM *Handbook,* 1959, p. 101, repr. p. 100; B. Dorival, "Musée National d'Art Moderne: trois mois d'activité," *La Revue du Louvre,* vol. II, no. 2, 1961, p. 86; C. Gray and M. Chamot, *Larionov and Gon-*

charova, exhibition catalogue, London, Arts Council, 1961, no. 33; C. Gray, *The Great Experiment: Russian Art 1863-1922,* New York, 1962, p. 124; R. Carrieri, *Futurism,* Milan, 1963, p. 135; W. George, *Larionov,* Paris, 1966, p. 116, repr. p. 123; F. Daulte, *Michel Larionov,* exhibition catalogue, New York, Acquavella Galleries, 1969, pp. [3-4]; L. Schafran, "Larionov and the Russian Vanguard," *Art News,* vol. 68, May 1969, p. 36; T. Loguine, *Gontcharova et Larionov,* Paris, 1971, p. 17, fn. 20; P. Vergo, "A Note on the Chronology of Larionov's Early Work," *Burlington Magazine,* vol. 114, July 1972, pp. 476-479; Idem, "Correspondence," Ibid., Sept. 1972, p. 634; J. E. Bowlt, L. Hutton, I. Hutton, S. Bodine, P. Vergo, "Correspondence," Ibid., Oct. 1972, pp. 718-720; A. Z. Rudenstine, "Correspondence," Ibid., Dec. 1972, p. 874.

2. A Der Sturm label removed from the back of the painting probably dates from this time. At the close of the exhibition the paintings were shipped back to Russia, but war broke out before they all arrived. Herwarth Walden claimed them as his property and thus preserved them from destruction at the hands of the German authorities. After the war he returned the works to the 2 artists.

3. The catalogue of this exhibition gives no city, and it has not been possible to verify whether the "Galerie L'Epoque" is in Paris or not. Nor is it certain that the picture listed as no. 32 is *Glass.* It is likely, however, that the present picture is the one listed.

Fernand Léger

Born February 1881, Argentan (Orne).
Died August 1955, Gif-sur-Yvette.

161   The Smokers.
ca. December 1911-January 1912.
(Les Fumeurs; The Smoker).

38.521

Oil on canvas, 51 x 38 (121.4 x 96.5)

Not signed or dated.

PROVENANCE:
D. H. Kahnweiler, Paris, 1912-14;[1] *Collection Henry Kahnweiler: troisième vente,* Hôtel Drouot, Paris, July 4, 1922, no. 103, repr. ("*Les Fumeurs,* signé au dos, daté 1911"); purchased by Galerie l'Effort Moderne (Léonce Rosenberg), Paris;[2] Georges Bernheim, Paris, by 1926 (*Indépendants* exhibition catalogue)—1938 (Mayor Gallery exhibition catalogue); purchased from Bernheim by Galerie Pierre (Pierre Loeb), Paris, 1938; purchased from Loeb by Solomon R.

Guggenheim, 1938; Gift of Solomon R. Guggenheim, 1938.

CONDITION:
In 1953 the picture was lined with wax resin and the surface cleaned. In 1970 active cleavage of paint along approximately 4 inches of the lower right margin was arrested by infusion of wax resin. Some inpainting of unspecified date has occurred along the lower third of the right margin, along the entire top margin, and in the lower left corner.

Apart from considerable wear in the upper corners, and some general areas of traction cracks, the condition is good. (Aug. 1972.)

The work has generally been dated 1911 (see below EXHIBITIONS and REFERENCES). Kahnweiler dated the work 1911 in his article of 1920, although his own photographic archives give the date as 1912 (the year he acquired the work, see fn. 1), and in his 1950 publication he also dated the picture 1912. Ozenfant and Jeanneret, writing on Cubism in the early 1920's, also dated the picture 1912. Léger himself, in a letter to the Guggenheim Museum dated April 25, 1945, referred to the picture as "*Les Fumeurs, 1912;*" on the other hand, his own signature and date on the reverse of the canvas apparently gave the date as 1911 (see fn. 4).

The question of the date is in one important respect related to the identification of the subject of the work and the evaluation of the influence of Futurist theories and paintings on its execution. Golding and others have associated the picture with the entry no. 3498: *Composition avec personnages,* in the *Salon des Indépendants* of March 1912 (see, for example, Golding, p. 153; Apollinaire, *Les Peintres cubistes,* ed. L. C. Breunig and J-Cl. Chevalier, Paris, 1965, pp. 85, 115, fn. 4; SRGM *Handbook,* 1970, p. 263). Spate, however, has argued (pp. 212-216) that the picture represents not two smokers but one—the double head expressing the notion of one figure in motion—and that there can thus be

1. The work appears in the Kahnweiler photographic archives in Paris dated 1912 and was acquired in that year. It was seized with the rest of Kahnweiler's collection as enemy property at the outbreak of the war. The collection was sold at auction in 4 sales between 1921 and 1923.

2. The picture appears in the Rosenberg photographic archives, Paris, as no. 434. He published the picture in *Bulletin de l'Effort Moderne,* no. 9, Nov. 1924 ("*Les Fumeurs 1911*").

no question of *"personnages"* in the plural (p. 212, fn. 24). She cites Apollinaire's 1912 reference to the work as *Le Fumeur* (Breunig and Chevalier, p. 85) —usually regarded as an error for *Les Fumeurs*—as one piece of supporting evidence for her interpretation. She suggests further that Léger's response to the Futurist exhibition of February 1912 and to the ideas expressed in its catalogue is to some extent responsible for the painting's conception, although she stresses that Futurist theories—many of which had been published earlier— probably exerted the greater influence. She sees the double head of the smoker as an attempt to reproduce the "movement of perception which could encompass the different 'simultaneous' views" of the figure and his ambience (p. 213). In thus placing the picture after February 1912, she also states that it must postdate *The Wedding* (Musée National d'Art Moderne, Paris), which she convincingly identifies as *Composition avec personnages* shown in the March *Indépendants* (p. 208).

Whereas Spate is undoubtedly correct in suggesting that *The Wedding* rather than *The Smokers* appeared in the March exhibition (see fn. 3), it is unlikely that the picture represents one smoker rather than two, or that the style of the work is dependent upon any direct influence of Futurist paintings. From a purely visual standpoint it is perhaps possible to describe the configuration either as one figure or as two. If it were seen as one, this might reflect not so much the influence of Futurist works as an exploration on Léger's part of the issues which were also preoccupying Duchamp at the end of 1911—figures seen simultaneously from several viewpoints (as in *Yvonne and Magdaleine Torn in Tatters*, September 1911, Philadelphia Museum of Art), or figures in motion (*Nude Descending a Staircase, I,* December 1911, Philadelphia Museum of Art). However, there is no evidence elsewhere in Léger's works of this period to suggest such preoccupations, and the fact that Léger himself (in his letter of April 1945, and in the inscribed title formerly on the reverse), as well as Kahnweiler and Rosenberg, identified the work as *Les Fumeurs,* argues for the existence of two figures rather than one.

Since the picture does not appear to reflect the influence of the February 1912 Futurist exhibition, its place within the development of Léger's style in 1911-12 remains to be established. M. Richet and Cl. Langier, like Spate, place *The Smokers* chronologically after *The Wedding,* although they date both works earlier—1910-11 for *The Wedding,* and 1911 for *The Smokers* (*Fernand Léger,* exhibition catalogue, Paris, 1971, nos. 5-7). C. Green has argued convincingly (in conversation with the author, November 1972, publication in preparation) that the Guggenheim picture follows the *Three Portraits* (Milwaukee Art Center), shown in the *Salon d'Automne* of 1911, and is approximately contemporary with the oil study for *The Wedding* (Private Collection, Paris, M. Raynal, *From Picasso to Surrealism,* Geneva, 1950, repr. color p. 74). *Smokers* is stylistically very much in tune with this study, and both works precede *The Wedding* itself, which Green, like Spate, identifies with the March *Salon* entry "*Composition avec personnages,*" and which must therefore have been completed by early March. (Green does accept Spate's interpretation of the subject of the picture as one smoker rather than two.) The scale and much more ambitious nature of *The Wedding* (which leads directly to *The Woman in Blue* of late 1912, Kunstmuseum Basel) suggests that it must have taken some months to complete, and it would seem likely, therefore, that *The Smokers* was painted between the end of 1911 and January 1912. Its creation at the turn of the year would explain Kahnweiler's and Léger's own uncertainties of recollection as to whether the picture was painted in 1911 or 1912, and indeed the picture was probably in process from late 1911 until some time early in 1912.

EXHIBITIONS:

Paris, Société des Artistes Indépendants, *Trente ans d'art indépendant 1884-1914,* Feb. 20-Mar. 21, 1926, suppl. no. 2798 ("*Les Fumeurs*-1911, app. à Georges Bernheim");[3] Dresden, *Internationaler Kunstausstellung,* June-Sept. 1926, no. 114 *(Die Räucher)*; Kunsthaus Zürich, *Fernand Léger,* Apr. 30-May 25, 1933, no. 55 ("*Les Fumeurs* 1911, verkäuflich");[4] Paris, Musée du Petit Palais, *Maîtres de l'art indépendant, 1895-1937,* June-Oct., 1937, no. 13 ("*Les Fumeurs, 1912*"); London, Mayor Gallery, *Fernand Léger 1912-1916,* June 1938, no. 2 ("*Les Deux fumeurs, 1912,* lent by Georges Bernheim"); Paris, Musée National d'Art Moderne, *L'Oeuvre du XXe siècle,* May-June, 1952, no. 55 ("*Les Fumeurs, 1911*"), traveled to London, Tate Gallery, July 15-Aug. 17, 1952, no. 47; New York, SRGM 78, 79 (checklists); 83 (no cat.); Toronto, SRGM 85-T, no. 46, repr.; Vancouver, SRGM 88-T, no. 46; Boston, SRGM 90-T (no cat.); Montreal, SRGM 93-T, no. 30; The Arts Club of Chicago, *Cubism,* Oct. 3-Nov. 4, 1955, no. 39; New York, SRGM 97 (checklist); London, SRGM 104-T, no. 39; Boston, SRGM 119-T, no. 36; Lexington, Ky., SRGM 122-T, no. 16, repr.; New York, SRGM 127 (checklist); 129 (checklist, repr.); Philadelphia, SRGM 134-T, no. 90; Worcester, Mass., SRGM 148-T, no. 24, repr.; New York, SRGM 151, 153 (checklists); 173, no. 21, repr.; 196 (checklist); 198-T (no cat.); 202, p. 44, repr. p. 45; The Baltimore Museum of Art, *From El Greco to Pollock: Early and Late Works by European and American Artists,* Oct. 22-Dec. 8, 1968, no. 121, repr.; New York, SRGM 216, 221 (no cats.); 232, pp. 263-264, repr. p. 262; Los Angeles County Museum of Art, *The Cubist Epoch,* Dec. 15, 1970-Feb. 21, 1971, no. 178 repr. color, traveled to New York, Metropolitan Museum of Art, Apr. 9-June 8, 1971; New York, SRGM 241, pp. 263-264, repr. p. 262; Paris, Grand Palais, *Fernand Léger,* Oct. 1971-Jan. 1972, no. 7, repr.; New York, SRGM 251 (no cat.); Cleveland, SRGM 258-T, pl. 5; New York, SRGM 276 (no cat.).

REFERENCES:

G. Apollinaire, *Les Peintres cubistes,* Paris, 1913, p. 65 *(Le Fumeur)*; D. Henry [Kahnweiler], "Fernand Léger," *Jahrbuch der Jungen Kunst,* ed. G. Biermann, Leipzig, 1920, p. 301, repr. p. 302 (dated 1911); *The Little Review,* vol. 9, spring 1923, repr. opp. p. 16 (dated 1911); A. Ozenfant and C. E. Jeanneret, "Le Cubisme," *L'Esprit Nouveau,* no. 23, repr. n.p. (dated 1912); Idem, *La Peinture moderne,* Paris, 1924, p. 97 (dated 1912); *Bulletin de l'Effort Moderne,* no. 9, Nov. 1924, repr. n.p. (dated 1911); E. Tériade, *Fernand Léger,* Paris, 1928, repr. p. 12 (*Les deux fumeurs,* [n.d.]); B. Cendrars, "F. Léger," *Cahiers d'Art,* vol. 8, no. 3-4, 1933, n.p. (dated 1911); D. Cooper, *Léger et le nouvel espace,* Geneva-Paris-London, 1949, repr. p. 44 (dated 1911); D. H. Kahnweiler, *Les Années héroiques du cubisme,* Paris, 1950, pl. 57 (dated 1912); C. Zervos, *Fernand Léger,* Paris, 1952, p. 16, repr. p. 30 (dated 1911); K. Kuh, *Léger,* Urbana, 1953, repr. p. 94 (dated 1911); F. Mathey, *F. Léger,* exhibition catalogue, Paris, 1955, p. 28 (dated 1911); F. Fosca, *Bilan du cubisme,* Paris, 1956, p. 38 (dated 1912); Golding, *Cubism,* 1968, p. 153, pl. 62 (dated 1911); Cooper, *Cubist Epoch,* 1970, no. 178, pp. 90, 296, color pl. 87 (dated 1911); Spate, 1970, pp. 212-214.

3. The entries in the catalogue include the notation *"IND"* for those works that had appeared in previous exhibitions of the *Salon des Indépendants.* There is no such reference in the present case, strongly suggesting that the picture did not, as has been generally supposed, appear in the 1912 Salon des Indépendants. Moreover, *The Wedding* is, according to the 1933 Kunsthaus Zürich exhibition catalogue (no. 56), inscribed on the reverse "*Composition avec personnages. Salon des Indépendants 1911-12.*" It is thus most probably the latter work that appeared in the 1912 *Salon.*

4. According to the catalogue of the Zurich exhibition, the picture is inscribed on the reverse: "*F. LEGER. LES Fumeurs (1911).*" This bears out the information in the Kahnweiler sale catalogue (see above PROVENANCE). However, it has been impossible to verify this fact since no such inscription was recorded when the work was acquired by the Guggenheim in 1938, and the picture has since been lined.

162   Nude Model in the Studio. 1912-1913.
(*Le Modèle nu dans l'atelier; Nude model*).

49.1193

Oil on burlap, 50⅜ x 37⅝ (127.8 x 95.7)

Signed: l.r.: *F. Léger;* inscribed c.l.: *EF.;* inscribed by the artist on reverse: *Le Modèle nu. ./dans l'atelier / Salon des indépen / dant. .1912-13 / (complémentaires de . . .) / F. Leger.*

PROVENANCE:

Early history unknown, but probably kept by Léger until after 1928;[1] Galerie de France, Paris, by 1946; purchased from Galerie de France by Louis Carré, Paris, February 1946 (information supplied by Carré, correspondence with the author, October 1972); purchased from Carré by Sidney Janis Gallery, New York, 1948; purchased from Janis, 1949.

CONDITION:

In 1971 the work was removed from its strainer, the back scraped, and the edges coated with BEVA to prevent raveling. It was noted that approximately ¾ in. of the upper margin had been tacked over the previous stretcher and heavily damaged. The surface of the work was cleaned with 5% Soilax, except for the red and blue areas which were soluble and cleaned only with dry cotton. Only the most discolored portions of the unevenly applied varnish were removed. The work was lined on fiberglass with ABCG adhesive and restretched on a new stretcher. The tack holes were filled with gesso and the losses inpainted. These were especially heavy in the ¾ in. margin along the upper edge. Other minor losses in the large black area left of center, the large white area left of center 14 in. from the left and 21 in. from the top, and the gray-white area at the lower right were also inpainted.

There is a heavy crackle throughout the white areas, and in a few other places. There is no ground, and the pigment has suffered from poor bonding with the support. These cracks are stable, however, and do not show any present danger of developing into cleavage. The overall condition is fair. (Mar. 1974.)

At some point between the 1913 Berlin exhibition and the 1946 acquisition of the work by Carré, Léger made some minor changes in the composition. (A photograph of the work supplied by Carré is the earliest located to date in which the changes are visible). The most notable of these changes are the puzzling addition of the letters *EF* at the center left and of some of the prominent lines immediately above these letters; several other scattered small lines, presumably added at the same time, are much less prominent and do not significantly alter the original conception. (For reproductions of the work prior to changes see below REFERENCES, all publications up to and including Zervos, 1952. Since the changes had definitely been made before 1946, Zervos must have been using an old photograph.) When he returned from the war in 1918, Léger began to include letters in his work and it is possible that he made the changes at approximately this time.

There are several studies of nudes in the studio which date from 1912-13. Two charcoal drawings and a gouache show the figure facing front or slightly

1. The picture did not belong to Kahnweiler, and it does not appear among the Rosenberg photographic archives in Paris, but these are incomplete. Tériade's publication of the work in 1928 without collection credit suggests that Léger still owned the work at that time.

fig. a.
Léger, study for *Nude Model in the Studio,* pencil and ink on paper, 18⅞ x 13⅜ in., 48 x 34 cm., Private Collection, Paris.

fig. b.
Léger, study for *Nude Model in the Studio,* gouache on paper (?), dimensions and present whereabouts unknown.

left with one arm across the chest and the hand resting on the opposite shoulder. These are a *Seated Nude* in a private collection in Stuttgart (formerly Galerie Beyeler, Basel, charcoal on paper, 19¼ x 12⅝ in., 49 x 32 cm., signed and dated *"FL 13,"* but probably datable 1912); a *Seated Nude* formerly in the Marie Cuttoli Collection, Paris (Galerie Beyeler, Basel, *Collection Marie Cuttoli, Henry Langier,* October-November 1970, no. 55, charcoal on paper, 25¼ x 19¼ in., 64 x 49 cm., signed and dated *"F.L 12"*); and a *Nude in the Studio* in a private collection in Paris (charcoal, ink, and gouache, 24 x 19¾ in., 61 x 50 cm., signed and dated *"F.LEGER 12,"* Galerie Louise Leiris, Paris, *Leger: dessins et gouaches,* February-March 1958, no. 4, repr.). Two further studies, one in ink and one in gouache, show the figure facing front, but in a much more abstract form than the above works, and clearly closer in time of execution to the painting itself (*Nude,* Galerie Louise Leiris, photo no. 30659, ink on paper, 12⅞ x 9¾ in., 32.7 x 24.8 cm., inscribed *"Ad.Basler,"* known as *Study for the Woman in Blue*; and *Nude,* formerly Silberman Galleries, Sale Sotheby Parke Bernet, New York, April 17, 1969, repr. no. 124, india ink, charcoal, and gouache on paper, 25 x 18½ in., 63.5 x 47 cm., signed and dated *"FL 12,"* known as *Contrastes de Formes*). Although these five works are clearly part of Léger's exploration of the subject depicted in the Guggenheim's *Nude Model,* they cannot be specifically described as studies for the work itself.

fig. c.
Léger, study for *Nude Model in the Studio,*
gouache on paper, 14⅛ x 11⅜ in., 36 x 29
cm., Sammlung Sprengel, Hanover.

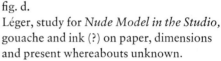

fig. d.
Léger, study for *Nude Model in the Studio,*
gouache and ink (?) on paper, dimensions
and present whereabouts unknown.

Several directly related studies do exist however. The earliest of these (fig. a) is a pencil and ink drawing which is signed and dated *"F.L.13 / Dessin pour le modèle nu,"* but which must surely date from 1912. Three gouaches, two of which are extremely close to the finished work, are also known. One (fig. b) was reproduced by Apollinaire in his March 18 *Montjoie!* review of the 1913 *Salon* (see fn. 2). A second is in the Sprengel Collection, Hanover (fig. c, Städtische Kunsthalle Düsseldorf, *Léger,* December 16, 1969-February 8, 1970, no. 2, erroneously captioned *"no. 3. Les toits"*). The third (fig. d, present whereabouts unknown) is among the photographic archives of Léonce Rosenberg in Paris (no. 1058).

In addition to the gouache reproduced by Apollinaire, several of the studies listed here may well have been included in the group exhibited in the 1913 *Salon* (see fn. 2). It is difficult to establish with certainty the exact sequence of the various studies, as well as the time the painting itself was started. The picture has been dated 1912, 1912-13, or early 1913 (see below REFERENCES). With the exception of Delevoy, authors have agreed that the picture was painted after *Woman in Blue* and before 1913 *Contrasts of Forms,* and that work on the picture must thus have begun in the last quarter of 1912. Apollinaire's March 18 review would suggest that Léger was at that point still not entirely happy with the painting, although it must by then have been close enough to completion to allow for its exhibition in that month, and it was apparently finished by March 25.

EXHIBITIONS:

Paris, *Salon des Indépendants,* Mar. 19-May 18, 1913;[2] Berlin, Der Sturm, *Erster Deutscher Herbstsalon,* Sept. 20-Nov. 1, 1913, no. 253, repr.; Hanover, Kestner Gesellschaft, *Französischer Malerei bis 1914 und Deutsche Künstler des Café du Dôme,* Sept. 7-Nov. 12, 1919, no. 94; Paris, Galerie Louis Carré, *Fernand Léger 1912-1939, 1946-1948,* June 11-July 11, 1948 (no cat.); The Art Institute of Chicago, *Léger,* Apr. 2-May 17, 1953, no. 9, repr., traveled to San Francisco Museum of Art, June 15-Aug. 23, 1953, New York, The Museum of Modern Art, Oct. 6, 1953-Jan. 3, 1954 (dated 1912); New York, SRGM 84, 87 (checklists); 89 (no cat.); 95 (checklist); Hartford, Wadsworth Atheneum, *Twentieth Century Painting from Three Cities,* Oct. 19-Dec. 4, 1955, no. 28 (dated 1912); New York, SRGM 107, 111, 112, 118, 129, 144, 196 (checklists); 202, p. 117, repr.; 221, 266 (no cats.).

REFERENCES:

Les Soirées de Paris, July-Aug. 1914, no. 26-27, frontispiece (dated 1913); H. Walden, *Expressionismus, die Kunstwende,* Berlin, 1918, repr. p. 61 (n.d.); D. Henry [Kahnweiler], "Fernand Léger," *Jahrbuch der Jungen Kunst,* ed. G. Biermann, Leipzig, 1920, repr. p. 303 (dated 1912-13); R. Blümner, *Der Geist des Kubismus und die Künste,* Berlin, 1921, repr. foll. p. 32 (n.d.); E. Tériade, *Fernand Léger,* Paris, 1928, repr. p. 14 (n.d.); D. Cooper, *Léger et le nouvel espace,* Geneva-Paris-London, 1949, repr. p. 54 (dated 1912); C. Zervos, *Fernand Léger,* Paris, 1952, p. 34 (dated 1912-13); K. Kuh, *Léger,* Urbana, Ill., 1953, p. 18, repr. (dated 1912); R. Delevoy, *Léger,* Geneva, 1962, p. 42 (dated 1912); Spate, 1970, pp. 225-226 (dated "early 1913"); C. Green, *Fernand Léger and the Parisian "Avant-garde," 1909-1921,* unpublished Ph.D. dissertation, Courtauld Institute of Art, University of London, 1973, pp. 84-87, 89.

2. The inscription on the reverse suggests that the picture did indeed appear in the *Salon des Indépendants,* and there is other evidence which helps to substantiate this point. Although Léger does not appear at all in the catalogue for that year, his entries are mentioned in two reviews of the exhibition by Apollinaire. In *Montjoie!* of Mar. 18, 1913, the critic refers to Léger's "studies" in Salle 45 as examples of the current Orphic tendencies of his style; in connection with the review Apollinaire reproduces a late gouache study for the *Nude Model in the Studio* (fig. b). He praises Léger's artistic conscience which led him to withhold the "large canvas" from the exhibition since it did not yet quite fulfill his aims, implying that he sent the studies for the picture instead. *("La lumière est içi dans toute sa vérité. C'est la nouvelle tendance du cubisme et nous retrouverons cette tendance à l'orphisme dans la salle suivante, dans presque toutes les toiles, mais surtout dans les études de Fernand Léger dont il faut louer la grande conscience artistique puisque, n'ayant pas encore atteint le but qu'il poursuivait, il n'a pas voulu envoyer sa grande toile.")*

In the review published on Mar. 25 in *L'Intransigeant,* however, Apollinaire implies that the picture itself was included after all. ("... *Cette nouvelle tendance se retrouve dans presque toutes les toiles de la salle suivante, notamment la toile de Fernand Léger. Il faut louer ce peintre, il expose pour la première fois un 'tableau.' C'est un très grand et très serieux effort.")*

The exhibition opened March 19; in order to publish a lengthy review on March 18, Apollinaire would have had to view the show at least three or four days before. It would seem, therefore, that some time between about March 14 (when Apollinaire saw the studies exhibited) and the following week (when he wrote his review for *L'Intransigeant*), Léger changed his mind and decided that the large picture was ready to be exhibited after all. Apollinaire, having first praised the conscience of the artist for withholding the work, now praises him for the quality of the work itself. It is difficult to know what he means by the statement that Léger is exhibiting *"un tableau"* for the first time, since he had shown major pictures in the *Salon des Indépendants* of 1911 and 1912. It does seem likely, however, that the *"tableau"* in question can be none other than the *Nude Model in the Studio.*

163   Contrast of Forms. 1913.
      (Contraste de formes; Variation de formes).

38.345

Oil on burlap, 38⅞ x 49¼ (98.8 x 125)

Signed l.l.: *F. Léger*; signed and dated on reverse (transcribed but not photographed before relining): *F. Léger. 1913*.

PROVENANCE:

D. H. Kahnweiler, Paris, 1913-14;[1] *Collection Henry Kahnweiler: quatrième vente,* Hôtel Drouot, Paris, May 7, 1923, no. 314 *("Eléments géometriques bleus et rouges,* 1m. x 1.25m."); probably purchased by Galerie l'Effort Moderne (Léonce Rosenberg), Paris;[2] Galerie Pierre (Pierre Loeb), Paris, by 1938; purchased from Loeb by

Solomon R. Guggenheim, 1938; Gift of Solomon R. Guggenheim, 1938.

CONDITION:

At an unspecified date (probably ca. 1953) the canvas was lined with wax resin.

Wax has penetrated the burlap in many places and darkened the ground to some extent. There is substantial wear along the 4 edges, and 2 losses of paint and ground, ½ and ¾ in. respectively. There are scattered cracks in the paint layer, especially in the heavy impasto, but this condition is not general. There are a few scattered minor abrasions, but the condition in general is good. (Sept. 1973.)

1. Kahnweiler photographic archives, Paris, no. 6003.
2. Rosenberg photographic archives, Paris, no. 1409.

This work and another formerly in the SRGM Collection (fig. a) belong to a group of more than nine oil *Contrasts of Forms,* all of which were painted in 1913 and all of which contain at the upper center what Green has called a "kite motif" (1973; an additional publication by Green specifically on this series is in preparation). Major examples in the group are as follows, though the listing is not intended to reflect a chronological sequence, the development within the group being difficult to establish:

fig. a.
Léger, *Contrast of Forms,* 1913, oil on burlap, 18 x 24 in., 45.7 x 61 cm., Perls Gallery, New York.

No. 1, a small horizontal canvas closely related to the present work and to fig. a (fig. b, Kahnweiler photo archives, Paris, no. 6014).

No. 2, a much larger horizontal canvas in the collection of S. Rosengart, Lucerne (fig. d). This version is closely related to the present work, but even more closely to the Philadelphia picture (No. 6 below).

A series of four vertical canvases in which the compositional elements of the present work are further developed:

No. 3, *Contrast of Forms,* 31⅞ x 25⅝ in., 81 x 65 cm., Galerie Beyeler, Basel, Beyeler, *Léger,* May-June 1964 (repr. color, no. 4);

No. 4, *Contrast of Forms,* 36¼ x 28¾ in., 92 x 73 cm., Collection Louis Carré, Paris (C. Zervos, *Léger,* Paris, 1952, color frontispiece);

No. 5, *Contrast of Forms,* 39½ x 32 in., 100 x 81 cm., The Museum of Modern Art, New York (Cooper, *Cubist Epoch,* 1970, color pl. 92);

No. 6, *Contrast of Forms,* 51⅜ x 38⅜ in., 133 x 119 cm., Philadelphia Museum of Art (Golding, *Cubism,* 1968, color pl. D).

A vertical and a horizontal canvas in which the "kite motif" is much less prominent, and which are in other respects less closely related to the other six works:

fig. b.
Léger, *Contrast of Forms,* 1913, oil on canvas, 15 x 18⅛
in., 38.1 x 46 cm., present whereabouts unknown.

fig. c.
Léger, *Contrast of Forms,* 1913, gouache on paper,
17⅝ x 21⅜ in., 44.8 x 54.2 cm., Collection S. Rosengart,
Lucerne.

fig. d.
Léger, *Contrast of Forms,* 1913, oil
on canvas, 66¾ x 69⅛ in.,
169.5 x 175.5 cm., Collection S.
Rosengart, Lucerne.

No. 7, *Contrast of Forms,* 21⅝ x 18⅛ in., 55 x 46 cm., Private Collection
(Galerie Berggruen, Paris, *Léger,* 1962, repr. color [no. 8]);

No. 8, *Contrast of Forms,* 23⅝ x 28¾ in., 60 x 73 cm., Collection Louis
Carré, Paris (Ibid., repr. color [no. 9]).

In addition Léger made several gouaches of the subject, some of which can
be directly related to finished paintings but most of which are independent.
Two are especially important within the development of the present group. A
gouache in the collection of S. Rosengart, Lucerne (fig. c), is closely related to

the present work, to fig. a, and to fig. b, although it cannot be described as a direct study for any of the three. A highly colored gouache in the collection of H. Berggruen (Galerie Berggruen, Paris, *Léger,* 1962, repr. color cover) is closely related to the series of vertical compositions nos. 2-4 above, but must be considered an independent composition within that group.

Green has argued convincingly (1973, pp. 96-101) that the *Contrasts of Forms,* Léger's most cogent and direct statement in the realm of *peinture pure,* emerge directly from and are clearly linked to the immediately preceding landscapes, such as *Houses under the Trees* (Museum Folkwang, Essen). The forms in the *Contrasts* are arranged to make their "origins in nature . . . almost unrecognizable as such" (p. 97), but the syntax or arrangement of elements is nonetheless basically the same. Green further suggests that the structure and organization of even the most "pure" *Contrasts* have a strong "figurative flavor" (p. 101) and he cogently analyzes the connection between works such as the Philadelphia *Contrast* (No. 6, above) and the gouache study (also in Philadelphia) for the 1914 *Woman in Red and Green.* While pointing out the demonstrable connections on the one hand to landscape and on the other to figuration, Green strongly emphasizes the quality of "pure pictorial contrasts" which Léger achieved in these *Contrasts of Forms* and gives a detailed analysis of the intellectual and visual stimuli which lay behind this development in the artist's work (pp. 102-134).

EXHIBITIONS:

New York, SRGM 74, no. 136; 78 (checklist); Toronto, SRGM 85-T, no. 47; New York, SRGM 87 (checklist); 89 (no cat.); Montreal, SRGM 93-T, no. 31; London, SRGM 104-T, no. 40; Boston, SRGM 119-T, no. 37; New York, SRGM 129 (checklist); 144, 151, 153 (checklists); 173, no. 31, repr.; 202, p. 39, repr. p. 38; 266, 276 (no cats.).

REFERENCES:

F. Léger, "Les Réalisations picturales actuelles," *Soirées de Paris,* June 15, 1914, pp. 349-354; E. Fry, *Cubism,* New York, 1966, pp. 31, 127, fig. 47; Golding, *Cubism,* 1968, p. 178, pl. 65; C. Green, *Fernand Léger and the Parisian "Avant-garde,"* 1909-1921, unpublished Ph.D. dissertation, Courtauld Institute of Art, University of London, 1973, pp. 96 ff.

164 The Clock. March 1918.
(L'Horloge).

38.522

Oil on burlap, 19⅞ x 24¼ (50.5 x 61.6)

Signed l.r.: *F. Leger*; inscribed by the artist on reverse (photographed before lining): *L'Horloge / Mars—18 / F. Leger.*

PROVENANCE:

Galerie l'Effort Moderne (Léonce Rosenberg), Paris, 1918-after 1926;[1] Rose Valland, Paris, by 1938; purchased from Valland by Solomon R. Guggenheim, 1938; Gift of Solomon R. Guggenheim, 1938.

CONDITION:

In 1954 the canvas was lined with wax resin and the strainer replaced with a new stretcher. The surface was superficially cleaned (varnish not removed); 2 small areas of paint loss (top right corner, and upper margin near right corner) were filled and inpainted. The canvas was surfaced with clear synthetic varnish.

Some chips of paint have been lost along the edges; the signature is worn and partially lost. The condition otherwise is good. (Feb. 1972.)

1. Rosenberg photographic archives, Paris, no. 865. Léger's contract with Rosenberg is dated July 15, 1918, and it is probable that this was among the works acquired by Rosenberg immediately afterwards. The picture is published by Rosenberg in his 1926 *Bulletin de l'Effort Moderne* (see below REFERENCES).

EXHIBITIONS:

Geneva, Galerie Moos, *La Jeune peinture française: les cubistes,* Feb. 1920, no. 88;[2] New York, SRGM 78 (checklist); Toronto, SRGM 85-T, no. 49; Vancouver, SRGM 88-T, no. 49; Montreal, SRGM 93-T, no. 32, repr.; London, SRGM 104-T, no. 41, pl. 6; New York, SRGM 118 (checklist); St. Louis, Washington University, *Fernand Léger,* circulating exhibition organized by The Museum of Modern Art, New York, traveled to Ithaca, N.Y., Cornell University, Ohio, University of Akron, Savannah, Georgia, Telfair Academy of Arts and Sciences, Hannover, N.H., Dartmouth College, Poughkeepsie, N.Y., Vassar College, Des Moines Art Center, 1967-68 (no cat.); Honolulu Academy of Arts, *Léger and the Machine,* Sept. 11-Oct. 26, 1969, no. 4; New York, SRGM 236 (no cat.); Rochester, N.Y., SRGM 263-T (no cat.); New York, SRGM 276 (no cat.).

REFERENCES:

Bulletin de l'Effort Moderne, Paris, no. 28, Oct. 1926, repr. n.p. (dated 1926); A. Salmon, "F. Léger," *Cahiers d'Art,* vol. 8, no. 3-4, 1933, n.p. ("*Composition 1918*"); SRGM *Handbook,* 1959, p.105, repr.

2. This exhibition was organized by Rosenberg.

---

165 The Stove. April 1918.
(Le Poèle).

38.525

Oil on canvas, 24 x 19¾ (61 x 50.1)

Inscribed by the artist on reverse (photographed before lining): *Le Poèle / Avril. 18 / F. Léger.*

PROVENANCE:

Early history unknown;[1] Galerie Pierre (Pierre Loeb), Paris, by 1938; purchased from Loeb by Solomon R. Guggenheim, 1938; Gift of Solomon R. Guggenheim, 1938.

CONDITION:

In 1954 the canvas was lined with wax resin and placed on a new stretcher. The surface was superficially cleaned (varnish not removed); areas of paint loss in the top left and top right corners, and right margin 1 in. from the top were filled and inpainted. There are 8 other scattered tiny touches of inpainting. The canvas was surfaced with clear synthetic varnish.

There is considerable wear in the 4 corners, and there are some other minor cracks in the paint film, but the condition in general is good. (Feb. 1972.)

1. The picture does not appear among the Rosenberg photographic archives in Paris, but these are incomplete. It was also not included, as many of Léger's 1918 works were, in Rosenberg's 1920 exhibition at the Galerie Moos in Geneva. It is possible, therefore, that Léger himself kept the picture for some time instead of selling it to Rosenberg.

165

The Clock and The Stove were both probably painted while Léger was recuperating in the hospital after being exposed to gas at the front in 1917. The dates and locations of his convalescence have yet to be completely documented, but some facts are known. A *"billet d'hôpital"* records his stay in a Paris hospital from March 16, 1918, to May 31, 1918 (*Fernand Léger, sa vie, son oeuvre, sa rêve,* Milan, 1972, repr. n.p.). In addition, two drawings inscribed *"Hôp. Villepinte"* were published in the April 1918 issue of *Nord-Sud.* (This latter fact was brought to my attention by C. Green.) It seems likely, therefore, that Léger started his recuperation period in Villepinte and was later moved to Paris. He was apparently completely discharged by July 1918, when he signed a contract with Rosenberg in Paris.

A preparatory drawing for *The Stove* (fig. a) contains hospital details such as a patient in bed at the right side. The cylindrical form diagonally placed in the center is clearly the stove pipe. The drawing thus probably dates from late in 1917 or early 1918. Various other works from this hospital period are closely related to the two Guggenheim pictures. Two versions of *The Barge-man* (one now in The Museum of Modern Art, Sidney Janis Collection, one sold at Christie's, July 2, 1974, lot 105) were both painted in March 1918. The *Pot of Herbal Tea* (Private Collection Paris, Grand Palais, Paris, *Léger*, exhibition catalogue, 1971-72, repr. no. 32) is inscribed on the reverse *"avril 18"* and was identified by Léger himself as having been painted in the hospital. A pencil and ink drawing for it in The Art Institute of Chicago is dated 1917 and is close in style to the preparatory study for *The Stove* (fig. a). A painting formerly in the Léonce Rosenberg Collection (Rosenberg photographic archives, Paris, no. 880, A. Salmon, *Cahiers d'Art,* vol. 8, no. 3-4, 1933, repr. n.p.) must be almost exactly contemporary with *The Stove;* the composition is almost identical in reverse, but it is less fragmented in its forms than the Guggenheim version and probably precedes it. Very shortly afterwards Léger must have painted *Factories* (Collection Robin D. Judah, London, *Léger and Purist Paris,* London, 1970-71, no. 5, repr. p. 46), the Cologne *Tugboat* (Ibid., no. 9, repr. p. 43), and the Paris *Tugboat* (Grand Palais, Paris, *Léger,* 1971-72, no. 40, p. 64), which is inscribed *"Etat définitif, juin 1918."*

fig. a.
Léger, *Interior of a Hospital,* 1917-18(?), ink on paper, 6⅜ x 5 in., 16.3 x 12.8 cm., present whereabouts unknown, reproduced courtesy Douglas Cooper and Heinz Berggruen.

EXHIBITIONS:

New York, SRGM 74, no. 135; 78, 79 (checklists); Toronto, SRGM 85-T, no. 50; Vancouver, SRGM 88-T, no. 50, repr.; Lexington, Ky., SRGM 122-T, no. 17; New York, SRGM 132 (checklist); Laguna Beach, Cal., SRGM 143-T (no cat.); Honolulu Academy of Arts, *Léger and the Machine,* Sept. 11-Oct. 26, 1969, no. 2; London, Tate Gallery, *Léger and Purist Paris,* Nov. 18, 1970-Jan. 24, 1971, no. 6, repr.; New York, SRGM 266, 276 (no cats.).

REFERENCE:

C. Green, *Léger and Purist Paris,* exhibition catalogue, London, 1970, pp. 45-46.

166   Mural Painting. 1924-1925.
       (Peinture murale).

58.1507

Oil on canvas, 71 x 31⅝ (180.2 x 80.2)

Signed and dated l.r.: *F. Léger. 25*; inscribed
by the artist on reverse: *Peinture Murale /
F. Léger—24.*

PROVENANCE:

Christian Zervos, Paris, by 1949 (Musée
National exhibition catalogue);[1] purchased
from Yvonne Zervos, Paris, 1958.

CONDITION:

The work has received no treatment since
its acquisition. At an unspecified date, inpainting of minor losses along the edges, in
the corners, and along the left edge of the
central dark red rectangle was performed.

Pentimenti are clearly visible along the left
sides of the lower red form and the right-
hand blue form, as well as along the left
edge of the central dark red rectangle. Some
ground cracks have caused cracks in the
paint film; these are in isolated areas and
the overall condition of the paint film is
good, though potentially fragile. (Mar.
1973.)

In October 1923 Léonce Rosenberg's Galerie l'Effort Moderne exhibited a
group of three De Stijl architectural projects. In each building the individual
walls, floors, and ceilings were colored in one of the three primaries or white.
Léger's immediate and enthusiastic response to the potentialities inherent in
such a "polychromatic architecture" is recorded by Le Corbusier in *L'Esprit
Nouveau*, no. 19, where Léger is placed in conversation with "X" and praises
the notion of a red, blue, or yellow wall, a black, blue, red, or yellow floor, as
"a total transformation of interior design." Léger's own first article on the subject appeared in *L'Architecture vivante*, Autumn / Winter 1924 (pp. 21-22). In
this piece, and in innumerable theoretical writings of the 1930's, 1940's, and
1950's, he expounded his developing notions of the role of color in architecture
and of the relationship between the work of the painter and that of the architect. (See, for example, "Le Mur, l'architecte, le peintre," 1933, first published
in *Fonctions de la peinture*, Paris, 1965, pp. 110-112; "Modern Architecture
and Color," *American Abstract Artists*, New York, 1946; "Un Nouvel espace
en architecture," *Art d'Aujourd'hui*, no. 3, Paris, 1949; "De la peinture murale," 1952, *Derrière le miroir*, no. 107-109, 1958; "La Couleur dans l'architecture," *Problèmes de la couleur*, Paris, 1954.)

The abstract "murals" of 1924-26 developed directly out of Léger's earliest
thinking on the subject and constituted a step beyond the notion of the colored
wall. They are conceived not as easel paintings but as complements to architecture, and it was in relation to the work of Le Corbusier in particular that he
evolved his theory of a specifically abstract mural art. In 1950 he wrote, "I believe and I maintain that abstract art is in trouble when it tries to do easel paint-

---

1. The picture was probably purchased directly from Léger, although no proof of this fact,
   or of Zervos' date of acquisition, has hitherto been found. The picture was never owned by
   Kahnweiler. It does not appear among the Rosenberg photographic archives in Paris, but
   these are incomplete.

ing. But *for the mural the possibilities are unlimited"* (*Functions of Painting: The Documents of 20th Century Art*, New York, 1973, p. 162 [not included in the 1965 French edition]). Le Corbusier regarded Léger's work of these years as an extension of his own desire to manipulate and vary apparently static space ("L'Architecture et Fernand Léger," *Sélection*, no. 5, Antwerp, 1929). Just as the colors of walls could effectively cause those walls to advance or recede, making the habitable rectangle an expandable one, so Léger's colored planes— with their "cunning play of colored forces moving on the surface of the wall" —could further expand the architect's possibilities. The flat areas of color in these paintings performed two functions: on the one hand they reinforced the flatness of the wall; on the other they broke into the flatness, thereby expanding and vitalizing the space around them and destroying what Léger felt was the intimidating rigidity of the blank wall. (See "De la peinture murale," *Derrière le miroir*, no. 44-45, March / April 1952, p. 6.)

Léger's theory of the function of abstract mural painting as a complement to architecture, the painter in a subservient role to that of the architect, is amply and clearly expressed in his writings, and Le Corbusier's corresponding theories suggest considerable exchange of ideas between the two. However, no evidence apparently survives to illustrate the actual results of Léger's collaboration with architects of the period. Two projects are widely cited in the literature as illustrative of this collaboration. The first is R. Mallet-Stevens' embassy for the 1925 *Exposition des arts décoratifs*. In this instance Léger and Delaunay provided paintings which were hung in the entrance hall (W. George, *L'Amour de l'art*, no. 8, August 1925, p. 289). Léger's "mural," present whereabouts unknown, is reproduced by George in its architectural context (p. 291). It belongs to the series of abstract paintings under discussion, but its origin as a commissioned work specifically conceived for the architectural setting in which it was hung is in doubt. Léger's name does not appear on the published list of artists who collaborated with Mallet-Stevens on the building (*Catalogue général officiel: exposition internationale des arts décoratifs et industriels modernes*, Paris, October 1925, p. 96, "*Hall composé par Mallet-Stevens . . . réalisé avec la collaboration de . . .*"). Moreover, though Léger in later years sometimes spoke of Mallet-Stevens' request that he produce a painting for the building (see, for example, "De la peinture murale," 1952), he elsewhere stated that the painting was already finished when Mallet-Stevens saw it for the first time and requested it for the building.

> *Je me souviens qu'à l'Exposition de 1925 j'avais travaillé à des choses abstraites en couleur pure, extrêmement rectangulaires, et Mallet-Stevens . . . venu chez moi, avait vu une grande peinture assez haute et large, absolument abstraite, en couleur assez forte, rectangulaire . . . il m'avait dit: "J'aimerais beaucoup avoir cela chez moi (dans l'ambassade)." J'ai donc mis chez lui cette chose qui n'était pas du tout appropriée, mais quand même cela constituait une attaque, une présence* (1954, first published in *Fonctions de la peinture*, Paris, 1965, p. 105; see also "Un Nouvel espace en architecture," pp. 123-124, first published 1949).

The second project which is generally cited as the prime example of Léger as mural painter working in collaboration with an architect is Le Corbusier's Pavillon de l'Esprit Nouveau also constructed for the 1925 *Exposition*. Léger himself stated on more than one occasion that his first murals were painted for Le Corbusier, implying thereby either that they were actually ordered by the architect to function within existing or projected structures, or that they were at least conceived in relation to such buildings. Surviving photographs of the interior spaces of the Pavillon de l'Esprit Nouveau do not, however, include any of Léger's abstract murals. The only paintings by him clearly visible in the interior are a 1924 *Composition*, present whereabouts unknown, which is closely related to works such as *The City* of 1919 or *The Large Tugboat* of 1923 (P. Selmersheim, *Le Village moderne, les constructions régionalistes et quelques autres pavillons*, Paris, 1925, pl. 40) and the 1925 *The Baluster*, The Museum of Modern Art, New York. The modeling and perspective in these works bring them into much closer relationship with Léger's contemporary still-lifes, and hence with his notion of easel painting, than with his expressed idea of an abstract mural art. (For an illuminating discussion of *The Baluster* and related works of this period see C. Green, *Léger and Purist Paris,* exhibition catalogue, London, 1970, p. 79.) Moreover, various pieces of additional evidence demonstrate that the Pavillon was apparently not the context for which Léger's first murals were designed. For example, in his own essay on the building, Le Corbusier specifically states that the works which hung on the walls were easel paintings, independently created, and not commissioned for the project. (*"Nous avons mis au mur des tableaux de Picasso, Braque, Léger, Gris, Ozenfant . . . des tableaux de chevalet dans des cadres. . . . Il est mieux que l'oeuvre peinte ou sculptée soit pas une 'commande' mais un produit direct de l'imagination." Almanach d'architecture moderne*, Paris [1925 or 1926?], pp. 145-146.) Likewise, Ozenfant's reminiscences about the project specifically rule out the notion that any murals were painted for it. (*"Personne ne fit aucune peinture murale pour ce pavillon. Le Tableau Léger—comme le mien d'ailleurs qui lui faisait face . . .—étaient des tableaux de chevalet, peint avant la construction du pavillon qui furent simplement prêtés pour y être accrochés." Mémoires 1886-1962*, Paris, 1968, p. 141. I am indebted to J. C. Di Meo for drawing this passage to my attention.)

Thus, although it is possible that some of the 1924-25 "murals" such as the Guggenheim painting were specifically conceived in relation to architectural contexts, either in collaboration with Le Corbusier or with other architects of the period, documentary records of such collaborative efforts have hitherto not come to light. The way any one of these pictures functioned within its architectural context, and the extent to which it reflected Léger's or Le Corbusier's theories of the relationship between painting and architecture remains, therefore, largely unresolved. Further research on the theory and practice of both must be undertaken before a satisfactory elucidation can be presented. Nonetheless, Léger's so-called mural paintings represent, as D. Cooper has suggested, his crucial exploration of the question of "whether or not art should have some representational content." For a discussion of this issue and of Léger's ultimate conclusion that for him a representational mural art was the only possible solution, see Cooper, *Fernand Léger et le nouvel espace,* Geneva-Paris-London, 1949, chapters iii, iv.

EXHIBITIONS:

Paris, Musée National d'Art Moderne, *Fernand Léger, 1905-1949,* Oct. 6-Nov. 13, 1949, no. 45; Kunsthalle Bern, *Fernand Léger,* Apr. 10-May 28, 1952, no. 31; Paris, Musée des Arts Décoratifs, *Fernand Léger, 1881-1955,* June-Oct. 1956, pp. 172-173, no. 51, repr.; New York, SRGM 111, 112 (checklists); Houston, Contemporary Art Museum, *Islands Beyond,* Oct. 2-19, 1958 (no cat.); New York, SRGM 118, 129 (checklists); Philadelphia, SRGM 134-T, no. 93; New York, SRGM 151, 153, 187, 195, 196 (checklists); 198-T, 227 (no cats.); 232, 241, p. 267, rep. p. 266; 260, 266, 276 (no cats.).

REFERENCE:

A. Verdet, *Fernand Léger, le dynamisme pictural,* Geneva, 1955, pl. 22.[2]

2. Verdet reproduces the Guggenheim painting together with a 1925 mural now in the collection of J. Müller, Solothurn (center), and a 1924 mural now in the collection of the Musée Fernand Léger, Biot (right). The group of 3 carries the caption *"Etude pour adaptation architecturale"* and the incongruous date *"1922-23."* The ensemble, which appears to be simply an installation photograph from the 1952 Bern exhibition (where the 3 works appeared as nos. 31, 32, and 30 respectively), would appear to have been arbitrarily designated by Verdet as a study for an architectural plan. There is hitherto no evidence to suggest that Léger himself was responsible for the combination of the 3 works under a single heading nor that he at any time conceived of them as a group destined for a particular architectural setting.

167   Composition (Definitive). 1925.
(*Composition [Définitif]*).

37.348

Oil on canvas, 51¼ x 38⅜ (130 x 97.4)

Signed and dated l.r.: *F. Léger. 25*; inscribed
by the artist on reverse: *Composition /
F. Leger. 25 / Definitif.*

PROVENANCE:

Early history and source of acquisition
unknown; purchased by Solomon R. Guggenheim by 1934 (Renaissance Society exhibition catalogue); Gift of Solomon R.
Guggenheim, 1937.

CONDITION:

In 1953 the picture was cleaned. Retouchings of an unrecorded date have been made
along the top and bottom edges and to a
lesser extent along the right and left edges.

There are also repaints in several abrasions
in the gray upper left and upper right; there
are a very few scattered small repaints in
other areas of the composition. In 1970,
while the picture was on loan to the Tate
Gallery, a small loss in the black near the
lower left corner was secured with wax and
retouched.

There are some ground and paint cracks
in the white and gray areas, and cleavage
appears to be developing in 1 or 2 of these.
There is some wear along the edges caused
by the rabbet of the previous frame. Under
UV several pentimenti, barely visible under
daylight, emerge clearly: the white-black-
white diagonal at the left originally extended to the top edge, curving parallel to
the diagonal at the right; the other vertical
elements which now stop short of the top
and bottom also originally extended to the
edges. Several other pentimenti are visible
under natural light. (Apr. 1972.)

At least two other versions of this composition exist, both of which probably
precede it and both of which show the central figure in reverse. The first version
contains three central diagonals instead of two (Collection J. Müller, Solothurn, formerly Collection Léonce Rosenberg, photographic archives no. 727,
Oskar Moll, *Cahiers d'Art*, vol. 8, no. 3-4, 1933, n.p., lower of two illustrations). The second version, present whereabouts unknown (Ibid., upper of two
illustrations; and in *Bulletin de l'Effort Moderne*, no. 25, May 1926, repr. n.p.),
is close to a mirror image of the Guggenheim composition prior to the latter's
pentimenti. The only difference is the substitution in the Guggenheim picture
of the wire "sculpture" in the lower right for the less prominent row of white
dots in the earlier version. All three works date from 1925.

    Green convincingly suggests that Léger's composition was inspired by Lis-
sitzky's *Machinery* lithograph from *Victory over the Sun*. The whole Lissitzky
portfolio was on view at the Kiesler exhibition in Vienna which Léger visited
in September 1924.

EXHIBITIONS:

Chicago, Renaissance Society at the University of Chicago, *Summer Exhibition: A Selection
of Works by 20th Century Artists,* June 20-Aug. 20, 1934, no. 18 ("Collection Mr. and Mrs.
S. R. Guggenheim;" the references given in the cat. entry refer to another version of the
composition); Charleston, S.C., SRGM 1-T, no. 96, repr. p. 57; Philadelphia, SRGM 3-T, no.
120; Charleston, S.C., SRGM 4-T, no. 154, repr. p. 121; New York, SRGM 74, no. 137;
78 (checklist; withdrawn Mar. 16); The Art Institute of Chicago, *Léger,* Apr. 2-May 17, 1953,
traveled to San Francisco Museum of Art, June 15-Aug. 23, 1953, New York, The Museum of
Modern Art, Oct. 6, 1953-Jan. 3, 1954, repr. p. 41; Toronto, SRGM 85-T, no. 54; New York,

SRGM 87 (checklist); Boston, SRGM 90-T (no cat.); Montreal, SRGM 93-T, no. 35; New York, SRGM 95, 97 (checklists); London, SRGM 104-T, no. 43; New York, SRGM 112 (not in checklist); 118, 195 (checklists); Vienna, Museum des 20. Jahrhunderts, *Léger,* Apr. 26-June 9, 1968, no. 18; Columbus, Ohio, SRGM 207-T, p. 28, repr. p. 29; London, Tate Gallery, *Léger and Purist Paris,* Nov. 18, 1970-Jan. 24, 1971, no. 54, repr.; Paris, Grand Palais, *Fernand Léger,* Oct. 1971-Jan. 1972, no. 85; New York, SRGM 276 (no cat.).

REFERENCES:

D. Cooper, *Fernand Léger et le nouvel espace,* Geneva-Paris-London, 1949, p. 133, repr. p. 98 *(Eléments mécaniques);* R. Delevoy, *Léger,* Geneva, 1962, repr. color p. 78; C. Green, *Léger and Purist Paris,* exhibition catalogue, London, 1970, p. 77.

168   Woman Holding a Vase. 1927.
       (Femme tenant une Vase).

58.1508

Oil on canvas, 57⅝ x 38⅜ (146.3 x 97.5)

Signed and dated l.r.: *F. Léger. 27*; inscribed
by the artist on reverse: *Femme tenant une
vase / etat definitif / F. Léger. 27.*

PROVENANCE:

Probably purchased directly from the artist
by Baron Napoléon Gourgaud (d. 1944),
Paris, late 1920's (information supplied by
M. Jardot, correspondence with the author,
August 1971); Baroness Gourgaud, Yerre,
1944-57; purchased from Baroness Gour-
gaud, Yerre, by Sidney Janis Gallery, New
York; purchased from Janis, 1958.

CONDITION:

At an unspecified date prior to acquisition
by the Museum, a repair, approximately
2⅛ x 1 in., was made in the hair adjacent to
the woman's right cheek; a patch was placed
on the reverse and the area was filled and
inpainted. In 1967 the surface was cleaned
and the natural varnish was partially removed. This process was continued in 1970
but not completed.

The canvas has suffered some stress along
the bottom margin and has pulled apart in
some places; but the condition is in general
very good. Pentimenti are visible in several
parts of the figure, suggesting that the outer
limits of the hair line and of both arms
were originally intended to be somewhat
narrower and the breast somewhat smaller.
(July 1972.)

There are several versions of this composition, the earliest oil being a painting
in the Statens Museum for Kunst, Copenhagen (36⅜ x 25½ in., 92.3 x 64.7 cm.,
signed and dated "*F. Léger. 24*," C. Zervos, *Léger*, Paris, 1952, repr. p. 59). Extremely close to this and to the Guggenheim version is a painting formerly in
the Collection Léonce Rosenberg, now in the Kunstmuseum Basel (51⅝ x 35½
in., 131 x 89.5 cm., dated "*24-27*," *Bulletin de l'Effort Moderne*, no. 37, June
1927, repr. n.p.; E. Tériade, *Léger*, Paris, 1928, p. 85, attributed to Collection
Vicomte de Noailles). Léger's inscription on the reverse of the Guggenheim picture describes it as the final version.

Three other works are related in subject matter, though not in style, to the
three works mentioned above. One is an undated pencil sketch on brown
paper, formerly Collection Helena Rubinstein (sold at Sotheby Parke Bernet,
New York, April 28, 1966, lot 789, to E. V. Thaw & Co., Inc.; I am indebted to
Z. Felix for drawing this work to my attention). The second, a gouache in the
collection of the Musée Fernand Léger, Biot (Musée des Arts Décoratifs, Paris,
Léger, 1956, no. 189, repr.), is dated 1920 and is probably the earliest work of
the series. A closely related oil was formerly in the Collection Léonce Rosenberg (present whereabouts unknown, photographic archives no. 701) and is
signed and dated "*F. Leger. 25*." All three works depict the same woman holding a comparable vase shown against a background of broken framing devices,
instead of a unified ground; all also lack the striking contrasts and dramatic
shading of the above three oils, as well as the latters' polished surfaces.

Villon engraved this composition for the Chalcographie du Louvre (colored
aquatint, 18¾ x 12⅝ in., 47.5 x 31.3 cm.). The edition of two hundred was
made in 1928 from the Guggenheim version of the composition (J. Auberty and
C. Pérussaux, *Jacques Villon: catalogue de son oeuvre gravé*, Paris, 1950, no.
523).

EXHIBITIONS:

Kunsthaus Zürich, *Fernand Léger*, Apr. 30-May 25, 1933, no. 116 (Collection Baron Napoléon Gourgaud); Paris, Galerie Louis Carré, *La Figure dans l'oeuvre de Fernand Léger*, June 6-July 12, 1952, no. 8; Paris, Musée des Arts Décoratifs, *Fernand Léger, 1881-1955*, June-Oct. 1956, no. 62, repr.; Amsterdam, Stedelijk Museum, *Léger Wegbereider*, Dec. 11, 1956-Jan. 28, 1957, no. 32; Munich, Haus der Kunst, *Fernand Léger 1881-1955*, Mar.-May, 1957, no. 49, repr.; Kunsthalle Basel, *Fernand Léger*, May 22-June 23, 1957, no. 53, repr.; Kunsthaus Zürich, *Fernand Léger*, July 6-Aug. 17, 1957, no. 68, repr.; New York, SRGM 111, 112, 118, 129 (checklists); Philadelphia, SRGM 134-T, no. 95, repr.; New York, SRGM 144 (checklist); Worcester, Mass., SRGM 148-T, no. 25, repr. color cover; New York, SRGM 151, 153 (checklists); 173, no. 58, repr. color; 187 (checklist); Or., Portland Art Museum, *75 Masterworks; Seventy-Fifth Anniversary Exhibition*, Dec. 12, 1967-Jan. 21, 1968, no. 65, repr.; New York, SRGM 227 (no cat.); 232, 241, pp. 268-269, repr. color; Cleveland, SRGM 258-T, pl. 23; New York, SRGM 276 (no cat.).

REFERENCES:

B. Dorival, *Les Peintres du XXe siècle*, Paris, 1957, repr. color p. 107; SRGM *Handbook*, 1959, pp. 108-109, repr.

---

169   Composition with Aloes, No. 4.
1934-1935.
(Composition à l'aloës).

41.877

Oil on canvas, 44⅝ x 57½ (113.3 x 146)

Signed l.r.: *F. Léger. 34-35*; inscribed by the artist on reverse (photographed before lining): *Composition à l'Aloës N⁰ 4 / F. Leger-35*; on stretcher: *Composition à l'Aloës N⁰ 4.*

PROVENANCE:

Purchased from the artist by Hilla Rebay, Greens Farms, Connecticut, 1941; Gift of Hilla Rebay, 1944.

CONDITION:

In 1955 the work was lined with wax resin and restretched on a new stretcher. The surface was cleaned with Soilax and benzine; some losses in the 4 corners and along the top, bottom, and left edges were inpainted, as was a 1 in. area 14 in. from the left side and 19 in. from the top.

Pentimenti are visible in the black forms, which have been enlarged somewhat. There is occasional scattered crackle over the surface, and there are some traction cracks at the edges of the black forms—especially in those areas where pentimenti occur. There are 3 diagonal scratches in the pigment (1 in., 2 in., and 3 in. in length), but the condition is otherwise good. (Dec. 1973.)

The aloe *(Aloe Vera)* is a plant with basal leaves which grows in the Mediterranean basin as well as in Southern Africa.

There are five other known oil versions of this theme. *Composition with Aloes, No. 1*, 1935, present whereabouts unknown (35 x 51⅛ in., 89 x 130 cm., P. Descargues, *Léger*, Paris, 1955, repr. p. 110), apparently postdates *No. 2* (1934), as well as possibly the Guggenheim's *No. 4* (1934-35), thus suggesting that the numerical designations are arbitrary.

Composition with Aloes, No. 2, 1934 (also known as *Composition with Two Profiles)*, was in the Collection Louis Clayeux and appeared in the Léger ex-

hibition at the Musée des Arts Décoratifs in 1956, where F. Mathey described it as being the second version of a theme which Léger worked on between 1933 and 1937 (repr., no. 87, 38¼ x 51¼ in., 97 x 130 cm.).

Composition with Aloes, No. 3, 1935, Galerie Louis Carré, Paris, appeared in the same exhibition (repr., no. 88, 38¼ x 51¼ in., 97 x 130 cm.). Since neither of these bears a numerical designation on its reverse, it is not clear how they have been identified as Nos. 2 and 3.

A fourth version is in the Collection José Luis Sert, Cambridge, Massachusetts, promised gift to the Museum of Fine Arts, Boston (oil on board, 15 x 18 in., 38.1 x 45.7 cm.). This version is dated 1935 but bears no numerical designation.

A fifth version (35 x 51⅛ in., 89 x 130 cm.), virtually but not quite identical to the Guggenheim picture, was published in 1949 by D. Cooper (*Léger et le nouvel espace,* Geneva-Paris-London, 1949, repr. p. 126). The picture belonged at that time to the artist himself. Since these two versions are so extraordinarily close, one might speculate that Léger made a copy for himself before selling his picture to Rebay.

EXHIBITIONS:

New York, SRGM 30 (no cat.); 74, no. 129; The Art Institute of Chicago, *Léger,* Apr. 2-May 17, 1953, traveled to San Francisco Museum of Art, June 15-Aug. 23, 1953, New York, The Museum of Modern Art, Oct. 6, 1953-Jan. 3, 1954, no. 42; Philadelphia, SRGM 134-T, no. 97; New York, SRGM 144 (checklist); St. Louis, Washington University, *Fernand Léger,* circulating exhibition organized by The Museum of Modern Art, New York, traveled to Ithaca, N.Y., Cornell University, Ohio, University of Akron, Savannah, Georgia, Telfair Academy of Arts and Sciences, Hannover, New Hampshire, Dartmouth College, Poughkeepsie, N.Y., Vassar College, Des Moines Art Center, 1967-68 (no cat.); New York, Whitney Museum of American Art, *The 1930's: Painting and Sculpture in America,* Oct. 15-Dec. 1, 1968, no. 65, repr.; New York, SRGM 276 (no cat.).

Kazimir Severinovich Malevich

Born February 1878, Kiev.
Died May 1935, Leningrad.

Kazimir Severinovich Malevich

170   Morning in the Village after
Snowstorm. 1912.
(Утро после вьюги в деревне, Utro posle
v'yugi v derevne; *Morning in the Country
after Rain*).

52.1327

Oil on canvas, 31¾ x 31⅞ (80.7 x 80.8)

Signed l.r.: *KM*; inscribed on reverse, not in
the artist's hand: "*K. Malevitch / Le matin à
la campagne d'après l'orage.*"; inscribed on
reverse, possibly by the artist (barely visible
through lining): "6(—) Пейзаж / зимой"
(Peizazh zimoi, *Landscape in Winter*). (According to Andersen [p. 88, no. 32], a
further inscription in the artist's hand was
faintly visible when he examined the painting in 1969. This is now lost. Andersen
transcribed it as: "Utro posle v'yugi"
[Morning after snowfall].)

PROVENANCE:

Owned by the artist until 1927;[1] acquired
from an unknown source by Rose Fried
Gallery, New York, by 1952;[2] purchased
from Fried, 1953.

CONDITION:

In 1953 the picture was placed on a new stretcher and given a surface cleaning.
Minor inpainting was done at this time in
the yellow and gray smoke upper left corner,
in the blue upper left corner, and in the red
sky upper center. In 1954 a label adhered to
the reverse with glue was removed, the glue
having caused blistering of paint in a light
blue triangular area left of center, below
and to the right of the base of the tree trunk.
In 1966 the canvas was lined with wax resin,
placed on a new stretcher, and the surface
sprayed with PVA.

Certain areas of the surface were specifically
left unpainted by the artist; in addition the
canvas is visible in scattered areas where
paint loss has obviously occurred. This condition is not active and there is no current
danger of flaking. There are some abrasions
in the grays and whites at the bottom of the
canvas, and considerable wear with loss in
the corners and along the edges. (Mar.
1972.)

The original Russian title used in the early exhibition catalogues (and often
erroneously translated as *Morning in the Village [Country] after Rain*) specifically refers to snow rather than rain. The Russian word "derevne," on the
other hand, is translatable either as "village" or "country."

The earliest evidence for the dating of *Morning in the Village after Snowstorm* is the *Union of Youth* exhibition of 1913-14, where the painting is dated
1912. Since its rediscovery in 1952, the picture has, for no apparent reason, us-

1. The picture appears in photographs of the 1927 Warsaw-Berlin exhibition published in the
Avantgarde Osteuropas, 1910-1930, exhibition catalogue, Akademie der bildenden Künste,
Berlin, Oct.-Nov. 1967, p. 22 (cited by Andersen, 1970, pp. 57-58). Andersen gives a detailed
description of the circumstances of this exhibition and of the available data regarding the
complete dispersal of the approximately 70 paintings after it closed. The Guggenheim picture was probably 1 of 12 pictures that were inexplicably lost some time between 1927
(when the paintings were left by Malevich in the hands of the architect Hugo Häring and
stored by him with the forwarding agent Gustav Knauer) and 1935, when Häring retrieved
the by then incomplete shipment. What became of these 12 pictures is not known.

2. The papers of Rose Fried were left to the Archives of American Art but are not yet available
for study. It is possible that some clue to her source for the picture, and hence its intervening history, may emerge from them.

ually been dated 1911 (see below EXHIBITIONS and REFERENCES). Gray and Calvesi without discussion date it 1912-13; Andersen dates it 1912.

Andersen's carefully documented chronology of Malevich's work convincingly places this picture in 1912. It has been frequently suggested in the literature that Malevich's 1912 style (as exemplified by the present work) was influenced by the Léger of 1910-11 and in particular by the *Nudes in a Landscape*. (See for example, G. Habasque, "Malevitch," *L'Oeil*, no. 71, November 1960, pp. 46, 88; Andersen, *Moderne Russisk Kunst 1910-25*, Copenhagen, 1967, pp. 60-61.) The *Nudes* was exhibited in Paris at the April 1911 *Salon des Indépendants* which Malevich did not see, and although it is well possible that Malevich saw a reproduction of the work by late in 1911 (as these and other authors have hypothesized), no definite proof of this has yet come to light. The earliest documented instance of Malevich's contact with Léger's work is February 1912, when Léger exhibited his 1911 *Three Portraits* (Milwaukee Art Center) at the *Jack of Diamonds* in Moscow. The four other works shown by Léger in that exhibition have so far not been identified.

There is, however, another possible source of contact with photographs or reproductions of Léger's work. Alexandra Exter was, between 1909 and 1914, as A. Nakov has pointed out, living half the year in Paris and half in Kiev and Moscow (*Alexandra Exter*, Paris, Galerie Jean Chauvelin, May-June 1972, p. 13; I am indebted to S. Compton for drawing this passage to my attention). According to Nakov, Exter regularly carried photographs and reproductions of works seen in Paris with her when she returned home. Since *Nudes in a Landscape* had caused a considerable stir when it was shown in Paris in April 1911, it seems likely that this would have been among the pictures Exter chose to show her Russian colleagues. Until further evidence on this point comes to light, however, one cannot be certain which Légers other than *Three Portraits* Malevich had seen by the time he painted *Morning in the Village after Snowstorm*.

Andersen's and Habasque's contention that works such as *Morning in the Village after Snowstorm* do betray the influence of Léger's 1910-11 style is compelling. The 1912 date for the present picture is thus entirely acceptable.

EXHIBITIONS:

Moscow, Мишень (Mishen, *Target*), Mar. 24-Apr. 7, 1913, no. 90; St. Petersburg, Союз молодежи (Soiuz Molodezhi, *Union of Youth*), Nov. 10, 1913-Jan. 10, 1914, no. 64 (dated 1912); Paris, *Salon des Indépendants*, Mar. 1-Apr. 30, 1914, no. 2156;[3] Moscow, *Sixteenth State Exhibition, K. S. Malevich, separate exhibition. His way from Impressionism to Suprematism*, 1919-20 (no cat. available);[4] Warsaw, Hotel Polonia, *Malevich*, Mar. 8-28, 1927, traveled to Berlin, *Grosser Berliner Ausstellung, Sonderausstellung Kasimir Malewitsch*, May 7-Sept. 30, 1927 (no cat.);[5] New York, Rose Fried Gallery, *Group Exhibition*, Dec. 15, 1952-Jan. 1953, no. 9; New York, SRGM 79 (checklist, "*Morning in the Country after Rain*, 1911;" the title and date by which the picture was known in all subsequent SRGM publications until 1970, SRGM 232, where it is dated ca. 1912; withdrawn Oct. 20); Toronto, SRGM 85-T, no. 55; New York, SRGM 87; Boston, SRGM 90-T (no cat.); Montreal, SRGM 93-T, no. 36; New York, SRGM 95 (checklist); London, SRGM 104-T, no. 44; New York, SRGM 118 (checklist); Philadelphia, SRGM 134-T, no. 101; New York, SRGM 144, 151 (checklists);

153 (checklist; commentary, repr. color); 173, no. 20, repr. color; The Museum of Fine Arts, Houston, *The Heroic Years: Paris 1908-1914,* Oct. 21-Dec. 8, 1965 (no cat.); New York, SRGM 196 (checklist); 232, 241, pp. 282-283, repr. color (dated c. 1912); New York, Leonard Hutton Galleries, *Russian Avant-Garde 1908-1922,* Oct. 16, 1971-Feb. 29, 1972, no. 68, repr. color (dated 1912); New York, SRGM 260 (no cat.); 272, *Kasimir Malevich,* no. 32, repr.

REFERENCES:

SRGM *Handbook,* 1959, p. 110, repr. (dated 1911); C. Gray, *The Great Experiment: Russian Art 1863-1922,* New York, 1962, pl. 92 (dated 1912-13); R. Carrieri, *Futurism,* Milan, 1963, pl. 47 (dated 1911); P. Courthion, "Les Grandes étapes de l'art contemporain 1907-1917," *XXᵉ Siècle,* nouv. sér., vol. 28, May 1966, repr. p. 87 (dated 1911); M. Calvesi, "Il Futurismo Russo," *L'Arte Moderna,* vol. 5, no. 44, 1967, repr. p. 319 (dated 1912-13); H. H. Arnason, *History of Modern Art,* New York, 1968, pl. 93 (dated 1911); T. Andersen, *Malevich,* Amsterdam, 1970, p. 88, no. 32 (dated 1912), repr.

3. A *Salon* label formerly on the stretcher now preserved in the Museum files inexplicably carries the number "2145."

4. For information on this exhibition see Andersen, pp. 62-63, 163; the present painting appears in an installation photograph reproduced on p. 62, fig. d.

5. For information on this exhibition see above fn. 1 and Andersen, 1970, pp. 57-58.

Franz Marc

Born February 1880, Munich.
Died March 1916, Verdun.

NOTE: K. Lankheit's catalogue raisonné (herein Lankheit, 1970) is the main source of accurate information on the work of Franz Marc. In addition to his own wide-ranging research into the artist's work, he was—as he states in his introduction—also aided by the research papers of A. Schardt, which were made available to him by the latter's son. Among those papers were the detailed questionnaires which Schardt had sent out to owners of pictures by Marc; many of these questionnaires were filled out by Maria Marc, the artist's widow. In addition, there were quotations in Schardt's hand from Franz Marc's *Merkbüchlein* (or house catalogue), which Lankheit had consulted in 1948-49, but which has since been lost (Lankheit, 1970, p. xi). Lankheit kindly allowed the author to consult Schardt's questionnaires and the quotations (where available) from the *Merkbüchlein*. Information from these sources in the following entries is specifically identified as such.

171   Sketch of Horses III. 1906.
(Pferdeskizze III).

71.1936R 104

Oil on paper mounted on board: painted surface, 5⅞ x 9⅞ (15 x 25); board sub-support, 6¼ x 10 (15.8 x 25.4)

Not signed or dated. Inscribed in black crayon on reverse by Maria Marc: *Aus dem Nachlass Franz Marc / bestätigs / Maria Marc*; in pencil, possibly by Maria Marc:[1] *Pferdeskizze II 1905.* Under the *II* is a *III* in red pencil. The word *skizze* is written in above the word *studie,* which has been deleted.

PROVENANCE:

Estate of Franz Marc, 1916-54; Otto Stangl, Munich (executor of the estate), 1954-55; purchased from Stangl by Hilla Rebay, Greens Farms, Connecticut, 1955; Hilla Rebay Collection, 1955-67; Estate of Hilla Rebay, 1967-71; acquired from the Estate of Hilla Rebay, 1971.

CONDITION:

At some point prior to 1936 (Schardt questionnaire) the top corners and the bottom right corner were torn off; the extent of the damage may be seen in Lankheit, 1970, p. 16, no. 43. Some time after 1950, probably after 1955, the corners were restored. (Lankheit, in conversation with the author, October 1972, felt that the picture was probably restored after Rebay acquired it, or possibly at her request while it was still with Stangl. Stangl was not in the habit of restoring works and would not have done so unless she specifically requested it.) The work was apparently first mounted on board; pieces of paper corresponding to the missing areas were added; these were then inpainted and the edges squared off with a blade (there are incisions in the board). The work was then coated with natural varnish. The paper has been torn in 2 places (both clearly visible in the photograph): the first tear extends from the bottom margin about 2 in. upwards; the second from the right edge about 2 in. diagonally down to the left. Both have been repaired and retouched. The work was apparently placed in a frame before the pigment was dry, causing distortion of the paint film on all 4 sides, especially the bottom. When the frame was removed, some white paper remained adhering to the paint film (visible in photo). Examination under UV indicates that minor retouching was performed in the rabbeted areas. There is a ¾ in. loss in the center of the lower margin.

There is a slight convex warp of the sub-support along the horizontal axis. Apart from 3 small punctures (left corner, center of left margin, and center of top margin), the condition of the paint film is good. (Sept. 1972.)

The three sketches of horses (Lankheit, nos. 41-43) were numbered either by
Maria Marc or by Schardt for purposes of identification and not to suggest
their sequence. They appear in Schardt's notebook, each accompanied by a
photograph and a description of the subject. The questionnaire for the present
work, completed by Maria Marc, contains the information: *"3 Ecken abge-
brochen. Pferdeskizze III. Kochel. 1906. 5 Pferde etwas in Walddunkel ver-
schwindend 1/3 des Bildes. Vordergrund stark besonnt in der grösste Teil des
vordersten Pferdes stärkerer Sonnenfleck. Stimmung starke Sonnenschweres
Waldesdunkel."* ("3 corners broken off. Sketch of horses III. Kochel. 1906. 5
horses disappearing somewhat into the darkness of the forest 1/3 of the picture. Foreground in strong sunlight; greater part of the foreground horse more
strongly highlighted. Tone strong sunlight and forest darkness.") Both Schardt
and Lankheit have accepted the date of summer 1906 when the Marcs spent the
summer in Kochel.

EXHIBITIONS:
Berlin, Galerie van der Heyde, *Franz Marc Gedächtnisausstellung*, opened May 3, 1936, no.
30 ("*Pferdeskizze III*, 1906. Privatbesitz," for sale); Munich, Moderne Galerie Otto Stangl,
Kandinsky, Marc, Münter; unbekannte Werke, 1954-55, no. 34; New York, SRGM 241 (addenda; "*Sketch for Horses, II*, 1905?"); Bridgeport, Conn., Carlson Gallery, University of
Bridgeport, *Homage to Hilla Rebay*, Apr. 18-May 10, 1972, no. 85; New York, SRGM 276
(no cat.).

REFERENCES:
Schardt, 1936, p. 162, 1906, no. 10; Lankheit, 1970, p. 16, no. 43, repr.

1. In consultation with the author, Oct. 1972, Lankheit compared the inscription with several
   examples of Maria Marc's handwriting and concluded that it was possibly, but not certainly, her hand.

172   Young Boy with a Lamb. 1911.
(Knabe mit Lamm; Der Hirte; Der gute Hirte; The Good Shepherd).

48.1172 x503

Oil on canvas, 34⅝ x 33 (88 x 83.8)

Not signed or dated.

PROVENANCE:

A. Flechtheim, Dusseldorf;[1] Alfred Hess, Erfurt, ca. 1920[2]-38; Hans Hess, London, 1938-39; given on consignment to Curt Valentin, New York, 1939; jointly owned by Valentin and Karl Nierendorf, New York, 1940 (Buchholz Gallery exhibition catalogue); acquired with the Estate of Karl Nierendorf, 1948.

CONDITION:

The work has received no treatment.

The edges show considerable wear in some places, especially at the corners. There is a slightly curved scratch in the paint, ca. 6 in. long, extending from the lamb's ear to the top of the shepherd's thigh. There are also visible traction cracks in various parts of the surface, the most noticeable being those in the dark areas near the bottom. The canvas is rather slackly stretched on the original strainer. The condition in general is good. (Sept. 1972.)

The picture is stylistically closely related to *Wood Carrier* (Private Collection, Krefeld, Lankheit, repr. no. 140); both were probably executed early in 1911.

EXHIBITIONS:[3]

Munich, Moderne Galerie Heinrich Thannhauser, *Kollektion Franz Marc,* May 1911 (no cat.);[4] Berlin, Nationalgalerie, *Franz Marc,* Mar.-Apr. 1922 (no cat.);[5] Olso, Kunstnernes Hus, *Nyere Tysk Kunst,* Jan. 1932, no. 113; New York, Buchholz Gallery, *Franz Marc,* Nov. 11-Dec. 7, 1940, no. 8; New York, SRGM 276 (no cat.).

REFERENCES:

Schardt, 1936, p. 163, 1911, no. 11; Lankheit, 1970, p. 47, no. 141, repr.

1. Schardt's notes contain the following quotation from Marc's *Merkbüchlein:* "*Knabe mit Lamm. A. Flechtheim Düsseld. 400.*"

2. According to Hans Hess (correspondence with the author, July 1972) his father Alfred purchased the picture in about 1920, possibly from Galerie Goldschmidt-Wallerstein; it seem likely that Flechtheim was the source involved, although it is possible that the picture went to Goldschmidt-Wallerstein in between. In 1938 Hans Hess took the picture to London with him, and lent it for a time to the Free German League of Culture. The following year he sent it to New York for sale.

3. The picture is reproduced in *Der Querschnitt,* 1921, p. 183, with the caption "*Leihgabe des Erfurter Sammlers Hess auf der Baseler Ausstellung,*" referring to an exhibition *Moderne Deutsche Malerei* held in Basel in Oct. 1921. The picture was not, however, in the catalogue, and according to the records of the Kunsthalle it definitely did not appear in the show (correspondence with the author, June 1972).

4. Lankheit's typewritten list of the works that appeared in the show was based on Schardt's notes from the *Merkbüchlein.*

5. Correspondence files for this exhibition still exist in Berlin, and Lankheit was able through these to put together a list of lenders and works lent. I am indebted to him for all information regarding it.

173 White Bull. 1911.
(Stier).

51.1312

Oil on canvas, 39⅜ x 53¼ (100 x 135.2)

Inscribed by the artist on reverse: *Fz. Marc ii / „Stier."*

PROVENANCE:
Bernard Koehler (1849-1927), Berlin, 1913[1]-27; Bernard Koehler, Jr. (1882-1964), Berlin, 1927-51; Otto Stangl, Munich, 1951; purchased from Stangl, 1951.

CONDITION:
In 1954 the canvas was given a light surface cleaning; a few minor losses along the left and top edges were retouched, and one 1¾ x ⅛ in. area to the left of the bull's eye. The picture was surfaced with PBM.

There are some traction cracks near the left edge and beneath the bull's hooves; a few minor cracks down the center of the painting may have been caused by a stretcher impression. Apart from some slight wear along the edges, the condition is excellent. (Oct. 1972.)

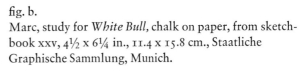

fig. a.
Marc, *Reclining Bull*, ca. 1910-11, pencil on paper, from sketchbook xxiv, 4⅛ x 6¾ in., 10.5 x 17.1 cm., formerly Estate of the Artist, no. 149.

fig. b.
Marc, study for *White Bull*, chalk on paper, from sketchbook xxv, 4½ x 6¼ in., 11.4 x 15.8 cm., Staatliche Graphische Sammlung, Munich.

Schardt's questionnaire (which appears to be in his own handwriting, suggesting that he went to Koehler's house to obtain the information on the large number of Marcs in the latter's collection) states that Marc was in England until the middle of June 1911 and that the picture was painted shortly after his return to Sindelsdorf. It must have been completed by August, when Marc mentioned it in a letter to Macke (see below fn. 2).

Lankheit lists two studies for the present painting. The first is a pencil study from sketchbook xxiv (fig. a). The second is a chalk drawing from sketchbook xxv (fig. b). Fig. b is also described by Lankheit as a study in reverse for *Reclining Red Bull* (Lankheit, no. 426). Fig. a probably served as a study not only for the present painting but also for a tempera painting (present whereabouts unknown, Lankheit, no. 425), which shows the bull in an identical pose in reverse.

EXHIBITIONS:
Weimar, Neue Künstler Vereinigung, Autumn, 1911;[2] Munich, Muenchner Neue Secession, *Franz Marc Gedächtnisausstellung,* Sept. 14-Oct. 15, 1916, no. 73; Wiesbaden, Nassauischer Kunstverein, Neues Museum, *Franz Marc Gedächtnisausstellung,* Mar.-Apr. 1917, no. 23;

1. When the picture was published in *Der Blaue Reiter Almanach* in 1912, it apparently did not yet belong to Koehler since it is not attributed to his collection in the list of illustrations, whereas Delaunay's *Eiffel Tower,* for example, is. Some time between late 1912 and May 1913 Koehler purchased the picture from Marc, since Macke lists it among the works he saw on a May visit to Koehler's house (*Briefwechsel,* 1964, p. 161, May 19, 1913). A label on the reverse bears Koehler's name.
2. Schardt's notes on this picture contain the following quotation from the *Merkbüchlein:* "*Stier (Juli 1911) im Herbst bei D u K Vereinigung in Weimar.*" Further reference to this Weimar exhibition is contained in a letter from Marc to Macke of Aug. 13, 1911: "*Von den Bildern die ich nach Weimar schicke, hätte ich Dir so gerne vor allem das eine (Stier) gezeigt.*" *Briefwechsel,* 1964, p. 69. ("Of the pictures I am sending to Weimar, I would have especially liked to have shown you one [Bull].") Further information about this exhibition has not yet come to light.

Berlin, Nationalgalerie, *Franz Marc,* Mar.-Apr. 1922 (no cat.);[3] Munich, Glaspalast, *Allgemeine Kunstausstellung,* June-Oct. 1926, no. 2224; Berlin, Nationalgalerie, *Ausstellung neuerer Deutscher Kunst aus Berliner Privatbesitz,* Apr. 1928, no. 111; Oslo, Kunstnernes Hus, *Nyere Tysk Kunst,* Jan. 1932, no. 112; Hanover, Kestner-Gesellschaft, *Franz Marc Gedächtnisausstellung,* Mar. 4-Apr. 19, 1936, no. 24; Berlin, Galerie Nierendorf, *Franz Marc,* May 1936, no. 19;[4] Munich, Galerie Günther Franke, *Franz Marc,* Nov.-Dec. 1946, no. 7; Städtische Kunsthalle Mannheim, *Franz Marc,* Apr.-May 1947, no. 6; Kunsthalle Bern, *Lehmbruck, Macke, Marc,* Aug. 21-Sept. 26, 1948, no. 133; Munich, Haus der Kunst, *Der Blaue Reiter,* Sept.-Oct. 1949, no. 230; Kunsthalle Basel, *Der Blaue Reiter,* Jan. 21-Feb. 26, 1950, no. 203; New York, SRGM 84 (checklist); Vancouver, SRGM 88-T, no. 55; Montreal, SRGM 93-T, no. 37; New York, SRGM 95 (checklist); London, SRGM 104-T, no. 46; Boston, SRGM 119-T, no. 38; Lexington, Ky., SRGM 122-T, no. 18; New York, SRGM 129 (checklist); Philadelphia, SRGM 134-T, no. 103; New York, SRGM 144 (checklist); Worcester, Mass., SRGM 148-T, no. 26, repr.; New York, SRGM 151 (checklist); Munich, Städtische Galerie, *Franz Marc,* Aug. 10-Oct. 13, 1963, no. 101, repr.; Kunstverein in Hamburg, *Franz Marc,* Nov. 9, 1963-Jan. 5, 1964, no. 29, repr.; New York, SRGM 173, no. 19, repr. color; 187, 196 (checklists); 232, 241, pp. 284, 285, repr. color; Cleveland SRGM 258-T, pl. 8; 276 (no cat.).

REFERENCES:

Der Blaue Reiter, ed. W. Kandinsky and F. Marc, Munich, 1912, repr. foll. p. 90; A. Macke, letter to Franz Marc, May 19, 1913, *Briefwechsel,* 1964, p. 161; C. Einstein, *Die Kunst des 20. Jahrhunderts,* 2nd ed., Berlin, 1928, repr. p. 408; Schardt, 1936, pp. 87, 163, 1911, no. 23, repr. p. 89; Lankheit, 1970, p. 51, no. 150, repr.

3. See above cat. no. 172, fn. 5.

4. A typed checklist for this exhibition is owned by Lankheit. I am indebted to him for this information.

---

174   Yellow Cow. 1911.
(Gelbe Kuh).

49.1210

Oil on canvas, 55⅜ x 74½ (140.5 x 189.2)

Signed on reverse: *Marc.*

PROVENANCE:

Purchased from Marc or Maria Marc by Herwarth Walden, Berlin, during World War I;[1] E. Kluxen, Berlin, 1916-ca. 1918 (Nell Walden, in conversation with the author, summer 1973, stated that Kluxen resold the picture to her approximately two years after he purchased it); Nell Walden, Berlin and Ascona, Switzerland, ca. 1918-49; purchased from Nell Walden, 1949.

CONDITION:

In 1953 the canvas was cleaned with 1% Soilax solution. A tiny area of cleavage in the green area at the lower center was set down with wax resin and retouched. Inpainting was also performed in scattered touches in the area of the cow's shoulder where the paint had been rubbed (an area approximately 2 x 4 in.). The canvas was placed on a new stretcher and portions of the left and right margins were inpainted (visible to the naked eye), since the original painted surface had been out of square. The painting was surfaced with PBM.

There are traction cracks visible in a few places, especially noticeable in the areas of the cow's udder and underbelly, the green plant lower center, and the blue/white of the mountain. There are 2 abrasions in the upper part of the far right black tree trunk. The condition in general is excellent. (July 1972.)

1. Schardt's questionnaire, in Maria Marc's handwriting, includes the sentence: *"im Krieg für 900 von Walden gekauft."* Marc, in a letter from the front dated Apr. 18, 1915, tells Maria that he has written to someone (presumably Walden) giving the net price he wants for the picture if a buyer can be found *(Franz Marc Briefe, Aufzeichnungen und Aphorismen,* Berlin, 1920, vol. 1, p. 55). The picture probably belonged to Walden by the time of the 1916 Der Sturm exhibition.

Like *White Bull,* cat. no. 173, this picture was painted in Sindelsdorf shortly after Marc's return from England in June 1911 (Schardt's notes, and questionnaire completed by Maria Marc).

Two studies for the work are known. One is a pencil study, formerly in sketchbook xxiii (fig. a). The second is a detailed oil study (fig. b).

A closely related work of the following year is *Cows Red, Green, Yellow* (Städtische Galerie, Munich, Inv. No. G13140, H. K. Röthel, *Sammlungskatalog, Der Blaue Reiter,* 3rd ed., Munich, 1970, color pl. 76). The yellow cow of the present picture is repeated almost exactly in the foreground of the Munich painting, which contains in addition a red and a green cow in the background.

The striking colors in both of these works inevitably bring to mind the correspondence between Macke and Marc in December 1910 on the subject of color. Marc's lengthy analysis of the effects of blue, yellow, and red is especially relevant in this context:

Blau *ist das* männliche *Prinzip, sanft, herb und geistig.*

Gelb *das* weibliche *Prinzip, sanft, heiter und sinnlich.*

Rot *die* Materie, *brutal und schwer und stets die Farbe, die von den anderen beiden bekämpft und überwunden werden muss! Mischt Du z.B. das ernste, geistige Blau mit Rot, dann steigerst Du das Blau bis zur unerträglichen Trauer, und das versöhnende Gelb, die Komplementärfarbe zu Violett, wird unerlässlich.*

fig. a.
Marc, study for *Yellow Cow,* pencil on paper, from sketchbook xxiii, dimensions and present whereabouts unknown.

fig. b.
Marc, study for *Yellow Cow,* oil on wood, 24⅝ x 34½ in., 62.5 x 87.5 cm., Private Collection.

(Das Weib als Trösterin, nicht als Liebende!)
Mischt Du Rot und Gelb zu Orange, so gibst Du dem passiven und weiblichen Gelb eine 'megärenhafte,' sinnliche Gewalt, dass das kühle, geistige Blau wiederum unerlässlich wird, der Mann, und zwar stellt sich das Blau sofort und automatisch neben Orange, die Farben lieben sich. Blau und Orange, ein durchaus festlicher Klang.

Mischt Du nun aber Blau und Gelb zu Grün, so weckst Du Rot, die Materie, die 'Erde,' zum Leben, aber hier fühle ich als Maler immer einen Unterschied: Mit Grün bringst Du das ewig materielle, brutale Rot nie ganz zur Ruhe, wie bei den vorigen Farbklängen. (Stelle Dir nur z.B. kunstgewerbliche Gegenstände vor, grün und rot!) Dem Grün müssen stets noch einmal Blau (der Himmel) und Gelb (die Sonne) zu Hilfe kommen, um die Materie zum Schweigen zu bringen (Briefwechsel, 1964, p. 28).

("Blue is the *male* principle, severe, bitter, spiritual and intellectual." [For a discussion of the meaning of the word *geistig*, which in German suggests a combination of both spiritual and intellectual, see Weiss, 1973, pp. 475 ff.] "Yellow is the *female* principle, gentle, cheerful, and sensual. Red is *matter*, brutal and heavy, the color which must be fought and overcome by the other two! For example, if you mix serious, intellectual-spiritual blue with red, you intensify the blue to a point of unbearable sadness, and comforting yellow, the complementary of violet, becomes indispensable. [Woman as comforter, not as lover!] If you mix red and yellow to make orange, you give the passive female yellow a 'turbulent' sensual power, so that the cool, spiritual and intellectual blue—the male principle—once again becomes indispensable; and blue immediately and automatically falls into place next to orange—these two being so drawn to one another. Blue and orange: a thoroughly festive resonance. If you then mix blue and yellow to make green, you bring red—matter, the 'Earth'—to life; but here, as painter, I always feel a difference. With green you never quite still the brutality and materiality of red, as was the case with the other color harmonies. [Just think, for example, how green and red are used in craft objects.] Green always requires the aid of blue [the sky] and yellow [the sun] to reduce matter to silence.")

Yellow Cow is a vibrant illustration of Marc's notion of the symbolic effects of color. The brilliant yellow cow with its two blue spots may be seen as the gentle, cheerful, sensual female principle, carrying within her an element of the male spiritual-intellectual. The earth (matter) under her feet is blue and orange (the festive resonance), violet and yellow (sadness and comfort), but most of all red (the essential color of matter) and green (which brings that matter to life). The Munich painting presents the same colors in different but equally brilliant juxtapositions; together the two works are an eloquent dramatization of Marc's theory.

EXHIBITIONS:[2]

Munich, Moderne Galerie Heinrich Thannhauser, *Der Blaue Reiter, die erste Ausstellung,* Dec. 18, 1911-Jan. 1, 1912, no. 30, repr.; Berlin, Der Sturm, *43. Ausstellung: Expressionisten, Futuristen, Kubisten,* July 1916, no. 45; Berlin, Der Sturm, *Sammlung Walden,* Oct. 1919, no. 236; Berlin, Der Sturm, *Zehn Jahre Sturm,* Sept. 1921, no. 71;[3] Berlin, Nationalgalerie, *Franz Marc,* Mar.-Apr. 1922? (no cat.);[4] Berlin, Galerie Flechtheim, *Nell Walden-Heimann und ihre Sammlungen,* Sept. 6-28, 1927, no. 95, repr.; Berlin, Nationalgalerie, *Ausstellung neuerer Deutschen Kunst aus Berliner Privatbesitz,* Apr. 1928, no. 116; Vienna, Kunstlerhaus, *Die Kunst in unserer Zeit,* Mar.-May 1930, no. 20; Berlin, Galerie Nierendorf, *Franz Marc,* May 1936, no. 8;[5] London, New Burlington Galleries, *Twentieth Century German Art,* July 1938, no. 164; Kunstmuseum Bern, *Sammlung Nell Walden aus den Jahren 1919-20,* Oct. 1944-Mar. 1945, no. 344; Kunsthalle Basel, *Francis Picabia: Sammlung Nell Walden,* Jan. 12-Feb. 13, 1946, no. 240; New York, SRGM 74, no. 140; 79, 129 (checklists); Paris, Galerie Maeght, *Der Blaue Reiter,* Oct. 26-Dec. 1962, no. 8 (cat. published as *Derrière le miroir,* no. 133-134); Munich, Städtische Galerie, *Franz Marc,* Aug. 10-Oct. 13, 1963, no. 100, repr.; Kunstverein in Hamburg, *Franz Marc,* Nov. 9, 1963-Jan. 5, 1964, no. 28, repr.; New York, SRGM 202, p. 119, repr. p. 118; 221 (no cat.); 232, 241, p. 286, repr. p. 287; 276 (no cat.).

REFERENCES:

Th. Däubler, "Franz Marc," *Die Neue Rundschau,* vol. xxvii, 1916, p. 564; Idem, "Franz Marc," *Die neue Standpunkt,* Hellerau, 1916, p. 141, quoted in K. Lankheit, *Franz Marc im Urteil seiner Zeit,* Cologne, 1960, pp. 83-84; W. Hausenstein, *Münchner Neuesten Nachrichten,* quoted in Lankheit, op. cit., p. 86; *Expressionismus die Kunstwende,* ed. H. Walden, Berlin, 1918, repr. p. 35; Idem, *Einblick in Kunst, Expressionismus, Futurismus, Kubismus,* Berlin, 1924, repr. p. 31; A. de Ridder, "L'Expressionisme—sur la déformation," *Le Centaure,* Mar. 1929, repr. p. 143; Schardt, 1936, pp. 86, 163, 1911, no. 22, repr. p. 88; N. Walden and L. Schreyer, *Der Sturm. Ein Erinnerungsbuch an H. Walden und die Künstler aus dem Sturmkreis,* Baden-Baden, 1954, repr. color bet. pp. 48-49; P. Selz, *German Expressionist Painting,* Berkeley, 1957, pp. 203, 263, pl. 81; Lankheit, 1970, p. 52, no. 152, repr.

2. Schardt's notes include the sentence: *"München-Köln-Sturm-Hagen."* It is not clear whether this was a single exhibition which traveled, or whether it refers in part to the *Blaue Reiter* exhibition of 1911, and to one of the Sturm exhibitions listed here. Exhibitions at Cologne and Hagen in which this picture appeared have not hitherto been traced. Schardt's questionnaire also contains a reference in Maria Marc's handwriting to the "Palais des Beaux Arts." This is substantiated by a fragmentary label on the stretcher of the picture which reads *"10 rue Royale / Franz Marc / La Vache jaune / collection Mme Walden-Heimann, Berlin,"* and indicates that the picture appeared in Brussels sometime between 1924 and 1940. However, it has so far proved impossible to find any record of the picture's appearance in an exhibition in Brussels (information supplied by S. Bertouille, correspondence with the author, Oct. 1972).

3. The entry reads *"Die gelbe Kuh"* but the reproduction is of the Munich picture *Kühe, Rot, Grün, Gelb (Cows, Red, Green, Yellow),* 1912. It has not been possible to establish which of the works actually appeared.

4. See above cat. no. 172, fn. 5. The correspondence inexplicably indicates that the picture was lent by Niestlé, Sindelsdorf. Neither the present picture, nor the Munich *Cows, Red, Green, Yellow* ever belonged to Niestlé as far as is known. The oil sketch was already in a private collection in Krefeld by 1922 and was indeed also lent to the 1922 exhibition. This problem of identification remains unsolved.

5. See above cat. no. 173, fn. 4.

175   Bos Orbis Mundi. 1913.
       (Die Weltenkuh).

46.1039

Oil on canvas, 27¾ x 55½ (70.5 x 141)

Signed l.r.: *M*; inscribed by the artist on reverse, partially obscured by stretcher: *„Die Weltenkuh" / Marc i3.*

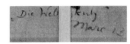

PROVENANCE:

Purchased from the artist by W. Beffie, Amsterdam and Brussels, before 1916;[1] purchased from Beffie by Karl Nierendorf, New York, after 1940 (Buchholz Gallery ex-hibition catalogue); purchased from Nierendorf, 1946.

CONDITION:

At some point prior to acquisition by the Museum, portions of the top, right, and bottom edges were inpainted. In 1954 surface dirt was removed with 3% Soilax solution and the surface coated with PBM.

There are noticeable traction cracks in various parts of the canvas but these are concentrated especially along the lower quarter of the surface and along the left margin. Apart from some general surface soil, the condition is good. (Oct. 1972.)

1. Schardt's notes from the *Merkbüchlein* read: *"Die Weltenkuh W.Beffie verkauft 800."*

On a postcard to Erich Heckel, dated April 4, 1913, Marc did a rather detailed study for the present work (fig. a). The painting itself was completed by May 22 (letter to Macke).

The colors in this work, like those in *Yellow Cow,* inevitably bring to mind Marc's analysis of color in his December 1910 letter to Macke. For the relevant passage from this letter, see above *Yellow Cow,* cat. no. 174. For a further discussion of this painting, see K. Lankheit, *Franz Marc* (in press).

fig. a.
Marc, study for *Bos Orbis Mundi,* ink over pencil, water-color, and chalk on postcard, 4⅛ x 5¾ in., 10.5 x 14.5 cm., Altonaer Museum, Hamburg.

EXHIBITIONS:

London, New Burlington Galleries, *20th Century German Art,* July 1938, no. 166; New York, Buchholz Gallery, *Franz Marc,* Nov. 11-Dec. 7, 1940, no. 14 ("*Red Cow,* lent W. Beffie, Brooklyn"); Munich, Haus der Kunst, *Der Blaue Reiter,* Sept.-Oct. 1949, no. 244, repr.; New York, SRGM 74, no. 142 (dated 1911); 78 (checklist); Toronto, SRGM 85-T, no. 56; San Francisco Museum of Art, *Art in the 20th Century,* June 17-July 10, 1955, p. 15, repr.; The Denver Art Museum, *Turn of the Century Masterpieces, 1880-1920,* Oct. 1-Nov. 18, 1956, no. 19; New York, SRGM 129 (checklist); Berlin, Akademie der Künste, *Symbol und Mythos in der zeitgenössischen Kunst,* Apr. 21-May 19, 1963, no. 17; Munich, Städtische Galerie, *Franz Marc,* Aug. 10-Oct. 13, 1963, no. 160, repr. color; Kunstverein in Hamburg, *Franz Marc,* Nov. 9, 1963-Jan. 5, 1964, no. 53, repr. color; New York, SRGM 202, p. 94, repr. 95; Columbus, Ohio, SRGM 207-T, p. 13, repr.; New York, SRGM 266, 276 (no cats.).

REFERENCES:

F. Marc, letter to August and Lisbeth Macke, May 22, 1913, *Briefwechsel,* 1964, p. 163; Schardt, 1936, pp. 128, 165, 1913, no. 21, repr.; K. Lankheit, *Franz Marc,* Berlin, 1950, pp. 29-32, repr.; Lankheit 1970, p. 73, no. 208, repr.

176   The Unfortunate Land of
        Tyrol. 1913.
        (Das arme Land Tirol).

46.1040

Oil on canvas 51⅝ x 78¾ (131.1 x 200)

Inscribed l.l.: *M. / das arme Land Tirol.*
Not dated.

PROVENANCE:

Purchased from the artist by W. Beffie,
Amsterdam and Brussels, before 1916;[1]
purchased from Beffie by Karl Nierendorf,
New York, after 1940 (Buchholz Gallery
exhibition catalogue); purchased from Nierendorf, 1946.

CONDITION:

In 1953 the painting was cleaned with 2%
Soilax solution, and 2 small losses at the
lower center were inpainted; the canvas was
surfaced with PBM and placed on a new
stretcher. In 1963 the reverse was cleaned
and the canvas lined with wax resin.

There are traction cracks in a number of
areas, mainly in the more thickly painted
blacks, blues, grays, and greens. There are
some abrasions in the black and blue paint
near the center of the left edge, and a 5 in.
vertical stain extending downwards from
the *M.* The condition is in general good.
(Oct. 1972.)

1. Schardt's notes from the *Merkbüchlein* read: *"Das arme Land Tirol W. Beffie verkauft
   1500."*

fig. a.
Marc, *Mountain Landscape*, 1913, pencil on paper, from
sketchbook xxxi, 4⅞ x 7⅞ in., 12.5 x 20 cm., Estate of
the Artist, no. 232.

fig. b.
Marc, *Tyrol*, 1913, pencil on paper, from sketchbook
xxxi, 4⅞ x 7⅞ in., 12.5 x 20 cm., Estate of the Artist,
no. 240.

On March 20, 1913, the Marcs, who were spending a few days in the Tyrol,
wrote to Lisbeth Macke: "... *wir schicken Euch herzliche Grüsse von einer
herrlichen Tour durch d. Vintschgau in Tirol. Neben Burg Montani ist eine
Kapelle mit den herrlichsten Fresken—wir wandern von Burg zu Burg und
haben viele schöne Kunst gesehen*" *(Briefwechsel*, p. 155). ("We send you our
best wishes from a wonderful journey through Vintschgau in the Tyrol. Close
to Castle Montani is a chapel with the most beautiful frescoes—we are walking
from one castle to the next and have seen many beautiful works of art.")

Two pencil sketches survive which must have been made on this journey
(figs. a and b). Although they have not hitherto been associated with *The
Unfortunate Land of Tyrol*, they must have formed the general basis for it.
When he returned to Sindelsdorf, Marc then proceeded to the preparatory
watercolor (fig. c), which has already been published by Lankheit as a study for
the painting. The watercolor corresponds closely to the final conception although it lacks the prominently placed border markers. The oil was completed
by the end of May, when Marc mentioned it in a letter to the Mackes *(Briefwechsel*, p. 163).

The presence of the Austro-Hungarian border sign, the rainbow, and the
heraldic eagle perched beneath it, together with the title, provide possible
clues to the painting's meaning, although ambiguities remain.

The history of the Tyrol in the nineteenth century is one of constant victim-
ization by its neighboring powers. After Austria's defeat by Napoleon in 1805
the Tyrol was annexed by Bavaria. When the new Austro-French war broke
out in 1809 the Tyrolean peasants under Andreas Hofer rose in a hopeless
struggle against the Bavarians and the French, but were predictably crushed,
and Hofer executed by the French. In 1814 the Tyrol was again united with

fig. c.
Marc, *Tyrol,* 1913, watercolor on paper, from sketch-
book xxxi, 4⅞ x 7⅞ in., 12.5 x 20 cm., Estate of the
Artist, no. 244.

Austria, but peace did not follow. Border disputes continued to erupt throughout the century. At the beginning of the twentieth century, tensions throughout
Europe were building up again. In 1912 the First Balkan War and in 1913 the
Second threatened to involve not Austria, but all of Europe. Thoughts and
fears of impending war are expressed throughout the writings of the period
leading up to 1914. The particularly vulnerable situation of the Tyrol (which
the Marcs had recently visited) and the generally threatening atmosphere in
Europe as a whole, were, thus, probably in Marc's mind as he developed the
composition. The ominous graveyard, the clear reference to a geographical
border zone, and the explicitly evocative nature of the title would support the
notion that this was his essential theme. The presence of the heraldic (German?) eagle perched just beyond the border and crowned by a rainbow may
thus suggest the potential unification of Europe, the destruction of borders,
through the purifying power of the impending war. On October 24, 1914, he
wrote to Kandinsky: "... *das gute Europäertum liegt m. Herzen näher als das
Deutschtum; ... Ich sehe [in diesem Krieg] sogar den heilsamen, wenn auch
grausamen Durchgang zu unsern Zielen; er wird die Menschen nicht zurück-
werfen, sondern Europa reinigen, bereit machen ... Europa thut heute dasselbe
an seinem Leibe, wie Frankreich in der grossen Revolution an sich that"*
(preserved in the Gabriele Münter und Johannes Eichner Stiftung, Munich,
Städtische Galerie, Munich; published by H. K. Röthel, *Franz Marc,* exhibition
catalogue, Munich, 1963). ("The sense of being a good European is closer to
my heart than is the sense of being a German; ... I even see in this war the
healing, if also gruesome, path to our goals; it will not set humanity back, but
on the contrary will purify Europe, and make it ready ... Europe is doing the
same things to her body that France did to hers during the Revolution.")

The letters written to Maria Marc from the front touch from time to time upon the potentially healing nature of war, upon the naturalness of war, and upon its spiritually regenerative aspects. It is not unlikely, therefore, that Marc already in 1913 was giving expression to some of these thoughts through the unusually explicit iconography and title of this painting.

(For a detailed discussion of the iconography and symbolism of Marc's immediately following paintings, see F. S. Levine, *The Apocalyptic Vision: An Analysis of the Art of Franz Marc within the Context of German Expressionism,* unpublished Ph.D. dissertation, Washington University, St. Louis, 1975. See also K. Lankheit, *Franz Marc* [in press].)

EXHIBITIONS:

London, New Burlington Galleries, *20th Century German Art,* July 1938, no. 15; New York, Buchholz Gallery, *Franz Marc,* Nov. 11-Dec. 7, 1940, no. 13; New York, SRGM 79 (checklist); Toronto, SRGM 85-T, no. 57; New York, SRGM 87 (checklist); Boston, SRGM 90-T (no cat.); Montreal, SRGM 93-T, no. 38, repr.; New York, SRGM 95 (checklist); London, SRGM 104-T, no. 47; New York, SRGM 118 (checklist); 129 (checklist, repr.); Munich, Städtische Galerie, *Franz Marc,* Aug. 10-Oct. 13, 1963, no. 159; Kunstverein in Hamburg, *Franz Marc,* Nov. 9, 1963-Jan. 5, 1964, no. 52, repr.; New York, SRGM 162, *Van Gogh and Expressionism* (checklist); 232, p. 288, repr. p. 289; 236 (no cat.); 241, p. 288, repr. p. 289; 266, 276 (no cats.).

REFERENCES:

F. Marc, letter to August and Lisbeth Macke, May 22, 1913, *Briefwechsel,* 1964, p. 163; Schardt, 1936, p. 165, 1913, no. 20; Lankheit, 1970, p. 72, no. 205, repr.

---

177   Stables. 1913.
      (Stallungen).

46.1037

Oil on canvas, 29 x 62 (73.6 x 157.5)

Signed l.r.: *M*; inscribed by the artist on reverse (photographed before lining): *Stallungen / Fz. Marc Sindelsdorf / Ob. Bayern.* Not dated.

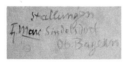

PROVENANCE:

Estate of the artist, 1916, until at least 1936;[1] Karl Nierendorf, New York, by 1939; purchased from Nierendorf, 1946.

CONDITION:

At an unrecorded date some inpainting was performed along most of the top edge (¼-½ in. in width), the upper third of the left edge (¼-½ in. in width), and in a diagonal area ⅝ x 3½ in. just below the center; in addition some scattered pinpoint losses were inpainted. In 1954 some cleaving paint lower left of center was set down with wax resin and the repaint in that area was probably performed at that time. In 1955 the canvas was lined with wax resin on natural linen and placed on a new stretcher.

The paint film is stained with a brownish substance (possibly varnish) in 3 places on the left side. The edges are somewhat worn, with some transfer material. Apart from some traction cracks in the impasto areas, the condition is good. (Oct. 1972.)

Schardt's notes[2] indicate that the picture was completed and sent to Dresden by the end of December 1913, in time for the opening of the January exhibition.

Lankheit drew attention to the pencil and ink study for the central section of the composition (fig. b). A pencil sketch from sketchbook xxix (fig. a) probably represents a preliminary study for the composition, with the vertical dividers already indicated, but the positions of the horses not yet finally established.

fig. a.
Marc, pencil on paper, from sketchbook xxix, ca. 1913, 4¾ x 5⅞ in., 12.1 x 14.9 cm., formerly Estate of the Artist, no. 196.

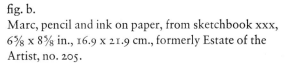

fig. b.
Marc, pencil and ink on paper, from sketchbook xxx, 6⅝ x 8⅝ in., 16.9 x 21.9 cm., formerly Estate of the Artist, no. 205.

1. Maria Marc is listed as the owner in Schardt as well as in the Hanover exhibition catalogue. Nierendorf had acquired the picture by 1939 and probably purchased it directly from Maria Marc, but no confirming evidence has hitherto come to light.

EXHIBITIONS:

Dresden, Galerie Arnold, *Die neue Malerei,* Jan. 1914, no. 98;[2] Berlin, Der Sturm, *43. Ausstellung: Expressionisten, Futuristen, Kubisten,* July 1916, no. 47; Munich, Neue Secession, *Franz Marc Gedächtnisausstellung,* Sept. 14-Oct. 15, 1916, no. 125; Berlin, Der Sturm, *Franz Marc Gedächtnisausstellung,* Nov. 1916, no. 22; Wiesbaden, Nassauischer Kunstverein, Neues Museum, *Franz Marc,* Mar.-Apr. 1917, no. 47; Berlin, Nationalgalerie, *Franz Marc,* Mar.-Apr. 1922 (no cat.);[3] Hanover, Kestner-Gesellschaft, *Franz Marc Gedächtnisausstellung,* Mar. 4-Apr. 19, 1936, no. 48; New York, Nierendorf Gallery, *German Expressionists,* May 1939 (no cat.); Boston, The Institute of Modern Art, *Contemporary German Art,* Nov. 2-Dec. 9, 1939, no. 39; San Francisco, Golden Gate International Exhibition, *Contemporary Art,* 1939, no. 683; Cincinnati Modern Art Society, *Expressionism,* Apr. 20-May 20, 1941, p. 10; New York, Nierendorf Gallery, *Art as Exhibited from 1922-1942 by the Nierendorf Gallery,* Nov. 1942 (checklist); New York, Nierendorf Gallery, *Gestation-Formation,* Mar. 1944 (checklist); New York, SRGM 74, no. 139; 78 (checklist; added Mar. 16); Toronto, SRGM 85-T, no. 58 (dated 1913-14; so dated in all subsequent publications until *Cubist Epoch,* 1970); Vancouver, SRGM 88-T, no. 57, repr.; Boston, SRGM 90-T (no cat.); San Francisco Museum of Art, *Art in the 20th Century,* June 17-July 10, 1955, p. 15; New York, SRGM 95 (checklist); Hartford, Conn., Wadsworth Atheneum, *Twentieth Century Painting from Three Cities: New York, New Haven, Hartford,* Oct. 19-Dec. 4, 1955, no. 34, repr.; New York, SRGM 97 (checklist); London, SRGM 104-T, no. 48; Boston, SRGM 119-T, no. 39; Lexington, Ky., SRGM 122-T, no. 19; Pasadena Art Museum, *German Expressionism,* Apr. 23-June 4, 1961, no. 72; New York, SRGM 129 (checklist); Philadelphia, SRGM 134-T, no. 105; New York, SRGM 144, 151 (checklists); Munich, Städtische Galerie im Lenbachhaus, *Franz Marc,* Aug. 10-Oct. 13, 1963, no. 221, repr.; Kunstverein in Hamburg, *Franz Marc,* Nov. 9, 1963-Jan. 5, 1964, no. 55, repr.; New York, SRGM 173, no. 33; 196 (checklist); Los Angeles County Museum of Art, *The Cubist Epoch,* Dec. 15, 1970-Feb. 21, 1971, no. 204, color pl. 144 (dated 1913), traveled to New York, The Metropolitan Museum of Art, Apr. 9-June 8, 1971; New York, SRGM 260, 266, 276 (no cats.).

REFERENCES:

Schardt, 1936, p. 165, winter 1913-14, no. 2; H. Bünemann, *Franz Marc, Zeichnungen Aquarelle,* Munich, 1948, p. 33; K. Lankheit, *Franz Marc,* Berlin, 1950, repr. p. 53 (dated 1913/14); Cooper, *Cubist Epoch,* 1970, pp. 147, 299, color pl. 144 (dated 1913); Lankheit, 1970, p. 77, no. 221, repr. (dated 1913).

2. Schardt's notes from the *Merkbüchlein* read in part: *"Stallungen . . . xii 13 Reiche—Arnold Coll. Dresden."* Richard Reiche was the director of the Kunstverein in Barmen and apparently the organizer of the Dresden exhibition, which has hitherto not been identified, but must be the Jan. 1914 one cited here. Further evidence for this is provided by Maria Marc's Dec. 2, 1913, letter to Lisbeth Macke which says: *"Franz hat viel gearbeitet und beteiligt sich an Dr. Reiche's Dresdner Ausstellung." Briefwechsel,* 1964, p. 175. ("Franz has been working hard and is taking part in Dr. Reiche's Dresden exhibition.")

3. See above cat. no. 172, fn. 5.

178   Broken Forms. 1914.
      (*Zerbrochene Formen*).

50.1240

Oil on canvas, 44 x 33¼ (111.8 x 88.4)

Not signed or dated.

PROVENANCE:

Maria Marc, Ried, 1916-50; purchased from Maria Marc through Otto Stangl, Munich, 1950.

CONDITION:

In 1953 the surface was cleaned with 1% Soilax solution, cleaving paint in 2 small areas was re-adhered with PVA emulsion, and the surface coated with PBM. In 1956 the canvas was impregnated from the reverse with wax resin (but not lined), and 2 tiny losses near the upper left corner were inpainted.

Traction cracks are visible in some areas and there are a few scattered pinpoint paint losses, but the condition is otherwise excellent. (Oct. 1972.)

fig. a.
Marc, pencil and ink on paper, from sketch-
book xxx, 8⅝ x 6⅝ in., 22 x 16.7 cm., formerly
Estate of the Artist, no. 208.

fig. b.
Marc, tempera on paper, from sketchbook
xxix, 6 x 4¾ in., 15.2 x 12.2 cm., formerly
Estate of the Artist, no. 198.

Early in 1914 the Marcs moved to Ried near the monastery of Benediktbeuren. He painted about twelve pictures there before he left for the front in August. Several of them, including the present one, are described by Schardt (presumably on the basis of Maria Marc's information) as unfinished and are accepted as such by Schmidt (1957), H. K. Röthel, and H. Platte (catalogues of 1963 Munich and Hamburg exhibitions). The fact that the work is neither signed nor dated might support their view. (Of the six "unfinished" works in Schardt, two are, however, signed.)

Lankheit has argued convincingly (in conversation with the author, October 1972) that the present work and some others from 1914 seem from an aesthetic standpoint complete. He suggests that Maria Marc might have had some anxieties about the quality of these late works. Marc himself had apparently described them as *Versuche* (experiments), possibly implying thereby that the whole venture into abstraction was, in a sense, unfinished. In this context, Lankheit suggests Maria Marc's description of the works as unfinished might be attributable to her own tentative feelings about them rather than to Marc's stated view. A reviewer of the 1917 Weisbaden exhibition (*Wiesbadener Tageblatt*, March 10, 1917, reprinted by Lankheit, *Franz Marc im Urteil seiner Zeit*, Cologne, 1960, p. 103) had said that Marc's last pictures represented the wanderings of a lost mind. Perhaps she was herself afraid that this might be so, and hence her cautious suggestion that they be judged as unfinished works.

The picture has been described as totally abstract by Lankheit (1960), P. Selz (*German Expressionist Painting*, Berkeley and Los Angeles, 1957, p. 307), and Röthel (*Modern German Painting*, New York, 1957, p. 47). While its effect is certainly abstract, it seems possible that it represents a transformation of the "house and garden" motif depicted in the 1913-14 sketchbooks (figs. a and b). Marc's ventures into abstraction were necessarily few since his life was cut short so soon after he began to work in this mode. His process of composition in these late works, and particularly the degree to which they may be evolved from representational sources, remains to be established.

EXHIBITIONS:
Munich, Haus der Kunst, *Der Blaue Reiter*, Sept.-Oct. 1949, no. 249 *("unvollendet")*; Kunsthalle Basel, *Der Blaue Reiter 1908-1914*, Jan. 21-Feb. 26, 1950, no. 216; New York, SRGM 74, no. 138; 87 (checklist); Montreal, SRGM 93-T, no. 40; The Newark Museum, *Abstract Art from 1910 to Today*, Apr. 27-June 10, 1961, no. 42; New York, SRGM 129, 144 (checklists); Munich, Städtische Galerie im Lenbachhaus, *Franz Marc*, Aug. 10-Oct. 13, 1963, no. 237 *("unvollendet")*; Kunstverein in Hamburg, *Franz Marc*, Nov. 9, 1963-Jan. 5, 1964, no. 59, repr. *("unvollendet")*; New York, SRGM 173, no. 34; New York, M. Knoedler & Co., Inc., *7 Decades of Modern Art*, Apr. 26-May 21, 1966, no. 95, repr.; Fine Arts Gallery of San Diego, *Color and Form 1901-1914*, Nov. 20, 1971-Jan. 2, 1972, no. 63, repr. color, traveled to Cal., The Oakland Museum, Jan. 26-Mar. 5, 1972, Seattle Art Museum, Mar. 24-May 27, 1972; Rochester, N.Y., SRGM 263-T (no cat.); New York, SRGM 276 (no cat.).

REFERENCES:
Schardt, 1936, p. 65, 1914, no. 4 *("unvollendet")*; K. Lankheit, *Franz Marc*, Berlin, 1950, pp. 50 ff., repr. color opp. p. 60; G. Schmidt, *Franz Marc*, Berlin, 1957, n.p.; K. Lankheit, *Franz Marc Watercolors, Drawings, Writings*, New York, 1960, p. 19; Idem, 1970, p. 82, no. 236, repr.

André Masson

Born January 1896, Balagny (Oise).
Lives in Paris.

179   Man in a Tower. 1924.
       *(Homme dans une tour; Homme tenant une
       corde).*

48.1172 x222

Oil on canvas, 37⅜ x 24 (95 x 60.8)

Signed on reverse (transcribed but not
photographed before lining, partially visible
in transmitted light): *André Masson.* Not
dated.

PROVENANCE:

Galerie Simon, Paris, 1924 (information supplied by M. Jardot, conversation with the
author, August 1972); purchased from
Galerie Simon by Gertrude Stein, 1924 (information supplied by Masson, conversation with the author, October 1971 and

Jardot, August 1972); acquired from an
unknown source by Karl Nierendorf, New
York, by 1948; acquired with the Estate of
Karl Nierendorf, 1948.

CONDITION:

In 1953 the work was cleaned with 1½%
Soilax and benzine and surfaced with PBM.
In 1959 it was lined with wax resin and
squared on a new stretcher. 6 in. of the top
edge and 4 in. of the bottom edge were
inpainted at this time.

The edges show slight wear but the condition in general is excellent. (Dec. 1973.)

Man in a Tower belongs to a group of works painted in 1923-25 in which
a single male figure in a tower or dungeon is surrounded by a group of clearly
symbolic objects. These are among the earliest works in which the artist—as
he himself expressed it—attempted to bring "philosophical ideas into a painting" (Leiris, "La Terre," *André Masson and his Universe,* p. 101).

André Masson, in conversation with the author (October 1971), gave probing thought to the symbolic nature of these works and offered an interpretation
of many of their essential ingredients. A summary of his comments follows:

> *The location of these men in underground, tower, or dungeon settings
> was highly significant; they had, in effect, something of the prisoner in
> them. The recurring rope suggests a way of escape, as do the steps at the
> right. The flame, which in the Guggenheim picture is at the center of the
> composition, and—significantly—over the heart of the man, represents the
> life which must not be extinguished. The knife, which appears again and
> again, is an expression of will power. The circular form at the upper left is
> the* boule de feu *—a reference to the astrological forces which so preoccupied
> all of us at the time; the large and small balls at the center left, on the other
> hand, are a totally frivolous addition—a "bilboquet" (cup and ball) which
> was in my studio and which I introduced into the scenery of many of my
> paintings. The dice are a reference to chance in general and, more specific-
> ally, to Mallarmé's poem "Un coup de dès n'abolira jamais le hasard."
> I regarded Mallarmé as one of the greatest of all poets, and I had done a
> series of illustrations for "Un coup de dès" in 1914. The notions of chance
> ("hasard"), luck ("chance"), and the absurd ("l'absurd") had preoccupied
> me and my war-time contemporaries constantly—they were, perforce, the
> three gods of every soldier.*

506

The man portrayed in the Guggenheim picture is not a direct portrait (in the sense that Man in an Interior [Portrait of Michel Leiris] *and* Man with an Orange [Self-Portrait] *are). Rather it is a composite portrait of the three more or less regular inhabitants of my studio at that time—Leiris, Georges Limbour, and Roland Tual. We four were close friends; the picture represents an imaginary man with the memory of each of them contained in him. The female silhouette behind the man's head is the ever-present allusion to woman which is a more or less explicit element in all of these apparently masculine paintings. The fish is perhaps the only enigma: it may represent, like the knife, a further suggestion of will power; or perhaps it is water. (Birds—air, and horses—earth, appeared in many of my paintings of this period.) Or perhaps freedom ["la liberté"]. But I cannot be sure.*

(The context in which the fish is most explicitly and clearly used by Masson to symbolize water is in *Les quatre éléments,* also of 1924, where a bird, a fish, a sphere, and a flame clearly represent air, water, earth, and fire [Leiris and Limbour, repr. p. 106].)

In a subsequent conversation with Rowell (June 1972), Masson raised the possibility that the notion of the prisoner, which is a factor in each of these paintings, may have been related to his own four years of military service, a time when he was "not free." Alternatively it might have been related to his post-war "incarceration" in a psychiatric hospital, where he was placed under temporary observation and surrounded by mad men (*"des fous"*). This preoccupation with imprisonment and with the rope as a means of escape reappears almost twenty years later in *Anatomie de mon univers* (1940-42, pl. xiii), *Tentative d'evasion,* where a man, clinging to a rope, tries to climb out of a seemingly endless tower. Masson has suggested that the prominence of this prisoner motif throughout his oeuvre is traceable to the influence of Piranesi's *Carceri,* to which he felt strongly drawn in the years 1923-25, and which provided a major source of inspiration in the gradual formulation of his own "personal mythology" (*"Piranèse et ses* Prisons . . . *Il a été une des portes d'initiation de ma mythologie personelle,"* interview with Georges Bernier, *L'Oeil,* no. 5, May 1955, pp. 12-17). His characterization of the imprisoned figure in *Man in a Tower* as a composite memory of his three close friends, and hence more the embodiment of an idea than a physical likeness, clarifies the relationship of this figure to the very similar ones in the related paintings of the period (*Man with an Orange,* 1923, Leiris and Limbour, repr. p. 13; *Man in an Interior,* 1924, Ibid., repr. p. 202; *Figure in a Dungeon,* 1924, Kahnweiler photo no. 10602; *Man surrounded by Birds,* 1924, Kahnweiler photo no. 10573). As Leiris has penetratingly argued, Masson's aim in all these so-called "portraits" is not simple description, but rather the expression of much deeper universal characteristics (pp. 195-199).

Masson's reference to the female form as a leitmotif hovering in the background of these male-dominated scenes throws new light on their content, since they have traditionally been regarded as exclusively male domains. (See, for example, Limbour, p. 116, or H. Juin, *André Masson,* Paris, 1963, p. 70.) The full symbolic implications of this female presence remain to be explored, although Masson's own expressed preoccupation with a potent sexual life and the developing Surrealist notions of sexual content are clearly involved.

Limbour has drawn attention to the fact that the large, angular kitchen knife which appears in most of these compositions prefigures those in so many of the later massacres and sacrifices, and he suggests that the formal juxtaposition of curved and angular forms underlines the strong sense of discord which pervades these works (pp. 116-117).

REFERENCE:
M. Leiris and G. Limbour, *André Masson and his Universe,* Geneva-Paris-London, 1947, repr. p. 43.

Jean Metzinger

Born June 1883, Nantes.
Died November 1956, Paris.

180   Woman with a Fan. 1912 (-1913?).
        (Femme à l'éventail).

38.531

Oil on canvas, 35¾ x 25¼ (90.7 x 64.2)

Signed l.l.: *Metzinger*. Not dated.

PROVENANCE:

Galerie l'Effort Moderne (Léonce Rosenberg), Paris, by 1937 (Petit Palais exhibition catalogue);[1] Galerie Garnier des Garets, Paris, 1937-38;[2] purchased from Garets by Solomon R. Guggenheim, 1938; Gift of Solomon R. Guggenheim, 1938.

CONDITION:

In 1953 the work was cleaned with 2% Soilax and inpainted with PVA; in 1967 it was glue lined, placed on a new stretcher, and the edges taped.

With the exception of some minor losses in the lower corners, the condition is excellent. (May 1974.)

A satisfactory chronology for Metzinger's work has not been established. Few of his works are dated and the difficulties are compounded by his conservative and academic tendencies which blur the lines of his stylistic development. In the case of *Woman with a Fan,* however, two related and documented works do exist to clarify the issue.

The first of these, *The Yellow Plume,* is signed and dated 1912 and was shown in the October 1912 *Section d'Or* exhibition (no. 119; *Painters of the Section d'Or,* exhibition catalogue, Buffalo, 1967, repr. color no. 35, Collection Mr. and Mrs. S. E. Johnson, Chicago). The second, *Dancer in a Café* (Albright-Knox Art Gallery, Buffalo), was convincingly associated by J. Golding with an entry in the 1912 *Salon d'Automne (Cubism,* 1968, p. 160) and it was probably painted shortly before *The Yellow Plume* in the summer of that year *(Salon d'Automne,* no. 1195, *Danseuse;* Cooper, *Cubist Epoch,* 1970, repr. color p. 78).

These two paintings and a second version of *The Yellow Plume* which was purchased by John Quinn in 1916 (later Collection R. Sturgis Ingersoll, Sotheby Parke Bernet, New York, sale catalogue, May 3, 1974, repr. color lot 371) are strikingly similar in style and conception to *Woman with a Fan.* The similarities are strongest among the two versions of *The Yellow Plume* and the Guggenheim painting. In these three portraits, all of which depict women wearing similar hats, the treatment of the figure and its relationship to the surrounding space are virtually identical. They and the slightly earlier *Dancer in a Café* demonstrate the extent to which Metzinger absorbed the example presented by Gris, whose recent work had been publicly exhibited for the first time at the *Salon des Indépendants* just a few months before. (See, for example,

1. The picture appears among the Rosenberg photographic archives in Paris, but there is no indication of when he acquired it. A Rosenberg label on the reverse bears only the information "*No.25112 J.Metzinger, 1913.*" Rosenberg was buying paintings by Metzinger by 1918 and may have acquired the picture soon afterwards.

2. Mlle. Garnier des Garets probably acquired the picture after the 1937 exhibition, possibly on behalf of Guggenheim.

Portrait of Picasso, 1912, Kahnweiler, *Juan Gris,* London, 1969, repr. p. 242, and a *Houses in Paris,* 1911-12 [destroyed, formerly Galerie Simon, Paris, photo no. 5012; see above cat. no. 67].) As Golding has pointed out, Metzinger's use of the superimposed linear grid lacks the structural rationale of the Gris models and creates instead a purely decorative surface pattern *(Cubism,* 1968, p. 160).

D. Cooper, who also comments on the decorative character of this phase in Metzinger's oeuvre, pointedly cites the artist's own warnings which were published at precisely the same period, but apparently ignored, on the dangers of such stylistic mannerisms: *"Toute préoccupation dérivant en art de la matière employée, nous devons tenir la préoccupation décorative, si nous la rencontrons chez un peintre, pour un artifice bon à cacher une impuissance."* ("As all preoccupation in art arises from the material employed, we ought to regard the decorative preoccupation, if we find it in a painter, as an anachronistic artifice, useful only to conceal impotence." *Du Cubisme,* Paris, 1912, English translation of 1913 quoted by Cooper, *Cubist Epoch,* 1970, p. 78.)

Metzinger's paintings of 1912 and later seem to demonstrate a fairly consistent and immediate response to the most recent work of Gris, which thus provides important guideposts for the dating of the former's work. The second version of *The Yellow Plume* and *Woman with a Fan* were both probably painted not long after the first version of *The Yellow Plume* and would thus date from late in 1912, or possibly early in 1913.

EXHIBITIONS:

Paris, Musée du Petit Palais, *Les Maîtres de l'art indépendant, 1895-1937,* June-Oct. 1937, no. 12 (dated 1912); New York, SRGM 78 (checklist; dated 1912?); 79 (checklist; dated 1913; so dated in all subsequent SRGM publications); 83 (checklist); Vancouver, SRGM 88-T, no. 60, repr.; Boston, SRGM 90-T (no cat.); Montreal, SRGM 93-T, no. 41; New York, SRGM 95 (checklist; withdrawn Sept. 12); The Arts Club of Chicago, *An Exhibition of Cubism on the Occasion of the Fortieth Anniversary of the Arts Club of Chicago,* Oct. 3-Nov. 4, 1955, no. 43; London, SRGM 104-T, no. 50; Boston, SRGM 119-T, no. 40; Lexington, Ky., SRGM 122-T, no. 20; New York, SRGM 144 (checklist); Worcester, Mass., SRGM 148-T, no. 28; The Museum of Fine Arts, Houston, *The Heroic Years: Paris 1908-1914,* Oct. 21-Dec. 8, 1965 (no cat.); Buffalo, N.Y., Albright-Knox Art Gallery, *Painters of the Section d'Or: The Alternatives to Cubism,* Sept. 27-Oct. 22, 1967, no. 37, repr. (dated 1913).

REFERENCES:

Art of Tomorrow, 1939, p. 174 (*"The Lady,* 1915"); L. Degand, "La Peinture cubiste," *Art d'aujourd'hui,* sér. 4, May-June 1953, repr. p. 14; SRGM *Handbook,* 1959, p. 118, repr.

181   Landscape. ca. 1913-1914.

40.841

Oil on canvas, 36⅛ x 28¾ (91.7 x 73)

Signed l.r.: *Metzinger*; on reverse (photographed before lining): *Metzinger*. Not dated.

PROVENANCE:

Purchased from Carroll Galleries, New York by John Quinn (1870-1924), by 1920;[1] purchased from the Quinn Collection by J. B. Neumann, New York, 1927 (Sale, American Art Galleries, New York, *The Renowned Collection of Modern and Ultra-Modern Art formed by the late John Quinn,* February 9-12, 1927, no. 509A); purchased from the J. B. Neumann Collection (Sale, Plaza Art Galleries, Inc., New York, *A Selection of Modern Art . . . from J. B. Neu-*

mann and others, May 8, 1940, no. 60, repr.).

CONDITION:

In 1956 the work was lined with wax resin and placed on a new stretcher; 7 losses (from ⅛ in. to 2 in. in width) were inpainted, and the canvas was surfaced with PBM.

The edges and corners were chipped in places with some loss of paint and ground. There are some minor areas of crackle and drying cracks, but no evidence of incipient cleavage. The present painting was almost certainly painted over an earlier work, but since the artist applied an intervening ground, it is impossible to determine what this composition was. UV, X-ray, and transmitted light have revealed extremely little beyond confirming the fact that a composition of some kind was present beneath the second ground layer. The condition in general is excellent. (May 1974.)

Metzinger's enclosure of the landscape within diagonally placed rectangular forms and his use of a high viewpoint characterize his direct dependence upon the work of Gris. Gris' 1913 paintings, such as the two landscapes at Céret (Private Collection, Paris, Golding, *Cubism,* 1968, pl. 54; and Moderna Museet, Stockholm, D.H. Kahnweiler, *Juan Gris,* London, 1969, repr. p. 247), are, in fact, more uncompromising than the Metzinger in their suppression of spatial recession. Metzinger, in retaining some clearly modeled three-dimensional forms, betrays his essentially more conservative adherence to traditional modes of representation. Nonetheless, the overall structure of the landscape is un-

1. On Mar. 23, 1920, W. Pach, Director of the Carroll Galleries since 1917, wrote to Quinn: "I am glad you got the Metzingers, as they are surely of the best of his work and will, I believe, rank very high in the art of their decade. Perhaps I should give you a temporary memorandum that they cost—for the Landscape—$300, The Head of a Woman 150. These are the prices that Gleizes put on them in 1915 or '16." Quinn owned 2 landscapes by Metzinger, the other having been purchased in Feb. 1916 (letter from Metzinger to Mrs. Bryant, Feb. 25, 1916, copy in Carroll Galleries Folder, Box 1 [Art Dealers], John Quinn Memorial Collection, Manuscripts and Archives Division, The New York Public Library, Astor, Lenox and Tilden Foundations).

It is impossible to say for certain which of the 2 is referred to in the Mar. 1920 letter. However, it is almost certain that Quinn must have owned both by Sept. 1920, when he wrote to Léonce Rosenberg, Sept. 24, 1920, "I have several examples of the work of Metzinger and would not be interested, I think, in any more of that." (See John Quinn Memorial Collection for correspondence cited.) He had purchased 4 other Metzingers from the Carroll Galleries in 1916 (see Quinn correspondence, New York Public Library), and owned 9 works by the artist in all.

mistakably indebted to Gris' example. A date of ca. 1913-14 for the present landscape is plausible, although it is possible that the picture was painted slightly later.

EXHIBITIONS:

Philadelphia, Pennsylvania Museum of Art, *Abstract Painting—1910,* May 11-June 19, 1935 (no cat.);[2] New York, Rains Auction Rooms, Inc., *Modern Paintings . . . from the Collection of J. B. Neumann,* Jan. 19-24, 1936, no. 65 (not sold); New York, SRGM 78 (checklist, dated 1914?); Philadelphia, SRGM 134-T, no. 110; New York, SRGM 144 (checklist).

REFERENCE:

The John Quinn Collection of Paintings, Watercolors, Drawings and Sculpture, New York, 1926, p. 11 ("*Landscape,* 28 x 36 in.").

2. A label on the reverse reads: "Pennsylvania Museum of Art, Fairmount, Metzinger, Paysage, lent Neumann." The records of the Philadelphia Museum contain a typed list of works included and their lenders. The present picture is listed as "Paysage. J.B. Neumann."

182   Coffee Grinder, Coffee Pot,
       Cigarettes, and Glass. ca. 1913-1916.
       (Still Life; Nature Morte).

59.1520

Oil on canvas, 27⅝ x 20⅝ (70.3 x 52.4)

Signed l.r.: *Metzinger.* Not dated.

PROVENANCE:

Probably purchased directly from the artist by Walter Pach (1883-1958), New York,[1] by 1924 (repr. *Masters of Modern Art);* purchased from the Estate of Walter Pach, 1948, by Peridot Gallery (Louis Pollack), New York; purchased from Peridot Gallery, 1959.

CONDITION:

At some time prior to acquisition by the Museum, the picture was glue lined and the edges taped. 4 areas of inpaint may date from this time: a 1 in. area at the lower left and upper right corners; a 1 in. area near the bottom edge; a 3 in. line 8 in. from the bottom and 9 in. from the left.

There are scattered irregular cracks in the heavy impasto and a severe vertical crack with some cupping in the white triangle at the upper left, but the condition is otherwise excellent. (May 1974.)

Although this work has been dated 1916 since its acquisition by the Museum, conclusive evidence for the date has not yet been established. The pervasive influence of Gris on Metzinger's post-1914 evolution provides clues for the establishment of *terminus ante quem* dates, but the precise sequence of works inspired by Gris' own development is not always easy to trace. The compositional structure of Metzinger's painting, which places the still-life within a diamond-shaped framing device, clearly owes something to a work such as Gris' *The Watch,* 1912 (Collection Hans Crether, Switzerland), which was shown at the *Section d'Or* in October 1912. The division of the surface into a series of vertical planes is reminiscent of Gris' 1912-13 pictures like *The Book,* 1913 (formerly Collection G. Henry, now Caisse Nationale des Monuments Historiques et des Sites, Paris), whereas the treatment of forms might be more clearly identified with Gris' coffee pots and coffee grinders in works such as *Breakfast* of 1915 (Musée National d'Art Moderne, Paris) or *The Coffee Grinder* of 1916 (Private Collection, Paris, *Juan Gris,* exhibition catalogue, Paris, 1974, repr. no. 51).

Until further evidence for a construction of Metzinger's chronology emerges, a date of ca. 1913-16 is the most plausible.

1. Both in his capacity as director of the Carroll Galleries and before, Pach had direct dealings with Metzinger. (See, for example, the John Quinn Memorial Collection, Manuscripts and Archives Division, The New York Public Library, Astor, Lenox and Tilden Foundations, letters dated Oct. 26, 1918, and Mar. 23, 1920.)

EXHIBITIONS:

New York, Peridot Gallery, *Second Annual Exhibition of European Paintings, Drawings and Sculpture,* Dec. 15, 1958-Jan. 10, 1959 (no cat.); New York, SRGM 118, 132 (checklists, dated 1916); Laguna Beach, Cal., SRGM 143-T (checklist, dated 1916).

REFERENCES:

W. Pach, *The Masters of Modern Art,* New York, 1924, pp. 109-110, repr. no. 24 (not dated); SRGM *Handbook,* 1959, p. 118, repr. (dated 1916).

Joan Miró[1]

Born April 1893, Barcelona.
Lives in Palma, Majorca.

183   Prades, the Village. Summer 1917.
       (Prades, el poble; View of Montroig).

69.1894

Oil on canvas, 25⅝ x 28⅝ (65 x 72.6)

Signed l.l.: *Miró.* Not dated.

PROVENANCE:

Purchased from Galeries Dalmau, Barcelona by Pedro Mañach, 1918;[2] purchased from Madame Mañach in 1951 by Pierre Matisse Gallery, New York; purchased from Matisse by Robert Elkon, New York, jointly with Albert Loeb and Krugier Gallery, 1969; purchased from Elkon, 1969.

CONDITION:

At some time prior to acquisition by the Museum, the canvas was glue lined; the edges of the original canvas were trimmed on all sides and taped. 3 areas of inpaint may date from this time: a 13 in. horizontal strip, 2 in. wide and 2 in. from the top edge; a 2 in. square area 5 in. from the top and 1½ in. from the right; a 1 in. area 3 in. from the top and 3 in. from the left.

The corners and edges show moderate wear with some loss of paint and ground, and there are some minor traction cracks in 2 or 3 areas, especially in the roofs below the spire. The lining process appears to have flattened the pigment to some extent, but the overall condition is good. (Dec. 1973.)

Although the scene has repeatedly been identified as Montroig (see below EXHIBITIONS and REFERENCES), the church is clearly that of Prades (fig. a). Miró himself has confirmed (in conversation with Rowell, May 1974) that during the summer of 1917, which he spent at Montroig, he went for several weeks to stay in an inn at Prades for a change of scene; every day during this period he made studies after nature. The clarity and objectivity with which Miró portrayed architectural forms at this stage in his development contrasts strongly,

fig. a.
Prades (photograph taken in 1974).

1. In May 1974 M. Rowell, Curator of Special Exhibitions at the Guggenheim Museum, interviewed Miró in Paris and on the author's behalf posed to him a series of detailed questions concerning his works in the SRGM Collection. Information supplied by Miró on this occasion is specifically cited in the individual entries which follow.

2. Pedro Mañach was a banker, as well as a friend and first dealer of Picasso. According to Miró (conversation with Rowell, May 1974), Mañach purchased the present painting out of the "disastrously unsuccessful" 1918 exhibition in order to help José Dalmau, who had presumably purchased the pictures from Miró.

as Dupin has pointed out, with the lyrical and decorative patterning of the landscape settings in which these structures are placed. The geometric regularity of the furrows in the foreground field occurs again and again in the subsequent landscapes, up to and including *The Farm,* 1921-22 (where it is barely visible on the extreme right edge), and *The Tilled Field,* 1923-24, in both of which the earlier vibrant Fauve colors have been transformed into a monochromatic brown.

Miró recently identified the colorful horizontal foreground bands as a field ploughed and ready for planting, and the wavy lines as string bean plants climbing up stakes. Moreover, he distinctly remembers having considerable difficulty resolving the problem of how to portray the latter (May 1974). Prades, approximately ten miles north of Miró's family farm at Montroig, was one of a group of villages (including Cornudella, Cambrils, and Ciurana) which Miró depicted in the paintings of this period.

183

Prades, the Village, which has always been dated 1917, is extremely close in style to *The Path, Ciurana,* which is signed and dated 1917 (Dupin, 1962, repr. color, p. 67) and must indeed have been painted the same year. (Miró himself recalls that he worked on it during his military service. As Dupin states [p. 62], this service began in 1915 and totaled ten months, but was fulfilled in short periods of duty extending over several years. This chronology would be consistent with the stylistic evidence which argues for a date of 1917.)

The use of juxtaposed stripes of bright color in these landscapes, and even more strikingly in the 1917 picture *North-South,* strongly suggests the influence of Robert Delaunay's paintings of 1916 such as *Portuguese Women,* where stripes similar in palette and mode of juxtaposition occur (Vriesen and Imdahl, 1969, color pl. 15). Delaunay spent the year 1916 in Spain and Portugal, and although it has hitherto not been possible to document a meeting between the two artists during that year, an exhibition of Delaunay's work did take place in Barcelona, and Miró must certainly have seen it. (See Delaunay's notes written ca. 1918-19 in *Du Cubisme à l'art abstrait,* Paris, 1957, p. 108, where he refers to the exhibition in Barcelona. Although he gives no date for it, the only possible occasion would have been his 1916-17 visit to that city. For the dating of the ca. 1918-19 notes see above cat. no. 36, fn. 3.) Which paintings Delaunay showed in this exhibition is not known. But the close relationship between his works of 1916 and aspects of Miró's 1917 style would suggest that pictures such as *Portuguese Women* must have been included.

EXHIBITIONS:

Barcelona, Galeries Dalmau, *Exposición Joan Miró,* Feb. 16-Mar. 3, 1918, no. 58 *(Prades. el poble);* Paris, Galerie La Licorne, *Expositions de peintures et dessins de Joan Miró,* Apr. 29-May 14, 1921, no. 10 *(Paysage)?;*[3] New York, Pierre Matisse Gallery, *The Early Paintings of Joan Miró,* Nov. 20-Dec. 15, 1951, no. 6, repr. (*"View of Montroig, 1917"*); New York, The Museum of Modern Art, *Joan Miró,* Mar. 18-May 10, 1959, no. 4 (*"View of Montroig, 1917"*), traveled to Los Angeles County Museum of Art, June 10-July 21, 1959; Paris, Musée National d'Art Moderne, *Joan Miró,* June 28-Nov. 4, 1962, no. 4 (*"Prades, le village, 1917"*); Tokyo, National Museum of Modern Art, *Joan Miró,* Aug. 26-Oct. 9, 1966, no. 12, repr. (*"Prades, le village, 1917"*), traveled to Kyoto National Museum of Modern Art, Oct. 20-Nov. 30, 1966; New York, Robert Elkon Gallery, *New Acquisitions,* Sept. 27-Oct. 29, 1969, no. 16, repr. (*"View of Montroig, 1917"*); New York, SRGM 227 (no cat.); 232, 241, p. 298, repr. p. 299 (*"The Village Prades [view of Montroig], 1917"*); New York, Acquavella Galleries, Inc., *Joan Miró,* Oct. 18-Nov. 18, 1972, no. 4, repr. (*"The Village, Prades, 1917"*); New York, SRGM 266 (no cat.).

REFERENCES:

J. Fitzsimmons, "Miró, Painter of Reality: An Early View," *Art Digest,* vol. 26, Dec. 1, 1951, p. 16 (*"View of Montroig, 1917,"* review of Pierre Matisse exhibition); J. T. Soby, *Joan Miró,* exhibition catalogue, New York, 1959, p. 14, repr. p. 12 (*"View of Montroig, 1917"*); J. Dupin, *Joan Miró: Life and Work,* New York, 1962, pp. 66, 68, 73, 504, no. 38 (*"Village, Prades, 1917"*); [M. Rowell], SRGM *Handbook,* 1970, p. 298, repr. p. 299 (*"The Village, Prades, 1917"*).

3. Miró recalls that the picture was included in this exhibition (conversation with Rowell, May 1974). The only entry which might correspond to it is no. 10.

184   Personage.   Summer 1925.[1]
(Personnage; Composition; Abstraction).

48.1172 x504

Oil and egg tempera (?) on canvas, 51¼ x
37⅞ (130 x 96.2). Miró, in correspondence
with the SRGM, 1967, specifically described
the medium of the blue background as egg
tempera. Tests conducted by O. H. Riley,
October 1974, have been unsuccessful in
confirming this. The medium appears rather
to be cobalt blue oil applied with a turpentine wash over a zinc ground.

Signed and dated l.l.: *Mirò. / 1925.*; on
reverse: *Joan Miró. / 1925.*

PROVENANCE:

Purchased from the artist by Galerie Pierre
(Pierre Loeb), Paris, ca. 1926-27;[2] Galerie
Beaune, Paris;[3] Walter P. Chrysler, Jr., New
York and Warrentown, Virginia, 1938-46;[3]
purchased from the Chrysler Collection
(Walter P. Chrysler Sale, Parke Bernet Galleries, Inc., New York, April 11, 1946, lot
36) by Karl Nierendorf, New York (information supplied by Parke Bernet, correspondence with the author, July 1974);
acquired with the Estate of Karl Nierendorf,
1948.

CONDITION:

In 1959, while the painting was on extended
loan to the Hackley Art Gallery, Muskegon,
Mich., it was accidentally sprayed in the
lower center and lower right with fire extin-
guishing fluid, causing scattered bleaching
of the blue pigment. The chemicals remaining on the surface were neutralized and the
tiny bleached spots inpainted with watercolor and gouache in PBM. 2 areas of old
repaint in the upper left were removed at
this time and the tiny losses inpainted. These
inpainted areas are mostly discolored and
visible to the naked eye; they have not substantially effected the appearance of the blue
background.

All the edges and corners show some slight
wear. A strong stretcher impression is
clearly visible on all 4 sides and horizontally
across the center. This may be partly due to
the effect on the wood, and hence on the
canvas, of the turpentine thinner mixed with
the pigment. Apart from this, the condition
in general is good. (Nov. 1973.)

This painting, like many works of 1925-27, has most often been known as
Painting or *Composition* (see below EXHIBITIONS and REFERENCES). Dupin,
who published it with the title *Painting,* drew attention to the fact that very few
of the works of this period were titled by Miró, and he specifically warned

1. Dupin (p. 157) describes the 1925 "dream paintings," of which this is one, as having been
painted in Paris. Miró specifically remembers, however, that the present work was painted
during the summer at Montroig (correspondence with SRGM, Feb. 1967). See W. Rubin,
Miró in The Museum of Modern Art, New York, 1973, p. 116, fn. 1, for a similar note on
The Birth of the World, which was also painted at Montroig in the summer of 1925.

2. Miró remembers that Loeb (who had by then acquired exclusive rights to his work)
acquired the picture shortly after it was painted and while the artist was living at rue
Tourlaque (conversation with Rowell, May 1974). This lends some support to R. T.
Doepel's contention that Miró's move to rue Tourlaque, usually dated 1927, may have
taken place in late 1925 or early 1926 (*Aspects of Miró's Stylistic Development, 1920-25,*
unpublished M.A. thesis, Courtauld Institute of Art, University of London, 1967, p. 53).

3. The 1946 Parke Bernet sale catalogue erroneously lists the previous owner as Lefèbvre-
Foinet, presumably on the basis of a Lefèbvre-Foinet shipping label on the reverse.
Lefèbvre-Foinet's records show that they shipped the painting to the United States in 1938,
although they have hitherto not been able to establish to whom it was sent (correspondence
with the author, July 1974). Chrysler, who had purchased other works from the Galerie
Beaune, was almost certainly the recipient, although this has not yet been confirmed.

against giving titles to those which lacked them. Moreover, he reported Miró's own strenuous objection to the misleading (and sometimes vulgarizing) titles currently attached to some of these works (pp. 166, 168). Even in those instances where titles do exist, or when Miró has provided the most explicit diagrams identifying every individual image (W. Rubin, *Miró in the Collection of The Museum of Modern Art*, New York, 1973, pp. 22, 28), the possibilities for multiple interpretations still exist. Miró's own perception of the original stimuli, sources, and ultimate meanings of his imagery has often grown more complex in the face of probing questions, and—as Rowell has suggested—the poetic nature of his enterprise is "a hieroglyph of infinite connotations" (*Art News*, vol. 73, January 1974, p. 96).

In spite of the openness and ambiguities of Miró's iconography, however, recent literature has contributed considerably to a clearer understanding of the multiplicity of sources from which the imagery is derived. (See especially Doepel, Rowell and Krauss, Rubin; M. Rowell, January 1974, pp. 94-96.) In particular it has been shown that enriching interpretations of the imagery can emerge if based as far as possible upon the clues offered by Miró himself—the painter's own comments, the titles of the pictures, inscriptions, recurring iconographic motifs, and, wherever possible, preparatory drawings for the works. Most of the drawings remain hitherto unpublished in the artist's collection, but those which have become available demonstrate their rich potential for elucidation of the finished work. (See, for example, Rubin pp. 40-50; also J. J. Sweeney's publication of an extremely revealing 1940's drawing from Miró's private sketchbook. The drawing is inscribed in part as follows: "This cloud is too realistic; interpret the clouds with the poetic symbols of 1940 . . . this figure is too realistic, make use of symbols [signs] to interpret it . . ." ["Miró," *Theatre Arts*, vol. xxxiii, March 1949, p. 40].) Clearly these notes suggest the extent to which Miró's drawings embody his gradual transformation of relatively realistic images into the symbolic sign language of the finished works. When drawings for other paintings from this 1924 to 1927 period become available they will almost certainly throw light on the origins of the often mysterious figures which inhabit them.

In the case of the present work, clues to an interpretation do exist, but they are ambiguous and inconclusive. The anthropomorphic designation *"Personnage"* is Miró's own. In correspondence with the Museum (February 1967), he specifically rejected the vagueness of *Composition* and substituted the more suggestive *"Personnage."* (*"Le titre marqué de Composition me semble gratuit, j'aimerais que vous mettiez Personnage."*) Attempts to probe further with Miró into the significance or background of this mysterious image have hitherto failed; he wished only to establish clearly that the figure was not an abstraction, but rather had some basis in the notion of person. In this sense the picture, and Miró's attitude to it, illustrates his well-known 1948 statement to Sweeney, "For me a form is never something abstract; it is always a sign of something" ("Joan Miró: Comment and Interview," *Partisan Review*, vol. xv, February 1948, p. 208). The amorphous "personage" suspended in a blue

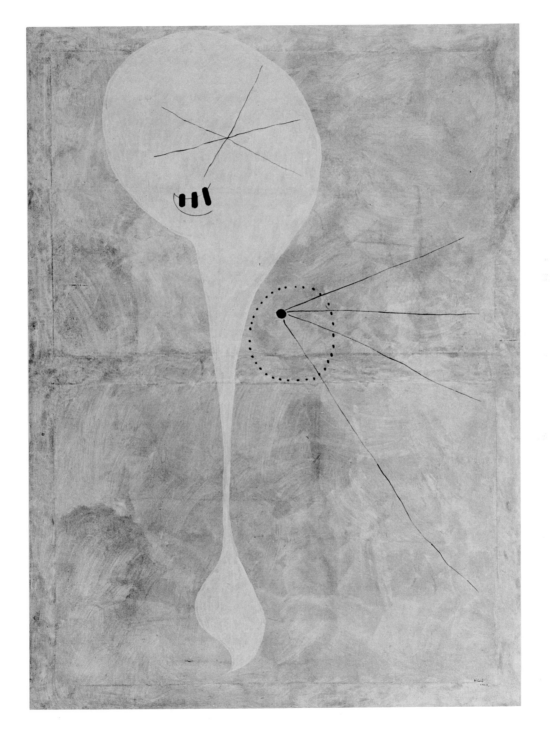

atmosphere is characteristic of a whole group of 1925 figures which Dupin has described as "devoid of all materiality, all corporeal density . . . They ignore the laws of gravitation; they hover in the clouds or glide through liquid or viscous matter. They are the very substance of dreams and hallucinations" (p. 164. For discussions of hallucinations in these paintings see Dupin, pp. 157ff.; also Doepel, pp. 3-4, 50-66, and Krauss, pp. 11-15, who focus upon the interrelated problems of automatism, so-called hallucinatory stimuli, and the clearly controlled quality of Miró's art in this period; for an illuminating analysis of the role of automatism in the creation of *The Birth of the World,* 1925, see Rubin, pp. 30-33).

Rowell has suggested that the blue backgrounds of these 1925 paintings are in themselves suggestive of Miró's break with physical reality: "the blue of the sky, namely, light, space, ether, infinity. Free from all associations with the earth, gravity, and form, blue appeared to be the most appropriate hue for the suspension and the diffusion of images which were Miró's poetic concern" (1972, pp. 61, 63). Rowell's illuminating discussion of the richly associative meanings of the color blue in Miró's 1925 paintings centers principally on its use in *"Photo: ceci est la couleur de mes rêves"* but is clearly applicable to the blue ground works such as *Personage.*

While it is clear that many of Miró's images carry similar meanings and associations in a number of paintings, his continual variation and modification of these motifs make any simple or mechanical interpretation of them impossible. While explication by analogy can throw light on their meanings, the images often remain open, ambiguous, or in some cases simply impenetrable. The iconography of the present painting, for example, is certainly susceptible of some elucidation, but it ultimately eludes detailed, explicit interpretation. Rowell and Krauss have stated: "The form is obviously meant to be an anthropomorphic figure, with an outsized head with teeth, and a large foot. The star-shaped sign on the head is usually a sign for the female genitals; here displaced to the head, it could be that, or an eye. The dotted circle around a spot radiating spokes also has two readings in keeping with Miró's private sign language: the male genitals or an eye projecting lines of vision. These unresolved ambiguities hold the viewer in a state of conceptual suspension" (p. 101).

The identification of the mouth and teeth is apparent, and indeed the motif bears a striking resemblance to the corresponding motif in Picasso's 1915 *Harlequin,* which Miró might well have known (The Museum of Modern Art, New York; the similarity was pointed out by L. Shearer, but it has hitherto not been possible to establish with certainty whether *Harlequin* was still in Picasso's collection in 1925). The other images referred to by Rowell and Krauss pose more complicated problems. Although the tail-like appendage at the base of the figure does not compare with the much more explicit feet of many of these imaginary figures (see, for example, *Person Throwing a Stone at a Bird,* or *Lovers* [Dupin, nos. 172, 117]), it clearly does correspond to those of other anthropomorphic images, where the emphasis on the foot is intentionally reduced. (See, for example, *The Siesta, Figure and Horse,* or *Nude,* [Dupin, nos. 119, 121, 178].) The "star-shaped sign" appears in a variety of contexts in Miró's work of the 1920's, though never demonstrably as an eye. Its identification as female genitals is, however, clearly documented in the 1924 *Woman and Insects* (Rowell and Krauss, repr. p. 114; as Rowell and Krauss have suggested, it appears here as a variation on Miró's more common usage of the spider as female genitals). Its appearance in the upper portion of the composition in *The Siesta, Painting,* and *"48"* (Dupin, nos. 119, 143, 216) is in each case highly ambiguous, although conceivably readable as an erotic symbol. If this symbol is indeed generally to be read as the female genitals, its presence prominently placed near the top edge of *Dutch Interior I* of 1928 (Rubin, p. 41) would presumably suggest the feminine and erotic nature of the diving bird for which it seems to serve as parachute.

Similar problems arise in connection with the dotted circle around a spot radiating spokes, in contrast to the star-shaped sign. The image appears in this particular form only rarely in Miró's work, and never demonstrably as male genitals. The latter are in fact represented in *The Hunter,* and elsewhere, as distinctly egg-shaped forms radiating arc-shaped lines. Furthermore, the reproductive overtones of the explicit egg shape have been emphasized by Rowell and Krauss as well as by Rubin (Rowell and Krauss, p. 114; Rubin, p. 24). It is therefore difficult to accept the notion, without further evidence, that the image of a simple dot radiating straight spokes carries the same sexual meaning. The use of this latter symbol to denote an eye, the spokes being sight-lines indicating "the cone of vision as it intersects with the portion of the external world seen from a given point" (Rowell and Krauss, p. 77), is clearly articulated as such in *The Hunter* (Rubin, p. 22, no. 34 in the diagram), in *Head of a Catalan Peasant* (Rowell and Krauss, p. 85), and elsewhere. This would seem, therefore, to be a more plausible explanation for its presence in the Guggenheim painting. A further meaning may be indicated by the disembodied eye: this image was, as Rowell and Krauss have demonstrated, a classic symbol in the vocabulary of Surrealism for the artist himself (p. 77). In this sense the eye here, or possibly the *Personage* in its entirety, may be intended as a metaphor for the persona of the artist. (For additional comments on the background to Miró's use of the disembodied eye, see Rubin, pp. 23-24.) (A dot with radiating spokes, but without a surrounding circle appears, among other places, in *The Birth of the World,* and it is seen by Rubin as "a spider-like little black star" [p. 33]; this is by analogy with the similar star, identified by Miró himself, in the upper left corner of *The Hunter* [p. 22, no. 6 in the diagram]. This image, which carries cosmic connotations, appears distinctly different in intention from that in the Guggenheim painting, where a circle surrounds the dot.)

The ambiguities presented by the imagery of *Personage* remain. Existing analogies would suggest that the most plausible origins for the two displaced motifs are the female genitals and the eye. The figure thus emerges as one defined primarily by its erotic aspect on the one hand, and its perceptual—

perhaps visionary—aspect on the other. Even if one allows for additional meanings to the two main symbols, the major iconographic significance of the *Personage* resides in its combination of the erotic and the visionary.

EXHIBITIONS:

Paris, Musée du Jeu de Paume, *Origines et développement de l'art international indépendant,* July 30-Oct. 31, 1937, no. 117 ("*Personnage, 1925*"); Richmond, The Virginia Museum of Fine Arts, *Collection of Walter P. Chrysler, Jr.,* Jan. 16-Mar. 4, 1941, no. 140 *(Abstraction),* traveled to Philadelphia Museum of Art, Mar. 29-May 11, 1941; New York, SRGM 79 (checklist; *Composition,* the title by which the picture was known until SRGM 196, 1967, when it was changed to *Personage*); Toronto, SRGM 85-T, no. 59; Boston, SRGM 119-T, no. 41; New York, SRGM 144 (checklists); 187, *Gauguin and the Decorative Style* (checklist); 195 (no cat.); 196 (checklist); 205, *Rousseau, Redon, and Fantasy* (checklist); 227 (no cat.); 232, 241, p. 300, repr. p. 301; 257, *Joan Miró: Magnetic Fields,* no. 17, repr. *(Painting [Personage]);* 266 (no cat.).

REFERENCES:

SRGM *Handbook,* 1959, p. 121, repr. *(Composition);* J. Dupin, *Joan Miró: Life and Work,* New York, 1962, pp. 156-158, 162-164, 512, no. 139, repr. *(Painting);* [M. Rowell], SRGM *Handbook,* 1970, p. 300, repr. p. 301 *(Personage);* M. Rowell and R. Krauss, *Joan Miró: Magnetic Fields,* exhibition catalogue, New York, 1972, pp. 100-101, repr. *(Painting [Personage]).*

185

185 Landscape (The Hare). Autumn 1927.[1]
(*Paysage [le lièvre]; Landscape; The Hare;
Scène; Peinture*).

57.1459

Oil on canvas, 51 x 76⅝ (129.6 x 194.6)

Signed and dated l.r.: *Miró / 1927*; inscribed
by the artist on reverse: *Joan Miró. /
"Paysage" / 1927*.

PROVENANCE:
Purchased from the artist by Galerie Pierre
(Pierre Loeb), Paris, 1927;[2] purchased from
Loeb by Max Pellequer, Paris, after 1933
(lent by Galerie Pierre to 1933 exhibition,
Rockefeller Center, New York); purchased
from Pellequer by Galerie Maeght, Paris, ca.
1950 (information supplied by Maeght,

correspondence with the author, May 1974);
purchased from Maeght, 1957.

CONDITION:
At an unrecorded date, probably prior to
acquisition by the Museum, some scattered
inpainting was carried out in the margin
areas; this is discolored and readily visible
to the naked eye.

The edges and corners show wear, abrasion,
and some scattered chipping of the paint
layer. The orange paint, which was applied
to the entire surface, shows through the
maroon in some places, causing the canvas
to appear abraded. The upper left half of
the orange area shows scattered stains and
drips; these, and the unevenly applied, discolored varnish, are almost impossible to
remove since the paint is dangerously susceptible to solvents. The overall condition is
fair. (Dec. 1973.)

As W. Rubin has stated, the landscapes of 1926 and 1927 are clearly more
anecdotal and "terrestrial" in nature than the ethereal conceptions of 1925
(*Miró in the Collection of The Museum of Modern Art*, New York, 1973, p.
37). The amorphous, intentionally indeterminate blue or bister space of the
1925 works (see above cat. no. 184) gives way to a landscape space explicitly
defined as such by the prominent horizon line which occurs in almost all of
these later paintings (Dupin, nos. 172, 173, 175-177, 179-183, and others). It
is interesting to note that Miró himself saw this clearly defined horizon as
deriving from the influence of his teacher, Modesto Urgell: "I remember two
paintings by Urgell in particular, both characterised by long straight twilit
horizons which cut the picture in halves . . ." (*Partisan Review*, vol. xv, February 1948, p. 209).

Dupin, who emphasizes that these landscapes had no titles, describes the
present painting as follows:
    . . . *there is nothing but a single odd creature, meticulously painted in sev-
    eral colors, apparently fascinated by the spiral path of a comet. All the rest*

---

1. Miró (in correspondence with the SRGM, Nov. 1966) dated the work "Autumn 1927,
   Montroig," suggesting that it was one of the very last of the 14 large "landscapes" executed
   during the summers of 1926 and 1927.
2. Loeb had exclusive rights to Miró's work in 1927, and he purchased the picture soon after
   it was painted (conversation with Rowell, May 1974). It has hitherto not been possible to
   establish when Pellequer purchased the picture from Loeb.

is sky or earth, the purplish red of the latter and the orange of the former presenting an especially intense contrast. The animal has been particularized by both the drawing and the color; Miró's point of departure was an elementary form, in a sense 'biological' . . . Like nature herself, he works from the embryo, from the mother cells which grow and develop, split up, take on various fixed forms, but always according to a continuous process, in obedience to laws of organic development.

Rowell (1970) defines the image more explicitly and attributes to it more cosmic implications: "The hare is a simple organic shape, symbolic of primal being. A falling comet with its fiery tail provides a pretext for the familiar dynamic (often circular or spiral) dotted line. The juxtaposition of hare and comet as well as the equality assigned to both earth and heavens express a reconciliation between earthly and cosmic forces, reality and dreams."

Rowell and Krauss relate the formal qualities of the painting and its imagery to *Landscape with Rabbit and Flower*, 1927, and suggest that both works share the erotic overtones of a "strange isolated animal transfixed by an apparition of female sexuality." The spiral form is read here as possibly representative of the "dazzle of evanescent fantasy."

Miró himself has recently testified (conversation with Rowell, May 1974) to the actual circumstances which surrounded the creation of this picture: while spending the summer at Montroig he was one evening looking across an unplanted brown field; as the sun was setting, a hare streaked across the scene before his eyes. The dotted spiral was intended to suggest the sun. Miró emphasizes that his title for the work is *Landscape (The Hare)*.

The fact that the original stimulus for the painting was an actual event which Miró can recall does not, of course, preclude the possibility that the image had poetic implications beyond the merely anecdotal. There are not, however, clear analogies elsewhere in Miró's oeuvre which might justify the reading of the dotted spiral as "an apparition of female sexuality." Rather it would seem that Dupin's emphasis on the essentially biological character of the creature corresponds more closely to Miró's own sense of having wanted to convey the impression of a specific animal's impact on his consciousness as he surveyed a deserted scene. The hare appears to be motionless, while the sun "streaks" through the sky; the dotted spiral of the sun's path seems thus to have become a metaphor for the hare's speed and links these two principal actors in the scene. The anecdotal aspect of the work is clearly secondary to the pictorial, which is conveyed by the juxtaposition of intense purple-red (the earth) and brilliant orange (the sky)—a dramatic effect which makes the picture closely comparable to the exactly contemporary *Landscape with Rabbit and Flower*, where an intense blue and red are similarly juxtaposed. (Rubin, p. 38, has given a striking analysis of precisely these pictorial aspects of the latter work; see also Krauss, p. 37, who, however, describes the rabbit as white instead of its actual yellow.)

EXHIBITIONS:

Paris, Galerie Georges Bernheim & Cie, *Miró,* May 1-15, 1928 (no cat.);[3] Brussels, Galerie Le Centaure, *Joan Miró,* May 11-22, 1929 (no cat.; repr. in exhibition review by W. George); New York, Rockefeller Center, *International 1933,* Feb. 6-26, 1933, no. 216 (*"Scène, 1927,* Coll. Galerie Pierre, Paris");[4] Krefeld, Kaiser Wilhelm Museum, *Joan Miró,* Jan. 10-Feb. 14, 1954, no. 3 (*"Der Hase, 1927"*), traveled to Stuttgart, Württembergische Staatsgalerie, Feb. 21-Mar. 28, 1954, Berlin, Haus am Waldsee, Apr. 18-May 2, 1954; Palais des Beaux-Arts de Bruxelles, *Joan Miró,* Jan. 6-Feb. 7, 1956, no. 32, repr. *(Le Lièvre);* Rome, SRGM 104-T (not in cat.; joined exhibition Dec. 26, 1957); Cologne, SRGM 104-T, no. 52, repr. *(Landschaft;* the picture is known as *Landscape* in all subsequent SRGM publications until SRGM 257, 1973, when the title was changed to *Landscape [The Hare]);* Paris, SRGM 104-T, no. 54, repr., New York, SRGM 106, 107, 118 (checklists); Paris, Musée National d'Art Moderne, *Joan Miró,* June 28-Nov. 4, 1962, no. 43; Boston, Museum of Fine Arts, *Surrealist and Fantastic Art from the Collections of the Museum of Modern Art and the Guggenheim Museum,* Feb. 14-Mar. 15, 1964, no. 44, repr.; London, Tate Gallery, *Joan Miró* (Arts Council of Great Britain), Aug. 27-Oct. 11, 1964, no. 70 *(Landscape - known as The Hare),* traveled to Kunsthaus Zürich, Oct. 31-Dec. 6, 1964; New York, SRGM 173, no. 57, repr. color; Tokyo, National Museum of Modern Art, *Joan Miró,* Aug. 26-Oct. 9, 1966, no. 32, repr., traveled to Kyoto, National Museum of Modern Art, Oct. 20-Nov. 30, 1966; New York, SRGM 195 (no cat.); New York, M. Knoedler & Co., Inc., *Space and Dream,* Dec. 5-29, 1967, repr. p. 69; New York, SRGM 205, *Rousseau, Redon, and Fantasy* (checklist); Columbus, Ohio, SRGM 207-T, p. 30, repr. color p. 31; New York, SRGM 227 (no cat.); 232, 241, p. 302, repr. p. 303; 257, *Joan Miró: Magnetic Fields,* no. 27, repr.; 266 (no cat.); Paris, Grand Palais, *Joan Miró,* May 17-Oct. 13, 1974, no. 3, repr. *(Paysage [Le lievre]).*

REFERENCES:

W. George, "Miró et le Miracle ressuscité," *Le Centaure,* 3ᵉ année, May 1, 1929, repr. p. 205 *(Peinture); Cahiers de Belgique,* 2ᵉ année, Miró issue, June 1929, repr. p. 207 *(Paysage);* E. Hüttinger, *Miró,* Stuttgart-Vienna, 1957, p. 22, pl. 16; J. Dupin, *Joan Miró: Life and Work,* New York, 1962, pp. 178-179, 515, no. 184, repr. *(Landscape [called The Hare]);* R. Penrose, *Joan Miró,* exhibition catalogue, London, 1964, p. 27; D. Robbins, *Painting between the Wars 1918-1940,* New York, 1966, p. 41, repr. color slide; [M. Rowell], SRGM *Handbook,* 1970, p. 302, repr. p. 303; M. Rowell and R. Krauss, *Joan Miró: Magnetic Fields,* exhibition catalogue, New York, 1972, p. 116, repr. p. 117.

3. Miró (in correspondence with the SRGM, Nov. 1966, and in conversation with Rowell, May 1974) confirmed the identification of this work as one of the 14 pictures exhibited at Georges Bernheim's gallery in 1928 under the auspices of Loeb. For further information on this exhibition, see Dupin, pp. 180, 189.

4. The picture is reproduced with this title in A. Schwob's review of the exhibition, "International 1933," *Creative Art,* vol. 12, Mar. 1933, p. 223.

Amedeo Modigliani

Born July 1884, Leghorn.
Died January 1920, Paris.

186   Nude. 1917.

(Nu; Nu couché; Dormeuse aux mains derrière la nuque; Nudo dagli occhi chiusi, con collana; La dormeuse).

41.535

Oil on canvas, 28¾ x 45⅞ (73 x 116.7)

Signed u.r.: *modigliani*; inscribed on reverse, probably by the artist (transcribed but not photographed before lining): *Modigliani / 3 Joseph Bara / Paris / 1917.*[1]

PROVENANCE:

Leopold Zborowski, Paris (Pfannstiel, 1929, p. 23, no dates of ownership given); Louis Libaude, Paris (Ibid., p. 23, no dates of ownership given);[2] Galerie Bing et Cie, Paris, by 1925 (Galerie Bing exhibition catalogue);[3] Félix Fénéon, Paris, by 1926 (*Société des Indépendants* catalogue); purchased from Fénéon by Solomon R. Guggenheim, 1938; Gift of Solomon R. Guggenheim, 1941.

CONDITION:

In 1955 the work was mounted on a new stretcher; in 1966 it was lined with wax resin and some superficial soil was removed.

The corners are badly worn with loss of paint and ground and the edges also show some losses. The condition is otherwise excellent. (Sept. 1973.)

Although dated 1918 by Salmon (and in the 1928 *Drawing and Design,* probably dependent upon the latter), the picture has otherwise consistently been dated 1917, which is corroborated by the inscription formerly visible on the reverse (see above).

Jeanne Modigliani characterized the final three years of the artist's life as ones in which various styles and techniques coexisted and overlapped, making the establishment of a reliable chronology almost impossible (pp. 82-83); and indeed the sequence and precise dating of the approximately twenty-six nudes which Modigliani painted during the years 1916 to 1919 remains problematic. F. Russoli, in an article published in 1958, also discussed the extensive problems that have been faced by all Modigliani scholars who have attempted to present a chronology of the artists's oeuvre ("Modigliani e la critica," *La Biennale di Venezia,* no. 33, October-November 1958, pp. 7-15). The recent publications by Ceroni (1970) and Lanthemann offer neither documentary evidence nor stylistic discussion to support their considerably different dating of these works, and other publications have similarly failed to cite documentary or stylistic evidence to support their presentations of the artist's late style. The artist's occasional practice of inscribing a work with the name of the place in which it was executed has provided one of the few reliable sources of documen-

1. 3, rue Joseph Bara was the address of Leopold Zborowski, whose apartment Modigliani used as his studio during 1917.

2. B. Weill (*Pan! dans l'Oeil!,* Paris, 1933, pp. 229-230) states that Libaude purchased a number of Modigliani paintings in 1920 when he heard the artist was dying, but that he had bought none before that. P. Sichel (*Modigliani,* New York, 1967, p. 402) records that Libaude came to Zborowski's apartment after the Weill exhibition of late 1917 to look at and to buy works by the artist; neither account can be verified. Part of the Libaude collection was sold at Hôtel Drouot, Paris, May 18, 1920, but the present picture was not in that sale.

3. No lenders are listed in the catalogue and the works apparently all belonged to Bing. See REFERENCES for additional evidence of Bing's ownership.

tation, and the inscription carried by the present work should, therefore, be treated as an important piece of corroborating evidence.

Since the Zborowskis only moved into their apartment in the rue Joseph Bara in the winter of 1916-17, and since Modigliani is known to have used space there as his studio during that winter (Ceroni, 1958, p. 25; F. Carco, *L'Ami des peintres,* Paris, 1953, p. 36; Sichel, p. 333), the inscription would support the 1917 date usually ascribed to the painting.

Two other oil portraits of the same unidentified model must have been painted at approximately the same time: *Seated Nude with Necklace* (Collection Mr. and Mrs. Ralph Colin, New York, 36¼ x 23⅜ in., 92.1 x 60 cm., Ceroni, 1970, repr. no. 187); and *Reclining Nude with Necklace* (Allen Memorial Art Museum, Oberlin, Ohio, 25⅝ x 39⅜ in., 65.1 x 100 cm., Ceroni, 1970, repr. no. 185). The Colin picture apparently is not inscribed, but the Oberlin version bears an inscription identical with that of the Guggenheim painting. Russell, who first suggested that these three works represented the same model, characterized her nature as "relatively withdrawn and inward," and as such distinct from all Modigliani's other late nudes (p. 19, no. 36). This characterization is especially true of the Guggenheim and Colin pictures, less so of the Oberlin version.

Both the Guggenheim and the Oberlin *Nudes* show to an unusual degree the influence of Titian, first noted in general terms by Jeanne Modigliani in relation to the entire group of 1917-19 *Nudes* (p. 83). The Oberlin *Nude* is very close to the Uffizi's ca. 1538 *Venus of Urbino,* not only in its similar pose, its diagonal placement, and its relationship to the pillows and drapery upon which it leans, but even more significantly in its almost identically conceived relationship to the viewer. The Guggenheim picture is similarly related—if somewhat less strikingly so—to the Dresden *Sleeping Venus* (probably begun by Giorgione and finished by Titian in about 1508).

While Modigliani is known to have studied the works in the Uffizi during his pre-1906 student days in Florence and to have been deeply impressed by Venetian art (Sichel, pp. 47, 56, 60), it is not known whether he was specifically drawn to the works of Titian. P. Alexandre recalls, however, from his many visits to Modigliani's studio, that the walls were covered with postcard reproductions of the old masters (C. Roy, *Modigliani,* Geneva, 1958, p. 30; see also Sichel, p. 124). Neither these reproductions, nor the books which Modigliani may have owned at the time appear to have been preserved. It is therefore impossible to establish with certainty whether the two Titians were among Modigliani's immediately available sources of inspiration, but the visual evidence offered by the *Nudes* themselves would strongly suggest that they were. (R. Salvini, "Appunti su Modigliani," *Emporium,* vol. cxxvii, January 1958, pp. 2-12, has offered some suggestive observations on the influence of Klimt and the Vienna Secessionist group on the development of Modigliani's linear style. Modigliani's access to these works, and others discussed by Salvini, would also have been dependent on reproductions—which were by then available—rather than on the works themselves.)

EXHIBITIONS:

Paris, Galerie B. Weill, *Exposition des peintures et de dessins de Modigliani,* Dec. 3-30, 1917, no. 17, 18, 30, or 31? (all *Nu*);[4] Paris, Galerie Bing et Cie, *Modigliani,* Oct. 24-Nov. 15, 1925, no. 2, 11, 21, 23, 26, or 29;[5] Paris, *Trente ans d'art indépendant,* Feb. 20-Mar. 21, 1926, no. 3104 (*"Dormeuse aux mains derrière la nuque—App. à M. Fénéon"*); New York, SRGM 78, 79 (checklists); 81, 83 (no cat.); 84, 87 (checklists); 89 (no cat.); 95, 97, 107, 111, 112, 118 (checklists); 127 (no cat.); 129, 144 (checklists); 173, no. 44, repr. color; 187, *Gauguin and the Decorative Style* (checklist); 196 (checklist); 202, p. 69, repr. color; 227 (no cat.); 232, 241, p. 314, repr. color p. 315; 251, 260, 266 (no cats.).

REFERENCES:

W. George, "Modigliani," *L'Amour de l'art,* vol. 6, Oct. 1925, repr. p. 388 (*"Collection Bing et Cie"*); G. Coquiot, "Modigliani," *Kunst und Künstler,* vol. 24, 1925/26, repr. p. 466 (*"Bes. Galerie Bing,"* dated 1917); A. Salmon, *Modigliani: sa vie et son oeuvre,* Paris, 1926, pl. 18 (dated 1918); *Drawing and Design,* vol. 4, June 1928, repr. p. 161 (dated 1918); A. Pfannstiel, *Modigliani,* Paris, 1929, pp. 22-23 of *catalogue présumé,* repr. foll. p. 108 (dated 1917); A. Pfannstiel, *Modigliani et son oeuvre,* Paris, 1956, no. 141 (dated 1917); J. Modigliani, *Modigliani: Man and Myth,* New York, 1958, pp. 82-83; A. Ceroni, *Amedeo Modigliani,* Milan, 1958, no. 122, repr. (dated 1917); J. Russell, *Modigliani,* exhibition catalogue, London, 1963, p. 19 (picture discussed, but not in exhibition); A. Ceroni, *Amedeo Modigliani: dessins et sculptures,* Milan, 1965, repr. pp. 18, 19 (installation photos of Galerie Bing exhibition); A. Ceroni, *I Dipinti di Modigliani,* Milan, 1970, no. 186, repr. (dated 1917); J. Lanthemann, *Modigliani: catalogue raisonné,* Barcelona, 1970, no. 214, repr. p. 217 (dated 1917); SRGM *Handbook,* 1970, repr. color p. 315 (dated 1917).

4. There is no way of establishing which *Nudes* by Modigliani were included in the exhibition, but it is possible that the present picture was among them. I am indebted to F. S. Wight for a copy of the checklist on which the dates are Dec. 3-30, 1917. According to Weill, however, the exhibition was closed for obscenity on Dec. 3rd by the police, whose attention was drawn to it by the display of a *Nude* in the window (op.cit.). No reports of the closing of the exhibition have hitherto been located in the French newspapers or periodicals of the period.

5. The Guggenheim *Nude* is visible in 2 installation photographs of this exhibition published by A. Ceroni (1965, pp. 18, 19). It is impossible to say which of the checklist entries corresponds to it.

187   Boy in Blue Jacket. 1918.
*(Garçon à la veste bleue; Le Gosse du
concierge).*

37.532

Oil on canvas, 36¼ x 24 (92.2 x 61)

Signed u.r.: *modigliani.* Not dated.

PROVENANCE:

Jacques Netter, Paris, ca. 1919?—before
1925;[1] Galerie Bing et Cie, Paris, by 1925
(W. George, October 1925)—at least 1928
(G. Scheiwiller, 1927 and 1928); Félix
Fénéon, Paris, by 1929 (Pfannstiel, 1929);
purchased from Fénéon by Solomon R.
Guggenheim, 1932 (a letter from Fénéon to
Hilla Rebay, October 8, 1932, refers to the
sale [The Hilla von Rebay Foundation
Archive]); Gift of Solomon R. Guggenheim,
1937.

CONDITION:

In 1957 the surface was cleaned with Soilax,
rinsed with petroleum benzine, and coated
with PBM. In 1958 the canvas was lined
with wax resin and the stretcher replaced. In
1962 superficial soil was removed and worn
areas along the 4 margins were inpainted
with colors in PBM.

There are a number of vertical paint cracks
in the blue jacket and in the light-colored
background on the right. The upper right
margins, the lower left and lower right corners, are severely abraded with losses and
some damage to the support. The condition
is otherwise good. (Nov. 1972.)

This portrait, as well as a closely related one of the same sitter now in the
John Herron Art Museum, Indianapolis (not in Pfannstiel; Ceroni, 1970, repr.
no. 297), dates from Modigliani's stay in the South of France between March
or April 1918 and May 31, 1919. The Indianapolis picture is inscribed
"Cagnes" and there is little doubt that both pictures were painted there. Jeanne
Modigliani *(Modigliani: Man and Myth,* New York, 1958, pp. 88, 92, 93, 95)
documents various addresses at which her father lived and worked in the Nice-
Cagnes area, but gives no specific dates for the Cagnes visit. Sichel (pp. 404-
405, 408-409, 414-415) documents the Cagnes period as dating specifically
from April to July 1918, when the family moved to Nice. Since the two towns
are so close, it is possible that Modigliani went back to Cagnes again after he
had moved to Nice; given his most precarious state of health, however, it seems
unlikely that he would have done much unnecessary traveling. The probability
that both pictures date from the spring or early summer of 1918 is thus considerable. (The present portrait has been consistently dated 1918 except by
Lanthemann, who dates it 1919 without documentation or discussion. The Indianapolis portrait is dated 1919 by both Ceroni and Lanthemann, in both
cases without discussion.)

    The identity of the sitter has not been established. Its designation in the 1925
and 1927 exhibitions as *Le Gosse du concierge* relates it directly to a portrait

1. The dates of Netter's ownership have not been finally established, but he had sold the
picture to Bing by 1925. Since he began to buy works by Modigliani in 1918, he may well
have purchased the picture soon after it was painted. (He still owned a large group of
1917-19 pictures in 1934, when he lent 21 of them to the Modigliani exhibition at the
Kunsthalle in Basel. For further information on Netter's support of Modigliani see P. Sichel,
Modigliani, New York, 1967, pp. 402-403, 420, and F. Carco, *L'Ami des peintres,* Paris,
1953, p. 38-39.)

with the same title in the collection of Jean Masurel (Pfannstiel, 1929, pp. 38-39 of *catalogue présumé*; 1956, no. 243; Ceroni, 1970, no. 239). Like the Indianapolis picture, this portrait is inscribed *"Cagnes,"* but the face is clearly that of another child. It is conceivable, thus, that the Masurel picture portrays one son, the Guggenheim and Indianapolis pictures a second son of the concierge at Modigliani's Cagnes address. According to Sichel, he stayed for part of that spring at Anders Osterlind's villa *La Riante,* Chemin des Colletes in Cagnes. For part of the time at least he also apparently stayed in a farmhouse located between Les Trois Soeurs and the Hotel Des Colonies. The boy in the Masurel portrait and the one in the Indianapolis picture sit on identical chairs

and may perhaps be posing in the same room. However, it has hitherto not been possible to establish either the location of this room or the identity of the two boys. (Jeffrey Robinson of St. Laurent-du-Var has kindly explored the area on behalf of the author and attempted to establish these facts. While several details have been clarified in the process, the precise evidence is still lacking.)

EXHIBITIONS:

Paris, Galerie Bing et Cie, *Modigliani,* Oct. 24-Nov. 15, 1925, no. 25 *(Le Gosse du concierge)* or no. 28 *(Jeune homme en blouse bleu);*[2] Kunsthaus Zürich, *Italienische Maler,* Mar. 18-May 1, 1927, no. 103 ("*Le Gosse du Concierge,* lent by Bing, dated 1918, for sale");[3] Charleston, S.C., SRGM 1-T, no. 118 (not dated; the picture is first dated in SRGM 79); Philadelphia, SRGM 3-T, no. 183; Charleston, S.C., SRGM 4-T, no. 257; Cleveland Museum of Art, *Modigliani: Paintings, Drawings, Sculpture,* Jan. 30-Mar. 18, 1951, p. 52, traveled to New York, The Museum of Modern Art, Apr. 11-June 10, 1951; New York, SRGM 79 (checklist, dated 1918; so dated in all subsequent SRGM publications); 83 (no cat.); 87 (checklist); 89 (no cat.); Montreal, SRGM 93-T, no. 42, repr. cover; New York, SRGM 95 (checklist); Hartford, Conn., Wadsworth Atheneum, *Twentieth Century Painting from Three Cities: New York, New Haven, Hartford,* Oct. 19-Dec. 4, 1955, no. 38, repr.; New York, SRGM 107 (checklist; withdrawn Oct. 16); San Antonio, Tex., Marion Koogler McNay Art Institute, *Modigliani,* Nov.-Dec. 1957, no. 2, repr.; New York, SRGM 111, 118 (checklists); 127 (no cat.); Vienna, Museum des 20. Jahrhunderts, *Kunst von 1900 bis heute,* Sept. 21-Nov. 4, 1962, no. 147, repr.; Worcester, Mass., SRGM 148-T, no. 30, repr.; Frankfurt, Steinernes Hus (Frankfurter Kunstverein), *Modigliani,* June 21-July 28, 1963, no. 23, repr. color; Edinburgh, Royal Scottish Academy (Arts Council of Great Britain), *Modigliani,* Aug. 17-Sept. 16, 1963, no. 38, repr., traveled to London, Tate Gallery, Sept. 28-Nov. 3, 1963; New York, SRGM 173, no. 47, repr.; The Baltimore Museum of Art, *Twentieth Century Italian Art,* Oct. 25-Nov. 27, 1966 (checklist); Providence, Museum of Art, Rhode Island School of Design, *Seven Centuries of Italian Art,* Apr. 12-May 21, 1967 (checklist); New York, SRGM 202, p. 26, repr.; 251, 266 (no cats.).

REFERENCES:

W. George, "Modigliani," *L'Amour de l'art,* vol. 6, Oct. 1925, repr. p. 385 ("*Portrait,* Collection Bing et Cie"); G. Scheiwiller, *Modigliani,* Milan, 1927, and Paris, 1928, pl. 4 *("Garçon,* Gal. Bing," dated 1917); A. Pfannstiel, *Modigliani,* Paris, 1929, pp. 45-46 of *catalogue présumé,* repr. color, opp. p. 96 (dated 1918);[4] S. Taguchi, *Modigliani,* Tokyo, 1936, color pl. iii, A. Pfannstiel, *Modigliani et son oeuvre,* Paris, 1956, no. 279 (dated 1918, attributed to private coll., Paris); A. Ceroni, *Modigliani,* Milan, 1958, no. 100 (dated 1918); Idem, *Amedeo Modigliani: dessins et sculptures,* Milan, 1965, repr. pp. 18-19 (installation photos of Galerie Bing exhibition); J. Russell, *Modigliani,* exhibition catalogue, London, 1963, pp. 9, 20, repr. (dated 1918); A. Ceroni, *I Dipinti di Modigliani,* Milan, 1970, no. 259, repr. (dated 1918); J. Lanthemann, *Modigliani: catalogue raisonné,* Barcelona, 1970, no. 368, repr. p. 257 (dated "Cagnes 1919").

2. The picture appears in the installation photographs published by Ceroni (1965, pp. 18-19).

3. An early photograph of the work preserved in the SRGM archives carries on the reverse, in Fénéon's hand, exhibition history and references for the picture; the Zurich exhibition and catalogue number are included. The work was returned to Bing after the exhibition (information supplied by Dr. A. Schlatter, correspondence with the author, Dec. 1972), and Fénéon probably purchased it shortly afterwards.

4. The wrong dimensions given by Pfannstiel (92 x 73 cm.), and thereafter repeatedly published elsewhere, were apparently inadvertently supplied by Fénéon, whose photograph of the work (see fn. 3) carries them.

188   Portrait of a Student. ca. 1918-1919.
       (*L'Etudiant*).

45.997

Oil on canvas, 24 x 18⅛ (60.9 x 46)

Signed u.r.: *modigliani*. Not dated.

PROVENANCE:

Dr. O. Sabouraud, Paris, by 1933 (Palais des Beaux-Arts exhibition catalogue) — at least 1934 (Kunsthalle Basel exhibition catalogue); Jacques Dubourg, Paris, by 1942; purchased from Dubourg by H. S. Southam, Ottawa, by 1942 (information supplied by Dominion Gallery, Montreal, correspondence with the author, January 1973); purchased from Southam by Dominion Gallery, Montreal, June 1945; purchased from Dominion by Fine Arts Associates, New York, 1945 (information supplied by Mrs. Otto Gerson, correspondence with the author, January 1972); Karl Nierendorf, New York, 1945; purchased from Nierendorf, 1945.

CONDITION:

At some point prior to 1954 (possibly prior to acquisition), a tear near the lower left corner was repaired by the application of a patch to the reverse with glue. In 1954 this patch was removed as it apparently caused blistering of the paint film in that area. In 1957 the glue residue in the area was removed, the canvas lined with wax resin and the area of loss (approximately 1 in. x ⅜ in.) filled and inpainted. The surface was then coated with PBM.

Apart from 2 small losses, and some fine horizontal cracks in the paint film, the condition is excellent. (Dec. 1972.)

The same sitter, who has not been identified, may be represented in a larger portrait, *Young Man with Red Hair,* now in the Cummings collection, Beverly Hills, although this is not certain (Pfannstiel, 1956, no. 345; Ceroni, no. 301; Lanthemann, no. 406). Lanthemann suggests that the Cummings picture (dated 1919 in all the sources), and the present portrait, may possibly represent a woman. However, the facial type and the barest indication of a moustache would suggest that the figure is male.

The problem of dating this work is similar in nature to that of *Jeanne Hébuterne with Yellow Sweater* (cat. no. 189). Whether *Portrait of a Student* and the Cummings portrait were painted in the South of France, or possibly after the return to Paris, is unclear. A date of ca. 1918-19, though inconclusive, is for the time being the most plausible.

EXHIBITIONS:

Palais des Beaux-Arts de Bruxelles, *Modigliani,* Nov. 1933, no. 39 ("*L'Etudiant,* dated 1917, Collection Sabouraud"); Kunsthalle Basel, *Modigliani,* Jan. 7-Feb. 4, 1934, no. 31 (dated 1917, Collection Sabouraud); Ottawa, National Gallery of Canada, *Paintings from the Collection of H. S. Southam of Ottawa,* May 27-July 2, 1944, no. 22 (not dated), traveled to Art Associates of Montreal, Aug. 27-Sept. 27, 1944; New York, SRGM 79 (checklist; withdrawn Nov.); Toronto, SRGM 85-T, no. 60, repr.; Vancouver, SRGM 88-T, no. 63, repr.; Boston, SRGM 90-T (no cat.); Montreal, SRGM 93-T, no. 44; New York, SRGM 97 (checklist); London, SRGM 104-T, no. 53, pl. 9; Boston, SRGM 119-T, no. 43 (dated 1917?; so dated in all subsequent SRGM publications); Lexington, Ky., SRGM 122-T, no. 22, repr.; New York, SRGM 129, 132, 144 (checklists); 173, no. 45, repr.; 196 (checklist); 202, p. 89, repr.; 227 (no cat.); 232, 241, p. 317, repr. p. 316; 251, 266 (no cats.).

REFERENCES:

P. Descargues, *Amedeo Modigliani,* Paris [1951], pl. 46 *(Portrait de femme);* A. Pfannstiel, *Modigliani et son oeuvre,* Paris, 1956, no. 158 ("*L'Etudiant,* 1917;" not in his 1929 *catalogue présumé*); (not in A. Ceroni, *I Dipinti di Modigliani,* Milan, 1970); J. Lanthemann, *Modigliani: catalogue raisonné,* Barcelona, 1970, no. 405, repr. ("*Portrait,* 1919").

189 Jeanne Hébuterne with Yellow
Sweater. 1918-1919.
(Le Sweater jaune; The Yellow Sweater).

37.533

Oil on canvas, 39⅜ x 25½ (100 x 64.7)

Signed u.r.: *modigliani*; inscribed on
stretcher, possibly, but not certainly by the
artist (transcribed but not photographed
before replacement of stretcher): *le sweater
jaune Ebuterne Amedeo Modigliani.* Not
dated.

PROVENANCE:

Leopold Zborowski, Paris?;[1] Galerie Bing et
Cie, Paris, possibly by 1925;[2] Félix Fénéon,
Paris, by 1929 (Pfannstiel, 1929); purchased
from Fénéon by Solomon R. Guggenheim,
1932 (a letter from Fénéon to Hilla Rebay,
October 8, 1932, refers to the sale [The Hilla
von Rebay Foundation Archive]); Gift of
Solomon R. Guggenheim, 1937.

CONDITION:

In 1953 the work was cleaned with 2%
Soilax and benzine and coated with Ozenfant's wax. Some small losses were inpainted
and the surface coated with PBM.

Apart from wear at the edges and corners,
and some minor stains and paint losses, the
condition is good. (Dec. 1972.)

This picture belongs to a group of portraits of Jeanne Hébuterne which have
been variously dated 1918, 1919, and 1920. However, no convincing evidence
has been presented for the sequence or dating of the more than twenty portraits
that Modigliani painted of Hébuterne between 1917 and 1920 (not one of
which was dated by the artist). The Guggenheim portrait does seem to belong
to that group of pictures painted in Nice and Cagnes between March or April
of 1918 and the end of May 1919; but it has as yet not been possible to establish
a firm date for it within this period. (For details about this year-long sojourn in
the South of France, see above cat. no. 187.)

An examination of the literature on Modigliani illustrates the lack of con-
sensus on this issue. Pfannstiel's 1956 catalogue contains nineteen portraits of
Hébuterne, three of which he assigns to 1917, nine to 1918, four to 1919, three
to 1920. Ceroni's 1970 catalogue contains twenty-six; four are placed in 1917,
ten in 1918, twelve in 1919. Lanthemann's 1970 catalogue contains twenty-
five; four are placed in 1917, two in 1918, eighteen in 1919, and one in 1920.
Lanthemann's and Ceroni's actual lists do not differ significantly from one
another, but neither they nor Pfannstiel have attempted to define or justify their
view of the artist's stylistic development during these years. It is not clear,
therefore, why Lanthemann has assigned almost all of the portraits to 1919,
whereas Ceroni has made a much more equal distribution of them over the
years 1918 and 1919.

1. Zborowski's ownership is recorded in Pfannstiel's 1956 catalogue, but not in the 1929
edition. It has hitherto not been possible to verify it from any other source.

2. Bing's ownership is recorded in Pfannstiel's 1929 and 1956 editions. It has hitherto not been
possible to establish whether Bing owned the work by the time of the 1925 Paris exhibition.
The painting is not visible in the installation photographs published by Ceroni (*Modigliani*,
Milan, 1965, pp. 18-19), but only 27 of the 36 exhibited works are reproduced there. It is
possible, therefore, that the present picture was included.

189

Both J. Modigliani and P. Sichel have gone far towards establishing the chronology of Modigliani's various addresses during the Nice-Cagnes year (see above cat. no. 187). But both have acknowledged that uncertainties remain; indeed Jeanne Modigliani suggested that many of the dating problems posed by her father's oeuvre might only be solved when details of furnishings and backgrounds in the individual paintings could be correlated with interiors in which the artist is known to have worked (*Modigliani: Man and Myth*, New York, p. 67). No research along the lines proposed has yet been published. Lanthemann states, without elaboration, in dating his no. 419, that the interior in which Jeanne is portrayed, and her pregnant state, prove that the picture was painted in January 1920. However, since the couple were living at rue de la Grande-Chaumière from the end of June 1919 until Modigliani's final departure for the hospital on January 18, 1920, and since Jeanne would certainly have been visibly pregnant by about October or November of 1919, it is difficult to know why January 1920 is a more certain date than, for example, any month between October 1919 and January 1920. Lanthemann's further claim that his catalogue raisonné finally establishes firm dates for the entire Modigliani oeuvre is similarly unsupported by evidence and is therefore difficult to evaluate.

In a study of the chronology of the Hébuterne portraits, six are especially close in style to the present version and should be taken into account in any attempt to establish a sequence. They are Pfannstiel, 1956, nos. 289, 290, 325, 337, 355, and Ceroni, 1970, no. 260 (not in Pfannstiel). All six are published by both Ceroni (nos. 218, 219, 260, 326, 328, 335) and Lanthemann (nos. 259, 339, 347, 355, 388, 419), and the dates for even this small group are the subject of considerable dispute. Until further research such as that proposed by Jeanne Modigliani has been carried out, a date of 1918-19 for all of these portraits remains the most plausible.

Jeanne Hébuterne was born in 1898 to Achille Casimir Hébuterne and Endoxie Anaïs Teller, natives of Meaux (Seine-et-Marne). When she met Modigliani in 1917, she lived with her parents at 8 bis, rue Amyot, in Paris; her father was chief cashier at a perfume shop, her brother was a painter, and she herself was a student at the Académie Colarossi where Modigliani had also studied in 1906. In July of 1917 Jeanne and Amedeo rented a joint studio at 8, rue de la Grande-Chaumière, and she remained his devoted companion until the day of his death. Their first child, Jeanne Modigliani, was born in the maternity hospital, Nice, November 29, 1918; she became pregnant for the second time in about May 1919. In a document dated June 7, 1919, Modigliani pledged that he would marry Jeanne as soon as the papers arrived, but the marriage never took place. Modigliani died on January 24, 1920, and the following morning Jeanne, in the ninth month of her pregnancy, jumped to her death from her parent's fifth floor apartment (biographical facts provided by Jeanne Modigliani, pp. 87-89, 95, 97-99; P. Sichel, *Modigliani*, New York, 1967, pp. 347-349, 357-358, 449, 493-507).

EXHIBITIONS:[3]

(Paris, Galerie Bing et Cie, *Modigliani,* Oct. 24-Nov. 15, 1925, no. 4 or no. 19? [both *Madame Modigliani*]);[2] Kunsthaus Zürich, *Italienische Maler,* Mar. 18-May 1, 1927, no. 109 ("*Ebuterne . . . 1919,*" lent by Bing, for sale);[4] Charleston, S.C., SRGM 1-T, no. 119; Philadelphia, SRGM 3-T, no. 184; Charleston, S.C., SRGM 4-T, no. 258; New York, SRGM 78 (checklist, dated 1915, added Mar. 16); Palm Beach, Fla., Society of the Four Arts, *Modigliani,* Jan. 8-31, 1954, no. 24, traveled to Miami, Lowe Gallery, Feb. 11-28; New York, SRGM 84 (checklists, dated 1919?; so dated in all subsequent SRGM publications until SRGM 202, 1968, when the date was changed to 1918); Vancouver, SRGM 88-T, no. 62, repr. color; Boston, SRGM 90-T (no cat.); Montreal, SRGM 93-T, no. 43; New York, SRGM 95 (checklist); London, SRGM 104-T, no. 52; Cincinnati, Contemporary Art Center, *Modigliani, Paintings, Sculpture, Drawings,* Apr. 18-May 20, 1959, no. 26, repr.; New York, SRGM 118 (checklist); Milan, Palazzo Reale, *Art Italiana del XX Secolo da Collezioni Americane* (International Council, The Museum of Modern Art), Apr. 30-June 26, 1960, no. 147, repr.; Hartford, Conn., Wadsworth Atheneum, *Salute to Italy,* Apr. 21-May 28, 1961, p. 32; New York, SRGM 129 (repr.); 144 (checklist); San Francisco Museum of Art, *The Human Form through the Ages,* Nov. 10, 1964-Jan. 3, 1965, no. 268; New York, SRGM 173, no. 48, repr.; 187, *Gauguin and the Decorative Style* (checklist); 202, p. 27, repr. (dated 1918); Columbus, Ohio, SRGM 207-T, p. 24, repr.; New York, SRGM 227 (no cat.); 232, 241, pp. 318-319, repr.; New York, Acquavella Galleries, Inc., *Modigliani,* Oct. 14-Nov. 13, 1971, no. 47, repr. color (dated 1919); New York, SRGM 251, 266 (no cats.).

REFERENCES:

A. Pfannstiel, *Modigliani,* Paris, 1929, p. 43 of *catalogue présumé,* repr. color foll. p. 104 (dated 1918); S. Taguchi, *Modigliani,* Tokyo, 1936, color pl. IV; A. Pfannstiel, *Modigliani et son oeuvre,* Paris, 1956, no. 268 (dated 1918); A. Ceroni, *Modigliani,* Milan, 1958, no. 151 (dated 1918); SRGM *Handbook,* 1959, p. 127, repr. (dated 1919?); F. Russoli, *Modigliani,* London, 1959, pl. 30 (dated 1919); Idem, *Modigliani,* Milan, 1963, pls. XIV-XV (dated 1919); A. Ceroni, *I Dipinti di Modigliani,* Milan, 1970, no. 220, color pl. LVI (dated 1918); J. Lanthemann, *Modigliani: catalogue raisonné,* Barcelona, 1970, no. 389, repr. (dated 1919); SRGM *Handbook,* 1970, pp. 318-319, repr. (dated 1918).

3. Portraits of Jeanne Hébuterne were shown in several early exhibitions of Modigliani's work, and it is impossible to establish whether the present picture was involved. For example: Geneva, *Exposition internationale d'art moderne,* Dec. 26, 1920-Jan. 25, 1921, no. 95 (*Portrait de la femme de l'artiste*); Paris, Bernheim-Jeune, *Modigliani,* Feb. 7-21, 1922, no. 9 (*Hébuterne*); Venice, Biennale, 1922, p. 57 (*Hébuterne*); etc.

4. Pfannstiel records the picture's appearance in the Zurich exhibition (although in his 1929 edition he erroneously gives it the catalogue no. 106 [*Sitzender Akt*]); the Kunsthaus records show that the picture was returned to Bing afterwards. Fénéon probably purchased both this painting and *Boy in Blue Jacket* on the same occasion shortly after the Zurich exhibition.

László Moholy-Nagy

Born July 1895, Borsod, Hungary.
Died November 1946, Chicago.

NOTE: Moholy-Nagy's Work on Plastic

Moholy-Nagy began to paint on transparent plastic materials in the early 1920's.[1] These "early celluloid and gallalith pictures before 1925 had been attempts to render *lighted* pigment, to give to the known color values a new radiance expressing the joy of perceiving an infinite variety of hues. But the media were unsatisfactory. Celluloid cracked and yellowed, gallalith warped easily, and the commercial dyes were too crude to blend with the carefully mixed oil paints."[2]

Moholy temporarily discontinued his experiments with transparent plastics around 1925, but wrote that this work was not only instrumental in changing his painting technique, but ". . . had inevitable repercussions on my thinking concerning light problems."[3] He found that "by producing real radiant light effects through transparent dyes on plastic, and through other means, one has no need for translating light into color by painting with pigment."[4]

In 1926 the patent on the American plastic Bakelite expired and its production under the name of Trolitan began in Germany.[5] Moholy, who was working at the Dessau Bauhaus from 1923-28, executed a number of works on this new opaque plastic.

After living for a few years in Berlin and Amsterdam, Moholy moved to London in 1935. Later in that year he began to experiment with transparent plastics once again.[6] His first "light modulator" was completed early in 1936 on a material called Rhodoid. (This picture, titled *Rho Transparent 51,* present whereabouts unknown, is illustrated by S. Moholy-Nagy, *Moholy-Nagy, Experiment in Totality,* New York, 1950, pl. 48.) Moholy is quite specific about his aims in these "light modulators":

There has been in the past a period of light painting, that of stained-glass windows. There, direct and reflected light and the shadow of the framing combined with projected colored light into a fascinating visual unity. Our technology offers new possibilities, no less impressive, and without imitating the old techniques. At present the central problem of painting on transparent sheets is the reality of direct light effects. In my first experiments I learned that I must have a screen upon which the light effects of the painting could be

1. S. Moholy-Nagy, *Moholy-Nagy, Experiment in Totality,* New York, 1950, pp. 198-199.
2. Ibid.
3. Ibid., p. 199.
4. Ibid.
5. *Encyclopedia of Chemical Technology,* vol. x, New York, 1969, p. 802.
6. S. Moholy-Nagy, op. cit., pp. 129-130.

projected. So I mounted the painted sheet several inches in front of plain white or light gray backgrounds. There I observed that solid shapes on transparent sheets cast solid shadows. To dissolve and articulate the heavy shadows one has to employ various means. There is a possibility of scratching the surface with fine lines of different density which throw shadows of varied gray values on the screen, similar to the fine gradations of grays in the photogram. To paint stripes similar to grill- or lattice-work, or to perforate solid surfaces, is another possibility. Such elements, if lighted, cast alternating shadows and light patterns on the background behind the painted surface. Upon these patterns the original painting is superimposed. If lighted from the side, the shapes of the original and its shadows appear shifted, creating a new relationship between the colors and their gray shadows. This intensifies considerably the effect of the usual shadowless paintings. It produces automatically a "light texture," especially if transparent dyes are used instead of pigments. The results, although very pleasing, bring some danger with them. The smooth perfection of the plastics, their light-flooded, sparkling planes, could easily lure one into an effective but decorative performance. I attempted to avoid this, especially when remembering my Louvre and Vatican visits, where I observed the "masterpieces" of late Roman sculptors who tried to outdo each other by using expensive polished marbles, colored bronzes, precious stones, ebony and gold.[7]

Moholy was pleased with the new plastic materials, but was aware of the difficulties in working with them:

Though plastics are new materials, not thoroughly tested, I had the feeling that one has to work with them, in spite of the danger of pretty effects. It may take decades until we will really know the material, and before we can develop a genuine technique to handle them. Even technical problems of painting on these new materials are yet unsolved. After doubtful experiments with industrial lacquers, which were not fast, I tried to paint with oil pigments on transparent sheets. In order to avoid the danger of the colors peeling off, I scratched hundreds and thousands of very fine lines into the plastic to be painted, hoping they would hold the pigment. I covered these engraved lines with oil paint which was held in and between the little crevices. I often painted on the front and back of the sheets too, so that my attempts to create space articulation by the relationships of receding and advancing colors were enhanced by the thickness of the sheet; that is, the real distance between the colors applied in front and in back. In addition I achieved differentiations in the appearance of the same color showing through or seen on the polished surfaces. The new material also needed a specific brush technique, which led to rather unexpected textures. Later, instead of covering and filling the fine engraved lines with a homogeneous color layer, I sometimes only rubbed color into them. By certain combinations of colored hair lines and their fine

7. L. Moholy-Nagy, *The New Vision and Abstract of an Artist*, New York, 1949, p. 83.

shadows, intensified, vibrating color effects appeared, an iridescence which I had admired so much in thin glass vessels buried thousands of years. Translated into oil pigment, Renoir was a great master of such effects. I felt happy to achieve a similar refinement in the handling of colors by simpler means. These new effects with their emotional content and spiritual aspirations can only be grasped, however, after their "novelty" aspect has been overcome by serious consideration of the problem involved.[8]

Moholy even went to the length of suggesting that "... the use of flaws and bubbles in the plastics, may lead to even more startling results."[9] (*Space Modulator*, cat. no. 196, in the Guggenheim Museum Collection may be an example of the artist's exploitation of such flaws in his material.) So pleased was Moholy with the new synthetic materials that he wrote that had he not been afraid that the plastics were not permanent, he would never have painted on canvas again.[10]

In 1936 the production of a new transparent plastic sheet, Plexiglas, was begun in America by Rohm and Haas, Inc.;[11] Moholy began to use it immediately. The new material was smoother than Rhodoid, but less flexible and did not require so firm a support.[12] The smoothness of the medium raised problems of paint adhesion, but the toughness, stability, and greater availability of Plexiglas ultimately recommended it to Moholy over all others.[13]

8. Ibid., p. 84.
   Moholy probably employed a technique similar to that used by engravers to rub color into his incised lines. The surface of the plate is completely covered with ink or paint and then wiped clean leaving pigment only in the incised areas.

9. Ibid., p. 84.

10. Ibid., p. 83.

11. *Encyclopedia of Chemical Technology*, p. 805.

12. S. Moholy-Nagy, op. cit., p. 201.

13. Ibid.

Plastic Materials Used by Moholy-Nagy

CELLULOID:[1]

Celluloid is the trade name of the Celanese Corporation of America for a plastic composed essentially of cellulose nitrate and camphor.

Celluloid was among the first plastic materials to be invented and was first produced in 1869 by the American chemist John Hyatt (1827-1920).

Properties:

1. Sheets of celluloid are clear, tough, and flexible.
2. Celluloid is easily pigmented.
3. Celluloid is easily soluble in alcohol, ketones, and esters and is decomposed by concentrated acids. The material is also affected by alkali.
4. Celluloid is dangerously flammable and has fallen from general use chiefly for this reason.
5. Celluloid quickly discolors in sunlight and, thus, does not weather well.

BAKELITE:[2]

Bakelite is a trade name currently owned by the Union Carbide Corporation for a phenol-formaldehyde resin. Bakelite was the first thermosetting plastic to be manufactured. The original Bakelite (the name now applies to a wide range of products) was first produced by the chemist L. H. Baekeland (1863-1944). He patented his discovery in 1907 and began commercial production three years later. The trade name was acquired by Union Carbide at a later date.

Properties:

1. Sheets of Bakelite are hard, opaque, and infusible.
2. Bakelite is black and cannot be pigmented easily.
3. Bakelite is highly resistant to moisture and to most solvents, both organic and acid. The material is decomposed only by concentrated oxidizing acids or hot alkali.
4. Bakelite is dimensionally stable and will resist high heat; to 400-600°F.
5. The material is virtually unaffected by weathering and sunlight.

TROLITAN:[3]

Trolitan is the trade name of the Dynamit Nobel Corporation of West Germany for a phenol-formaldehyde resin virtually identical to Bakelite in its appearance and properties.

Production of Trolitan in Germany began in 1926 with the expiration of Baekeland's patent on his formula for Bakelite.

GALALITH:[4]

Galalith (artificial horn) is a trade name for a casein-formaldehyde thermoplastic. Invention of Galalith was made in Germany around 1885; commercial production began shortly thereafter.

Properties:

1. Sheets of Galalith are tough, horny, and may be either translucent or opaque.
2. Sheets of Galalith can be pigmented.
3. Galalith is not resistant to moisture, swelling and softening when wet.
4. Galalith is relatively unaffected by most organic liquids, but is decomposed by concentrated acids and alkali.
5. Heat causes Galalith to swell and ultimately char.
6. Galalith discolors rapidly in sunlight.

RHODOID:[5]

Rhodoid is a trade name for a cellulose acetate polymer.

1. J. R. Scott and W. J. Roff, *Handbook of Common Polymers,* London, 1971, pp. 159-160; J. A. Brydson, *Plastic Materials,* London, 1969, p. 363.
2. Scott and Roff, pp. 299-304, 309; H. R. Simonds and J. M. Church, *A Concise Guide to Plastics,* New York, 1963, p. 41.
3. Scott and Roff, p. 299.
4. Ibid., pp. 197, 202.
5. Ibid., p. 149.

Properties:

1. Sheets of Rhodoid are clear, tough, and flexible.
2. Rhodoid may be easily pigmented.
3. Rhodoid is soluble in only a very limited range of organic liquids, chiefly ketones. Concentrated acid will decompose Rhodoid.
4. Rhodoid does not burn or distort readily with heat.
5. Rhodoid is relatively unaffected by either weathering or sunlight.

PLEXIGLAS:[6]

Plexiglas is the trade name of the Rohm and Haas Company for its poly-methyl-methacrylate plastic sheet.

Plexiglas was the first so-called acrylic resin to be produced. First synthesized in Germany in 1910 by the chemist, Röhm, the material was not produced commercially in sheet form until 1936 in America.

Properties:

1. Sheets of Plexiglas are light in weight, tough, flexible, and clear.
2. Plexiglas is easily pigmented.
3. Plexiglas is soluble in organic liquids such as ketones, esters, and aromatic hydrocarbons, but is resistant to most acids and alkali.
4. Plexiglas is slow to burn, but distorts at ca. 180°F.
5. Plexiglas is resistant to weathering and virtually unaffected by sunlight.
6. Plexiglas has unique optical properties which allow it to be used for making lenses. Sheets and rods of this material are also capable of transmitting light through the interior of the plastic from edge to edge.

CELON:[7]

Celon is the trade name of the Dynamit Nobel Corporation of West Germany for its polycaproamide (essentially Nylon) plastic.

Properties:

1. Celon is tough and horn-like; usually slightly yellow in color and translucent to opaque.
2. Celon is not easily pigmented.
3. Celon is relatively unaffected by organic solvents and alkalies. It is decomposed by concentrated acids.
4. Celon will oxidize and discolor after prolonged exposure to heat and sunlight.

Information given above for all plastics is for their sheet form. Each, however, is available in other forms (liquid, molding compound, etc.).

Moholy used other plastics, now out of production, in his work. Among these are Zellon, Neolith, and Coulou.

6. Ibid., p. 87; *Plexiglas Design and Fabrication Data*, Rohm and Haas Company Brochure, 1967.
7. Scott and Roff, p. 209.

190 A II. 1924.

43.900

Oil on canvas, 45⅝ x 53⅝ (115.8 x 136.5)

Inscribed by the artist on reverse: *Moholy-Nagy / A^{II} (1924) Moholy = Nagy* (the latter covered by stretcher).

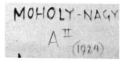

PROVENANCE:

Purchased from the artist, 1943.

CONDITION:

The work has received no treatment since its acquisition.

The geometric composition is painted directly onto a sized but unpainted brownish canvas; there are several stains in the lower right-hand quarter of this unpainted surface. There is a very fine crackle pattern in the upper yellow area and in the red section of the large circle. There are several abrasions, the most serious of which are: a 5½ in. diagonal abrasion, ½ in. wide in the large circle; a 24 in. abrasion (partially inpainted) running vertically 26 in. from the right starting 12 in. from the top; 2 diagonal 2 in. lines in the lower black area; a 2 in. and a 3 in. line in the gray area. The canvas has not been varnished and there is some soil both in the painted and unpainted areas. The overall condition is fair. (Oct. 1973.)

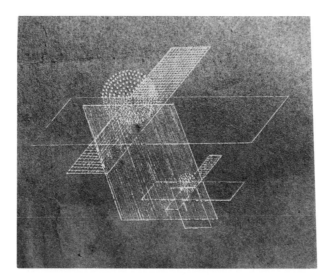

fig. a.
Moholy-Nagy, woodcut, 9 x 11⅝ in., 23 x 29.5 cm.,
Collection Dr. Hans Klihm, Munich.

It was in 1923 that Moholy painted his first transparent painting—a work on a
Galalith sheet (see above "Moholy-Nagy's Work on Plastic"). As he explored
the possibilities of overlapping forms, transparency, and light in this new medium, he also continued to deal with them in his canvases. S. Moholy-Nagy has
described the experience of seeing one of these canvases (*A17*, 1923) for the first
time (*Experiment in Totality,* New York, 1950, pp. 69-70). As Moholy-Nagy
himself moved a light back and forth across its surface a disc in the center of the
painting appeared to move out from the surface of the canvas and to recede
into it. The canvas thus provided a dramatic illustration of Moholy's concept
of "light-chronology"—a notion which preoccupied him continuously in the
following years.

Moholy-Nagy's own writings contain innumerable references to the significance of transparency, which he felt was "one of the most spectacular features
of our time" ("Space-Time Problems in Art," *American Abstract Artists,* 1946,
Yearbook reprint, New York, 1969, p. 186). For further comments on this subject, see below cat. no. 196.

At an unknown date Moholy-Nagy made a small black-and-white woodcut
of this composition (fig. a). Two colored drawings of 1945, although more
loosely structured than the 1924 painting, are clearly reminiscent of it and illustrate Moholy's continuing preoccupation with a similar range of compositional issues (Collection Bauhaus-Archiv, Berlin, negative no. F6242; Private
Collection, Berlin, Bauhaus-Archiv negative no. F6243).

EXHIBITIONS:

Dresden, *Internationale Kunstausstellung,* June-Sept. 1926, no. 420; London, London Gallery,
L. Moholy-Nagy, Dec. 31, 1936-Jan. 27, 1937, no. 19, repr. (listed as tempera, for sale, 75 gns.);
New York, The Museum of Modern Art, *Bauhaus 1919-1928,* Dec. 7, 1938-Jan. 30, 1939

(no cat.); New York, SRGM 32, no. 44; 34, no. 38; Utica, N.Y., SRGM 52-T (no cat.); Indianapolis, Ind., John Herron Art Museum, *Cubist and Non-Objective Paintings*, Dec. 29, 1946-Feb. 2, 1947, no. 36; New York, SRGM 57, repr. p. 11 (no. 33, listed as "A 2B"); Paris, Palais des Beaux Arts de la Ville de Paris, *Troisième salon internationale des réalités nouvelles*, July 23-Aug. 29, 1948 (not in cat.); New York, SRGM 87 (checklist); Montreal SRGM 93-T, no. 45; London, SRGM 104-T, no. 54; New York, SRGM 118 (checklist); Cleveland Museum of Art, *Paths of Abstract Art*, Oct. 4-Nov. 13, 1960, no. 33, repr.; New York, SRGM 151 (checklist); 153 (checklist; commentary, repr. color); 173, no. 54, repr. color; New York, Perls Gallery, *Seven Decades 1895-1965, Crosscurrents in Modern Art*, Apr. 26-May 21, 1966, no. 149, repr.; New York, SRGM 195 (no cat.); 196 (checklist); 202, p. 78, repr. color p. 79 (upside down); Chicago, SRGM 218 (not in cat.); New York, SRGM 277 (no cat.); 232, pp. 320-321, repr. color; 236 (no cat.); 241, pp. 320-321, repr. color; 266 (no cat.).

REFERENCES:

Telehor [international review], Brno, 1936, Moholy-Nagy issue with text by the artist, repr. p. 61 ("*a 20*, tempera"); S. Giedion, "Notes on the Life and Work of Moholy-Nagy," *Architects Yearbook*, vol. 3, 1949, repr. p. 34 (*Circle*); D. Robbins, *Painting Between the Wars*, New York, 1966, no. 22, repr. color slide; I. Finkelstein, *The Life and Work of Josef Albers*, unpublished Ph.D. dissertation, Institute of Fine Arts, New York University, 1967, pp. 87-88; SRGM *Handbook*, 1970, pp. 320-321, repr. color.

---

191   T1. 1926.

37.354

Oil on Trolitan,[1] 55 x 24¾ (139.8 x 61.8)

Inscribed by the artist on reverse: *Moholy / T1 (26)*; stenciled twice: *L. Moholy-Nagy*.

PROVENANCE:

Purchased from the artist by Solomon R. Guggenheim before 1936; Gift of Solomon R. Guggenheim, 1937.

CONDITION:

The picture has received no treatment.

All edges show a ½ in. rabbet mark from former frame and are rubbed and scratched. There are fine scratches scattered over the entire surface, but these are barely visible. There is some soil in the large white circle, and there are some abrasions elsewhere, but the condition in general is good. (Jan. 1974.)

T1 and other works of this period were clearly influenced, as S. Moholy-Nagy has suggested (*Experiment in Totality*, New York, 1950, p. 29), by Moholy's own experiments with photography and especially with the making of photograms. The treatment of surface, light, and form in these paintings closely approximates the effects created in the photograms of the same period. One ca. 1926 photogram (present whereabouts unknown) is so strikingly similar in de-

1. See above "Plastic Materials Used by Moholy-Nagy."

sign to the present painting as to suggest a direct relationship between the two (*Experiment in Totality*, 2nd ed., Cambridge, Massachusetts, 1968, fig. 29).

EXHIBITIONS:

Charleston, S.C., SRGM 1-T, no. 98, repr. p. 37; Philadelphia, SRGM 3-T, no. 122, repr. p. 42; Charleston, S.C., SRGM 4-T, no. 158, repr. p. 50; New York, SRGM 57, *Laszlo Moholy-Nagy*, no. 38; Chicago, SRGM 218, *Laszlo Moholy-Nagy*, no. 22.

191

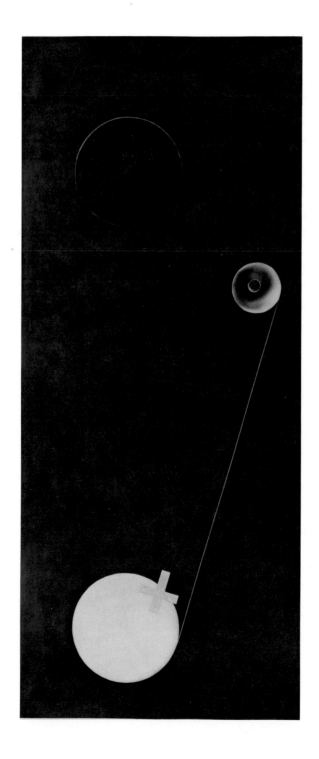

192 Axl II. 1927.

64.1754

Oil on canvas, 37 x 29⅛ (94.1 x 73.9)

Inscribed by the artist on reverse: *Axl II*
(obscured by stretcher) / *Moholy- / Nagy /
1927.*

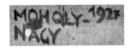

PROVENANCE:

Sibyl Moholy-Nagy, 1946-60; purchased
from S. Moholy-Nagy by Galerie Chalette,
New York, 1960; purchased from Galerie
Chalette by Mr. and Mrs. Andrew P. Fuller,
New York, 1961; Gift of Mrs. Andrew P.
Fuller, 1964.

CONDITION:

No treatment is recorded but the canvas
was at some point restretched and a patch
placed in the reverse 8 in. from the bottom
and 13 in. from the left side. A ½ in. area
of inpaint on the front of the canvas corresponds to this patch.

The black circle shows overall drying cracks
and there is a very fine crackle scattered in
other impasto areas. Apart from some general soil, and some minor abrasions, the
condition is good. (Jan. 1974.)

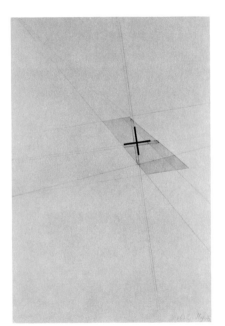

fig. a.
Moholy-Nagy, watercolor, pencil, India ink,
and collage on paper, 17¾ x 7⅞ in., 45 x 20 cm.,
Stedelijk van Abbemuseum, Eindhoven.

A watercolor in the collection of the Stedelijk van Abbemuseum, Eindhoven,
signed and dated 1922, is closely related to the present work and probably
served as a preparatory study for it (fig. a). It is a characteristic example of
Moholy's 1921-22 experiments with superimposed planes and spatial definition which were inspired by the example of Lissitzky and Malevich. Moholy-
Nagy describes the problem he set for himself in the years 1921-22 as stemming
from "severe simplification of form in two-dimensional space, to the creation
of visual depth through color transparencies" (S. Moholy-Nagy, *Experiment
in Totality,* New York, 1950, p. 18). He suggested that his choice of purely
geometric forms during these years was part of his desire to achieve total "objectivity" (*The New Vision and Abstract of an Artist,* New York, 1946, p. 75).
This preoccupation continued into the mid and late 1920's as is demonstrated
by the close relationship between the 1922 watercolor and the present painting.

EXHIBITIONS:

Kunsthaus Zürich, *Abstrakte und Surrealistische Malerei und Plastik*, Oct. 6-Nov. 3, 1929, no. 90; New York, SRGM 57, *Laszlo Moholy-Nagy*, no. 47; 176, 195 (no cats.); 196 (checklist; listed as *ACL II*); Chicago, SRGM 218, *Laszlo Moholy-Nagy*, no. 25, repr. p. 29; Venice, *35 Biennale internazionale d'arte*, June 24-Oct. 25, 1970, no. 26; New York, SRGM 260, 266 (no cats.).

REFERENCE:

R. Kostelanetz, *Moholy-Nagy*, New York, 1970, repr. no. 6.

193   Tp 2. 1930.

37.357

Oil and incised lines on blue Trolitan,[1]
24¼ x 56¾ (61.5 x 144.3)

Inscribed by the artist on reverse:
Moholy = Nagy / Tp 2 (1930) / m = n.

PROVENANCE:

Purchased from the artist by Solomon R.
Guggenheim by 1936; Gift of Solomon R.
Guggenheim, 1937.

CONDITION:

In 1969 the work was cleaned with distilled
water.

The support is slightly warped, and there
are many tiny scratches and abrasions
scattered over the surface; there are 4 major
scratches (varying in length from ½ in. to
5 in.). The painted areas are in good condition, and the overall condition is fair to
good. (Jan. 1974.)

EXHIBITIONS:

Charleston, S.C., SRGM 1-T, no. 101, repr. p. 38; Philadelphia, SRGM 3-T, no. 124, repr.
p. 43; Charleston, S.C., SRGM 4-T, no. 162, repr. p. 104; New York, SRGM 57, *Laszlo
Moholy-Nagy,* no. 55; New York, The Museum of Modern Art, *Moholy-Nagy* (traveling
exhibition), Feb. 1964-May 1965 (checklist); Chicago, SRGM 218, *Laszlo Moholy-Nagy,*
no. 26.

REFERENCES:

Telehor [international review], Brno, 1936, Moholy-Nagy issue with text by the artist, repr.
p. 57; H. Rebay, "Beauté de l'inobjectivité," *Innovation,* Paris, June 25, 1937, repr. p. 62.

1. See above "Plastic Materials Used by Moholy-Nagy."

194   Sil 2. 1933.

48.1157

Oil and incised lines on silverit,[1] 19¾ x 23⅝
(50.1 x 60.1)

Inscribed by the artist on reverse (incised,
barely visible): *Moholy = Nagy / 1933 /
Sil 1*; in paint (partially obscured by clamp):
L. Moholy = Nagy / Sil 2; in crayon
(barely visible): *Moholy = Nagy / 1933.*

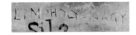

PROVENANCE:

Estate of the artist, 1946-48; purchased
from the Estate, 1948.

CONDITION:

In 1963 the work was superficially cleaned.

The polished surface of the work shows a
large number of fine scratches and a few
more serious ones. Apart from some minor
chips lost from the black areas, the overall
condition is good. (Sept. 1973.)

EXHIBITIONS:

The Art Institute of Chicago, *L. Moholy-Nagy*, Sept. 18-Oct. 26, 1947, no. 5 (dated 1939;
so dated in all subsequent SRGM publications); New York, The Museum of Modern Art,
Moholy-Nagy (traveling exhibition), Feb. 1964-May 1965 (checklist); Chicago, SRGM 218,
Laszlo Moholy-Nagy, no. 40; Venice, *35 Biennale internazionale d'arte,* June 24-Oct. 25, 1970,
no. 27.

REFERENCE:

Telehor [international review], Brno, 1936, Moholy-Nagy issue with text by the artist, repr.
p. 72 (dated 1933).

1. The nature of this support (which Moholy described as "silverit") has not been definitely
   established, although it appears to be a highly polished aluminum. There is no trace of a
   plastic or metallic film on top of the polished surface.

195   Ch Beata 1. 1939.

48.1128

Oil on canvas, 46⅞ x 47⅛ (118.9 x 119.8)

Inscribed by the artist on reverse (photographed before lining): *L. Moholy = Nagy / Ch Beata I / (39)*; on stretcher: *L. Moholy = Nagy (39)*.

PROVENANCE:

Estate of the artist, 1946-48; purchased from the Estate, 1948.

CONDITION:

In 1954 the work, which had not been previously varnished and was very dirty, was cleaned and surfaced with synthetic varnish. In 1972 it was removed from the stretcher, and a patch removed from the back. Cleavage was developing in the black areas, and the condition was fragile. The varnish was removed, cleavage set down, and the work was lined with fiberglass with BEVA using no penetration. The small losses in the black area were filled with gesso and inpainted; and the work was then varnished.

There are 8 tack holes in a diagonal line along the right edge extending 20 in. down from the top. The canvas was apparently at some point stretched considerably out of square and a rabbet mark in this area is clearly visible. The edges are in general in good condition, but there are some abrasions with losses, chiefly at the lower left and upper right corners. Compass-point holes are visible in the center of each of the small circles. The artist apparently applied a second coat of paint to the red areas to achieve a more crimson tone. Apart from some scattered minor losses, the condition in general is good. (Sept. 1973.)

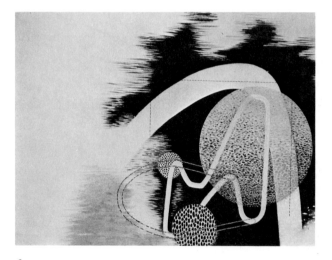

fig. a.
Moholy-Nagy, *Ch xiv*, 1939, oil on canvas, 36¼ x 47⅛ in., 92 x 119.5 cm., Collection Hattula Moholy-Nagy Hug, Courtesy Galerie Klihm, Munich.

Many of the canvases produced by Moholy in Chicago in 1939 are variations on the structural vocabulary, textures, and transparencies of *Ch Beata 1*. See, for example, *Ch xiv* (fig. a).

EXHIBITIONS:

Chicago, The Katherine Kuh Gallery, *L. Moholy-Nagy*, Jan. 4-Feb. 4, 1940, no. 27 *(Chicago Beata)*; New York, SRGM 57, *Laszlo Moholy-Nagy*, no. 75 *(CH Beta)*; Minneapolis, University Art Gallery, University of Minnesota, *Contemporary American and European Painters*, June 30-July 30, 1954 (no cat.); Vancouver, SRGM 88-T, no. 64, repr.; Palais International des Beaux-Arts de Bruxelles, *50 ans d'art moderne*, Apr. 17-July 21, 1958, no. 228, repr.; New York, The Museum of Modern Art, *Moholy-Nagy* (traveling exhibition), Feb. 1964-May 1965 (checklist); New York, SRGM 195 (no cat.); 196 (checklist); Chicago, SRGM 218, *Laszlo Moholy-Nagy*, no. 36, repr. color; Venice, *35 Biennale internazionale d'arte*, June 24-Oct. 25, 1970, no. 28; New York, SRGM 266 (no cat.).

195

196   Space Modulator. 1939-1945.

47.1064

Oil on incised Plexiglas, mounted in 2 wood rails 1 in. from white plywood background. Plexiglas: 24¾ (63.0) x bottom 25⅞ (65.9); top, 26¼ (66.6)

Signed and dated l.r. (incised): *L. Moholy = Nagy 39-45*; inscribed by the artist on reverse: *L. Moholy = Nagy / L. Moholy = Nagy / Space modulator 1939-45 / (this painting requires a strong / spotlight).*

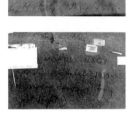

PROVENANCE:

Sibyl Moholy-Nagy, Chicago, 1946-47; purchased from S. Moholy-Nagy, 1947.

CONDITION:

In 1954 the work was cleaned with water, and in 1955 the artist's frame and backing were repaired.

Extending down from the upper edge are many cracks in the plastic, some of which do not penetrate the surface. It is impossible to say whether these flaws were already present when Moholy began to work, or whether they have occurred since. The same is true of the bubbles near the lower right corner and along the left side. The edges show some rubs and scratches, and the paint of the frame is cracked in places, but the condition is otherwise good. (Jan. 1974.)

Moholy-Nagy's preoccupation with the notion of shadow as a necessary element in the creation of a living work of art was reflected strongly in his film-making and photography experiments of the early 1930's. S. Moholy-Nagy quotes from the artist on this subject as follows: "All human life has its shadow. Without it, it stops being human. But the typical studio lighting—this insane cross fire of illumination—creates a shadowless world that is without appeal because it is unfamiliar" (*Experiment in Totality,* New York, 1950, p. 83).

In 1923 Moholy produced his first painting on transparent plastic; forms were painted on the surface and their shadows were actually painted on the underside of the plastic and on the wood substructure to which the plastic was attached (Ibid., p. 69). In 1935 he painted his first "light modulator"—an oil painting on a Rhodoid sheet, mounted two inches from a white plywood background, to produce a mobile shadow play. Variations on these early ideas were produced throughout the next twenty years. Moholy saw the potential of plastic materials in two main areas: transparency and sensitivity to light. "In working with these materials—uniformly colored, opaque or transparent plastics—I made discoveries which were instrumental in changing my painting technique. This had inevitable repercussions on my thinking concerning light problems" (*The New Vision and Abstract of an Artist,* New York, 1946, p. 83).

Moholy's own detailed explanation for his use of these plastic materials, and for their invaluable capacity to cast real shadows is cited above ("Moholy-Nagy's Work on Plastic"). His technique in *Space Modulator* included incising and painting on both sides of the sheet in order, as he put it, "to create space articulation by the relationships of receding and advancing colors...enhanced by the thickness of the sheet; that is the real distance between the colors applied in the front and in the back." In addition, his specific directions on the reverse of this and other paintings ("this painting requires a strong spotlight") must be

seen as an integral part of the work itself. The lighting—as he makes clear—is a crucial ingredient in his use of the medium: "Such elements, if lighted, cast alternating shadows and light patterns on the background behind the painted surface . . ."; and again: "If lighted from the side, the shapes of the original and its shadows appear shifted, creating a new relationship between the colors and their grey shadows. This intensifies considerably the effect of the usual shadowless paintings . . ." (see above "Moholy-Nagy's Work on Plastic").

A pen and ink drawing dated 1945 (fig. a) represents an elaboration of the present work, rather than a study for it, and bears witness to his continuing preoccupation over a period of six years with the same theme.

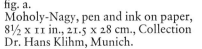

fig. a.
Moholy-Nagy, pen and ink on paper, 8½ x 11 in., 21.5 x 28 cm., Collection Dr. Hans Klihm, Munich.

EXHIBITIONS:

New York, SRGM 64 (no cat.); Tulsa, Okla., SRGM 159-T, Richmond, Va., SRGM 188-T (no cats.); Chicago, SRGM 218, *Laszlo Moholy-Nagy*, no. 42, repr. color (described as "oil on incised plaster"); Venice, *35 Biennale internazionale d'arte*, June 24-Oct. 25, 1970, no. 29.

197   Mills 1. 1940.

44.958

Oil on incised Plexiglas, mounted in 4 wood
rails, 1 in. from white plywood background.
Plexiglas (sight only): 34¾ x 25¾
(87.4 x 65.4)

Inscribed by the artist u.r. (incised):
Moholy = Nagy 40 / Mills 1; formerly on
reverse in pencil (transcribed but not photographed before discarding of back): *L.
Moholy = Nagy 1940 / Mills No. 1.*

PROVENANCE:

Purchased from the artist, 1944.

CONDITION:

In 1963 and 1969 the work was superficially
cleaned with water and Soilax.

There is a ½ in. loss in the support near the
lower right corner. There are some scattered
minor abrasions of the Plexiglas, and some
scattered pinpoint losses in the black area.
The condition is otherwise very good.
(Jan. 1974.)

The title of this work refers to Moholy-Nagy's residence during the summer of
1940 at Mills College in Oakland, California, where, at the invitation of A.
Neumeyer, he conducted an intensive summer school course in the Bauhaus
curriculum (S. Moholy-Nagy, *Experiment in Totality*, New York, 1950, p.
180). The ambiguous spatial relationship between the two arcs is similar to
that of two arcs in another 1940 *Space Modulator* of which Moholy-Nagy
wrote: "This painting introduces a psychologically determined motion if one
tries to define whether the black or the white arc is in front of the other. There
is a feeling of a definite movement of the arcs forward and backward" (*Vision
in Motion*, Chicago, 1947, p. 150). As in *Space Modulator*, above cat. no. 196,
Moholy has further complicated the interrelationships by alternating his application of paint and his incising of the surface on the obverse or the reverse
of the Plexiglas. The upper portion of the larger arc is painted on the obverse,
the lower portion on the reverse; the lower half of the smaller arc is incised on
the obverse, the upper half of the reverse. The spatial effects are clearly intended to be visually provocative and ambiguous.

EXHIBITIONS:

New York, SRGM 39, no. 101; 57, *Laszlo Moholy-Nagy*, no. 85, repr.; 64 (no cat.); New
York, The Museum of Modern Art, *Moholy-Nagy* (traveling exhibition), Feb. 1964-May
1965 (checklist); Chicago, SRGM 218, *Laszlo Moholy-Nagy*, no. 44; New York, Finch College
Museum of Art, *Art Deco*, Oct. 14-Nov. 30, 1970, no. 26.

198   Ch 4. 1941.

48.1109

Oil on incised Plexiglas, mounted with
chromium clamps on white plywood background. Plexiglas: 35 ⅞ x 35 ⅞ (91.2 x 91.1)

Signed and dated l.l. (incised): *L.
Moholy = Nagy 41.*

PROVENANCE:

Estate of the artist, 1946-48; purchased from
the Estate, 1948.

CONDITION:

The work has received no treatment.

Apart from some minor scratches and abrasions throughout the Plexiglas, and some
slight soil in the white painted area, the
condition is excellent. (Nov. 1972.)

fig. b.
Ch 4, photograph by Moholy-Nagy, The Solomon R. Guggenheim Museum, New York.

 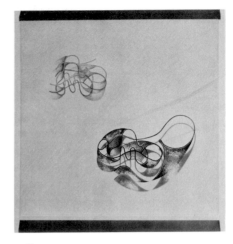

fig. a.
Moholy-Nagy, pen, ink, and pencil on paper, 8½ x 11
in., 21.5 x 28 cm., Collection Hattula Moholy-Nagy Hug,
Courtesy Galerie Klihm, Munich.

198

Moholy-Nagy's own photograph of *Ch 4* (fig. b) captured the light cast on the
work and the resulting series of shadows in such a way as to illustrate his notion of "vision in motion," which he defined in part as "a new *kinetic* concept
of spatial articulation" (p. 153).

In an unpublished letter to Hilla Rebay, dated March 11, 1942, he urged her
to show this photograph (a copy of which he enclosed) to the Museum photog-
rapher so that the latter might attempt to introduce the same lighting effects
into his reproductions of Moholy-Nagy's work (letter preserved in the SRGM
archives).

A pen, ink, and pencil drawing in the collection of Hattula Moholy-Nagy
Hug (fig. a), dated October 26, 1941, is closely related to the present work, but
it is unclear whether it is preparatory to it or a subsequent variation.

EXHIBITIONS:

New York, SRGM 57, *Laszlo Moholy-Nagy*, no. 94 (with incorrect dimensions); The Art
Institute of Chicago, *L. Moholy-Nagy*, Sept. 18-Oct. 26, 1947, no. 9 (*Chicago 4* with incorrect
dimensions); New York, SRGM 64 (no cat.); Chicago, SRGM 218, *Laszlo Moholy-Nagy*,
no. 46.

REFERENCE:

L. Moholy-Nagy, *Vision in Motion,* Chicago, 1947, repr. p. 152 (dated 1940).

199 Ch 7. 1941.
(Chicago Space 7).[1]

41.882

Oil on canvas, 47 x 47¼ (119.7 x 119.9)

Inscribed by the artist on reverse:
*Moholy = Nagy; L. Moholy = Nagy /
Ch 7 (41).*

PROVENANCE:

Purchased from the artist, August 1941.

CONDITION:

In 1953 some small losses in the white areas were apparently inpainted, but these are not visible either under UV or the naked eye. In 1954 some spots of gray paint and some dark brown stains were removed, and the surface was lightly coated with PBM. In 1956 the canvas was removed from its stretcher, the reverse cleaned, and the picture was then restretched on the same stretcher with edges waxed. At some time prior to 1953 the frame was painted with the painting still in it and some paint dripped onto the edges of the canvas. These drips are whiter than the adjacent priming which forms the background of the composition.

Apart from some general surface dirt, the condition is excellent. (Nov. 1972.)

A preparatory study for this work suggests something of Moholy's method for establishing the variety of spatial interrelationships he wished to create (fig. a). Straight lines, dotted lines, flat areas of color and pasted paper are used in the

1. The title of the work has been alternatively given by Moholy as *Ch 7* (on the reverse) and *Chicago Space 7* (*The New Vision and Abstract of an Artist*).

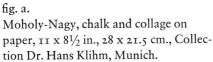

fig. a.
Moholy-Nagy, chalk and collage on
paper, 11 x 8½ in., 28 x 21.5 cm., Collection Dr. Hans Klihm, Munich.

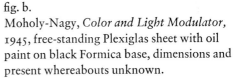

fig. b.
Moholy-Nagy, *Color and Light Modulator*,
1945, free-standing Plexiglas sheet with oil
paint on black Formica base, dimensions and
present whereabouts unknown.

initial stage to suggest the variety of possible textural and spatial interrelationships, which are later incorporated into the final work.

In 1945 Moholy-Nagy produced a variation on this composition in the form
of a free-standing Plexiglas sheet which had been painted with oil paint,
molded while hot, and mounted on a Formica base (fig. b). The movement of
forms in space, so clearly demonstrated in this molded work, had already been
anticipated to a considerable extent in the present painting on canvas, which
was completed four years earlier. It is interesting to note that Moholy himself,
in "Abstract of an Artist," specifically explains how he had tried to create on
canvas the same complex effects he was achieving with molded plastics (see
below cat. no. 200).

EXHIBITIONS:

Andover, Mass., Addison Gallery of American Art, *European Artists Teaching in America,*
Sept.-Nov. 1941, no. 28 ("*Chicago Space 1941*"); New York, SRGM 30, Utica, N.Y., SRGM
52-T (no cats.); New York, SRGM 57, *Laszlo Moholy-Nagy,* no. 89; 64 (no cat.); Minneapolis,
Walker Art Center, *The Classic Tradition in Contemporary Art,* Apr. 24-June 28, 1953, no.
87, repr. (*Chicago Space No. 7*); New York, SRGM 118 (checklist); New York, The Museum
of Modern Art, *Moholy-Nagy* (traveling exhibition), Feb. 1964-May 1965 (checklist);
Chicago, SRGM 218, *Laszlo Moholy-Nagy,* no. 47; Venice, *35 Biennale internazionale d'arte,*
June 24-Oct. 25, 1970, no. 31; Rochester, N.Y., SRGM 263-T (no cat.).

REFERENCE:

L. Moholy-Nagy, *The New Vision and Abstract of an Artist,* New York, 1946, repr. p. 78
(*Chicago Space 7*).

200   B-10 Space Modulator. 1942.

47.1063

Oil on incised and molded Plexiglas,
mounted with chromium clamps 2 in. from
white plywood backing. Plexiglas: 17¾ x 12
(45.1 x 30.5). The Plexiglas has been molded
by the artist up to 3 in. out of plane.

Signed and dated l.l. (incised): *L.
Moholy = Nagy 42*; inscribed by the artist
on reverse mount: *L. Moholy-Nagy / 1942 /
B-10 Space Modulator.*

PROVENANCE:

Sibyl Moholy-Nagy, Chicago, 1946-47; purchased from S. Moholy-Nagy, January 1947.

CONDITION:

The work has received no treatment.

There are some scattered scratches on the
surface, and a major 1 in. scratch 3½ in.
from the top, 5 in. from the right side. Apart
from considerable soil, the work is otherwise in good condition. (Jan. 1974.)

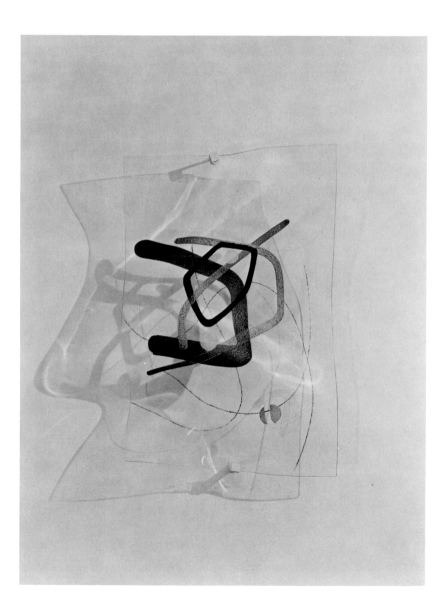

In his 1944 essay "Abstract of an Artist," Moholy-Nagy describes his use of plastics in some detail, dwelling in particular on the advantages to be derived from their transparency (see above "Moholy-Nagy's Work on Plastic," and cat. no. 196). In the final section of the essay, he describes both his technique for working with molded plastic and the motives that led him to this development:

Thermoplastics, when heated, can be easily shaped. One day it occurred to me that by painting on flat plastic sheets, I neglected this essential property of the material. Thus I heated, bent, and twisted a transparent sheet after painting on it. With this manipulation I arrived at complex concave and convex shapes, rich compound curvatures which created a constantly changing relationship between the painted and engraved transparent planes and the background, resulting in a new type of "related" distortions. The bends and curves made the plastics structurally more resistant to breakage. At the same time, the bends caught high lights. They could be made a part of the light compositions themselves. These could hardly be called paintings or sculpture. . . . For me they were "space modulators." The distorted shapes of my "modulators" produced spatial effects, not only through the curved surfaces which were either protruding or receding, but also through the lines flowing in all directions of the weather cock, formed by the thickness of the sheets themselves. . . . I tried to achieve similar effects with painting on canvas. There the free 'motion' forward and backward of color prepared a new type of spatial perception. This was in clear opposition to the renaissance method of producing illusionistic space by the illusionistic relationships of volumes. In this way my experiments seemed to become a part of the general tendencies of contemporary painters. Many of us have departed from the old canons and obsolete conventions, to a new space articulation, trying to define intuitively and to satisfy more adequately the specific need of our time for a vision in motion.

The problems encountered by Moholy in applying paint to the smooth Plexiglas surface, and the measures he took to counteract these problems are described in some detail by him and S. Moholy-Nagy (see above "Moholy-Nagy's Work on Plastic"). The paint and incised lines were, in this as in other instances, applied to both sides of the Plexiglas.

EXHIBITIONS:
New York, SRGM 57, *Laszlo Moholy-Nagy*, no. 104 (with incorrect dimensions); 64 (no cat.).

REFERENCE:
L. Moholy-Nagy, *The New Vision and Abstract of an Artist*, New York, 1946, repr. p. 86 (dated 1943).

201   Leuk 4. 1945.

48.1124

Oil and watercolor on canvas, 49⅛ x 49⅛
(124.7 x 124.7)

Inscribed by the artist on reverse: *L.
Moholy = Nagy / Leuk 4 (45) / Moholy.*

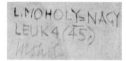

PROVENANCE:

Estate of the artist, 1946-48; purchased
from the Estate, 1948.

CONDITION:

In 1954 the white and yellow areas were
cleaned with ½% Soilax solution; the other
areas, which are water soluble, were dusted
with a dry brush.

White paint transfer is visible on all edges
about ⅜ in. in width, apparently the result
of attempts to paint the former frame while
it was still in place. There are virtually invisible hairline cracks in a few places, and
some general soil, but the condition is otherwise good. (Feb. 1974.)

The title refers to the disease which was ultimately fatal to Moholy: the leuke-
mia was diagnosed in November 1945 and the painting followed shortly
thereafter.

A colored chalk drawing in the collection of Hattula Moholy-Nagy Hug
(fig. a), dated 1945, almost certainly represents the artist's preliminary ideas for
the picture. The composition is also closely related to a painting dated 1939
(present whereabouts unknown, S. Moholy-Nagy, *Experiment in Totality,*
New York, 1950, repr. p. 197).

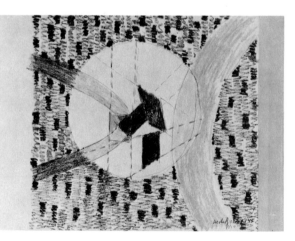

fig. a.
Moholy-Nagy, colored chalk and pencil on paper,
8½ x 11 in., 21.5 x 28 cm., Collection Hattula Moholy-
Nagy Hug, Courtesy Galerie Klihm, Munich.

EXHIBITIONS:

New York, SRGM 57, *Laszlo Moholy-Nagy,* no. 128 ("*Leuk* 1946"); Chicago, SRGM 218,
Laszlo Moholy-Nagy, no. 64, repr. p. 38; New York, SRGM 232, 241, p. 322, repr. p. 323.

REFERENCE:

SRGM *Handbook,* 1970, p. 322, repr. p. 323.

Piet Mondrian

Born March 1872, Amersfoort.
Died February 1944, New York.

202 Composition VII. 1913.

49.1228

Oil on canvas, 41⅛ x 44¾ (104.4 x 113.6)

Signed l.l.: *Mondrian*; on reverse: *Mondrian*; inscribed by the artist, later deleted by him: *Tableau / N:2*;[1] on stretcher: *Composition. N:VII. Mondrian.Haut.* Not dated.

PROVENANCE:

Rev. Hendricus van Assendelft (1875-1928), Gouda, 1914[2]-28; Mrs. Jacoba van Assendelft-Hoos (1876-1954), Gouda, 1928[3]-47; purchased from Mrs. Assendelft-Hoos by Jon Nicholas Streep, New York, 1947;[4] purchased from Streep by Sidney Janis Gallery, New York, 1948; purchased from Janis, 1949.

CONDITION:

In 1953 some surface dirt was removed with 2% Soilax solution. Some inpainting along 2¾ in. of the bottom edge, left of center, is of unrecorded date, but may have been done at this time.

A dark greenish-brown line, which frames the composition along much of all 4 sides ca. 7⁄16 in. from the edge of the canvas, apparently derives from a bronze gilding powder used to color an early frame. Owing to the fragility of the paint layer beneath, no attempt has hitherto been made to remove this. Whether the frame was still wet when the picture was placed in it, or whether the frame was painted with the picture already in place is not known. There is minor cracking of the paint film along most of the bottom edge, and some scattered small losses along all 4 edges. Some other areas of very fine crackle are visible in a raking light. In certain places where the paint was thinly applied, or where it has become more transparent with age, underdrawing in two shades of blue is visible, revealing extensive pentimenti. The overall condition is excellent. (Jan. 1973.)

The picture's appearance in the November 1913 *Moderne Kunstkring* gives it a firm *terminus ante quem*. Terpstra dates it, together with *Tableau I* (Seuphor, 1956, repr. cc 266) and *Oval Composition with Trees* (Ibid., repr. cc 200),

1. Mondrian's use of numerical designations as titles for his paintings was usually directly related to exhibitions of his work. He numbered his entries to a given exhibition consecutively, irrespective of any titles they might have carried previously. Thus, the present work was entitled *Tableau N: 2* when it appeared in the Nov. 1913 *Kunstkring*. Half a year later when he sent 16 paintings from Paris to The Hague for the 1914 Walrecht exhibition he numbered them I-XVI (inscribed in roman numerals on the stretchers), and it was at this time that he deleted the *Tableau N: 2* on the reverse of the present work, substituting the *Composition VII* on the stretcher. There was no catalogue of the Walrecht exhibition, but the list of works exhibited has been reconstructed by Joosten on the basis of the roman numerals *(Centennial Catalogue, 1971, p. 62; also correspondence with the author, Mar. 1973).*

2. Joosten has convincingly established (correspondence with the author, Mar. 1973) that *Composition VII* was 1 of 3 works purchased by van Assendelft from the 1914 Walrecht exhibition.

3. Mrs. van Assendelft-Hoos inherited the collection upon her husband's death.

4. Information supplied by Mrs. E. J. Schijvens-van Assendelft, Zeist, correspondence with the author, Mar. 1973. Streep apparently purchased this and some other works by Mondrian (see below cat. nos. 203 and 204) after the Nov.-Dec. 1946 Stedelijk Museum exhibition.

both of which also appeared in that exhibition, to the second half of 1913. Welsh allows for the possibility that *Oval Composition with Trees* and *Composition VII* were completed by the spring of that year (1966, p. 140).

The fact that all three paintings cited above derive from Mondrian's tree studies of the immediately preceding period has been widely acknowledged (Terpstra, p. 161; Welsh, 1966, p. 138; Joosten, p. 59; Welsh, 1973). Moreover, it seems clear that Mondrian himself attached some importance to the representational origins of the 1913-14 pictures. In at least two instances he specifically identified the tree sources (Terpstra, fn. 3; Welsh, 1966), suggesting thereby the extent to which the connections were present in his own mind. N. H. Wolf's report of a 1913 conversation with Mondrian in which the artist seemed to suggest that the subjects of his paintings did not as such interest him, but rather awakened "his interest because of line and color relationships" (*De Kunst,* vol. 7, February 20, 1915, pp. 251-252, cited by Welsh, 1966) does not preclude the notion that he nonetheless felt the importance of the relationship between that subject, once chosen, and his pictorial conception of it.

The specific sources for *Composition VII* have been convincingly identified by Welsh as *Study: Trees I* (fig. a) and *Study: Trees II* (fig. b). He dates both during the 1912-13 Paris period, most likely during early 1913, a date accepted by C. Blok (*GM,* 1968, 131).

Although the dating of Mondrian's two published sketchbooks does not bear directly on the development or dating of *Composition VII*, the presence in *Sketchbook I* of tree studies closely related in style to some of the 1912-13 drawings and paintings of this subject does raise the issue of how long Mondrian continued to be preoccupied with the tree motif, and how consistent his development towards increasingly abstract renderings of the motif was. Welsh has argued convincingly that the drawings in this first sketchbook date from 1912-13, but the argument has been contested by J. Baljeu, who suggests that the drawings and texts in *Sketchbook I* probably date from as late as 1916 (Welsh and Joosten, *Two Mondrian Sketchbooks: 1912-1914,* Amsterdam, 1969, pp. 9-14; correspondence by J. Baljeu and R. P. Welsh in *Museumjournaal,* no. 6, December 1971, pp. 315-319, 320-323; no. 4, August 1972, pp. 180-181, 182-183).

If Baljeu were correct, Mondrian would have been producing sketches of trees, related in style to 1912-13 drawings such as figs. a and b, when he had otherwise long abandoned the tree motif, examples of which are not found among the paintings beyond 1913. As Welsh has pointed out, it is difficult to imagine (as Baljeu would have it) that there is no functional relationship at all between the sketchbook drawings and the paintings of the period, and that the sketches were illustrations of the philosophical ideas contained in the text, but at the same time rapid reminders *a posteriori* of what Mondrian had been doing several years before. Rather it seems more likely that the tree drawings in the sketchbook are intimately tied to Mondrian's developing Cubist style of the years immediately preceding the First World War. (For more detailed discussion of the development of the tree motif in Mondrian's oeuvre as it was pro-

202

gressively influenced by Cubist works, see Joosten, 1971, pp. 58-60; also Wilmon-Vervaerdt, 1913, p. 86, who describes Schelfhout as *"toute intellec-tualité,"* Mondrian as *"tout sentiment. Son art ne raisonne pas, ni ne compose; il rêve dans l'abstraction. Avec abandon et laisser-aller il distribue les gentil-lesses charmantes de ses sentiments vagues dans des harmonies de gris et de jaunes...."*)

EXHIBITIONS:

Amsterdam, Stedelijk Museum, *Moderne Kunstkring*, Nov. 7-Dec. 8, 1913, no. 167, repr. *(Tableau II)*; The Hague, Galerie Walrecht, *Mondrian*, ca. June-July 31, 1914 (no cat.);[1] Rotterdam, *Rotterdamsche Kunstkring, Alma, Le Fauconnier, Mondriaan*, Jan. 31-Feb. 28, 1915, no. 58 *(Compositie E*, private collection);[5] Rotterdam, Museum Boymans-van-Beuningen, *Kersttentoonstelling*, Dec. 23, 1931-Jan. 18, 1932, no. 43 *(Compositie VII*; information supplied

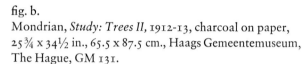

fig. a.
Mondrian, *Study: Trees I*, 1912-13, black chalk on paper, 25⅝ x 35 in., 65 x 89 cm., Haags Gemeentemuseum, The Hague, GM 124.

fig. b.
Mondrian, *Study: Trees II*, 1912-13, charcoal on paper, 25¾ x 34½ in., 65.5 x 87.5 cm., Haags Gemeentemuseum, The Hague, GM 131.

by W. van Dam, The Hague, correspondence with the author, Mar. 1973); New York, SRGM 64 (no cat.); New York, Sidney Janis Gallery, *Mondrian*, Oct. 10-Nov. 12, 1949, no. 7; New York, SRGM 74, no. 159; 78, 79, 84, 87 (checklists); 89 (no cat.); 97, 108, *Piet Mondrian*, 118, 129 (checklists); Philadelphia, SRGM 134-T, no. 117; New York, SRGM 144 (checklist); Worcester, Mass., SRGM 148-T, no. 31; New York, SRGM 151, 153 (checklists); New York, Sidney Janis Gallery, *Piet Mondrian*, Nov. 4-30, 1963, no. 17; Cal., The Santa Barbara Museum of Art, *Piet Mondrian*, Jan. 12-Feb. 21, 1965, no. 42, repr.; New York, SRGM 173, no. 32, repr.; New York, M. Knoedler & Co., Inc., *Seven Decades, 1895-1965: Crosscurrents in Modern Art*, Apr. 26-May 21, 1966, no. 52, repr.; New York, SRGM 196 (checklist); Berlin, Nationalgalerie, *Piet Mondrian*, Sept. 15-Nov. 20, 1968, no. 32; New York, SRGM 198-T (no cat.); 202, p. 125, repr.; Paris, Orangerie, *Mondrian*, Jan. 18-Mar. 31, 1969, no. 42, repr.; New York, SRGM 221 (no cat.); 232, 241, pp. 329-330, repr. p. 328; 244, *Piet Mondrian: Centennial Exhibition*, no. 56, repr. color; Cleveland, SRGM 258-T, no. 11, repr.; New York, Sidney Janis Gallery, *25th Anniversary Exhibition*, Oct. 2-Nov. 3, 1973, no. 85, repr.; New York, SRGM 276 (no cat.).

REFERENCES:

Wilmon-Vervaerdt, review of *Moderne Kunstkring, De Kunst*, vol. 6, no. 302, Nov. 8, 1913, p. 86; review of *Rotterdamsche Kunstkring, De Kunst*, vol. 7, Feb. 20, 1915, p. 252; Seuphor [1956], repr. cc 265, p. 254; A. B. Loosjes-Terpstra, *Moderne Kunst in Nederland*, Utrecht, 1959, pp. 158, 161, fig. 140; R. P. Welsh, *TM*, 1966, pp. 138, 140; M. Seuphor, *L'Art abstrait*, Paris, 1971, repr. color p. 198; J. M. Joosten, *Centennial Catalogue*, 1971, pp. 59-60; 62, cat. no. 56; R. P. Welsh, "The Birth of de Stijl, Part I: Piet Mondrian," *Artforum*, vol. xi, Apr. 1973, p. 50.

5. I am indebted to Joosten for the information that this and all of the other works in the Walrecht exhibition (except for 2 purchased by Mrs. Kröller-Müller) traveled to Rotterdam. Some items, but not the works owned by van Assendelft, then went on to Groningen. (See review of the Rotterdam exhibition in *De Kunst*, vol. 7, Feb. 20, 1915, and *De Kunst*, vol. 7, Feb. 27, 1915, p. 264.) Joosten convincingly identified the Guggenheim *Composition VII* as no. 58 in the Rotterdam catalogue on the basis of combined information from Rotterdam museum records, reviews, and the catalogue itself. Once again the title of the work has been changed *(Compositie E)* to fit in with the sequence of entries for this specific exhibition.

203   Composition No. 8. 1914.

49.1227

Oil on canvas, 37⅛ x 21⅞ (94.4 x 55.6)

Signed and dated l.l.: *Mondrian. 1914.*;
inscribed on reverse, probably by the artist:
Compositie / 8 / P. Mondriaan.[1]

PROVENANCE:

Vilmos Huszár (1884-1960), Hierden, ca.
1918-47;[2] purchased from Huszár by Jon
Nicholas Streep, New York, 1947; purchased from Streep by Sidney Janis Gallery,
New York, 1948; purchased from Janis,
1949.

CONDITION:

In 1953 the canvas was placed on a new
stretcher. The surface was cleaned with 1%
Soilax and benzine and coated with Ozenfant's wax.

There is considerable wear along all 4 edges
with some losses, especially at the corners.
Extensive crackle throughout the surface,
probably due to the artist's repeated reworking of the surface, is stable, although
there are a few areas of possible incipient
cleavage. Pentimenti are visible in several
places. The gray pigment used along 13½
in. of the bottom of the painting is darker in
tone than the gray used elsewhere in the
painting. This area was apparently retouched
by the artist soon after the completion of
the picture. Apart from some light surface
soil, the overall condition is good. (Sept.
1973.)

Welsh first convincingly suggested that *Composition No. 6* (Gemeentemuseum,
The Hague, *GM* 134a), to which the present work is extremely closely related,
was based upon an architectural source (*TM,* 1966, p. 150). Although *Composition No. 6* is squarer in format and retains a more articulated oval framework for its composition, the two pictures clearly relate to the same source and
are executed in a similar technique and range of colors. It has hitherto not been
possible to identify the particular building involved or even to point to drawings which might help to trace the development of the composition. It is not
impossible, however, that both paintings derive in part from a drawing such
as *Paris Façade* of ca. 1912 from Mondrian's third, presently unlocated sketchbook (R. P. Welsh and J. M. Joosten, *Two Mondrian Sketchbooks,* Amster-

1. J. M. Joosten has established that nine of the paintings exhibited at the Walrecht
   exhibition and the *Rotterdamsche Kunstkring* (see fn. 3) were subsequently sent to a 1915
   exhibition in Amsterdam. The *"Compositie 8"* inscribed on the reverse of the canvas is the
   picture's title for the Amsterdam exhibition; roman numerals were used in the catalogue
   but arabic numerals on the works themselves and on Mondrian's list sent to L. Schelfhout,
   the organizer of the exhibition. (I am indebted to Joosten for this information and for a
   copy of the list, the original of which is preserved in the Rijksbureau voor Kunsthistorische
   Documentatie in The Hague.) The handwriting on the reverse of these paintings is difficult
   to identify with certainty, but is probably Mondrian's own.

2. Huszár's ownership of the work has been established by Mrs. E. J. Schijvens-van Assendelft,
   Zeist (correspondence with the author, Mar. 1973), and he was the lender to the 1946
   exhibition in Amsterdam. In 1947 the work was hanging in her house, on loan from
   Huszár, when J. Streep saw and subsequently purchased it. Mrs. Schijvens-van Assendelft
   was unable to say how long Huszár had owned it; however, it is probable that he acquired
   it from Mondrian (possibly in exchange for one of his own pictures) during the period of
   their close association in the *De Stijl* years.

dam, 1969, p. 11, fig. 5; see p. 11 of this publication for a note on the lost sketchbook and on the dating of some of the known extracted leaves from it). The vertical format of the sketch, its emphasis on specific horizontals and verticals which are strongly echoed in *Composition No. 6* and *No. 8*, and the curved bases of several of its windows, suggest a possible source for the Guggenheim and Gemeentemuseum pictures, in both of which the composition has been transformed into an abstract grid. The drawings in *Sketchbook 1* and *2* do not provide any clues to the origin of *Composition No. 8*, but it is possible that others in *Sketchbook 3* might throw some light on the development of

both paintings, further substantiating, or disproving their association with *Paris Façade.* For the time being one can merely affirm that both *Composition No. 6* and *Composition No. 8* belong to the group of Paris façades which Mondrian produced late in 1913 and early in 1914. Other examples are *Composition No. 7* (Seuphor, cc 271), *Composition with Color Planes* (Ibid., cc 284), and *Oval Composition* (Ibid., cc 283), all of which predate *Composition No. 6* and *Composition No. 8.* In the first three works cited, diagonals and slanting lines are still present to a greater or lesser degree. In the latter two, although pentimenti reveal that such lines were part of the original conception, they have been painted out in the final realization. As Welsh has pointed out, *Composition No. 6* represents "a slightly greater suppression of subject matter" than its immediate predecessors, and the literal elements of the building are thus somewhat less readily identifiable; but the architectural background for the composition is still apparent.

A drawing formerly in the collection of V. Huszár (who also owned the present painting) has recently been published by A. de Jongh, who suggested that it might be a sketch by Mondrian for *Composition No. 8,* or perhaps more likely a sketch by Huszár after the present painting (*Museumjournaal,* no. 6, December 1972, p. 265). Although it is more plausible to attribute this drawing to Huszár than to Mondrian, as de Jongh suggests, the relationship between it and the painting seems too tenuous to allow for any specific connection.

EXHIBITIONS:

The Hague, Galerie Walrecht, *Mondrian,* ca. June-July 31, 1914 (no cat.);[3] Rotterdam, *Rotterdamsche Kunstkring, Alma, Le Fauconnier, Mondriaan,* Jan. 31-Feb. 28, 1915, no. 53, 63 or 64?;[4] Amsterdam, Stedelijk Museum, *Schelfhout, Mondriaan, Sluyters, Gestel, Le Fauconnier, van Epen,* Oct. 3-25, 1915, no. 114 *(Composition VIII);*[1] Amsterdam, Stedelijk Museum, *Piet Mondrian,* Nov.-Dec. 1946, no. 76, traveled to Kunsthalle Basel, Feb. 6-Mar. 2, 1947; New York, Sidney Janis Gallery, *Mondrian,* Oct. 10-Nov. 12, 1949, no. 11; New York, SRGM 64 (no cat.); 74, no. 161; 78 (checklist); Vancouver, SRGM 88-T, no. 65; San Francisco Museum of Art, *Art in the Twentieth Century,* June 17-July 10, 1955, p. 15; New York, SRGM 95, 97, 98 (checklists); Boston, SRGM 119-T, no. 45; New York, SRGM 129 (checklist); Philadelphia, SRGM 134-T, no. 118; New York, SRGM 144, 151, 153 (checklists);

3. Joosten reconstructed the Walrecht Gallery exhibition of 16 paintings on the basis of the roman numerals inscribed on the stretchers (see above cat. no. 202, fn. 1). Stretchers bearing the numbers III, IV, and XIII have not been found, suggesting that—as in the present case— these numbers were inscribed on stretchers which have since been replaced. It is impossible to state with certainty that the present *Composition No. 8* originally bore such an inscription, but Joosten's hypothesis that it did is a plausible one.

4. See cat. no. 202, fn. 5. Joosten (in correspondence with the author, Jan. 1973) identifies *Composition No. 8* as no. 53, 63, or 64 in the Rotterdam catalogue on the basis of a review which alludes to the dominant colors in various pictures: "... *no. 53 in een gamma van blauw, bruin, rose en grijs. . . . Sommige werken zijn overwegend rose: no. 63 en no. 64*" (*De Kunst,* vol. 7, Feb. 20, 1915, p. 252). ("... no. 53 is painted in a scale of blue, brown, pink, and gray. . . . Some works are mainly pink: no. 63 and no. 64.") Since 53 and 63 both belonged to private collections by this time, the entry for no. 64 probably applies.

The Baltimore Museum of Art, *1914: An Exhibition of Paintings, Drawings and Sculpture,* Oct. 6-Nov. 15, 1964, no. 167, repr.; New York, SRGM 173, no. 35, repr.; 196 (checklist); 202, p. 124, repr.; 221 (no cat.); 232, 241, pp. 330-331, repr.; 244, *Piet Mondrian: Centennial Exhibition,* no. 60, repr.; 266, 276 (no cats.).

REFERENCES:

N. H. Wolf, review of *Rotterdamsche Kunstkring, De Kunst,* vol. 7, Feb. 20 1915, p. 252; Seuphor [1956], p. 404, repr. cc 274, and p. 259 (Collection The Museum of Modern Art, New York); [M. Rowell], SRGM *Handbook,* 1970, p. 331, repr.

---

204 Composition 1916. 1916.

49.1229

Oil on canvas, with wood strip nailed to bottom edge, 46⅞ x 29⅝ (119 x 75.1), including ⁷⁄₁₆ (1.2) wood strip

Signed and dated on wood strip l.l. (apostrophe and "6" extending onto canvas): *P. Mondriaan. '16.*[1]

PROVENANCE:

Rev. Hendricus van Assendelft (1875-1928), Gouda, 1916[2]-28; Mrs. Jacoba van Assendelft-Hoos (1876-1954), Gouda, 1928-47;[3] purchased from Mrs. Assendelft-Hoos by Jon Nicholas Streep, New York, 1947; purchased from Streep by Sidney Janis Gallery, New York, 1948; purchased from Janis, 1949.

CONDITION:

The work has received no treatment since its acquisition. Examination under UV reveals a small area of inpainting, ca. ⅝ x 1⅜ in., located near the bottom edge, 10 in. from the left edge.

A brownish substance has stained the surface in the upper right corner. Considerable cracking of the paint film in scattered locations is due to the repeated reworkings of the composition by the artist. These areas are stable and show no present danger of cleavage. There are 19 tiny punctures through the paint and support scattered along the left and top margins. These may have been made by miniature nails used to solidify the painting's adherence to the frame. Pentimenti are visible throughout; these are especially noticeable in the black bands, many of which have been widened or narrowed in the course of the painting's development. The overall condition is good. (Jan. 1973.)

Blok first drew attention to the fact that the Guggenheim's *Composition 1916* was derived from a series of studies of the Domburg church façade, beginning with the 1914 ink drawing in the collection of the Haags Gemeentemuseum (*GM*, 1964, 135). This initial study was followed, according to Blok's note, by three others (Seuphor, repr. cc 253, 255, and 257), an argument which Welsh also accepted.

1. Although Mondrian dropped the second 'a' from his name upon his arrival in Paris in 1912, it was not unusual for him to revert to the Dutch spelling when he was signing a picture for a Dutch client or sending it to a Dutch exhibition.
2. Joosten, on the basis of unpublished correspondence between van Assendelft and Mondrian, has established that this work was probably purchased soon after van Assendelft saw it at the Mar.-Apr. 1916 Stedelijk exhibition.
3. See above cat. no. 202, fns. 3, 4.

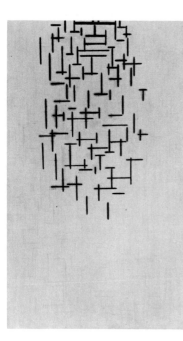

fig. a.
Mondrian, *Plus and Minus: Study for Composition 1916*, oil and pencil on canvas, 49 x 21½ in., 124.4 x 54.6 cm., Sidney Janis Gallery, New York.

The four drawings cited by Blok illustrate Mondrian's gradual elimination of the specific architectural details of the building, as well as his developing emphasis upon the strong horizontals at the upper center of the composition. *Plus and Minus: Study for Composition 1916* (fig. a), which surely followed the drawings, further demonstrates his continuing conviction, so clearly expressed in the final painting, that the powerful horizontal emphasis near but not at the top of the picture was of central importance. Furthermore, the existence of this unfinished study establishes the fact that Mondrian worked out the composition from the top downwards. The study has usually been reproduced upside down, thereby obscuring its relationship to the present painting. But a comparison of the distinctive configuration of horizontals and verticals at the upper edge of the study with those of the painting clearly demonstrates their interdependence.

Related to the question of Mondrian's process of composition in this work is his construction for it of a specific frame. The artist's original frame has been lost, but a photograph of it was discovered and recently published by Joosten, who noted that it probably represented the earliest documented use of a strip frame (1973, p. 55). Joosten also published some comments on the effects of the frame, extracted from the review of a 1916 exhibition in which the picture had been prominently displayed. The reviewer noted that *"Er is een schoon overvloeien van toon in, waarvan het effect nog verhoogd wordt, doordat het doek op de lijst gezet is, inplaats van er in. Mondriaan toont door deze manier van omlijsten, dat het hem wel degelijk om een decoratief geheel te doen is, hetgeen men langen tijd heeft moeten betwijfelen." Nieuwe Rotterdamsche Courant,* March 22, 1916, p. 11. ("There is a beautiful overflow of tones in the picture, the effect of which is enhanced because the canvas is placed upon the frame rather than within it. With this framing device, Mondrian proves that he is concerned with the decorative whole—something which has been in doubt for some time.")

Mondrian himself must surely have been referring to this same framing device (although ascribing to it a very different effect) when he stated to J. J. Sweeney: *"A ma connaissance, j'ai été le premier à faire décoller un tableau de son cadre, plutôt que de le laisser enserré dans celui-ci. J'avais remarqué qu'un tableau sans cadre a un effet plus pur qu'un tableau encadré et que l'encadrement semble ajouter une troisième dimension. Le cadre donne une*

204

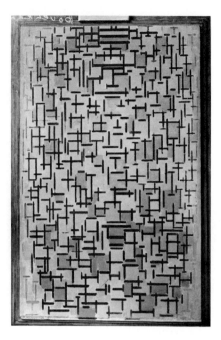

fig. b.
The picture in Mondrian's original frame, now
lost. Photograph, Stedelijk Museum, Amsterdam.

*illusion de profondeur. J'ai donc pris un cadre de bois naturel et j'ai monté
mon tableau dessus. De cette façon, j'ai donné au tableau une existence plus
réelle."* Transcript of original interview, as recalled by J. J. Sweeney, partially
preserved in files of SRGM. ("So far as I know, I was the first painter to bring
a picture forward from its frame, as opposed to setting it within one. I had
noticed that a picture without a frame has a purer effect than a framed one, and
that framing seems to add a third dimension. The frame gives an illusion of
depth. So I took a plain wooden frame and mounted my picture upon it. By
doing this I gave the picture a more real existence.")

Mondrian's discussion of his strip frame, and the degree to which he felt
it drew attention to the picture's surface (and hence away from the three-
dimensional quality of a "decorative whole"), becomes even more revealing if
one examines his method of attaching the canvas to it. As has been noted
above, there is a narrow wooden strip attached to the lower edge of the
stretcher. This strip is fully integrated into the composition and carries the
artist's signature and date, which extend in part onto the canvas above it.
Examination of Joosten's early photograph (fig. b) reveals that there was
originally a similar strip of wood attached to the top edge, but that this was
not incorporated into the composition. It seems likely, therefore, that Mondrian may have initially fixed both strips to the canvas in order to facilitate the
mounting of the painting upon the frame. After having nailed the two strips
firmly to the recessed plain wooden frame, he apparently decided that the
composition needed additional weight at the lower edge. Thus, he extended
the gray background onto the lower wooden strip and—more importantly—
added two black horizontals near the center of it, thus firmly closing off the
composition at its base and reinforcing the barely suggested oval shape of the

painting. The top edge, by contrast, remains more open (as it had in all of the earlier studies), and the strong verticals bisecting the edge extend by implication into the space beyond. Since Mondrian worked out the composition from the top downwards, his decision to include the wooden strip, endowing it with the particularly important role of anchoring the picture at its base, becomes comprehensible as a final, significant step in completing the composition.

EXHIBITIONS:

Amsterdam, Stedelijk Museum, *Hollandsche Kunstenaarskring,* Mar. 11- Apr. 2, 1916;[4] Amsterdam, Stedelijk Museum, *Piet Mondrian,* Nov.-Dec. 1946, no. 78, traveled to Kunsthalle Basel, Feb. 6-Mar. 2, 1947; New York, Sidney Janis Gallery, *Mondrian,* Oct. 10- Nov. 12, 1949, no. 13; New York, SRGM 64 (no cat.), 78, 79 (checklists); Toronto, SRGM 85-T, no. 61; New York, SRGM 87 (checklist); Boston, SRGM 90-T (no cat.); Montreal, SRGM 93-T, no. 46, repr.; New York, SRGM 97, 108 (checklists); 111 (no cat.); New York, Sidney Janis Gallery, *10 Years of Janis,* Sept. 29-Nov. 1, 1958, no. 50, repr.; New York, SRGM 129 (checklist); Philadelphia, SRGM 134-T, no. 119; New York, SRGM 144, 151 (checklist); 153 (checklist; commentary, repr. color); New York, Sidney Janis Gallery, *Piet Mondrian,* Nov. 4-30, 1963, no. 19, repr.; The Santa Barbara Museum of Art, *Piet Mondrian,* Jan. 12-Feb. 21, 1965, no. 49; New York, SRGM 173, no. 41, repr. color; The Art Gallery of Toronto, *Piet Mondrian,* Feb. 12-Mar. 20, 1966, no. 80, repr.; New York, SRGM 196 (checklist); 202, p. 126, repr. color p. 127; Columbus, Ohio, SRGM 207-T, p. 22, repr. color p. 23; New York, SRGM 227 (no cat.); 232, p. 333, repr. p. 332; 236 (no cat.); 241, p. 333, repr. p. 332; 244, *Piet Mondrian: Centennial Exhibition,* no. 69, repr. color; Cleveland, SRGM 258-T, no. 13, repr.; New York, SRGM 276 (no cat.).

REFERENCES:

Review of *Hollandsche Kunstenaarskring* (unsigned), *Nieuwe Rotterdamsche Courant,* Mar. 22, 1916, p. 11; W. Steenhoff, review of *Hollandsche Kunstenaarskring, De Nieuwe Amsterdammer,* Apr. 1, 1916; N. H. Wolf, review of *Hollandsche Kunstenaarskring, De Kunst,* vol. viii, Apr. 1916, p. 317; F. M. Huebner, *Moderne Kunst in den Holländischen Privatsammlungen,* Leipzig, 1922, repr. n.p. (wood strip cropped in reproduction); Seuphor [1956], no. 424, repr. p. 260; C. Blok, *GM,* 1964, no. 135; R. P. Welsh, *TM,* 1966, p. 160, repr. p. 161; H.L.C. Jaffé, *Piet Mondrian,* New York [1970], pp. 32, 118, repr. p. 119; J. M. Joosten, *Centennial Catalogue,* 1971, pp. 63-66, repr. color p. 151; Idem, "Abstraction and Compositional Innovation," *Artforum,* vol. xi, Apr. 1973, p. 55, repr. color p. 51.

4. J. M. Joosten has identified this picture as the subject of comments made by two reviewers of the exhibition. See his "Abstraction and Compositional Innovation," *Artforum,* vol. xi, Apr. 1973. It must have been cat. no. 42, 43, 44, or 45.

205   Composition 2. 1922.
       (Tableau 2).

51.1309

Oil on canvas, 21⅞ x 21⅛ (55.6 x 53.4)

Signed with monogram and dated l.r.:
PM 22; inscribed by the artist on reverse:
Tableau 2.

PROVENANCE:

Private collection, Germany;[1] Galerie
Springer (Rudolf Springer), Berlin, 1947;
purchased from Springer by Jon Nicholas
Streep, New York, 1947; purchased from
Streep, 1951.

CONDITION:

In 1956 the surface was lightly cleaned with
benzine and surfaced with PBM. Some
minor losses were retouched in the blue
edge area, the corner red area, the yellow
area, and the gray/white edges and corners.
Older discolored retouchings in the gray/
white area to the left of center were retouched. The yellowish tone of the background was very slightly reduced, and the
frame was retouched with watercolor. It
was noted that the work needed lining, and
that other discolored inpaints remained.

All edges show considerable wear and
heavily inpainted losses extending ¾ in.
into the painting in places. Numerous horizontal cracks in the paint film cover most of
the surface; these are due to repeated reworking of the surface and also possibly in
part to the presence on the reverse of an
earlier composition. Crackle in the yellow
is especially severe; it is not present in the
blacks, except in the black line immediately
below the yellow (where yellow had been
applied underneath). There are several old
repairs and retouched areas scattered over
the surface. The condition in general is fair
to good. (Sept. 1973.)

The gray background, which Mondrian did not entirely abandon until 1931,
is characteristic of several closely related works of 1921-22, all of which are
dominated by a central gray square or rectangle. (Seuphor [1956], p. 152, suggests that Mondrian used only white backgrounds from 1922 onwards.) In the
Haags Gemeentemuseum's *Composition with Red, Yellow, and Blue*, 1921
(*GM* 1968, repr. 154), for example, three different grays are used, and the
composition—with minor variations in the proportions of the color planes—
is an inversion of the Guggenheim picture. Another closely related work is
Composition 1922 in the Rothschild Collection (Seuphor [1956], repr. color
p. 169, where the colors are, however, inaccurate). Here, while the central
square and the one above it are almost white, the two adjoining areas on the
left are nearly identical in color to the gray of the Guggenheim picture. In
Composition with Red, Yellow, and Blue, 1922 (Stedelijk Museum, Amsterdam, Seuphor [1956], repr. cc 326), the large central square tends slightly more
towards bluish-gray, but the remaining colors are identical to those of the
Guggenheim and related paintings.

R. Welsh has drawn attention to the fact that Mondrian's lines at this stage
frequently stop short of the edge: "According to the late Georges Vantonger-

1. It has so far proved impossible to discover the identity of this collection, or the dates of
   ownership. The information conveyed by Springer was limited to the fact that the picture
   came to him from a private collection in Germany.

loo, the practice originated from a fear that the abstract composition would lose its organic compactness if all lines were carried through to the edge of the composition, bisecting it completely" (*TM*, 1966, p. 178). Mondrian did not adhere to this practice consistently, however, even during the *De Stijl* period, and by the late 1920's he had abandoned it.

EXHIBITIONS:

New York, SRGM 74, no. 160; 78 (checklist); Toronto, SRGM 85-T, no. 62; Vancouver, SRGM 88-T, no. 66, repr.; Boston, SRGM 90-T (no cat.); New York, SRGM 97 (checklist); Boston, Museum of Fine Arts, *European Masters of Our Time,* Oct. 10-Nov. 17, 1957, no. 100, repr.; Palm Beach, Fla., The Society of the Four Arts, *The School of Paris,* Mar. 4-Apr. 5, 1960, no. 24, repr.; The Cleveland Museum of Art, *Paths of Abstract Art,* Oct. 4-Nov. 13, 1960, no. 25, repr.; New York, SRGM 129 (checklist); Philadelphia, SRGM 134-T, no. 120; New York, SRGM 144 (checklist); Worcester, Mass., SRGM 148-T, no. 32, repr.; New York, SRGM 151, 153 (checklists); 160, 195 (no cats.); 196 (checklist); Buffalo, N.Y., Albright-Knox Art Gallery, *Plus by Minus: Today's Half-Century,* Mar. 3-Apr. 14, 1968, no. 131; Berlin, Nationalgalerie, *Piet Mondrian,* Sept. 15-Nov. 20, 1968, no. 50, repr., traveled to Paris, Orangerie, Jan. 18-Mar. 31, 1969, no. 73, repr. cover; New York, SRGM 227 (no cat.); 232, p. 334, repr. color p. 335; 236 (no cat.); 241, p. 334, repr. color p. 335; 244, *Piet Mondrian: Centennial Exhibition,* no. 93, repr. color; 266, 276 (no cats.).

REFERENCES:

D. Robbins, *Painting Between the Wars,* New York, 1966, repr. color slide no. 19; [M. Rowell], SRGM *Handbook,* 1970, p. 334, repr. color p. 335.

206 Composition. 1929.

53.1347

Oil on canvas, 17¾ x 17⅞ (45.1 x 45.3)

Signed and dated l.r.: *PM 29*; inscribed by the artist on stretcher: *Haut / Composition / P. Mondrian.*

PROVENANCE:

Katherine S. Dreier, West Redding, Con-
necticut;[1] Gift of the Estate of Katherine S. Dreier, 1953.

CONDITION:

In 1953 the edges of the canvas were retouched at the top left, top right of center, and right center.

There are approximately 11 more or less vertical cracks and 1 horizontal crack in the white areas; these appear stable, although there is some indication of possible incipient cleavage. Some drying cracks are visible in the black area at the bottom edge near the right corner. There is some soil throughout, especially in the upper white area. The paint on all 4 frame miters is chipped and cracked, and there is additional cracking with paint loss on the lower edge of the frame. The overall condition is good. (Sept. 1973.)

The enclosed gray square which dominates this composition is characteristic of the paintings produced between 1921 and 1928, but has almost disappeared by 1929, when the dominant square has usually been pushed into the corner and enclosed on two adjacent sides instead of four (e.g., Seuphor [1956], repr. cc 341-344; for a brief note on this development see Welsh, *TM*, 1966, pp. 192-194). The present picture and *Foxtrot B* (Yale University Art Gallery, Seuphor [1956], repr. cc 337) are the final examples of this earlier compositional type and are the only ones painted in 1929 known to the present author.

EXHIBITIONS:

Kunsthaus Zürich, *Abstrakte und Surrealistische Malerei und Plastik,* Oct. 6-Nov. 3, 1929, no. 95? ("*Composition III,* 46 x 46, 1929. 1300 fr.");[2] New York, SRGM 79 (checklist); 81 (no cat.); 83, 87 (checklists); 89 (no cat.); Montreal, SRGM 93-T, no. 47; London, SRGM 104-T, no. 55; New York, SRGM 112 (checklist); Boston, SRGM 119-T, no. 46; New York, SRGM 132 (checklist); 173, no. 59, repr.; Cincinnati, The Taft Museum, *Color: Light to Palette,* Oct. 22-Dec. 6, 1965, no. 55; New York, SRGM 195, 196, 198-T, 227 (no cats.); 232, 241, p. 337, repr. p. 336; 244, *Piet Mondrian: Centennial Exhibition,* no. 105, repr.; 266, 276 (no cats.).

REFERENCE:

[M. Rowell], SRGM *Handbook,* 1970, p. 337, repr. p. 336.

1. The date of Dreier's acquisition of this work is unknown. She had purchased works directly from the artist by 1929 and may have acquired this soon after it was painted, but no records of her purchase have yet come to light.

2. No additional data that would confirm the present painting's appearance in the Zurich exhibition has hitherto come to light.

207 Composition 1 A.[1] 1930.

71.1936R 96

Oil on canvas (lozenge), 29⅝ x 29⅝
(75.2 x 75.2)

Signed and dated at center of l.l. edge (on
black bar): *P M 30*; inscribed by the artist
on stretcher: *P Mondrian accrocher /
losangiquement Nᵒ· I.*

PROVENANCE:

Purchased from the artist by Hilla Rebay,
Greens Farms, Connecticut, by October
1930;[2] Estate of Hilla Rebay, 1967-71; acquired from the Estate of Hilla Rebay, 1971.

CONDITION:
The picture was lined with wax resin on
natural linen at an unrecorded date. There
is a considerable amount of old inpainting
along all edges and in scattered locations
throughout the surface, the majority over
cracks in the pigment.

Long irregular pigment cracks, some with
cupping, are scattered over the surface.
These are the result of the artist's practice
of applying the pigment in successive layers.
It is interesting to note that Mondrian
looked upon the successive layers of paint—
its thickness—as a potential source of resis-
tance to damage.[2] There is some slight
chipping and wear at all edges, especially
in the blacks. The condition in general is
fair but stable. (Apr. 1974.)

1. It is not clear whether this title (first used in print in the 1946 exhibition catalogue) is
   Mondrian's own, or whether it was given to the picture by Hilla Rebay.
2. A letter from Mondrian to Rebay, expressing delight at her purchase of the painting, is
   dated Oct. 10, 1930. In it Mondrian tells Rebay that he has brought the picture to Fénéon's
   house, where several other paintings were awaiting shipment to her. He continues:
   *"J'espère que le tableau vous parvienne en bon état, mais si on le salit quand-même vous
   pouvez toujours avec un peu d'eau et du savon blanc le nettoyer. La peinture est assez
   épaisse pour supporter cela."* The Hilla von Rebay Foundation Archive. ("I hope that the
   picture will arrive in good condition, but if it does get dirty you can always clean it with a
   little water and white soap. The paint is sufficiently thick to withstand this.")

Mondrian's reference to the lozenge-shaped canvas as an illustration of his explicit rejection of van Doesburg's 1925 reintroduction of the diagonal into his work has often been cited. He said to J. J. Sweeney:

Doesburg, in his late work, tried to destroy static expression by a diagonal arrangement of the lines of his compositions. But through such an emphasis the feeling of physical equilibrium which is necessary for the enjoyment of the work of art is lost. The relationship with architecture and its vertical and horizontal dominants is broken. If a square picture, however, is hung diagonally, as I have frequently planned my pictures to be hung, this effect does not result. Only the borders of the canvas are on 45° angles, not the picture. The advantage of such a procedure is that longer horizontal and vertical lines may be employed in the composition ("Eleven Europeans in America," *The Museum of Modern Art Bulletin,* vol. xiii, no. 4-5, 1946).

Both statements imply that the viewer's tendency to see the lines as continuing beyond the limits of the canvas edge is not only unavoidable but desirable (although R. P. Welsh has correctly drawn attention to the fact that Mondrian probably regarded this as a secondary phenomenon and never explicitly mentioned it in his published writings; *TM,* 1966, p. 198).

M. Bill was unaware of these statements by Mondrian when he suggested in his essay on the 1925 *Composition I with Blue and Yellow* that the crucial quality of the lozenge-shaped pictures was the inevitable extension into the surrounding space of their horizontals, their verticals, and even of their colored planes. Precisely because their horizontals and verticals did not correspond to the edges of the canvas, Bill implied, they acquired an added independent momentum which allowed them infinite possibilities for extension beyond the framing edge (*Zürcher Kunstgesellschaft, Jahresbericht,* 1956, trans. M. Wolf, *Centennial Catalogue,* 1971, pp. 74-76).

The fact that most of Mondrian's approximately twenty lozenge-shaped canvases were produced in the years 1925-26, when his break with van Doesburg over the issue of the diagonal and his own renewed emphasis on the primary importance of the vertical and horizontal were foremost in his mind, cannot be insignificant.

Composition 1 A is the earlier of only two paintings by Mondrian in which none of the verticals and horizontals intersect within the confines of the canvas: two of them touch at the center of the lower right edge, but they intersect only outside it. This particular element takes even more extreme form in the Haags Gemeentemuseum's *Composition with Yellow Lines* of 1933 (*GM* 155, Seuphor [1956], repr. cc 410), where none of the four colored bars touch at all.

EXHIBITIONS:

Amsterdam, Stedelijk Museum, *Piet Mondrian,* Nov.-Dec. 1946, no. 107, traveled to Kunsthalle Basel, Feb. 6-Mar. 2, 1947; New York, SRGM 64 (no cat.); New York, Sidney Janis Gallery, *Piet Mondrian,* Oct. 10-Nov. 12, 1949, no. 22; New York, SRGM 241 (addenda); 244, *Piet Mondrian: Centennial Exhibition,* no. 111, repr.; 260, 266, 276 (no cats.).

REFERENCE:

Seuphor [1956], repr. cc 408.

Amédée Ozenfant

Born April 1886, Saint-Quentin, Picardy.
Died May 1966, Cannes.

208   Still Life. 1920.
(Nature morte; "L'Esprit Nouveau [2]").[1]

55.1423

Oil on canvas, 31⅞ x 39⅜ (80.9 x 100.0)

Signed l.r.: *ozenfant.* Not dated.

PROVENANCE:
Purchased from the artist, 1955.

CONDITION:
In 1964 the work was restretched on a new stretcher. Surface dirt was removed in 1973, but the work was not varnished due to the danger of possible cross-linking with varnish already mixed with the pigment. Minor inpainting was mostly confined to the extreme left edge with scattered minor touches on the other edges.

Apart from some scattered minor chips at the edges and corners, scattered ground cracks at the left side of the picture, and moderate scratches and abrasion in the lower margin, the condition is good. (Apr. 1974.)

1. The picture appears with this title in the "Suggestion for purchase" memorandum submitted to the trustees of the SRGM in 1955. Although no document in Ozenfant's hand has hitherto come to light in which the picture is so designated, it seems certain that the title originated with him. The inclusion of the 1940 Chicago show in the present exhibition history is based upon this title.

The 1920 date for this work appears in the 1921 *L'Esprit Nouveau* illustration caption and is entirely consistent with the stylistic evidence.

At least two other versions of the composition exist, both also painted in 1920. One, now in the collection of Peggy Guggenheim in Venice, is identical in size to the present work and is signed and dated (N. and E. Calas, *The Peggy Guggenheim Collection of Modern Art,* New York, 1966, repr. p. 43). The table top in this latter version is divided into dark and light areas, and the molding in the upper left corner is a single rounded form. Certain areas of light and dark are reversed in this painting, and the value relationships are altered in some places, but the compositions are otherwise identical.

In the third version (present whereabouts unknown, *L'Esprit Nouveau,* no. 7, 1921, repr. p. 827) the molding at the upper left corner takes yet another slightly modified form, but the table top is, like that of the present painting, uniform. Although the colors in this work are unknown, the value relationships appear to be closer to those of cat. no. 208 than to those of the Peggy Guggenheim picture.

A comparison among these three works and representative related works of 1919 corroborates Golding's point that Purism reached its maturity in 1920 (p. 12). A 1919 still-life illustrated in *L'Esprit Nouveau* (no. 7, 1921, p. 819), though incorporating many of the same elements as cat. no. 208, is not yet characterized by the economy, simplicity, and lucidity of the latter.

Ozenfant's designation of the Guggenheim painting as *Esprit Nouveau (2)* (the "2" apparently describing its relationship to another picture of 1920 included in the Chicago exhibition as *Still Life Esprit Nouveau,* but hitherto otherwise unidentified) suggests the extent to which this painting epitomized for him the important developments of 1920. In that year the first issues of his periodical *L'Esprit Nouveau* appeared (jointly edited with Jeanneret), and the new style which they had both been gradually refining became fully established and articulated in the pages of their journal.

EXHIBITIONS:

Paris, Galerie Druet, *Ozenfant et Jeanneret,* Jan. 22-Feb. 5, 1921, possibly one of nos. 6-20? (all "*Natures mortes 1919-1920*"); The Arts Club of Chicago, *Amédée Ozenfant,* Jan. 2-27, 1940, no. 17 ("*Esprit Nouveau [2]* for sale"),[1] traveled to San Francisco Museum of Art, Mar. 5-Apr. 9, Minn., St. Paul Gallery and School of Art, Oct. 3-20, 1940; New York, SRGM 95 (checklist); London, SRGM 104-T, no. 58; Worcester, Mass., SRGM 148-T, no. 34; New York, SRGM 151, 153 (checklists); 195 (no cat.); 196 (checklist); 260 (no cat.); New York, M. Knoedler & Co., Inc., *Ozenfant,* Apr. 5-28, 1973, no. 8, repr.

REFERENCES:

M. Raynal, "Ozenfant et Jeanneret," *L'Esprit Nouveau,* no. 7, 1921, repr. color p. 816 (dated 1920); SRGM *Handbook,* 1959, p. 141, repr. (dated 1920); J. Golding, *Ozenfant,* exhibition catalogue, New York, 1973, pp. 12-13, repr. p. 18, checklist p. 47 (dated 1920).

François Marie Martinez Picabia

Born January 1879, Paris.
Died November 1953, Paris.

209 Portrait of Mistinguett (?).
ca. 1908-1911.

66.1801

Oil on canvas, 23⅝ x 19⅜ (60 x 49.2)

Signed and dated l.c.: *Francis Picabia 1907.*

PROVENANCE:

Early history unknown; "M. Axel," Paris, 1952;[1] purchased from Axel by Pierre Granville, Paris, 1952;[1] purchased from Granville, 1966.

CONDITION:

The painting was lined and cleaned prior to its acquisition by Granville (conversation between Granville and Rowell, Paris, 1970). Cracks in the paint film are considerable in the right background, and there is a prominent vertical crack slightly left of center; both of these areas have been partially filled and inpainted. Minor paint losses and cracks are visible elsewhere. Examination under high magnification revealed that the signature and date were applied over cracks in the original paint film, establishing that they were added after the completion of the canvas. Since the artist's handwriting did not alter significantly over the years, it is impossible to determine with any precision when this addition might have taken place. The condition is in general good. (Dec. 1971.)

Although the 1907 date was added in the artist's hand, it must be treated with some caution (see above CONDITION). The style of the painting tends to indicate a slightly later date, since the majority of the paintings securely dated 1907 reveal a much greater dependence on Impressionism. By late 1908 and early 1909, and perhaps to an even greater extent in the first part of 1911, the influence of Fauvism and Japonisme—so clearly present in the *Portrait of Mistinguett*—had become prominent in Picabia's style. Works such as *Woman with Mimosas* of 1908 (Galleries Maurice Sternberg, Chicago), or *Adam and Eve* of 1911 (Collection Simone Collinet, Paris) are examples of this development that would lend support to a later date for the *Mistinguett*. At the same time it is important to note, as Camfield has, that Picabia's paintings of 1908-11 were marked by a somewhat quixotic experimentation with various styles, making it difficult to pinpoint the dates of individual pictures exactly. Furthermore, since the date of the Guggenheim painting was inscribed substantially after the completion of the canvas, it is possible that other signed and dated paintings of this period might pose similar problems. Until further evidence on this point emerges, a date of ca. 1908-11 would seem most convincing.

The identification of the sitter as Mistinguett cannot be established with certainty, but various factors contribute to its plausibility. Simone Collinet, who included the portrait in an exhibition of Picabia's work at her Galerie Furstenberg in 1956, suggested at that time that it might represent Mistinguett; Gabrielle Buffet-Picabia, who had married the artist in 1909, agreed that the identification was plausible (conversation between Rowell and Simone Col-

---

1. Conversation between M. Rowell and Granville, Paris, 1970. Granville specified that he purchased the painting from a Mr. Axel, who had the painting on consignment from a foreign collector. He did not know anything further about Mr. Axel or about the earlier history of the painting.

linet, Paris, 1971). Gabrielle Buffet-Picabia subsequently indicated in a letter to Granville (April 7, 1962, copy in the SRGM files) that Picabia knew Mistinguett very well at the time this picture was painted, and she added that the portrait seemed to her to be a good likeness. Denise de Lima, daughter-in-law of Mistinguett, also offered confirmation of the identification (letter to Granville, March 15, 1962, copy in the SRGM files). Olga Picabia, who married the artist in 1940, was not able to identify the sitter from personal acquaintance, but stated (in conversation with T. M. Messer, New York, September 1970) that Picabia had several times spoken of his portrait of Mistinguett and wondered what had become of it.

Comparison of the profile with photographs of the actress are suggestive but inconclusive. Since the painting is clearly an evocative likeness, however, rather than a portrait painted from a posed model, the representation is necessarily somewhat generalized. Gabrielle Buffet-Picabia (in conversation with Rowell, Paris, 1971) stated in relation to the picture that the artist's portraits were almost always painted from memory and not based on sittings. While this would seem unlikely in relation to works such as the portraits of Soupault and Breton (*Les Champs magnétiques,* Paris, 1920, frontispiece) or the portrait of Ernest Walsh (*This Quarter,* Monte Carlo, no. 3, 1927, p. 2), it is convincing in relation to the present portrait.

Mistinguett (née Jeanne Marie Bourgeois) was born at La Pointe Raquet in 1875 and made her first music hall appearances in the 1890's. In 1907 she began to appear in straight comedy, but shortly thereafter moved to the Moulin Rouge, of which she become part proprietor. Her later appearances at the Folies-Bergère and the Casino de Paris, usually with Maurice Chevalier as her dancing partner, were world famous. She appeared in the United States (1923-24) and on the London stage (1947 and later), and she made eight films between 1910 and 1936. Her early successes derived largely from the originality of her comedy style; afterward she became the undisputed queen of revue artists. Her writings include her own memoirs *(Mistinguett and her Confessions,* ed. and trans. H. Griffith, London, 1938) and a short piece in the spring 1922 issue of *The Little Review,* an issue devoted entirely to Picabia. This last piece is additional evidence for the connection of Mistinguett with Picabia's literary and artistic circle. She died in January 1956.

EXHIBITIONS:

Paris, Galerie Furstenberg, *Picabia,* June 5-July 5, 1956, *hors catalogue* (information supplied by Simone Collinet in conversation with Rowell, Paris, 1971); New York, SRGM 187, 196 (checklists); 221 (no cat.); 232, p. 358, repr. p. 359; 233, *Francis Picabia,* no. 9, repr.

REFERENCE:

W. A. Camfield, *Francis Picabia,* exhibition catalogue, New York, 1970, pp. 17-18, 54, no. 9, repr.

210 The Child Carburetor. 1919.
(*L'Enfant carburateur*).

55.1426

Oil, enamel and metallic paint, gold leaf, pencil, and crayon on stained plywood, 49¾ x 39⅞ (126.3 x 101.3)

Signed l.r.: *Francis Picabia*; inscribed u.l.: *L'Enfant Carburateur*; elsewhere on surface (left to right and top to bottom): *méthode crocodile; dissolution de prolongation; flux et reflux des résolutions; sphère de la migraine; détruire le futur; valse en jaquette* (barely visible l.c., hitherto published as *Value en Jaquette*).

PROVENANCE:

Gabrielle Buffet-Picabia, 1919-40;[1] [Lucien Lefebvre-Foinet, Paris];[2] Peggy Guggenheim, New York, 1940-43;[3] purchased from Art of this Century (Peggy Guggenheim), by Patricia Matta (later Patricia Matisse), New York, 1943;[4] purchased from Patricia Matta by Rose Fried, New York, by 1954;[5] purchased from Fried, 1955.

CONDITION:

The black enamel areas have been retouched with matte black paint, the gold-painted areas with slightly different color gold. It is impossible to say when these reworkings took place and whether they are by the artist; examination under UV indicates only that they were made at some date after the original paint application.

The plywood support is slightly warped at the top and bottom edges, resulting in a separation of the top layer of plywood from those below. There is considerable vertical cracking in the panel, especially at the top and bottom edges. The gold leaf is wrinkled throughout and there is some flaking. (Mar. 1972.)

The painting has been variously dated 1915 (Rose Fried exhibition catalogue); 1916 (P. Guggenheim); 1917 (Barr, 1946); 1918 (Barr, 1936); and ca. 1919 (Camfield, 1966, 1970; Hultén; SRGM *Handbook,* 1970). The two earliest exhibition catalogues (1919 and 1920), as well as the earliest known repro-

1. Gabrielle Buffet-Picabia, in correspondence with the author, Dec. 1970, revealed that she had been given the painting by Picabia in 1919 and that she had sold it to Peggy Guggenheim in 1921. Peggy Guggenheim, in correspondence with the author, Dec. 1970, stated that she had purchased the picture from Gabrielle in 1940. Since she was not in fact buying modern art until the late 1930's, it seems most likely that Mrs. Guggenheim's memory of the date is the correct one. Germaine Everling-Picabia believes that the picture hung in the dining room at Mougins, the château built by Picabia in 1925 (letter dated Nov. 24, 1970, SRGM files). It is possible that she intended to refer to the dining room of the apartment on rue Emile Augier, where the picture was actually painted; or alternatively, that Picabia at some point between 1925 and 1940 borrowed the picture back from Gabrielle and brought it to Mougins.

2. Lucien Lefebvre-Foinet is listed as the lender in the catalogue of the 1936 Museum of Modern Art exhibition, and letters addressed to him as lender exist in The Museum of Modern Art files. He, however, denies ever having owned the picture, although he has clear records of having shipped it (correspondence with the author, Feb.-Apr., 1971). It seems possible that at some time in the 1930's Gabrielle deposited the painting with Lefebvre-Foinet (who stored many of Picabia's other pictures), either as a loan, or in payment for some services rendered, and that he subsequently returned it to her.

3. Letter from Peggy Guggenheim cited in fn. 1. See also P. Guggenheim, 1942, p. 60; and Barr, 1947, p. 257, repr. p. 195.

4. Letter from Peggy Guggenheim cited in fn. 1; also letter from Pierre Matisse Gallery, Nov. 10, 1972.

5. Letter from Pierre Matisse Gallery cited in fn. 4. See also Rose Fried's exhibition catalogue of 1954.

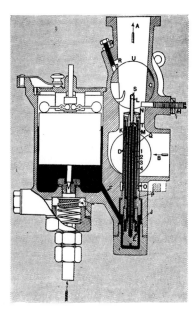

fig. a.
Racing Claudel Carburetor (from R. W. A. Brewer, *Carburetion Theory and Practice,* 2nd ed., London, 1918, p. 189).

duction of the work *(The Little Review,* 1922), provide no information on the date.

Only Camfield (1970, p. 107) discusses the date, suggesting that although the style is reminiscent of works of 1915 such as *This Thing is Made to Perpetuate My Memory* (The Arts Club of Chicago; Camfield, 1970, repr. no. 44) or *Paroxysm of Sadness* (Collection Simone Collinet, Paris; Camfield, 1970, repr. no. 46), its asymmetrical composition indicates a later date. He also refers to the testimony of Germaine Everling-Picabia (1955) and to the fact that the picture was exhibited for the first time at the *Salon d'Automne* in November 1919.

Very few of Picabia's machine paintings—most of which were produced between 1915 and 1922—are securely dated, so it is difficult to establish a firm date on stylistic grounds alone. External evidence, however, strongly supports Camfield's 1919 date. Everling-Picabia describes Picabia's work on the picture at her apartment on rue Emile Augier, into which he did not move until the fall of 1919 (Camfield, 1970, p. 27, fn. 39). In addition, the symbolic significance of the painting's title and iconography, and the relationship of these to certain biographical facts lend support to the theory that the picture was painted shortly before the opening of the November 1919 *Salon* (see below).

Picabia's machine paintings were in many instances directly dependent upon engineering diagrams or other technical sources (see Camfield, 1966, p. 314 et passim; also Everling-Picabia, 1955 and Idem, *L'Anneau de saturne,* Paris, 1970, p. 90). Camfield first suggested that this particular painting was based on a diagram of an actual carburetor and cited a 1920 illustration as a possible model (1966, p. 320). Although Camfield's suggestion was undoubtedly correct in principle, the model he illustrated indicated that Picabia's adaptation had been a fairly free one. Comparison of the painting with the diagram of a 1918 Racing Claudel carburetor (fig. a), however, reveals that Picabia's dependence on his technical source was actually far closer.

The significance of the painting's title and inscriptions is difficult to establish, but several factors should be taken into account in a consideration of the iconography. Both Camfield and Hultén have argued convincingly that Picabia's expressed attitude towards his titles must play a role in the examination of his iconography and symbolism. Two statements by the artist are important in this connection: "I have been profoundly impressed by the vast mechanical development in America. The machine has become more than a mere adjunct of human life. It is really a part of human life—perhaps the very soul. In seeking forms through which to interpret ideas or by which to expose human characteristics I have come at length upon the form which appears most brilliantly plastic and fraught with symbolism. I have enlisted the machinery of the modern world, and introduced it into my studio" ("French Artists Spur on American Art," *New York Tribune,* October 24, 1915, pt. iv, p. 2, cited by Camfield, 1966, p. 313). And: "In my work the subjective expression is the title, the painting the object. But this object is nevertheless somewhat subjective, because it is the pantomime—the appearance of the title" (statement in *291,* no. 12, February 1916, quoted by Camfield, 1966, pp. 314-315; Hultén, p. 85).

W. Rubin has argued that the relationship between title and image in the anti-art of Picabia is usually obvious and the "symbols themselves are so exaggeratedly prosaic as to suggest that it was Picabia's intention to telescope the process of association which might give them richness, and thus arrive at the greatest commonplace" *(Dada and Surrealist Art,* New York, 1968, p. 56). Furthermore, Camfield, while not discussing *The Child Carburetor,* has argued for the relationship in some of the other paintings between iconographical features and events in Picabia's own life (1966, pp. 313 ff.).

The present painting is on one level immediately comprehensible in the terms suggested by Rubin's analysis: the machine parts of the carburetor readily lend themselves to interpretation in sexual terms, with the male organ so obviously poised above the female. On another level, the painting's meaning is more elusive. The inscriptions within the painting remain something of a mystery even though they suggest the macabre ability of the machine to act in human ways, and conversely the potential for humans to take on the qualities of machines. The title, however, can be interpreted on yet another level.

Picabia's passion for automobiles is well-known. During 1919 alone he owned in succession a Peugeot, an English Singer (for which he paid by selling Germaine Everling's pearl necklace), and an American Mercer. Furthermore, the Singer, which he still owned in the early fall of 1919 (Sanouillet, 1966, p. 97), almost certainly contained the type of Racing Claudel carburetor on which the design of the present painting is based (information supplied by Chrysler, United Kingdom, Ltd., correspondence with the author, December 1971). As has already been suggested above, the machine parts in the painting have explicit sexual analogies which are both visually and intellectually obvious. Related biographical facts which most probably have a bearing on the interpretation of the painting concern Picabia's simultaneous involvement at this time with two women, Gabrielle Buffet and Germaine Everling. In September 1919 his wife Gabrielle gave birth to a son, Vincente; three months later his mistress Germaine gave birth to a son, Lorenzo.

In the light of these biographical facts, the title of the painting lends to the prosaic sexual imagery a more complex significance: what is presented, in essence, is a comment upon the involved human relationships between the artist and the two women. It suggests that in the autumn of 1919, while his wife and mistress were giving birth to human children, he was preoccupied with another kind of child—his automobile, a child conceived in machine terms. Through the symbolism of the machine, and his relationship to it, he was giving expression to the infinite complexities of his own emotional and sexual life.

EXHIBITIONS:

Paris, *Salon d'Automne,* Nov. 9-Dec. 10, 1919, no. 1533;[6] Paris, Galerie de la Cible (Galerie Povolotzky), *Picabia,* Dec. 10-25, 1920, no. 44 (see M. de la Hire, *Francis Picabia,* Paris, Galerie de la Cible, 1920, published on occasion of the exhibition; includes checklist of works exhibited); New York, The Museum of Modern Art, *Fantastic Art, Dada and Surrealism,* Dec. 7, 1936-Jan. 17, 1937, p. 229, no. 462, repr. (dated 1918);[2] New York, Rose Fried Gallery, *Group Exhibition,* Nov. 2-Dec., 1954, no. 11 (dated 1915); New York, SRGM 95 (checklist); The Newark Museum, *Abstract Art 1910 to Today,* Apr. 27-June 10, 1956, no. 55; New York, SRGM 196 (checklist); 205, *Rousseau, Redon and Fantasy* (checklist; commentary, repr. color, n.p.); New York, The Museum of Modern Art, *The Machine as Seen at the End of the Mechanical Age,* Nov. 25, 1968-Feb. 9, 1969, pp. 85, 93, 95, repr. (dated c. 1919); New York, SRGM 227 (no cat.); 232, p. 360, repr. p. 361; 233, *Francis Picabia,* no. 63, repr. color; 241, p. 360, repr. p. 361; 260 (no cat.).

REFERENCES:

The Little Review, spring 1922, repr. bet. pp. 16 and 17; A. H. Barr, Jr., *Fantastic Art, Dada and Surrealism,* 1st ed., New York, 1936, p. 229, no. 462, repr., 3rd ed., New York, 1947, p. 257, repr. p. 195 (listed as "Collection Matta"); *Art of this Century,* ed. P. Guggenheim, New York, 1942, p. 60; G. Everling-Picabia, "C'était hier Dada," *Les Oeuvres libres,* Paris, June 1955, p. 129; W. A. Camfield, "The Machine Style of Francis Picabia," *The Art Bulletin,* vol. 48, Sept.-Dec. 1966, p. 320, fig. 32; K. G. P. Hultén, *The Machine as Seen at the End of the Mechanical Age,* exhibition catalogue, New York, 1968, pp. 85, 93, 95, repr.; SRGM *Handbook,* 1970, p. 360, repr. p. 361; W. A. Camfield, *Francis Picabia,* exhibition catalogue, New York, 1970, pp. 27, 107, repr. color.

6. Picabia's 4 entries in the 1919 *Salon,* all examples of his "machine" style which was hitherto unknown in Paris, caused consternation among the conservative officers of the *Salon.* Unable to refuse the work of a *Salon* Associate, they exhibited the pictures virtually out of sight under a staircase. Camfield has described the emerging conflict in which Picabia and Ribemont-Dessaignes launched an attack in 2 successive issues of *391;* the officers of the *Salon* demanded Ribemont-Dessaignes' resignation and Louis Vauxcelles challenged him to a duel (1970, p. 27; see also *391,* no. 9, Nov. 1919, and *391,* no. 10, Dec. 1919; M. Sanouillet, *Francis Picabia et "391,"* vol. ii, Paris, 1966, p. 107). Reviews of the *Salon* mentioning Picabia's entries appeared in *Le Matin,* Paris, Nov. 1, 1919; *La France libre,* Paris, Nov. 5, 1919; *La Petite Gironde,* Nov. 24, 1919; *Images de Paris,* Paris, Dec. 1919. Picabia's open letter of protest to Frantz Jourdain was published in *Journal du Peuple,* Paris, Nov. 2, 1919. I am indebted to W. Camfield for drawing these reviews to my attention.

Pablo Ruiz Picasso

Born October 1881, Malaga.
Died April 1973, Mougins.

211 Carafe, Jug, and Fruit Bowl.
Summer 1909.
(Carafon; Pot et Compotier; Compotier).

37.536

Oil on canvas, 28¼ x 25⅜ (71.6 x 64.6)

Not signed or dated.

PROVENANCE:

Probably purchased directly from the artist by G. F. Reber, Lausanne, sometime after 1918;[1] purchased from Reber by Zwemmer Gallery (A. Zwemmer), London, 1935 (information supplied by Zwemmer, correspondence with the author, May 1971); purchased from Zwemmer by Solomon R.

Guggenheim, September 1936; Gift of Solomon R. Guggenheim, 1937.

CONDITION:

Prior to its acquisition by the Museum, the painting was placed on a new stretcher and the edges were taped, apparently to hide unpainted and tacked margins that became visible in the restretching process. In 1953 there was a surface cleaning, but the varnish was not removed.

The overall condition is excellent.
(Jan. 1972.)

The earliest known publication of the picture is Zwemmer's exhibition catalogue of 1936, where it is dated 1908; Barr concurred with this date. Zervos placed the picture in the spring of 1909 as do G. Aust (SRGM 104-T, 1957, Cologne catalogue) and F. Mathey (Ibid., Paris catalogue). Until 1968 the Museum accepted the 1908 date, but evidence provided subsequently by Sabartés argued for redating the picture to 1909: in his book of documents relating to Picasso's life and work Sabartés reproduces a photograph of Picasso's summer 1909 studio at Horta de San Juan; the left side of the present painting is clearly visible hanging on the wall.

Stylistically the painting belongs to the late spring and early summer of 1909. It clearly follows by at least some months the *Vase, Gourd, and Fruit on a Table* in the John Hay Whitney Collection (Zervos, 2*, repr. no. 126), dated by Zervos spring 1909, but more convincingly dated by M. Jardot to the winter of 1908-09, or the first months of 1909 (*Picasso*, exhibition catalogue, Musée des Arts Décoratifs, Paris, 1955, repr. no. 17). It also clearly follows the Moscow *Fruit Bowl, Fruit, and Glass* (Zervos, 2*, repr. no. 124, dated there spring 1909), which cannot be later than the earliest months of 1909, and The Museum of Modern Art *Fruit Dish* (Zervos, 2*, no. 12, dated there winter 1908). Kahnweiler and Barr push the latter forward into the spring of 1909 (Barr, 1946, p. 65); J. Golding convincingly dates it "probably early spring 1909" (*Cubism*, 1959, revised ed., 1968, p. 71), as does W. Rubin, although he does not rule out the possibility that it might be a few months earlier (*Picasso in the Collection of The Museum of Modern Art*, New York, 1972, p. 201). Whether or not the Whitney, Moscow, and The Museum of

1. The picture was never owned by Kahnweiler; it appears neither in his own photo archive in Paris nor in any of the 4 Kahnweiler Sales. Léonce Rosenberg's photographic archives in Paris do not include it either, but these are incomplete and it cannot be altogether ruled out that the picture once belonged to him. Daix feels that the picture is more likely to have been purchased by Reber directly from Picasso (correspondence with the author, June 1972). In any event, it is clear that Picasso himself kept the picture in his own collection for at least 9 years after he painted it and perhaps considerably longer.

Modern Art still-lifes fall in the later part of the winter, or as late as February-March of 1909, they are clearly distinct from the developments that occurred in Picasso's work starting in May, when he moved to Horta for over four months. The present picture is in certain respects clearly reminiscent of the earlier group: the treatment of the rounded fruits in the bowl, the bowl simultaneously shown from various viewpoints, and the tilting forward of the table top are reminiscent of The Museum of Modern Art still-life (see Golding, p. 72, for a discussion of these elements). But in the carafe, and even more strongly in the draperies, the angular faceting brings the work much closer to the developed Cubism of *Woman with Pears* (on extended loan to The Museum of Modern Art), which dates from some time well into the summer (Rubin, 1972, p. 61). Nothing in the present picture is quite so broken down into complex fragmentary planes as the head in this latter painting; but a comparison of the background drapery in the two pictures, as well as the arrangement of tablecloth and napkins in the present picture with the tablecloth and even with Fernande's forehead in The Museum of Modern Art work, tends to indicate that the Guggenheim painting was in process not very long before the other, and after the first of the Horta landscapes. Daix has stated (in correspondence with the author, June 1972) that Picasso remembered painting the Guggenheim still-life some time after he arrived at Horta. His recollection is borne out by the stylistic evidence, which would place the painting after the landscapes (Zervos, 2*, repr. nos. 157, 158, 161), shortly before the *Woman with Pears,* and rather more substantially before The Museum of Modern Art *Still Life with Liqueur Bottle* painted in the late summer (Rubin, 1972, p. 62).

Daix places the picture late in the Horta series and draws attention to the fact that the carafe, which does not appear in any of the Paris still-lifes, is visible in truncated form in the upper right corner of *Portrait of Fernande* (Zervos, 6, repr. no. 1071), which he also places in this period.

EXHIBITIONS:
London, Zwemmer Gallery, *Picasso,* May-June, 1936, no. 29 (*Compotier,* 1908); Philadelphia, SRGM 3-T, no. 190; Charleston, S.C., SRGM 4-T, no. 260; New York, SRGM 78 (checklist); 79 (checklist; withdrawn Nov.); 81, 83 (no cats.); 87 (checklist); Boston, SRGM 90-T (no cat.); Montreal, SRGM 93-T, no. 49, repr.; New York, SRGM 95 (checklist; withdrawn Sept. 12); The Arts Club of Chicago, *An Exhibition of Cubism on the Occasion of the Fortieth Anniversary of The Arts Club of Chicago,* Oct. 3-Nov. 4, 1955, no. 14; New York, SRGM 97 (checklist); London, SRGM 104-T, no. 59 (dated 1908 in London, The Hague, Helsinki, Rome cats.; dated 1909 in Cologne, Paris cats.); New York, SRGM 118, 129, 144, 151, 153 (checklists); 173, no. 12, repr.; Museum of Fine Arts, Houston, *The Heroic Years: Paris 1908-1914,* Oct. 21-Dec. 8, 1965 (no cat.); New York, SRGM 196 (checklist); 202, p. 29, repr. p. 28 (dated 1909); 221 (no cat.); 232, 241, pp. 363-364, repr. p. 362 (dated 1909); 251, 266, 276 (no cats.).

REFERENCES:
C. Zervos, *Histoire de l'art contemporain,* Paris, 1938, repr. p. 206 (dated "1909"); A. H. Barr, Jr., *Picasso: Forty Years of His Art,* New York, 1939, p. 195 (dated 1908); C. Zervos, *Pablo Picasso: oeuvres de 1906 à 1912,* vol. 2*, Paris, 1942, no. 164, pl. 81 (dated "Spring 1909"); A. H. Barr, Jr., *Picasso: Fifty Years of His Art,* New York, 1946, p. 283 (dated 1908); J. Sabartés, *Picasso: documents iconographiques,* Geneva, 1954, pl. 187; U. Apollonio, *Fauves et Cubistes,* Bergamo and Paris, 1959, repr. color p. 58 (dated 1908); P. Daix, *Picasso: le cubisme, 1907-1916, catalogue raisonné,* Neuchâtel [in press], no. 277 (dated "summer 1909").

212   Accordionist. Summer 1911.
(Homme assis; Pierrot; Harlequin).

37.537

Oil on canvas, 51¼ x 35¼ (130.2 x 89.5)

Signed l.l.: *Picasso*; inscribed by the artist on reverse: *Picasso / Ceret.* The signature on the face must have been added at a later date, probably in the 1920's or 1930's when the picture was sold. (See Jardot, 1955, p. 46, for a discussion of the fact that Picasso and Braque rarely signed their pictures on the obverse between the years 1907 and 1914.)

PROVENANCE:

Possibly purchased directly from the artist by Paul Guillaume, Paris, ca. 1920;[1] purchased from Guillaume by Valentine Gallery (Valentine Dudensing), New York, before 1936; purchased from Dudensing by Solomon R. Guggenheim, 1936; Gift of Solomon R. Guggenheim, 1937.

CONDITION:

The work has received no treatment since its acquisition. There is some paint loss along the left margin which was inpainted before 1936, and a few small areas of loss elsewhere on the canvas.

The edges are worn and soiled from contact with the rabbet of a previous frame, and the support, which is thin and fragile, shows some tears and losses in the corners. The overall condition of the paint film is excellent. (Jan. 1971.)

The picture was painted during the summer of 1911 when Picasso and Braque were working in close collaboration at Céret in the Pyrenees. As has often been noted, their work during these months was strikingly similar. (See, for example, Braque's *Man with a Guitar,* The Museum of Modern Art, Golding, *Cubism,* 1968, pl. 37B, which is extremely close in vocabulary and style to the present painting.) During the years 1911-12 the two painters came closer to total abstraction than at any other time, and the images, though still containing elusive references to recognizable forms and objects, are increasingly difficult to decipher. Paintings such as *Glasses, Violin, and Fan* (Zervos, 2*, no. 263), *Man with a Pipe* (Zervos, 2*, repr. no. 280), *The Poet* (Zervos, 2*, no. 285), all painted in the summer of 1911, pose problems of legibility similar to those of the *Accordionist.* (For discussion of this particular development in Picasso's work see Rubin, *Picasso in the Collection of The Museum of Modern Art,* New York, 1972, pp. 68-70; R. Rosenblum, "Picasso," *Bulletin, Philadelphia Museum of Art,* vol. lxii, January-March 1967, pp. 175-178.) Daix places the present painting at the very end of the summer in Céret.

The identification of the subject of the present painting as Pierrot (Dudensing, letter to S. R. Guggenheim, November 1936; SRGM exhibition catalogues

1. A label formerly on the stretcher (transcription only preserved) reads "Dudensing Paul Guillaume." D. Cooper confirmed (in correspondence with the author, July 1971) that Guillaume purchased pictures of this sort from Picasso in the 1920's and sold them to Dudensing in the 1930's. Daix (in correspondence with the author, June 1972) concurred with this hypothesis.

212

of 1937 and 1938; *Art of Tomorrow*, 1939, no. 537; Barr, 1939) is unconvinc-
ing, since the figure wears no hat. Zervos (2*, no. 277) first identified the figure
as an accordionist, an identification that had been suggested as an alternative
by Barr in 1939 and was fully accepted by him by 1946. As Barr describes the
figure, he faces front, head slightly tilted to the right, his left arm clearly bent
at the elbow, his fingers and the keys of the instrument visible just below the
center, and the curled volutes of the armchair in which he is seated emerging
near the bottom of the canvas. In addition to the three keys, one can also
discern the folds of the instrument's concertina-like bellows.

EXHIBITIONS:

Philadelphia, SRGM 3-T, no. 187 *(Pierrot)*; Charleston, S.C., SRGM 4-T, no. 261 *(Pierrot)*;
New York, The Museum of Modern Art, *Picasso: Forty Years of His Art*, Nov. 15, 1939-
Jan. 7, 1940, traveled to The Art Institute of Chicago, Feb. 1-Mar. 30, 1940, p. 76 *(Pierrot
[Seated Man; Accordionist])*; The Art Gallery of Toronto, *Picasso*, Apr. 1949, no. 7 *(Pierrot)*;
New York, SRGM 78, 79 (checklists, *Accordionist*, the title by which the picture has sub-
sequently been known); 81, 83 (no cats.); 84, 87 (checklists); 89 (no cat.); Paris, Musée des
Arts Décoratifs, *Picasso*, June-Oct., 1955, no. 24, repr. (definitive ed. cat., no. 26); The Arts
Club of Chicago, *An Exhibition of Cubism on the Occasion of the Fortieth Anniversary of
The Arts Club of Chicago*, Oct. 3-Nov. 4, 1955, no. 15, repr.; New York, SRGM 97 (checklist); London, SRGM 104-T, no. 60; New York, SRGM 118 (checklist); 127 (no cat.); 129
(checklist); Philadelphia, SRGM 134-T, no. 128, repr.; New York, Saidenberg Gallery,
Picasso: An American Tribute, Apr. 24-May 15, 1962, no. 5, repr.; New York, SRGM 144,
151, 153 (checklists); 173, no. 22, repr. p. 30; 202, p. 29, repr. p. 28; 221 (no cat.); 232, pp.
365-366, repr. p. 367; 240 (no cat.); 241, pp. 365-366, repr. p. 367; 251, 260, 266, 276 (no cats.).

REFERENCES:

A. H. Barr, Jr., *Picasso: Forty Years of His Art*, New York, 1939, p. 76, no. 97, repr. *(Pierrot)*;
C. Zervos, *Pablo Picasso: oeuvres de 1906 à 1912*, vol. 2*, Paris, 1942, no. 277, pl. 135; A. H.
Barr, Jr., *Picasso: Fifty Years of His Art*, New York, 1946, p. 74, repr. p. 75 *(Accordionist)*;
M. Jardot, *Picasso*, exhibition catalogue, Paris, 1955, no. 26, repr.; J. Palau i Fabre, *Picasso en
Cataluña*, Barcelona, 1966, p. 162; P. Daix, *Picasso: le cubisme, 1907-1916, catalogue
raisonné*, Neuchâtel [in press], no. 377.

213 Landscape at Céret. Summer 1911.
(Paysage de Céret).

37.538

Oil on canvas, 25⅝ x 19¾ (65.1 x 50.3)

Signed l.l.: *Picasso*; inscribed by the artist on reverse (visible through lining): *Picasso / Ceret*. The signature on the face was added at a later date, probably in the 1930's (see above *Accordionist*).

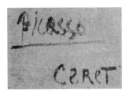

PROVENANCE:

Possibly purchased directly from the artist by Pierre Loeb or Pierre Colle, ca. 1930 (hypothesis suggested by D. Cooper in correspondence with the author, July 1971);[1] purchased from Loeb or Colle by Valentine Gallery (Valentine Dudensing), New York, before 1936; purchased from Dudensing by Solomon R. Guggenheim, November 1936; Gift of Solomon R. Guggenheim, 1937.

CONDITION:

In 1960 the picture was superficially cleaned, lined with wax resin, and placed on a new stretcher; it was surfaced with synthetic varnish and had apparently not been varnished previously.

The edges are worn and soiled from contact with previous frame and there is some retouching in these areas. In the upper left quarter of the painting there are five areas in which dark green is used in conjunction with black. These appear to have been applied by the artist some time after the original completion of the canvas. Apart from a few extremely small abrasions with paint loss, the condition is excellent. (Dec. 1971.)

Although Barr dated the picture 1914, a date accepted for some years by the Guggenheim (see below EXHIBITIONS, and *Art of Tomorrow,* 1939, no. 538), it undoubtedly belongs to the most abstract phase of the 1911 summer at Céret. Elliptical suggestions of curtained windows in the upper center, a flight of steps below, several archways on the left, and some roofs are the only clues to deciphering the landscape represented. Braque's *Rooftops at Céret* (Collection Ralph Colin, New York, R. Rosenblum, *Cubism and Twentieth-Century Art,* New York, 1960, fig. 31), with its somewhat clearer references to architectural forms, provides some further indications of the architectural sources for Picasso's much more shadowy rendering. Daix places the Picasso landscape early in the summer of 1911, before Braque's arrival at Céret in mid-August, implying thereby that Braque was strongly influenced by Picasso's already completed work when he painted the Colin picture.

EXHIBITIONS:

New York, Valentine Gallery, *Picasso,* Oct.-Nov. 1936, no. 33 or 35 (" *Paysage à Céret—1911*" or "*Paysage—1911;*" information that the picture appeared in this exhibition supplied by Cooper); Philadelphia, SRGM 3-T, no. 186 ("*Landscape Seret* [sic], 1914"); Charleston, S.C.,

1. The picture was not owned by Kahnweiler. It does not appear in the Rosenberg photographic archives in Paris, but these are incomplete. The picture must have remained in Picasso's hands until at least 1918, but in conversation with Daix, the artist gave the impression that he owned the picture for a good deal longer than this (information supplied by Daix, correspondence with the author, June 1972). Cooper's hypothesis is based upon the fact that Valentine Dudensing was buying pictures from both Loeb and Colle in the 1930's and that both bought Cubist works from Picasso in those years.

SRGM 4-T, no. 262 (as "*Landscape Seret, 1914*"); New York, The Museum of Modern Art, *Picasso: Forty Years of His Art,* Nov. 15, 1939-Jan. 7, 1940, traveled to The Art Institute of Chicago, Feb. 1-Mar. 30, 1940, p. 195 (dated 1914); New York, SRGM 78 (checklist; dated 1911; so dated in all subsequent SRGM publications); Toronto, SRGM 85-T, no. 64; Vancouver, SRGM 88-T, no. 68; New York, SRGM 89 (no cat.); Montreal, SRGM 93-T, no. 50; New York, SRGM 95 (checklist; withdrawn Sept. 12); London, SRGM 104-T, no. 61; Boston, SRGM 119-T, no. 48; New York, SRGM 129 (checklist); University of California at Los Angeles Art Galleries, *Years of Ferment: The Birth of Twentieth Century Art,* traveled to San Francisco Museum of Art, Mar. 28-May 16, 1965, Cleveland Museum of Art, July 13-Aug. 22, 1965, no. 51, repr. p. 48; Tel Aviv Museum, *Picasso,* Dec. 1965-May 18, 1966, no. 14, repr.; New York, SRGM 196 (no cat.); 202, p. 31, repr. p. 30; Columbus, Ohio, SRGM 207, p. 12, repr.; New York, SRGM 240 (no cat.); New York, Marlborough and Saidenberg Galleries, *Homage to Picasso,* Oct. 1971, no. 14, repr.; New York, SRGM 251, 266, 276 (no cats.).

REFERENCES:

A. H. Barr, Jr., *Picasso: Forty Years of His Art,* New York, 1939, p. 195 (dated 1914); C. Zervos, *Pablo Picasso: oeuvres de 1906 à 1912,* vol. 2*, Paris, 1942, no. 281, pl. 137 (dated "summer 1911"); A. H. Barr, Jr., *Picasso: Fifty Years of His Art,* New York, 1946, p. 283 (dated 1914); P. Daix, *Picasso: le cubisme, 1907-1916, catalogue raisonné,* Neuchâtel [in press], no. 365.

214 Bottles and Glasses. Winter 1911-1912.
(Bouteilles et Verres; Le Percolateur).

38.539

Oil on paper mounted on canvas,
25⅜ x 19½ (64.4 x 49.5)

Signed l.r.: *Picasso*; inscribed on stretcher,
not in the artist's hand: *Tableau signé en
1937*. Like *Accordionist*, Summer 1911, cat.
no. 212, the picture would not have been
signed when it was painted, and the style of
the signature corresponds with those of the
1930's. Zervos (2*, no. 299) refers to the fact
that the picture was signed in 1937.

PROVENANCE:

Gift of the artist to Max Pellequer, Paris,
some time between 1920 and 1937;[1] Galerie
Pierre (Pierre Loeb), Paris, 1937-38;[2] purchased from Loeb by Solomon R. Guggenheim, September 1938; Gift of Solomon R.
Guggenheim, 1938.

CONDITION:

The picture was at an unrecorded date
taped on all sides. It has not been cleaned.

There is a light soil and some discoloration
over the entire surface. The edges and
corners are worn and some repairs have
been made where the paper was torn. There
are minor abrasions, and occasional minor
cracking in the impasto areas resulting in
very small paint losses, but the overall condition is good. (Dec. 1971.)

The picture dates from Picasso's most hermetic period and is not easy to
decipher. Loeb called it *Le Percolateur* (bill of sale to Guggenheim), but it is
difficult to locate such an object. Two liqueur bottles appear at the top center
and left of the canvas, and a glass on the left side, near the center. On the right
is some kind of a poster or sign, possibly the name of a theater or shop. W.
Rubin's proposal (in conversation with the author, June 1972) that the second
line of lettering reads *"[f]er[m]eture an[nuelle],"* suggesting that it is indeed
a shop sign, is convincing. The first line remains hitherto undeciphered. Daix
suggests that the letters may derive from a newspaper; however, on the basis
of conversations with Picasso regarding a similar picture, he feels that the
letters were not intended to be deciphered (correspondence with the author,
September 1973. Picasso apparently said, *". . . je ne voulais pas qu'on puisse
lire les lettres. Il fallait que ce soit des lettres et rien d'autre"*).

Zervos' date of winter 1911-12 is convincing. The vocabulary and style place
the painting close to works such as *The Carafe* (Zervos, 2*, no. 286, dated by
him winter 1911-12), which is a modified version of the upper left quarter of
the present composition and probably just precedes it. The closeness in style
between these pictures and works such as The Museum of Modern Art *Still
Life: The Torero* (Zervos, 2*, repr. no. 266), painted at Céret in the summer
of 1911, and *"Ma Jolie"* of winter 1911-12 (W. Rubin, *Picasso in the Collection of The Museum of Modern Art*, New York, 1972, pp. 68-70) illustrates

---

1. Loeb apparently provided the information that the picture came from Pellequer, although
   no records currently exist to prove this point. Pellequer was Picasso's banker, and, starting
   in 1920, the artist apparently occasionally gave him paintings (information supplied by
   D. Cooper, correspondence with the author, July 1971). Since the signature dates from
   1937 (see above), it was probably at this time that Pellequer decided to sell the painting,
   asking Picasso to sign it before he did so.

2. It is not clear whether the transaction between Loeb and Pellequer was a sale or exchange.
   Cooper (July 1971) indicated that the 2 often exchanged pictures.

the continuity in Picasso's style from the summer of 1911 into the beginning of 1912 as well as the difficulty inherent in establishing a more detailed chronology for these months. (Zervos, 2*, no. 244, unconvincingly dates *"Ma Jolie"* spring 1911; Golding, pl. 14, dates it 1912.)

In the summer of 1911 Braque for the first time introduced stenciled letters into his composition *The Portuguese* (Kunstmuseum Basel, Golding, pl. 39), a technique that Picasso began to use only in the winter of 1911-12. (Daix has pointed out in correspondence with the author, June 1972, that the oft-stated notion that Braque first introduced lettering into his pictures as early as 1910 has not been documented. Picasso's *Torero* and *The Bottle of Rum* were probably the earliest examples of the use of letters as such.) Braque himself analyzed the importance of the new development: the letters were forms which could not be distorted because, being flat, they existed outside space and their presence in the painting, by contrast, enabled one to distinguish between objects situated in space and those outside it (D. Vallier, "Braque, la peinture

et nous," *Cahiers d'Art,* vol. xxix, no. 1, 1954, p. 16). The function and effect of this new element in the Cubist compositions of both Braque and Picasso have been widely discussed. (See especially C. Greenberg, "The Pasted Paper Revolution," *Art News,* vol. lvii, Sept. 1958, pp. 47 ff., reprinted in *Art and Culture,* Boston, 1961, pp. 72 ff.) In Braque's *The Portuguese* or Picasso's *"Ma Jolie"* the letters appear, as Greenberg says, to lie on top of the Cubist flatness, between the representation and the spectator. "Wherever this printing appears, it stops the eye at the literal plane, just as the artist's signature would" (1961, p. 73).

The lettering in the present painting (and to a lesser extent in some earlier ones) plays a slightly more complex role, for the letters are *not* stenciled and are not entirely outside the context of the painting. In the second line of printing, the end of the line is cut off by an apparently overlapping plane. Below are three illegible letters which bridge both planes. The larger letters above stand in an even more ambiguous relationship to the surrounding planes, as well as to the lines below. The *"G"* is partially hidden by the plane in which the *"A"* is embedded; the *"W,"* larger in scale than the other letters, seems suspended alongside, or perhaps slightly behind the *"A,"* but is cut off at the left by yet another plane. The interweaving of frontal letters with the composition itself thus creates the same kind of ambiguity of interrelationships that was to be fully explored in the collages of the coming months. In The Museum of Modern Art's *Still Life with Chair Caning* of no earlier than May 1912 "every part and plane of the picture keeps changing place in relative depth with every other part and plane; and it is as if the only stable relation left among the different parts of the picture is the ambivalent and ambiguous one that each has with the surface" (Greenberg, 1961, p. 76). Although it is extremely difficult to date with precision, the present picture with its painted rather than stenciled letters may precede the developments of the later winter. (I am indebted to Daix for having raised important questions regarding the dating of this work.)

EXHIBITIONS:

New York, SRGM 78 (checklist); 83 (no cat.); 84 (checklist); Vancouver, SRGM 88-T, no. 69, repr.; Boston, SRGM 90-T (no cat.); Montreal, SRGM 93-T, no. 51, repr.; New York, SRGM 95 (checklist; withdrawn Sept. 12); The Arts Club of Chicago, *An Exhibition of Cubism on the Occasion of the Fortieth Anniversary of The Arts Club of Chicago,* Oct. 3-Nov. 4, 1955, no. 16; The Newark Museum, *Abstract Art 1910 to Today,* Apr. 27-June 10, 1956, no. 57; The Art Gallery of Toronto, *Comparisons,* Jan. 11-Feb. 3, 1957, no. 14c; London, SRGM 104-T, no. 62; Boston, SRGM 119-T, no. 49; Lexington, Ky., SRGM 122-T, no. 23, repr.; New York, SRGM 129 (checklist); Dallas, Museum of Fine Arts, *The Arts of Man,* Oct. 6-Dec. 31, 1962 (not in cat.); Worcester, Mass., SRGM 148-T, no. 35, repr.; New York, SRGM 173, no. 23, repr.; 196 (checklist); 202, p. 46, repr.; 221 (no cat.); 232, p. 368, repr. p. 369; Or., Portland Art Museum, *Picasso for Portland,* Sept. 20-Oct. 25, 1970, no. 16, repr.; New York, SRGM 240 (no cat.); 241, p. 368, repr. p. 369; 251, 266, 276 (no cats.).

REFERENCES:

C. Zervos, *Pablo Picasso: oeuvres de 1906 à 1912,* vol. 2*, Paris, 1942, no. 299, pl. 145 (dated "winter 1911-12"); Golding, *Cubism,* 1968, p. 113, pl. 13A (dated "late 1911"); P. Daix, *Picasso: le cubisme, 1907-1916, catalogue raisonné,* Neuchâtel [in press], no. 402.

215   Glass and Pipe. 1918.
       (Verre et Pipe; Nature Morte; Pipe;
       Composition).

37·379

Oil with sand on canvas, 13¾ x 10⅝
(35 x 27)

Signed and dated u.r.: *Picasso / 18.*

PROVENANCE:

Galerie l'Effort Moderne (Léonce Rosenberg), Paris, by 1921 (*L'Esprit Nouveau,* no.
9, frontispiece *"Nature morte, Coll Léonce
Rosenberg;"*[1] a photograph of the work appears in the Rosenberg photographic archives, Paris); G. F. Reber, Lausanne,
probably mid-1920's-1936;[2] purchased from
Reber by Zwemmer Gallery (A. Zwemmer),
London, 1936 (information supplied by
Zwemmer, correspondence with the author,
1971); purchased from Zwemmer by
Solomon R. Guggenheim, September 1936;
Gift of Solomon R. Guggenheim, 1937.

CONDITION:

In 1953 the picture was superficially cleaned
without removal of the varnish, and the
strainer was replaced. An old ½ in. tear in
the upper left corner (approximately 2½ in.
from the left, 3¼ in. from the top) was repaired and the area inpainted.

There is extensive cracking in the paint film
of the white areas. Tiny hair cracks in the
black areas are probably drying cracks since
they were already visible in Rosenberg's
photograph, presumably of about 1920 (fig.
a, no. 014N-205). The latter also reveals that
there was originally a stronger differentia-
tion in value between the rectangle within
which the hexagon is placed and the framing areas surrounding it. Examination under
UV suggests that the artist applied a heavier
coat of varnish to the inner rectangle and
thus created a clear separation between the
2 areas. General discoloration of the varnish
has blurred this distinction. (Dec. 1971.)

fig. a.
Early photograph of *Glass and Pipe.*

1. I am indebted to D. Cooper for bringing this reference to my attention. The picture still
   belonged to Rosenberg in 1924 when it was reproduced in color in *La Peinture moderne.*
2. Cooper suggested (in correspondence with the author, July 1971) that Reber purchased the
   picture either from Léonce or Paul Rosenberg as early as 1920 or 1921. However, it is reproduced in Léonce Rosenberg's journal *Bulletin de l'Effort Moderne,* no. 8, Oct. 1924,
   without indication of collection, suggesting that at that time Rosenberg himself still owned
   it. Cooper said, however, that Reber started in the early 1920's exchanging Cézannes and
   Impressionist works for more modern pictures in the Rosenberg collection, so it would
   seem possible that the *Glass and Pipe* was one of the latter, and that Reber acquired it soon
   after 1924.

215

Although Léonce Rosenberg's earliest publication of the picture identified it only as a *Nature morte (L'Esprit Nouveau,* no. 9 [1921?]), he had by 1924 more precisely described it as *Verre et Pipe (Bulletin de l'Effort Moderne,* no 8). Guggenheim clearly accepted Zwemmer's designation of the work as a more abstract *Composition,* as have most subsequent publications (see below EX-HIBITIONS). Notable exceptions are Zervos, who called the picture *Pipe,* and Fry, who correctly identified it as *Still Life with Pipe and Glass.*

The particular compositional and textural concerns of the Guggenheim *Glass and Pipe* are the subject of a whole series of 1918 canvases (Zervos, 3, nos. 143-146, 120, 121, 138, 140; a further example in the Huber Collection, Glarus [Zervos, 6, no. 1408], dated there 1920, must surely also be of 1918). In all of these, a still-life is placed on an asymmetrical ground and seen against either a vertically divided background with one or two rectangular framing edges, or within a series of receding framing rectangles. In each one highly textured areas of oil mixed with sand are juxtaposed with smoother areas of pure paint, heavily varnished areas with unvarnished ones, striped areas with plain ones, and so on. The *trompe l'oeil* "frames" in these pictures and the variety of textural qualities used as if in imitation of collage are particularly characteristic of the 1918 series, although certain of the ingredients are to be found in both earlier and later works.

EXHIBITIONS:

Geneva, Galerie Moos, *La jeune peinture française: les cubistes,* Feb. 1920, no. 133 or no. 135 ("*Nature morte,* 1918");[3] Paris, Galerie Paul Rosenberg, *Picasso 1905-1921,* 1921 (no cat.);[4] London, Zwemmer Gallery, *Picasso,* May-June, 1936, no. 32 *(Composition)*; Phil-adelphia, SRGM 3-T, no. 130, repr. p. 44 *(Composition;* the title by which the picture has been known in all subsequent SRGM publications); Charleston, S.C., SRGM 4-T, no. 175, repr. p. 112; Savannah, Ga., SRGM 50-T (no cat.); New York, SRGM 79 (checklist); Toronto, SRGM 85-T, no. 66; New York, SRGM 87 (checklist); 89 (no cat.); Montreal, SRGM 93-T, no. 52; New York, SRGM 95 (checklist); London, SRGM 104-T, no. 63; New York, SRGM 132 (checklist); Jacksonville, Fla., Cummer Gallery of Art, *Spanish Art from the Middle Ages to the Present,* Oct. 26-Nov. 30, 1965 (no cat.); New York, SRGM 240, 266, 276 (no cats.).

REFERENCES:

L'Esprit Nouveau, no. 9 [1921?] color frontispiece *(Nature morte)*; A. Ozenfant and C.-E. Jeanneret, *La Peinture moderne,* Paris, 1924, repr. color unpag. section foll. p. 172 *(Nature Morte)*; *Bulletin de l'Effort Moderne,* no. 8, Oct. 1924, n.p. *(Verre et Pipe)*; C. Zervos, *Pablo Picasso: oeuvres de 1917 à 1919,* vol. 3, Paris, 1949, no. 161, pl. 60 *(Pipe)*; E. Fry, *Cubism,* New York and Toronto, 1966, fig. 51 *(Still Life wth Pipe and Glass).*

3. The exhibition consisted of works lent by Léonce Rosenberg, who wrote the catalogue in-troduction. Since the Guggenheim picture was entitled *Nature morte* when it was lent to the Paul Rosenberg exhibition the following year, it is possible that it was also included in the Geneva exhibition with this title. There is, however, no conclusive evidence to further substantiate the hypothesis.

4. In *L'Esprit Nouveau,* no. 9, the picture is published in connection with an article by M. Raynal on the Paul Rosenberg Picasso exhibition.

216 Mandolin and Guitar. 1924.
(Chambre à Juan-les-Pins; Nature morte devant la fenêtre; Guitares et Compotier).

53.1358

Oil with sand on canvas, 55⅜ x 78⅞ (140.6 x 200.4)

Signed and dated l.l.: *Picasso / 24.* The signature and date were added some time after 1927, since the picture is reproduced without signature in O. Schürer's 1927 monograph.

PROVENANCE:

Purchased from the artist by Paul Rosenberg, Paris, 1924;[1] purchased from Rosenberg by G. F. Reber by 1927 (Schürer [p. 67]); purchased from Reber by Jon Nicholas Streep, New York, 1953; purchased from Streep, 1953.

CONDITION:

Prior to its acquisition by the Museum, the canvas was lined with glue and the edges were taped with brown paper tape. In 1953 the painting was superficially cleaned, but the varnish was not removed. In 1957 the canvas was placed on a new stretcher. In 1960 cleavage between the 2 canvases (approximately 24 in. along lower right margin) was repaired with wax resin, and the corresponding area on the face lightly inpainted. There is evidence of considerable filling and inpainting along the top and bottom margins, probably dating from the lining and restretching of the canvas. Minor retouchings in 2 or 3 other areas probably date from the same time.

The overall condition of the paint film is excellent. (Jan. 1971.)

Picasso's earliest paintings on the theme of a still-life on a table in front of an open window date, as Jardot has stated, from the summer of 1919, when he spent his first summer on the Côte d'Azur (1955, nos. 48, 58, 60, 61, 62, 64). The theme recurs again and again during the subsequent summers, up to, but not beyond, 1925. Jardot has drawn attention to the fact that the majority of those painted in 1919 are small verticals, whereas the later ones are almost all horizontal and much larger. During the summers of 1924 and 1925, both of which were spent at Juan-les-Pins, Picasso produced at least nine large oils of this subject (Zervos, 5, nos. 224, 225, 252, 268 (vertical), 376, 377, 380, 445—all 38¼ x 51¼ in., 97 x 130 cm.—and no. 228—39¾ x 62¼ in., 101 x 158 cm.). The Guggenheim picture is considerably larger than any of the others. There are also at least eight watercolors and gouaches dating from these years, but none of them is specifically related to the present painting.

Léonce Rosenberg's 1925 publication of the picture carries the date "1925." This is improbable in view of the fact that Picasso would have been in Juan-les-Pins just at the time the magazine was going to press, and had the picture been painted that summer, rather than the previous one, it would not have been available to be photographed until some months later. Zervos' date of summer 1924, borne out by Picasso's own, is undoubtedly correct.

1. Information supplied by A. Rosenberg (correspondence with the author, Feb. 1973.) The picture was probably acquired soon after it was painted as part of the contract Rosenberg signed with the artist in 1918. It appears in the Paul Rosenberg photo archives among the works of 1924 and with the title *Chambre à Juan-les-Pins.*

EXHIBITIONS:

Paris, Galerie Paul Rosenberg, *Exposition d'oeuvres récentes de Picasso,* June-July 1926, no. 29? (*"Nature morte à la mandoline* 1924");[2] Paris, Galerie Georges Petit, *Exposition Picasso,* June 16-July 30, 1932, p. 53, repr. p. 156 *(Nature morte devant la fenêtre);* Kunsthaus Zürich, *Picasso,* Sept. 11-Oct. 30, 1932, no. 149; New York, SRGM 79 (checklist); 81, 83 (no cats.); 84, 87 (checklists); 89 (no cat.); Paris, Musée des Arts Décoratifs, *Picasso,* June 3-Oct. 14, 1955, no. 57 (definitive ed., cat. no. 61), repr.; New York, SRGM 97 (checklist); London, SRGM 104-T, no. 64, pl. 7; New York, SRGM 118, 129, 132 (checklists); Philadelphia, SRGM 134-T; New York, Paul Rosenberg & Co., *Picasso, An American Tribute,* Apr. 25-May 12, 1962, no. 35, repr.; New York, SRGM 144 (checklist); Worcester, Mass., SRGM 148-T; New York, SRGM 151, 153 (checklists); 160 (no cat.); 173, no. 55, repr. p. 53; Paris, Grand Palais, *Hommage à Pablo Picasso,* Nov. 18, 1966-Feb. 13, 1967, no. 133, repr.; Amsterdam, Stedelijk Museum, *Picasso,* Mar. 4-Apr. 30, 1967, no. 62, repr.; New York, SRGM 196 (checklist); 198-T, 216, 227 (no cats.); 232, p. 375, repr. color p. 374; 240 (no cat.); 241, p. 375, repr. color p. 374; New York, Marlborough and Saidenberg Galleries, *Homage to Picasso,* Oct. 1971, no. 37, repr. color; Cleveland, SRGM 258-T, pl. 20; New York, SRGM 276 (no cat.).

REFERENCES:

Bulletin de l'Effort Moderne, July 1925, n.p. (dated 1925); O. Schürer, *Picasso,* Berlin and Leipzig, 1927, repr. [p. 67]; C. Zervos, *Pablo Picasso: oeuvres de 1923 à 1925,* vol. 5, Paris, 1952, no. 220, pl. 107; M. Jardot, *Picasso,* exhibition catalogue (definitive ed.), Paris, 1955, no. 61, repr.

2. This entry cannot with certainty be associated with the present picture, but its appearance in the exhibition is plausible. Reber might have seen and purchased it on that occasion.

Hilla Rebay

Born May 1890, Strasbourg, Alsace.
Died September 1967, Greens Farms, Connecticut.

217 Composition. ca. 1915.
(Komposition 1).

71.380

Oil on canvas, 52 x 39¼ (131.9 x 99.8)

Signed l.r.: *v Rebay*; on stretcher: *Hillav. Rebay / 1915.*

PROVENANCE:

Hilla Rebay, Strasbourg, Alsace, and Greens Farms, Connecticut-1967; Estate of Hilla Rebay, 1967-71; acquired from the Estate of Hilla Rebay, 1971.

CONDITION:

At an unknown date the picture was lined with wax resin. Some minor touches of repaint may date from this time.

The edges and corners are worn and chipped with scattered losses of paint and ground. There are scattered drying cracks and some more serious pigment cracks, as well as some scattered abrasions. The canvas is separating from the lining in several places. The condition in general is fair. (July 1974.)

The chronology of Rebay's early development is difficult to establish. Few dated paintings from before 1920 survive and those, almost always dated on the stretchers, may have been inscribed at a much later time when the artist no longer remembered the exact date of execution. The ca. 1915 date of the present work is thus tentative.

EXHIBITIONS:

Berlin, Der Sturm, *Hugo Händel, Hilla von Rebay,* opened Apr. 6, 1919, no. 19 *(Komposition 1)*;[1] Grenoble, Musée de Peinture et de Sculpture, *Hilla Rebay,* 1948 (no cat.);[2] New York, SRGM 67, no. 49 *(Composition,* not dated); 74, no. 180 ("Composition 1915").

1. A Der Sturm label on the reverse corroborates the information contained in the exhibition catalogue.
2. The museum in Grenoble has been unable to locate records of this exhibition. However, the Registrar's files at the SRGM indicate the picture was sent to such an exhibition.

---

218   Animato.   1941-1942.

49.1315

Oil on canvas, 37 x 50 (94.0 x 127.0)

Signed l.r.: *Rebay*; inscribed by the artist on reverse: *Rebay / 1941-42 Animato.*

PROVENANCE:

Hilla Rebay, Greens Farms, Connecticut-

1949; acquired by bequest under the will of Solomon R. Guggenheim, 1949.

CONDITION:

The central black area has been repaired and inpainted, probably by the artist.

There are a few scattered drying cracks and abrasions, but the condition is otherwise very good. (July 1974.)

EXHIBITIONS:

New York, SRGM 30 (no cat.); Fort Worth, Tex., SRGM 42-T, no. 2; New York, SRGM 202, p. 129.

REFERENCE:

"American Non-Objective Painting Reviewed," *Art Digest,* vol. 16, Aug. 1, 1942, p. 12, repr.

219   Yellow Lines. ca. 1942-1943.
(Vibration).

71.1936R M189

Oil on canvas, 50 x 39 (126.8 x 99.1)

Signed l.r.: *Rebay*; inscribed by the artist on reverse: *Hilla Rebay / Yellow Lines / 1942*; on stretcher: *To: Maresia* [1] *Hilla Rebay*.

PROVENANCE:

Hilla Rebay, Greens Farms, Connecticut-1967; Estate of Hilla Rebay, 1967-71; acquired from the Estate of Hilla Rebay, 1971.

CONDITION:

The painting has received no treatment.
The condition is very good. (July 1974.)

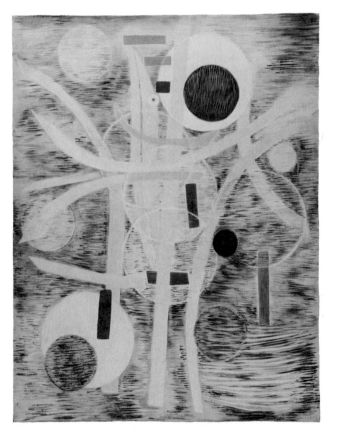

EXHIBITIONS:

New York, SRGM 36, no. 71 (*"Vibration,* 1943"); 64 (no cat.; *"Yellow Lines,* 1942"); Munich, Art Group Zen, untitled exhibition, opened Mar. 15, 1950 (no cat.);[2] 73, no. 72 *(Vibration)*; 74, no. 187 (*"Yellow Lines,* 1943").

REFERENCES:

M. Lowengrund, "Non-Objective Anniversary Exhibition," *Art Digest,* vol. 23, Aug. 1, 1949, p. 11; *Art of Tomorrow: Bauer / Kandinsky / Rebay. Exhibition of Non-Objective Painting,* Lakeland, Fla., Florida Southern College, exhibition catalogue, 1955, repr. n.p.

1. Maresia von Rebay is the artist's German niece.
2. Museum records indicate that the works were returned from Munich in May 1951.

220   Crosses. 1944.

71.1936R M267

Oil on canvas, 59 x 79 (149.7 x 203.0)

Signed l.r.: *Rebay*; inscribed by the artist on stretcher: *Hilla Rebay Crosses*. Not dated.

PROVENANCE:

Hilla Rebay, Greens Farms, Connecticut-1967; Estate of Hilla Rebay, 1967-71; acquired from the Estate of Hilla Rebay, 1971.

CONDITION:

Many of the blue areas were apparently reworked by the artist.

There are scattered minor drying cracks, some abrasions, and losses. The condition in general is good. (July 1974.)

EXHIBITIONS:

New York, SRGM 39, no. 110 ("*Crosses, 1944*"); Scranton, Pa., SRGM 45-T, no. 32; Zurich, SRGM 60-T, no. 29, repr. ("*Crosses, 1944*").

REFERENCES:

Art Digest, vol. 18, July 1, 1944, repr. p. 21 (advertisement for SRGM 39); F. Roh, "Bemerkungen zu Compositionen von Hilla von Rebay," *Die Kunst und das Schöne Heim,* vol. 2, Nov. 1960, repr. p. 49, fig. 6.

Henri Rousseau

Born May 1844, Laval, France.
Died September 1910, Paris.

221   Artillerymen. c. 1893-1895.
       (*Les Artilleurs*).

38.711

Oil on canvas, 31⅛ x 39 (79.1 x 98.9)

Signed l.r.: *H. Rousseau*. Not dated.

PROVENANCE:

Benoit Bénoni-Auran, Paris?;[1] Georges-
Edouard Dorival, Paris?;[2] Maurice Renou,
Paris, before 1926;[3] purchased from Renou
by Galerie van Leer, Paris, by 1926;[4] purchased from van Leer by M. Knoedler &
Co., Inc., New York, July 1929;[5] purchased
from Knoedler by Roland Balaÿ, Paris,
December 1937; purchased from Balaÿ et
Carré, Paris, by Solomon R. Guggenheim,
1938; Gift of Solomon R. Guggenheim,
1938.

CONDITION:

Prior to its acquisition by the Museum, the
painting was lined; the edges were cut on all
4 sides, built up with plaster, and taped. The
painting was cleaned in 1953, but owing to
the thinness of the paint film, the varnish
was treated rather than fully removed.

Inpainting is visible along all 4 edges extending approximately ¼ in. to ¾ in. from
the tape. Some cracking and paint loss along
these edges has also occurred.

The overall condition is good and the paint
loss insignificant. (June 1971.)

The picture has been variously dated between 1893 and 1895. Vallier (1969)
dates it ca. 1893, citing the purity of composition, the treatment of color, and
the aerial perspective as evidence for a date closer to 1893 than to 1895. The
date ca. 1895 has been given, without comment, by Rich; Uhde (who does not
mention the picture in his monographs of 1911, 1914, and 1923, suggesting
that he did not discover the work until later); J. J. Sweeney (SRGM *Handbook*,
1959); Bouret; Shattuck.

Relatively few of Rousseau's works are dated. Only eight of the ninety
paintings ascribed in Vallier's oeuvre catalogue to the decade 1890-1900 actually bear a date. Six more can be dated on the basis of their appearance in
exhibitions of the *Salon des Indépendants* during those years. Within the general outline provided by these dated works many problems still remain unsolved, and until further evidence emerges, therefore, an approximate date of
ca. 1893-95 seems most acceptable.

1. Verbal information obtained by H. Certigny, Paris, from a friend and contemporary of
   Bénoni-Auran named Lavergne (correspondence with the author, Jan. 1970). Bénoni-Auran
   was a painter who lived in Montparnasse, and who, according to Certigny, owned at least
   1 other painting by Rousseau (*Harvest at the Château*, Musée de Laval).
2. Verbal information obtained by Certigny from F. Fels (correspondence with the author,
   Dec. 1971). Dorival (1871-1939) was an actor of some repute at the Comédie Française and
   is known to have had an art collection.
3. Information supplied in part by Knoedler (correspondence with the author, Mar. 1971), in
   part by A. D. Mouradien, who was a partner of van Leer at the time and confirmed that he
   and van Leer had purchased the picture in the mid-1920's (conversation with the author,
   Paris, Nov. 1972).
4. The painting is reproduced in *Der Querschnitt*, vi Jg., Heft 9, Sept. 1926, foll. p. 688, with
   the caption "Galerie van Leer, Paris."
5. This and the following details of provenance were supplied by Knoedler (Mar. 1971).

Rich first suggested that the formal group arrangement of the artillerymen with their cannon was probably derived from a photograph. Comparison of the picture with group photographs of the late nineteenth century certainly supports this notion. Although Rich's hypothesis has been widely accepted, no actual photograph has so far come to light.

Rousseau's own military experience was with the infantry rather than the artillery; he served from 1863-70 as a private in the fifty-first regiment (H. Certigny, *La Vérité sur le Douanier Rousseau*, Paris, 1961, pp. 59 ff. Certigny has scrupulously traced every piece of documentary information about all aspects of Rousseau's military service and established, among other things, that he did not, as is generally stated, travel to Mexico in 1862 with Emperor Maximilian's army). The artist's only known connection with the artillery was through his friendship with an artillery officer, Frumence Biche, of whom he painted two portraits (Certigny, *Le Douanier Rousseau et Frumence Biche*, Paris, 1973, where a complete study of the life of Biche, his friendship with Rousseau, and the discovery of the two portraits in the collection of Biche's daughter is to be found).

The first of these portraits, executed about 1891, shows Biche in civilian dress, and Certigny argues convincingly that it might have been a wedding present. Biche was married to Rousseau's friend, Marie Foucher, on March 3, 1891. A daughter, Cécile, was born to them December 31, 1891; and on May 10, 1892, Biche died suddenly at the early age of thirty-seven. Rousseau's second painting of his friend was a full-length military portrait dated 1893 and exhibited at the *Salon des Indépendants* that year (now Collection Joachim J. Aberbach, Sands Point, Long Island). Certigny has suggested that this work was painted from a photograph and was clearly intended as a memorial. It was not for sale at the *Salon,* and it remained in the collection of Biche's family until its discovery by Certigny.

It seems possible that the present picture is also a memorial tribute to Biche's military career. The photograph from which Rousseau derived his composition might have been given to the artist by the widow together with the more formal individual photograph which must have been the basis for the 1893 portrait. Although it is known that Biche was a sergeant in the thirty-fifth artillery regiment, the military records do not specify which battery he commanded. The inscription "*4ème Batterie 3ème Pièce,*" so clearly legible on the cannon in the present picture, does not, therefore, provide any substantiating evidence of a connection with Biche. Indeed, there is no record of who commanded this battery. Biche did, it should be noted, also serve some time as an instructor teaching military exercises, and it is possible that the photograph and the painting date from this phase of his career.

One further fact should be taken into account: Frumence Biche was, for a man of this period, unusually tall—1.82 m. (almost 6 feet). M. Chamla, in a statistical study of the stature of French soldiers, has shown that the height of Frenchmen in the Paris area in 1890 was 1.48 m. minimum to 1.81 maximum ("L'accroissement de la stature en France 1880-1960," *Bulletins et mémoires de la Societé d'Anthropologie de Paris,* vol. vi, April-June, 1964, p. 266 [Seine], Tableau A). This fact might identify Biche as the prominently placed figure in white on the far right of the *Artillerymen.* Comparison of this man's features with those of Biche suggests that the figure may well represent Biche but until further evidence is found, the identification of this soldier in the Guggenheim picture must remain conjectural.

EXHIBITIONS:

Dusseldorf, Galerie Flechtheim, *Degas, Henri Rousseau, Nauen, usw.,* winter, 1926?;[6] Berlin, Galerie Thannhauser, *Erste Sonderausstellung in Berlin,* Jan. 9-Feb. 14, 1927, no. 229; London, Arthur Tooth & Sons, Ltd., *Les Maîtres populaires de la réalité,* Feb. 17-Mar. 12, 1938, no. 3; The Art Institute of Chicago, *Henri Rousseau,* Jan. 22-Feb. 23, 1942, traveled to New York, The Museum of Modern Art, Mar. 18-May 3, 1942, repr. p. 29; New York, SRGM 79 (checklist; withdrawn Oct. 20); 81, 83 (no cats.); 84, 87 (checklists); Boston, SRGM 90-T (no cat.); Montreal, SRGM 93-T, no. 53; New York, SRGM 95, 97 (checklists); London, SRGM 104-T, no. 67; New York, SRGM 112, 118, 129, 144 (checklists); New York, Wildenstein & Co., Inc., *Henri Rousseau,* Apr. 17-May 25, 1963, no. 9, repr.; Rotterdam, Museum Boymans-van Beuningen, *De Lusthof der Naïeven,* July 10-Sept. 6, 1964, traveled to Paris, Musée National d'Art Moderne, *Le Monde des naifs,* Oct. 14-Dec. 6, 1964, no. 4, repr.; New York, SRGM 160 (no cat.); 173, no. 5, repr. color; New York, Paul Rosenberg & Co., *Seven Decades 1895-1965: Crosscurrents in Modern Art,* Apr. 26-May 21, 1966, no. 43, repr.; New York, SRGM 202, p. 48, repr. color; 205, *Rousseau, Redon and Fantasy* (checklist); 216, 221 (no cats.); 232, 241, pp. 385-386, repr. p. 384; 251 (no cat.); Amsterdam, Stedelijk Museum, *De grote Naïeven,* Aug. 23-Oct. 20, 1974, no. 4, repr.

REFERENCES:

D. C. Rich, *Henri Rousseau,* exhibition catalogue, New York, 1942, revised ed., 1946, p. 29, repr.; W. Uhde, *Rousseau,* Bern, 1948, repr. p. 17; SRGM *Handbook,* 1959, p. 154, repr.; J. Bouret, *Henri Rousseau,* Neuchâtel and New York, 1961, pp. 50, 254, no. 86, repr. p. 190; D. Vallier, *Henri Rousseau,* Cologne and Paris, 1961, New York, 1962, repr. color p. 51; G. Artieri and D. Vallier, *L'Opera completa di Rousseau il Doganieri,* Milan, 1969, no. 65, color pl. XIV; R. Shattuck, *The Banquet Years: The Origins of the Avant-Garde in France, 1885 to World War I,* N.Y., 1958, revised ed., London, 1969, pp. 104, 362 no. 21a.

6. In the issue of *Der Querschnitt* cited above, there is an advertisement for the Galerie Flechtheim exhibition which is separated by 50 pages from the reproduction of the *Artillerymen.* However, since there is no reference to Rousseau in the entire issue except for this advertisement, it seems likely that the reproduction is to be directly associated with the forthcoming exhibition, for which no catalogue has been located.

222 The Football Players. 1908.
(Les Joueurs de football).

60.1583

Oil on canvas, 39½ x 31⅝ (100.5 x 80.3)

Signed and dated l.r.: *Henri Rousseau / 1908.*

PROVENANCE:

Justin K. Thannhauser, Munich, 1912-17;[1] purchased from Thannhauser through Wilhelm Uhde by Edwin Suermondt (d. 1923), Burg Drove, Die Eifel, Germany, 1917;[2] Mrs. Edwin Suermondt, 1923-26;[3] Galerie Flechtheim, Berlin and Dusseldorf, 1926 (?)-28;[3] purchased from Flechtheim by Paul Rosenberg, Paris, 1928;[4] purchased from Rosenberg by Mrs. Henry D. Sharpe, Providence, Rhode Island, May 1943;[4] purchased at Sotheby and Co., London (*Paintings, Drawings and Sculpture by Modern and* *Impressionist Masters,* lot 70, November 23, 1960).

CONDITION:

The painting was lined prior to its acquisition by the Guggenheim, and cleavage between the original canvas and the lining has since occurred. 2 repairs, one on the left of the figure tossing the ball, the other in the sky and trees right of center, were also made prior to the painting's acquisition. A puncture in the left sky (approximately 1 in. by ⅝ in.) was repaired in 1967.

The varnish, which has not been removed, is considerably discolored. The overall condition is good, although extensive cracks in the paint film exist, notably in the sky and in the lower right-hand portion of the canvas. (June 1971.)

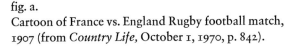

fig. a.
Cartoon of France vs. England Rugby football match, 1907 (from *Country Life,* October 1, 1970, p. 842).

1. Thannhauser (in conversation with D. C. Rich, New York, June 1971) stated that he bought the picture in 1912 from B. Weill. In 1917, on the occasion of his marriage, he needed money and was forced to sell it. Uhde arranged the sale to Suermondt for him. See also Uhde, *Henri Rousseau,* Dusseldorf, 1914 [pl. 15], where the picture is reproduced as "coll. Thannhauser."

2. W. Uhde, *Henri Rousseau,* Dresden and Berlin, 1923, repr. [p. 42] "Samml. Suermondt."

3. After Suermondt's death his widow presumably inherited the collection, and she is listed as one of the lenders to the Mar. 1926 exhibition at Galerie Flechtheim in which this picture appeared. However, in A. Basler's 1927 article on Rousseau (*The Arts,* vol. 11, Jan.-June 1927, p. 315), the picture is reproduced "Courtesy of the Galerie Flechtheim, Berlin and Düsseldorf." Suermondt's widow married A. Vömel, Co-Director of the Galerie Flechtheim, in 1926, and it is difficult to know exactly when the picture passed from her personal collection into the possession of the gallery.

4. Information supplied by A. Rosenberg, New York (in conversation with the author, Feb. 1973). Mrs. Henry Sharpe (in correspondence with the author, Aug. 1971) specified that she purchased it from Rosenberg in May 1943. Uhde erroneously recorded in the 1948 edition of his monograph that the picture had passed into the collection of Mrs. Murray Danforth.

The question of whether Rousseau's four athletes are engaged in a game of Rugby football, of Soccer (Football Association, as it was commonly called in France at this time), or possibly even just a game of handball has been the subject of some dispute in the literature on Rousseau. In fact the evidence clearly identifies the sport as Rugby. Not only is the ball an oval one, but the players are most explicitly using their hands, something which only the goalie is permitted to do in Soccer.

Whether Rousseau was inspired by any specific event (such as England's first Rugby match against France held in Paris in the spring of 1908), or whether he was responding more generally to the enormous rise in popularity of this sport in the early part of this century in France is not clear. His conception of the players is not far removed from that of a newspaper cartoonist of January 1907 who was recording his impressions of the previous year's match between France and England played at Richmond (fig. a; I am indebted to U. A. Titley for per-

mission to reprint this cartoon which he published in *Country Life,* October 1970, p. 842. Titley also provided me with the dates of various international Rugby events of the years 1908-13).

Gleizes' *Football Players* of 1912-13, and Robert Delaunay's *Cardiff Team* of 1913, where once again the ball is oval and the hands are being used, are equally clearly identifiable as depictions of Rugby games, although here again the identification with Soccer has commonly been made. In the case of the Gleizes it is possible that the 1912 match of England and Ireland against France was the inspiration; in the Delaunay it was certainly the 1913 match between Wales and France held in Paris. (A newspaper photograph of this event, published by Vriesen and Imdahl [1969, Documents, p. 108], although erroneously identified in the caption as of a Soccer game, definitely records the 1913 Rugby match cited above. The newspaper clipping belonged to Delaunay and clearly served as the basis for his painting.)

What is more important than the specific identification of the events which served to inspire these three paintings is the reflection in each of them of the general popularity of Rugby during the early years of the century. More significant still is the fact that sport as such, and Rugby in particular, was felt by these and other artists to be a suitable subject for major works of art. (For a fuller discussion of the comparative popularity of Rugby and Soccer see E. Weber, "Gymnastics and Sports in Fin de Siècle France," *American Historical Review,* vol. 76, February 1971, pp. 82-90; on the subject of sport in the art and literature of this period see Pär Bergman, *"Modernolatria" et "Simultaneita,"* Studia Litterarum Upsaliensia, II, ed. Gunnar Tideström, Uppsala, 1962.)

Rousseau's depiction of the scene, which has been aptly described by Rich as more reminiscent of a ballet than a game of football, is perhaps the quintessential illustration of G. de Saint-Clair's claim that "when played by young, well-bred men, Rugby football is not dangerous" (*Football [Rugby],* Paris, 1894, p. 20).

EXHIBITIONS:

Paris, *Salon des Indépendants,* Mar. 20-May 2, 1908, no. 5261;[5] Berlin, Galerie Flechtheim, *Ausstellung Henri Rousseau,* Mar. 1926, no. 11, repr. p. 12; Dusseldorf, *Grosse Ausstellung für Gesundheitspflege, Kunst und Sport,* May 8-Oct. 1926, no. 679, repr. p. 8 *(Ballspieler);* Paris, Galerie Paul Rosenberg, *Exposition Henri Rousseau,* Mar. 3-31, 1937, no. 12; London, Arthur Tooth & Sons, Ltd., *Les Maîtres populaires de la réalité,* Feb. 17-Mar. 12, 1938, no. 2; The Art Institute of Chicago, *Henri Rousseau,* Jan. 22-Feb. 23, 1942, traveled to New York, The Museum of Modern Art, Mar. 18-May 3, 1942, repr. p. 51; Boston, The Institute of Modern Art, *An Exhibition of Paintings by Henri Rousseau,* Oct.-Nov. 15, 1942, no. 2; New York, Wildenstein & Co., Inc., *A Loan Exhibition of Six Masters of Post Impressionism,* Apr. 8-May 8, 1948, no. 41, repr. p. 54; Venice, *XXV Biennale di Venezia,* Salle Rousseau, 1950, no. 15;[6] New York, Sidney Janis Gallery, *Henri Rousseau,* Nov. 5-Dec. 22, 1951, no. 17, repr.; New York, Paul Rosenberg & Co., *Masterpieces Recalled,* Feb. 6-Mar. 2, 1957, no. 28, repr. p. 30; Knokke-Le-Zoute, Belgium, Casino Communal, *Les Peintres naïfs du douanier Rousseau à nos jours,* June 29-Aug. 31, 1958, p. 15, no. 2, repr. p. 7; New York, SRGM exhibition 129 (checklist); Philadelphia, SRGM 134-T, no. 135, repr.; 144 (checklist); New York, Wildenstein & Co., Inc., *Henri Rousseau,* Apr. 17-May 25, 1963, no. 49, repr.; New York, SRGM 160 (no cat.); Rotterdam, Museum Boymans-van Beuningen, *De Lusthof der Naïeven,* July 10-

Sept. 6, 1964, traveled to Paris, Musée National d'Art Moderne, *Le Monde des naïfs,* Oct. 14-Dec. 16, 1964, no. 22, repr.; New York, SRGM 173, no. 13, repr. color; 205 *Rousseau, Redon and Fantasy* (checklist; commentary, repr. color, n.p.); 216, 221 (no cats.); 232, 241, pp. 387-388, repr. color p. 389; 251, 260 (no cats.); Amsterdam, Stedelijk Museum, *De grote Naïeven,* Aug. 23-Oct. 20, 1974, no. 11, repr.

REFERENCES:

[L. Vauxcelles], "Le Douanier persécuté," *Gil Blas,* Mar. 22, 1908; W. Uhde, *Henri Rousseau,* Paris, 1911, p. 65; D. C. Rich, *Henri Rousseau,* exhibition catalogue, New York, 1942, p. 50, repr. p. 51; W. Uhde, *Rousseau,* Bern, 1948, p. 16, pl. 47 ("coll. Mrs. M. S. Danforth"); A. Werner, *Henri Rousseau,* New York, 1957, pl. 25; R. Shattuck, *The Banquet Years,* N.Y., 1958, revised ed., London, 1969, pp. 94, 96, 103n, 107, 110, 363 no. 45, pl. XIII; J. Bouret, *Henri Rousseau,* New York, 1961, no. 37, p. 251, repr. p. 133; H. Certigny, *La Vérité sur le Douanier Rousseau,* Paris, 1961, p. 315; D. Vallier, *Henri Rousseau,* Cologne and Paris, 1961, New York, 1962, repr. color p. 111.

5. The picture did not appear, as is stated in SRGM *Handbook,* 1970, p. 387, in the 29th *Salon des Indépendents,* Apr.-June 1911.

6. The picture did not appear, as is stated in SRGM *Handbook,* 1970, p. 387, in the *XXVII Biennale di Venezia* of 1954.

Egon Schiele

Born June 1890, Tulln, Austria.
Died October 1918, Vienna.

223   Portrait of Johann Harms. 1916.

69.1884

Oil with wax on canvas, sight dimensions:
54½ x 42½ (138.3 x 108)

Signed and dated l.r.: *Egon / Schiele / 1916*.[1]

PROVENANCE:

Acquired from the artist by Karl Grünwald, Vienna, by 1918;[2] purchased from Grünwald by Otto Kallir (-Nirenstein), Vienna, 1921 (information supplied by Kallir, in correspondence, May 1975); acquired from

Dr. and Mrs. Otto Kallir, New York, by purchase and partial gift, 1969.

CONDITION:

The work has received no treatment since its acquisition.

There is a ¼ in. repair 11½ in. from top and 5 in. from left. The presence of wax in the medium gives the colors their matte appearance. There are a few scattered minor cracks in the paint and ground layers, but without signs of incipient cleavage. The condition is excellent. (May 1974.)

Johann Harms was born December 23, 1843, in Rullsdorf, Hanover. He became a well-to-do master locksmith in Vienna, and in 1884 he married Josefine Bürzner (1850-1939). They had three children: Adolf (d. 1938); Adele (d. 1968); Edith (1893-1918). The family Harms lived at 114 Hietzinger Hauptstrasse in Vienna, directly opposite Schiele's studio, which was at no. 101. In spite of opposition from her parents, who did not want their daughter to become the wife of a mere artist, Edith married Schiele on June 17, 1915. Subsequently Schiele appears to have developed a good relationship with his father-in-law, who sat for this portrait and its various preparatory drawings. The old man died on January 5, 1917, just nine months after the completion of the painting. A few days later Schiele, in reporting the death to his brother-in-law Anton Peschka, made a brief reference to the improved relations between the two men: *"Ich hatte ihn sehr gerne."* A. Roessler, 1921, p. 116. ("I liked him very much.")

Schiele was drafted into the Austrian army in June 1915, and remained on active duty until January 1917. As his war diaries make clear, however, he spent most of his time in the immediate vicinity of Vienna in Liesing, Atzgersdorf, Mauer, and Mödling, and was able to spend his weekends and many of his afternoons and evenings with his wife "Did." at home. (See Comini, 1966, pp. 86-102; the diaries are preserved in the Egon Schiele Archiv, Albertina, Vienna.) It was during these off-duty visits to his own home that he apparently worked on the portrait of his father-in-law, to which there are three references in the diaries. The first is dated April 17, 1916: *"ich kam um 11h nach Liesing, —Wachabteilen war schon um ½2h ich hatte keinen Dienst.—nachmittags war ich bei Did.—das Wetter war etwas besser.—ich zeichnete klein und gross auf Leinwand meinen Schwiegervater."* ("I arrived at Liesing at 11 a.m.,—Guard assignments were already at 1:30 p.m. I had no duty.—I spent the afternoon

1. The format of this signature, in which the name and date are ornamentally inscribed within a frame, was intermittently used by Schiele between 1913 and 1918 (Kallir, 1966, p. 505).
2. When Roessler published the picture in 1918, he listed it as *"Privatbesitz."* The art dealer Grünwald, who was a friend of Schiele's and whose portrait had been painted by the artist in 1917, must have owned it by this time, but it has not been possible to verify the exact date of acquisition.

fig. a.
Schiele, study for *Portrait of Johann Harms,* charcoal on paper, Collection James Kirkman, London.

fig. b.
Schiele, study for *Portrait of Johann Harms,* pencil and gouache on paper, 18½ x 12¼ in., 47 x 31 cm., Private Collection.

with Did.—the weather was somewhat better.—I drew on canvas the details and overall conception of my father-in-law.") The meaning of this last sentence is unclear. Leopold's translator, A. Lieven, has suggested that it should read: "I drew my father-in-law in outline and detail" (Leopold, p. 593). Another possible reading, which would require inserting a comma after *"klein,"* would be: "I made a small drawing (or small drawings?) and then a large one on canvas of my father-in-law." The interpretation of the sentence has thus considerable bearing on Schiele's method of composition and on the relationship between the drawing and painting phases.

On April 22 he continues: *"ich bekam für Ostersonntag dienstfrei. um 1/2 10h war ich bei Did.—ich malte an dem Porträt meines Schwiegervaters.—"* ("I was off-duty for Easter Sunday. At 9:30 a.m. I was with Did.—I worked on the painting of my father-in-law.") On April 24 he mentions the portrait for the last time: *"ich fuhr nach Liesing bei einem elenden Regenwetter.—ich hatte keinen Dienst, folglich war ich schnellstens wieder bei Did.—ich malte an dem Porträt meines Schwiegervaters den dunklen Grund."* ("I drove to Liesing in the rain.—I was not on duty, so as quickly as possible I was back with Did.—I painted the dark background of the portrait of my father-in-law.")

These three letters (April 17, April 22, April 24) are the only known references to Schiele's progress on the picture. Whether they indicate that he actually completed the work between April 17 and April 24 cannot be said with certainty, but seems probable. Close examination of the background reveals that the dark gray paint is applied over a considerably lighter greenish gray, and that the darker gray was in part at least applied after the completion of the

fig. c.
Schiele, study for *Portrait of Johann Harms,* pencil
on paper, Graphische Sammlung, Albertina, Vienna.

figure. It is possible, therefore, that Schiele's decision to place the figure against
a very dark background came after the figure was essentially complete, and that
the diary entry for April 24 thus represents the final stage of his work on the
picture. The fact that his entry for April 17 refers to drawing rather than painting would indicate that he was at that date still involved with preliminaries,
and it is possible, therefore, that the entire portrait was indeed completed
within that one week.

Seven drawings of Johann Harms have so far come to light. Two of these
(Leopold, no. 270, studies 2 and 6) have not been published and were unavail-
able for study; they are therefore excluded from discussion. Of the remaining
five, three are fully developed finished drawings of a man seated firmly up-
right, formally attired with wing collar, tie, vest, and coat (figs. a-c). In the first,
a bust-length charcoal study, the figure faces three-quarters left, and both
thoughtfully focused eyes are clearly visible. In the second, a half-length charcoal and gouache study, the head is turned slightly further left and only one eye
is distinct. In the last of the three, a half-length pencil study, the head is turned
in almost complete profile and the left eye is barely indicated. It is difficult to
establish the sequence of these three drawings with certainty. The present
sequence is based upon the fact that the first two drawings are dated 1915, the
third 1916; and furthermore upon the premise that Schiele would almost certainly have started with a charcoal study and only then proceeded to a more
elaborate gouache version. Neither of these arguments is conclusive, however,
and a further study of this group of drawings remains to be made.

All three of the above are described by Leopold as studies for the Guggenheim portrait (no. 270, studies 1, 3, 4). The drawing in the Albertina (fig. c) had
already been identified as a portrait of Harms by 1965 (SRGM 170, exhibition
catalogue, no. 34). The drawing in a private collection (fig. b) was identified in the 1965 exhibition catalogue merely as *Portrait of an Old Man* (Ibid.,

no. 33), but it too had by then been recognized by some scholars as a Harms portrait. Although these drawings are surely preparatory in nature, they represent a totally different conception of the sitter from that of the Guggenheim painting, in which the old man is shown as frail and aged, slumped in his chair, and possibly even asleep. Thus by the time Schiele embarked upon the actual painting of his father-in-law, probably in April 1916, his conception was utterly different from that expressed in the three drawings.

Two further sketches which are clearly associated with the Guggenheim portrait may possibly have additional implications. Both are on sketchbook pages. One has only recently come to light (fig. d) and is hitherto unpublished, although Leopold includes a note on its existence in his Addenda (p. 687) and describes its three figures, two of which overlap, as preliminary studies for the Guggenheim portrait. This identification had been previously made by Dr. F. Gerstel, New York, in whose collection the sheet was at the time. The other drawing (fig. e) has been known for some time and is reproduced on the lower half of page 112 of the facsimile edition of *A Sketchbook by Egon Schiele* (edited by Otto Kallir, Johannes Press, New York, 1967). In this publication Kallir convincingly suggested that the drawing represented an early idea for the Guggenheim portrait (p. 10 of his accompanying commentary), and Leopold has since concurred with this view (no. 270, study 5). The upper figure on this page (fig. e) has been variously described as anticipatory of Schiele's poignant self-portrait in *The Family* of 1918 (Kallir, 1967, commentary, p. 10), or as possibly related to his early experiments with the composition of *Mother with Two Children* of 1915-17 (Leopold, 1973, p. 594). Although the pose of this figure with one arm awkwardly raised does occur in both these as well as other contexts, it corresponds most closely to the figure at the end of the table in the sketch here reproduced as fig. f. This latter drawing (the reverse of fig. d) is an early study for Schiele's important late work *Round the Table (The Friends),* which provided the subject for the March 1918 Secession poster, as well as for two oils, one of which is reproduced here (fig. g). Thus, on the obverse and reverse of one sketchbook page (figs. d, f) and on the upper and lower portions of another (fig. e), sketches for the Harms portrait are juxtaposed with early ideas for *Round the Table (The Friends).*

Schiele's first reference to *Round the Table* occurs in a January 13, 1917, letter to his brother-in-law, Peschka. The letter was written eight days after Harms' death and conveys the sad news of that event. In the sentence immediately following Schiele writes: *"ich hatte ihn* [Harms] *sehr gerne. . . . Ich habe vor, ein grosses Figurenbild zu malen, mit allen meinen Nächstbekannten, lebensgross, bei einer Tafel sitzend."* A. Roessler, 1921, p. 116. ("I liked him very much. . . . I am planning to paint a large figure composition with all of my closest acquaintances seated life-size around a table.") Here again an allusion to Harms is juxtaposed with one to *Round the Table*. Although it is perfectly possible that in both cases the juxtaposition of allusions was totally fortuitous, it cannot be ruled out that a tenuous relationship between the Harms sketches (figs. d, e) and Schiele's early ideas for *Round the Table* does in fact exist.

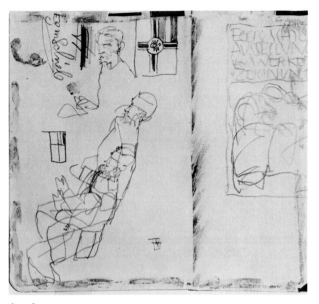

fig. d.
Schiele, sketchbook page, 6 x 6¾ in., 15.2 x 17.2 cm.,
formerly Collection Dr. F. Gerstel, New York.

fig. e.
Schiele, sketchbook page from
A Sketchbook by Egon Schiele,
pencil on paper, 6⅞ x 4⅜ in.,
17.5 x 11 cm., Private Collection,
New York.

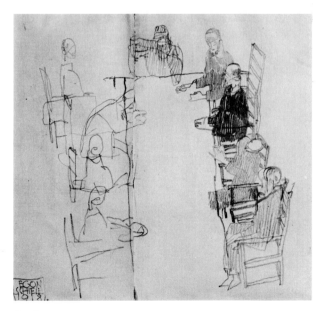

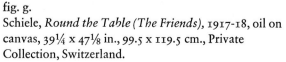

fig. f.
Schiele, sketch for *Round the Table (The Friends),* 1918,
pencil on paper, 6 x 6¾ in., 15.2 x 17.2 cm., reverse of
fig. d.

fig. g.
Schiele, *Round the Table (The Friends),* 1917-18, oil on
canvas, 39¼ x 47⅛ in., 99.5 x 119.5 cm., Private
Collection, Switzerland.

The striking characteristic shared by these sketches of Harms is the treatment of the sitter's left arm and hand, which project rather forcefully out from the body at an upward angle, as if resting upon the arm of a chair, or upon a table. Comparison of these figures with the figure seated second from the front at the right side of the table in the sketch for *Round the Table* (fig. f) would tend to support the notion that something of the Harms studies lingered in the artist's mind as he began to develop his conception for the large composition. Comini has suggested that the group of *"Nächstbekannten"* are artists, with Schiele at their head (1974, pp. 184-186, 250-251, fns. 96, 97), and although several questions about the identity of all of the participants remain unresolved, the basic premise is totally convincing. It is thus not as an actual member of the group that Harms' presence may be felt. Rather it is his physical outline, as recorded by Schiele on the very sketchbook pages he was using to explore ideas for the new composition, which appears to have injected itself into the artist's thoughts. This physical outline, perhaps imbued with new meaning in the light of Harms' recent death, may thus represent a tenuous link between the 1916 portrait and the important group composition begun almost a year later.

EXHIBITIONS:

Munich, Glaspalast, *Sezession,* July-Sept. 1917, no. 2400 (*Porträt J.H.* for sale);[3] Vienna, *XLIX Ausstellung der Vereinigung Bildender Künstler Österreichs Secession,* Mar. 1918, no. 6 *(Bildnis Herr J.H.);* Vienna, Neue Galerie, *Egon Schiele Gemälde und Handzeichnungen,* Nov. 20-Dec. 31, 1923, no. 6 ("Porträt des Herrn H. 1916"); Dresden, *Internationale Kunstausstellung,* June-Sept. 1926, no. 262 ("Der Schwiegervater, 1,39 x 1,09"); Vienna, Hagenbund, *Gedächtnisausstellung zum 10. Todestag,* Oct.-Nov. 1928, no. 62 ("Porträt eines alten Herrn [J.H.] 1916, Coll. Otto Nirenstein, Wien"); New York, Galerie St. Etienne, *Egon Schiele,* Nov. 1941 (no cat.); New York, Galerie St. Etienne, *Egon Schiele,* Apr. 5-May 1, 1948, no. 8, repr. ("Portrait of an Old Man, 1916"); Boston, Institute of Contemporary Art, *Egon Schiele,* Oct. 6-Nov. 6, 1960, no. 52, traveled to New York, Galerie St. Etienne, Nov. 15-Dec. 15, 1960, Louisville, Ky., J. B. Speed Art Museum, Jan. 3-31, 1961, Pittsburgh, Carnegie Institute, Mar. 1-Apr. 2, 1961, The Minneapolis Institute of Arts, Apr. 19-May 21, 1961; New York, Galerie St. Etienne, *25th Anniversary Exhibition,* Oct. 17-Nov. 14, 1964, no. 43, repr.; New York, SRGM 170, *Gustav Klimt and Egon Schiele,* Feb. 5-Apr. 25, 1965, no. 40, repr.; 227 (no cat.); 232, 241, pp. 390-391, repr.; 260 (no cat.).

REFERENCES:

A. Roessler, *Kritische Fragmente, Aufsätze über Österreichische Neukünstler,* Vienna, 1918, repr. p. 149 ("Bildnis des Herrn H. Privatbesitz"); *Briefe und Prosa von Egon Schiele,* ed. A. Roessler, Vienna, 1921, p. 116 (letter of Jan. 13, 1917); F. Karpfen, *Das Egon Schiele Buch,* Vienna, 1921, pl. 20 *(Bildnis des Herrn H.);* A. Faistauer, *Neue Malerei in Österreich, Betrachtungen eines Malers,* Vienna, 1923, pl. 5 ("Altmännerbildnis, Privatbesitz, Wien"); O. Nirenstein, *Egon Schiele, Persönlichkeit und Werk,* Vienna, 1930, p. 67, no. 153, pl. 114 ("Bildnis eines alten Mannes [J. Harms]"); O. Kallir, *Egon Schiele, Oeuvre Catalogue of the Paintings,* New York, 1966, no. 213, repr. color p. 421; A. Comini, "Egon Schieles Kriegstagebuch 1916," *Albertina Studien,* vol. 4, no. 2, 1966, pp. 86, 98; R. Leopold, *Egon Schiele: Paintings, Watercolors, Drawings,* London, 1973, pp. 16, 416, no. 270, pl. 192; A. Comini, *Egon Schiele's Portraits,* Berkeley, Los Angeles, London, 1974, pp. 147-148, color pl. 142.

3. Schiele showed 8 paintings in this exhibition and his entries were mentioned by K. Mittenzwey: *"Recht stark ist diesmal Egon Schiele vertreten"* (*Deutsche Kunst und Dekoration,* vol. xli, Nov. 1917/18, pp. 108-109).

Kurt Schwitters

Born June 1887, Hanover.
Died January 1948, Kendal, near Ambleside, England.

224   Mountain Graveyard. 1919.
       (Hochgebirgsfriedhof).[1]

62.1617

Oil on board mounted on cork, 36 x 28½
(91.6 x 72.4)

Signed and dated l.l.: *KS / 19.*

PROVENANCE:

Herwarth Walden, Berlin, by 1921; purchased from Walden by Frederick M. Stern,
Berlin, 1921 (information supplied by Stern,
correspondence with the author, March
1974); Gift of Frederick M. Stern, New
York, 1962.

CONDITION:

All edges have been inpainted, as have some small losses near the lower left corner.
These repairs pre-date acquisition by the
Museum. In 1964 a small green area at the
upper right was inpainted; in 1970 the top
center edge was inpainted; and in 1973 an
area of cleavage near the top center was set
down with AYAF.

There are extensive drying cracks scattered
over the entire surface, and some small paint
losses. All edges and corners are considerably worn and chipped. There is a heavy
coat of unevenly applied natural varnish
which is somewhat discolored. The overall
condition is fair to good. (Mar. 1974.)

In the years 1918 and 1919 Schwitters was simultaneously producing his first
abstract pictures, his first Merz collages, his first Merz poems, and works such
as *Mountain Graveyard.* These last were essentially based on nature, though—
as Schwitters himself put it—they were subjective expressions rather than direct impressions of natural forms. "The personal grasp of nature now seemed
to me the most important thing. The picture became an intermediary between
myself and the spectator. I had impressions, painted a picture in accordance
with them; the picture had expression" ("Merz," *Der Ararat,* 1921, written
December 19, 1920, trans. R. Manheim, *The Dada Painters and Poets,* ed. R.
Motherwell, New York, 1951, p. 59). While asserting the importance of
consistently striving for "expression," Schwitters clearly felt a contradictory
drive to hold meaning in the conventional sense at arm's length; the imagery of
expression must, he asserted, be as inexplicable as life, indefinable and without
purpose (Ibid.). In this sense, the imagery of works such as *Mountain Graveyard* or *Expression 2, Sun in the High Mountains* (present whereabouts unknown, Schmalenbach, fig. 8) must be treated with some caution, and the temp-

1. A Der Sturm label on the reverse reads: *"Kunstausstellung Der Sturm / Lietung Herwarth
Walden / Berlin W 9, Potsdamer Strasse 134 / Name Kurt Schwitters / Titel Hochgebirgsfriedhof / Katalog nr. 25."* Inscribed on the stretcher in crayon is: *"E 19 / Hochgebirgs- /
friedhof / K. Schwitters / Januar 1919."*
Schwitters exhibited at Der Sturm for the first time in 1919 and had his first 1-man show
there in 1920; he participated in 3 other group exhibitions there between 1919 and 1922.
It has so far not been possible to establish whether any of these exhibitions other than that
of 1920 included the present painting, although Stern remembers buying the picture out of
a Der Sturm exhibition in about 1921.

224

tation to interpret it as evocative of the recently ended First World War, or of the artist's ensuing sense of death or tragedy, must be resisted.

As early as 1919, C. Spengemann was issuing warnings along these lines: *"Immer wiederkehrende Figuren werden ohne jede gedankliche Bedeutung benutzt. Es sind Dinge, die in des Künstlers Totalerlebnis insofern eine Rolle spielen, als sich ein bestimmtes Gefühl mit ihnen verbindet . . ."* (*Der Cicerone,* 1919, p. 580). Thus, recognizable forms may appear in the paintings, but their "meaning" is probably pictorial rather than symbolic. In the Merz poetry of 1919, Schwitters incorporates many of the images which he used in pictures such as *Mountain Graveyard* (mountains, graveyards, sun, church), but here the conventional message of the imagery is totally obscured. (See, for example, "Welt voll Irrsinn," first published in *Der Zeltweg,* November 1919, pp. 19-20; or "Erhabenheit," *Gedicht Nr. 8,* first published in *Anna Blume: Dichtungen,* Hanover, 1919.) As Schwitters himself stated in relation to poems such as these: "Elements of poetry are letters, syllables, words, sentences. Poetry arises from the interaction of these elements. Meaning is important only if it is employed as one such factor. I play off sense against nonsense. I prefer nonsense . . ." ("Merz," pp. 59-60).

Precisely because the imagery of *Mountain Graveyard* cannot be so clearly designated as lacking in conventional "meaning" or Expressionist content, it must be seen within the context of Schwitters' exactly contemporary preoccupation with a developing abstraction and with his clearly Merz poetic style. As Schmalenbach has stated, objective painting had artistic relevance in Schwitters' life only so long as the artist was moving towards abstraction (p. 76), and it is in this intermediate sense that the imagery and "Expressionist" quality of *Mountain Graveyard* should be seen.

EXHIBITIONS:

Berlin, Der Sturm, *85. Ausstellung: Kurt Schwitters,* 1920, no. 25 *(Hochgebirgsfriedhof)*;[1] New York, SRGM 144 (checklist); 176, 236 (no cats.); Dusseldorf, Städtische Kunsthalle, *Kurt Schwitters,* Jan. 15-Mar. 3, 1971, no. 8, repr. color, traveled to Berlin, Akademie der Künste, Mar. 12-Apr. 18, Staatsgalerie Stuttgart, May 14-July 18, Kunsthalle Basel, July 31-Sept. 5, 1971; New York, SRGM 266 (no cat.).

REFERENCE:

W. Schmalenbach, *Kurt Schwitters,* Cologne, 1967, p. 78, repr. color p. 19.

Kurt Seligmann

Born July 1900, Basel, Switzerland.
Died January 1962, New York.

225   Portrait. 1932.

64.1697

Oil on plywood, 31⅞ x 25⅝ (80.9 x 65)

Signed and dated on reverse: *K. Seligmann / 1932.*

PROVENANCE:

Estate of the artist, 1962-64; purchased from the Estate through D'Arcy Galleries, New York by A. Chauncey Newlin as a gift to the Museum, 1964.

CONDITION:

Examination under UV reveals certain minor scattered areas of strengthening and some inpainting of dents in the support; these were probably the work of the artist. Pentimenti are clearly visible under UV: at the top of the picture there was originally a triangle, the base of which rested on the brownish vertical now serving as a flagpole; the green triangle at the lower edge was originally 1½ in. wider on the left, ¾ in. wider on the right.

There are vertical cracks throughout the surface caused by the expansion and contraction of the support; these are especially severe along the lower edge. Traction cracks in the light background are visible to the right of the green triangle. Apart from some general soil, the condition is good. (Mar. 1973.)

EXHIBITIONS:[1]

New York, Iolas Gallery, *Seligmann,* Feb. 3-22, 1953 (not in cat., possibly mentioned in review);[2] New York, D'Arcy Galleries, *Kurt Seligmann,* Apr.-May 1961, no. 11, repr.; New York, D'Arcy Galleries, *Kurt Seligmann: The Early Years,* Jan. 27-Feb. 15, 1964 (no cat.; repr. in pamphlet by M. Schapiro); New York, SRGM 176, 186, 195 (no cats.); 196 (checklist).

REFERENCES:

L. C[ampbell], review of exhibition at Iolas Gallery, *Art News,* vol. 51, Feb. 1953, p. 74;[2] M. Schapiro, "Kurt Seligmann," exhibition pamphlet published by D'Arcy Galleries, 1964, repr.

1. Catalogues or other records of Seligmann's 1932 and 1935 Paris exhibitions, 1933 London exhibition, 1934 exhibitions in Milan and Rome have hitherto not been found.

2. Campbell's review of the exhibition describes *Portrait* as the only picture in the exhibition which "comes to terms more or less successfully with the idea of a two-dimensional surface." It has so far not been possible to verify whether the present picture, or another *Portrait,* was the work involved, although Mrs. Seligmann believes that the picture did appear in the exhibition (conversation with the author, Mar. 1974).

Georges Pierre Seurat

Born December 1859, Paris.
Died March 1891, Paris.

226   Peasant with Hoe. 1882.
       (Paysan à la houe; l'Homme à la houe).

41.716

Oil on canvas, 18¼ x 22⅛ (46.3 x 56.1)

Not signed or dated.

PROVENANCE:

Emile Seurat (1846-ca. 1905), brother of the artist, 1891-?;[1] "Mme. J. D." by 1908 (lender to Bernheim-Jeune exhibition); Mme. Camille Platteel (de Hauke, no. 103); Félix Fénéon, Paris, by 1934 (lender to Durand-Ruel exhibition)-38; purchased from Fénéon by Solomon R. Guggenheim, 1938; Gift of Solomon R. Guggenheim, 1941.

CONDITION:

In 1954 surface dirt was removed, the painting was lined with wax resin on natural linen, stretched on a new stretcher, and surfaced with clear varnish. A coat of natural varnish, which was never used by Seurat himself, was applied at an unknown date. It has not been removed, and it has darkened to some extent. There are extremely minor repairs with inpainting, one in the lower left foreground, one close to the upper left corner, one in the upper right of the haystack; also some very minor cracks in the paint film in some areas.

The condition of the picture poses certain problems. Herbert suggested (in conversation with the author, July 1970) that it is one of the pictures retouched in the winter of 1885-86, when, at the suggestion of Pissarro, Seurat experimented with the unstable pigments of a certain "Maître Edouard." Seurat's reworking of *La Grande Jatte* at this period resulted in a considerable darkening of the overall effect. (See, among others, Fénéon, *Chat noir*, April 2, 1892: *"Du fait des couleurs dont Seurat se servait à la fin de 1885 et en 1886, ce tableau,* *d'importance historique, a perdu son charme lumineux: si les roses et les bleus se sont maintenus, les véronèse sont maintenant olivâtres, et les orangés qui représentaient la lumière ne représentent plus que des trous."* ["Because of the pigments which Seurat used at the end of 1885 and during 1886 this historic painting has lost its luminous charm: while the pinks and blues have survived, the veronese greens are now olives, and the oranges which represented light are now mere holes."]) Some of the other early canvases were probably subjected to the same treatment. (See E. Demolder, "Chronique artistique: exposition des XX à Bruxelles," in J. Guillerme, *L'Atelier du temps,* Paris, 1964, p. 18: *"Quelques toiles [de Seurat] ont poussé au noir, et on s'est permis de dire que la faute en était au procédé et à la facture. Affirmation absurde, c'est la couleur même qui a noirci. Le coupable c'est le fabricant de couleurs, rien que lui."* ["Some canvases have significantly darkened, and it has been suggested that it is due to the artist's technique—an absurd suggestion. It is the pigment which has darkened. The manufacturer of the paints is to blame—no one else."]) The overall effect of the present canvas is unusually somber and dulled. In particular, the presence of the dark olive strokes in sunlit areas (especially to the left of the tree trunk) are impossible to explain within the context of Seurat's color practice, even in the early years. Had this color originally been a vivid orange it would have formed a logical part of the sunlight reflected from the grassy field. Examination under UV indicates that these olive brush strokes were added after the completion of the original picture. (Apr. 1972.)

---

1. De Hauke lists Emile Seurat as the first owner, but gives no date of acquisition or sale. He also records that the picture was no. 22 in the posthumous inventory taken in the atelier on May 3, 1891, by Signac, Fénéon, and Luce. (See R. Rey, *La Renaissance du sentiment classique,* Paris, 1921, p. 144, for a general description of the contents.) No systematic list of the inventory was made, but each canvas, panel, and drawing was inscribed on the back with the name of Seurat, an inventory number, and the initials P. S., L., or F. F. Some notes

were also made in a notebook indicating the number of works in each category, and
referring by name to some of the more important canvases. The SRGM's files have no
record of any such notation found on the back of the present picture prior to the relining
of 1957, but according to de Hauke the crayon used did not survive well and would in most
cases have worn away. His entry does not indicate whether the information establishing
the present picture as no. 22 in the inventory derived from the notebook or from other notes
given to him by Fénéon, on whose material de Hauke's book is largely based. All the documentation is presumably to be found among de Hauke's research materials which were
placed in the Bibliothèque Doucet with a 25-year interdiction and will not be available for
study until about 1990. It is thus for the time being impossible to confirm whether the
picture was in the atelier at the time of Seurat's death. However, since Emile undoubtedly
acquired some of his brother's works at this time (the paintings were all distributed by the
artist's mother, Ernestine Faivre Seurat, d. 1898), it is plausible to assume that it was among
the artist's effects and that his brother owned it from 1891.

The variety of dates proposed for this picture (see below EXHIBITIONS and REF-ERENCES) highlights the problem of establishing a chronology for Seurat's early work. The approximately eighty-five small oils which Seurat painted before his first major work—*La Baignade Asnières* (National Gallery, London) of 1883-84—are, like the present canvas, all undated, and few were exhibited before 1900. Furthermore, the dates assigned to them by Fénéon in the catalogues of the exhibitions of 1900 and 1908-09 must, as Homer has pointed out (review of Dorra-Rewald, *The Art Bulletin,* vol. xlii, September 1960, p. 229), be treated with some caution since Fénéon did not meet Seurat until 1886, and it has not been determined whether the evidence he used came directly from the artist. The fact that Fénéon himself offered conflicting dates at various times for various canvases suggests that he may have been uncertain about this early period of Seurat's work. Both Homer and Herbert have done much to pinpoint the influences absorbed by Seurat in his early years (Herbert, "Seurat in Chicago and New York," *Burlington Magazine,* vol. c, May 1958, pp. 149-151; Homer, "Seurat's Formative Period: 1880-84," *Connoisseur,* vol. cxlii, September 1958, pp. 58-62, and *Seurat and the Science of Painting,* Cambridge, Massachusetts, 1964). In addition, Herbert has made considerable progress towards the establishment of a specific chronology (1958, pp. 149-150; 1968; and in a longer study now in progress) and has concluded that the most convincing evidence derives from the dates of Seurat's exposure to various theories of color and from his gradual incorporation of these theories into his own work.

In this regard, one crucial fact is Seurat's own statement that he had seen Blanc's and Chevreul's writings, including the former's essay on Delacroix, while he was still a schoolboy. From these materials and from a study of Delacroix's paintings, he absorbed the theory of color contrasts, including the idea that one should strive to create a vibration rather than a fusion of color. In 1881 he read the French translation of Rood's *Modern Chromatics,* with its analysis of divided color. (For a detailed analysis of these theoretical writings and their relationship to the works of Seurat see Homer, 1964, and Herbert, "Les Théories de Seurat et le néo-impressionnisme," in J. Sutter, *Les Néo-impressionnistes,* Neuchâtel, 1970.) Herbert argues that the post-1881 pictures show not only an awareness of divided color theory, but also a gradually brightening palette and a gradually decreasing use of earth colors, which totally disappear by the end of 1884. The brushwork is characterized in the early work by "broomswept" *(balayé)* strokes, but becomes progressively tighter and finer, acquiring by the end of 1882 a fairly consistent "chopped straw" quality. Herbert also conjectures that while Seurat may well have seen the Impressionist exhibition of 1879, it did not at the time make the dramatic impact upon him often attributed to it (see L. Rosenthal, "Ernest Laurent," *Art et décoration,* March 1911; and Dorra-Rewald, p. xxxv). Indeed, Impressionism did not emerge as the dominant influence in Seurat's work until the spring of 1883, when he started the studies for the *Baignade.*

Within this framework it is possible to identify—at least tentatively—works that were painted prior to Seurat's reading of Rood, and others that follow closely thereafter. Still other paintings relate more clearly to the intense experiments in Impressionist styles that typify the early stages of the work on *La Baignade*.

According to Herbert's analysis, several canvases can be confidently assigned to 1881. *Peasants at Montfermeil* (Mellon Collection, Upperville, Virginia, de Hauke 34), with its flat centerground of pale olive green, slightly brighter green, and some darker green, its brown underpainting—especially in the clothes of the women—its use of tans and browns, and its broad crisscross brush stroke is typical of the early stage. Similarly, as Herbert points out (1958, p. 150), *The Diggers* (Mellon Collection, de Hauke 62) is characterized by its use of tan-brown, darker brown, and muddy ochres; moreover, there is no trace of divided color. A *Peasant at Work* (Mellon Collection, de Hauke 61), while less somber in its overall effect, shows the same dependence on browns and the same lack of divided color. Herbert also makes a detailed and convincing case (1968, no. 64) for dating the *Forest at Pontaubert* (Collection Sir Kenneth Clark, London, de Hauke 14) in 1881, although this picture had previously posed a number of problems (see Homer, 1960, p. 230, and B. Nicolson, "Seurat's *La Baignade*," *Burlington Magazine*, vol. lxxix, November 1941, p. 146, fn. 29; Herbert's point was later substantiated by Sutter's discovery of the inn receipt, which records Seurat's Pontaubert visit as October 1881).

A *Stonebreaker* in the Mellon Collection (de Hauke 31) represents the beginning of the post-Rood development (1881-82). The earth colors are to some extent still present, but divided color—if not consistently applied—is evident. In the foreground, orange, orange-tan, brownish orange, and pink indicate the bright sunlight reflected from the stone; the pale blue of the trousers (the color opposite of the orange) heightens the latter's intensity; the bushes in the background shadow are dark green (the local color which is not subjected to sunlight), blue (the quality of indirect light and again the color opposite of orange), with some touches of dark reddish-purple (the color opposite of the light green touches in the trousers). Two other pictures—which have a very similar palette and technique must date from approximately the same time—*Two Stonebreakers* (Yale University Art Gallery, New Haven, de Hauke 35) and *Stonebreaker* (Mellon Collection, de Hauke 30).

A *Stonebreaker* in the Phillips Collection, Washington, D.C. (J. Russell, *Seurat*, London, 1965, repr. color no. 105, de Hauke 100), represents perhaps a slightly later phase. The cream-beige color of the stones is juxtaposed with its color opposite, a pale violet in the adjacent shadows; the sunlit orange of the man's forearm is opposed to and intensifies the blue of his hat, belt, and sleeve-line; the dark green local color of the shaded bushes in the background and the grass in the left foreground, touched with blue and purple, indicate the indirect light, as well as the color opposite of the adjacent yellow-ochres. Browns, ochres, and a generally somber palette, however, are still strong here, as they are in the obviously contemporary Guggenheim painting *Peasant with Hoe*.

Although the condition of the present painting makes it difficult to judge the palette with accuracy, the general scheme is discernible. The patch of ground being hoed has a green undercoat but is predominantly brown, ochre, and orange (local color combined with pure sunlight and sunlight reflected from the surface). The adjacent shadow in the foreground contains a strong brown (the local color without sunlight) and ultramarine (the quality of indirect light as well as the color opposite of the adjacent orange). Similarly the blues in the shirt and trousers of the man serve as heightening contrasts to the sunlit orange of his arm. In the background the greens of the bushes and hedge contain touches of orange (sunlight), and the three horizontal shadow areas on the right are dark green with touches of blue and dark red. Like the Phillips picture, the overall impression is still somber and dull; earth colors are present, as are olive greens and rather muddy ochres. The brush stroke is still the "broomswept" one of the previous year, but the organization is tighter, and divided color is beginning to be more consistently applied. The picture probably dates from not long after Seurat's absorption of Rood's theories—early in 1882.

In relation to this and other works of the early 1880's, Pissarro's immediately preceding work was clearly of prime importance for Seurat. See, for example, Pissarro's *Father Melon Cutting Wood in Pontoise* of 1879 (formerly Stoll Collection, Zurich, Venturi no. 499, repr.).

EXHIBITIONS:

Paris, *Expositions de La Revue blanche: Seurat*, Mar. 19-Apr. 5, 1900, no. 8 (dated 1884); Paris, Galerie Bernheim-Jeune, *Georges Seurat*, Dec. 14, 1908-Jan. 9, 1909, no. 29 (dated 1884; lent by "Mme. J. D."); Paris, Galerie Durand-Ruel, *Quelques oeuvres importantes de Corot à van Gogh*, May 11-June 16, 1934, no. 56 (dated 1884; no lender listed, but lent by Fénéon); Paris, Galerie Paul Rosenberg, *Georges Seurat*, Feb. 3-29, 1936, no. 28 (dated 1884; no lender listed, but lent by Fénéon); New York, SRGM 79 (checklist; dated 1884; so dated in all subsequent SRGM publications until SRGM 198, 1968; withdrawn Oct. 20); 83 (no cat.); 84 (checklist); Vancouver, 88-T, no. 75, repr.; 95 (checklist); London, SRGM 104-T, no. 70; The Art Institute of Chicago, *Seurat: Paintings and Drawings*, Jan. 16-Mar. 7, 1958, traveled to New York, The Museum of Modern Art, Mar. 24-May 11, 1958, no. 34, repr.; Lexington, Ky., SRGM 122-T, no. 24, repr.; New York, SRGM 129 (checklist); Philadelphia, SRGM 134-T, no. 141; New York, SRGM 144 (checklist); Kunstverein in Hamburg, *Seurat, Cezanne, van Gogh, Gauguin*, May 4-July 14, 1963, no. 99 repr.; New York, SRGM 160 (checklist); 173, no. 4, repr. p. 14; 186 (checklist); 199, *Neo-Impressionism*, no. 69, repr. color (dated c. 1882); 202, p. 73, repr. color p. 72; 221 (no cat.); 232, 241, p. 399, repr. p. 398; 251 (no cat.).

REFERENCES:

L. Cousturier, "Georges Seurat," *L'Art décoratif*, June 20, 1912, repr. p. 359; J. Sacs, "En Seurat, el lluminisme i els pobres lluministes," *Vell I Nou*, vol. 4, Mar. 1, 1918, repr. p. 90; J. Rewald, *Georges Seurat*, New York, 1946, repr. p. 85, Paris, 1948, repr. p. 32 (dated ca. 1884); D. C. Rich, *Seurat: Paintings and Drawings,* exhibition catalogue, Chicago, 1958, no. 34, repr. (dated ca. 1882); H. Dorra and J. Rewald, *Seurat: l'oeuvre peint, biographie et catalogue critique*, Paris, 1959, p. 41, repr. (dated ca. 1882); SRGM *Handbook*, 1959, p. 161 (dated 1884); C. M. de Hauke, *Seurat et son oeuvre*, Paris, 1961, vol. 1, no. 103, repr. (dated ca. 1884); W. I. Homer, "Seurat's Paintings and Drawings," (review of De Hauke), *Burlington Magazine*, June 1963, p. 284; R. L. Herbert, *Neo-Impressionism*, exhibition catalogue, New York, 1968, no. 69, repr. color (dated ca. 1882); A. Chastel and F. Minervino, *L'Opera completa di Seurat*, Milan, 1972, no. 48, repr. (dated ca. 1882); A. Bowness, *Modern European Art*, London, 1972, repr. no. 42, p. 48 (dated 1884).

227 Farm Women at Work. ca. 1882.
(Paysannes au travail).

41.713

Oil on canvas, 15⅛ x 18¼ (38.5 x 46.2)

Not signed or dated.

PROVENANCE:

Emile Seurat (1846-ca. 1905), brother of the artist (de Hauke, vol. 1, no. 60); Mme. Vve. Emile Seurat (Ibid.);[1] Félix Fénéon, Paris, by 1930 (lender to Stedelijk exhibition)-1938; purchased from Fénéon by Solomon R. Guggenheim, 1938; Gift of Solomon R. Guggenheim, 1941.

CONDITION:

In 1965 the surface dirt was removed, the painting was lined with wax resin on natural linen and restretched on a new stretcher. It was surfaced with clear varnish; it had not been varnished by Seurat.

There are a few minor paint losses at the worn edges. The wax resin has penetrated and darkened the original canvas in places (visible in those areas where little or no paint was applied or where tiny paint losses have occurred), but the colors in general have remained unharmed. The overall condition is excellent and the pigments exceptionally fresh. (Apr. 1972.)

This picture (like the *Peasant with Hoe,* above cat. no. 226) has been variously dated between 1882 and 1884. (See below EXHIBITIONS and REFERENCES).

The palette is much brighter than that of the *Peasant with Hoe* and the handling of color contrast and divided color is almost entirely consistent with Rood's theories. In the field, bands of bright pale green (local color) and orange and yellow (reflected and partly absorbed sunlight) alternate with the shaded areas of dark green (local color without sunlight), purple and blue (indirect light as well as the color opposites of the adjacent yellow and orange), and a few touches of dark magenta (complementary of the adjacent green). The addition of gray strokes in the sunlit areas recalls a sentence from Chevreul which Seurat is known to have copied: "if one puts gray next to a color it makes the latter more brilliant; at the same time the gray becomes tinted with the complementary of that adjacent color." The fact that the gray seems indeed to be slightly tinged with pale violet is the effect created by the adjacent yellow. The shadows behind the two women are dark green, dark blue, and violet—entirely consistent with the neighboring sunlit areas. The overall impression here is one of bright vivid blues and greens—colors that lead directly to the *Baignade.*

The palette and handling of the *Farm Women at Work* is closely paralleled in the *Gardener* (The Metropolitan Museum of Art, New York, Bequest of Adelaide de Groot, 1967, de Hauke 101). In the latter the brush stroke is perhaps a little less tight, but the palette and organization of color are comparable. Both pictures probably date from late in 1882 or early in 1883.

As Herbert has pointed out (1958, p. 150), Millet's *The Gleaners* provided the source for Seurat's motif in *Farm Women at Work.* The picture was exhibited at the *Salon* of 1857 and at the *Exposition Universelle* of 1867, but was not actually given to the Louvre until 1890 (Bequest of Mme. Pommeroy). An

1. It has not been possible to verify this information from any other source.

227

Farm Women at Work

229

Horse

etching was made of it in 1857 and must have been widely known by 1880 (Moreau-Nélaton, *E. Millet raconté par lui-même,* II, fig. 136); moreover, A. Sensier's book on Millet, in which the etching is reproduced, was published in 1881 (*La Vie et l'oeuvre de J.-F. Millet,* Paris, repr. p. 177). Seurat's source was thus almost certainly the etching rather than the original oil.

EXHIBITIONS:

Paris, *Expositions de la Revue blanche: Seurat,* Mar. 19-Apr. 5, 1900 (not in cat., but in hand-written *"Liste des oeuvres de G. Seurat, peintes et dessinées, exposées et non cataloguées"* on the back of Fénéon's own annotated copy of the catalogue); New York, Joseph Brummer Galleries, *Georges Seurat,* Dec. 4-27, 1924, no. 5 (dated ca. 1883); [erroneously recorded in SRGM *Handbook,* 1959 and 1970 as having appeared in 1926 Galerie Bernheim-Jeune exhibition of Seurat drawings];[2] Amsterdam, Stedelijk Museum, *Tentoonstelling Vincent van Gogh en zijn Tijdgenooten,* Sept.-Oct. 1930, no. 273 (dated ca. 1884); Paris, Galerie Paul Rosenberg, *Georges Seurat,* Feb. 3-29, 1936, no. 13 (dated 1882-84); London, Leicester Galleries, *Artists who Died Young,* Mar.-Apr. 1938, no. 32 (dated ca. 1884); Vancouver, SRGM 88-T, no. 73; New York, SRGM 95 (checklist); The Art Institute of Chicago, *Seurat: Paintings and Drawings,* Jan. 16-Mar. 7, 1958, traveled to New York, The Museum of Modern Art, Mar. 24-May 11, 1958, no. 21; New York, SRGM 129 (checklist); Philadelphia, SRGM 134-T, no. 137; San Francisco, California Palace of the Legion of Honor, *Barbizon Revisited,* Sept. 29-Nov. 4, 1962, traveled to The Toledo Museum of Art, Nov. 20-Dec. 27, 1962, Cleveland Museum of Art, Jan. 15-Feb. 24, 1963, Boston, Museum of Fine Arts, Mar. 14-Apr. 28, 1963, no. 11, p. 20, repr. p. 205; New York, SRGM 160 (no cat.); 173, no. 1, repr. p. 14; 186 (no cat.); 202, p. 70, repr. p. 71; 221 (no cat); 232, 241, p. 400, repr. p. 401; 251 (no cat.).

REFERENCES:

D. C. Rich, "Seurat's Paintings," *Seurat: Paintings and Drawings,* exhibition catalogue, Chicago, 1958, no. 21 (dated 1881-82); R. L. Herbert, "Seurat in Chicago and New York," *Burlington Magazine,* vol. c, May 1958, p. 150, fig. 8 (dated 1882); H. Dorra and J. Rewald, *Seurat: l'oeuvre peint, biographie et catalogue critique,* Paris, 1959, pp. lxxx, 40, detail repr. p. lxxxi (dated ca. 1882); SRGM *Handbook,* 1959, p. 158, pl. 136 (dated 1882); C. M. de Hauke, *Seurat et son oeuvre,* Paris, 1961, vol. 1, no. 60, repr. (dated ca. 1883); R. L. Herbert, *Barbizon Revisited,* exhibition catalogue, San Francisco, 1962, no. 111, repr. p. 205 as no. 110 (dated 1882); J. Russell, *Seurat,* London, 1965, p. 45, repr. (dated ca. 1883); A. Chastel and F. Minervino, *L'Opera completa di Seurat,* Milan, 1972, no. 28, repr. (dated 1882-83).

2. A Bernheim-Jeune label removed from the back of the painting during the 1957 lining carried the handwritten information: "Seurat / 1926." The only exhibition of Seurat's work held at the Gallery in that year contained 140 drawings, but no paintings. A list of 10 additional drawings, which arrived too late to be included in the printed catalogue, appears in Fénéon's handwriting on the back of his own annotated copy of the catalogue (see de Hauke, p. 254). Fénéon habitually kept meticulous records of the works included in his exhibitions and resorted to *hors catalogue* lists on his own annotated copy if necessary (see de Hauke, p. 232 for a detailed list of this sort appended to the 1900 *Revue blanche* exhibition catalogue). It seems unlikely, therefore, that in this instance he would have omitted any paintings that did appear. The information on the label indicates only that the picture was brought into the Gallery in 1926 and does not relate it specifically to the exhibition. It is possible that Fénéon brought the picture to Bernheim-Jeune at the time of the exhibition with the intention of including it (and other paintings) but that it was ultimately omitted. Alternatively, since Fénéon was on the staff of Bernheim-Jeune at this time, it is more than likely that his own works came in and out of the gallery for various reasons and that they were sometimes recorded.

228 Seated Woman. 1883.
*(Paysanne assise dans l'herbe; Femme assise;
Paysanne assise).*

37.714

Oil on canvas, 15 x 18 (38.1 x 46.2)

Not signed or dated.

PROVENANCE:

Léo Gausson (1860-1944), Paris, 1891(?)-?;[1]
Félix Fénéon, Paris, by 1912 (L. Cousturier, "Georges Seurat," *L'Art décoratif,*
no. 174, June 20, 1912, p. 363); purchased
from Fénéon by Solomon R. Guggenheim,

1932 (letter from Fénéon to Hilla Rebay,
October 8, 1932, preserved in The Hilla
von Rebay Foundation Archive); Gift of
Solomon R. Guggenheim, 1937.

CONDITION:

The picture was lined with wax resin and
put on a new stretcher in 1957. It had not
been previously varnished, but a coat of
synthetic varnish was applied at this time.

The condition is excellent. (Apr. 1972.)

Like the two preceding pictures, cat. nos. 226, 227, this work has been variously
dated between 1882 and 1884 (see below EXHIBITIONS and REFERENCES),
and, as in other instances, Fénéon proposed two different dates, the first 1882
(catalogues of the exhibitions at Bernheim-Jeune 1908-09 and 1920, and
Prague, 1923), and the second ca. 1883 (if, as seems probable, he was the
lender to the Brummer Gallery exhibition in 1924). Dorra accepts Fénéon's
original 1882 date for this and a group of other works but suggests that they
may have been started even earlier. He does not analyze the chronological
development of Seurat's style within the years 1880-84.

Herbert's association of the *Seated Woman* with the *Baignade* phase of
Seurat's development is convincing and makes it difficult to accept a date
earlier than the spring of 1883, when work on the studies for the large composition began. Herbert has referred to the similarity in palette and technique
between the two works (1968, p. 105). The "broomswept" *(balayé)* brush
strokes in the field of the *Seated Woman,* as well as the smooth strokes used
for the figures, are indeed almost identical to the technique of *La Baignade.*
Both paintings also reveal a preoccupation with silhouettes shown in strict
profile, and the present picture shares some of the monumentality of one of
the major studies for the large work—the Yale *Seated Boy with Straw Hat* (de
Hauke 595)—although the latter, like most of Seurat's drawings from this
period, is considerably subtler than the painting in its handling of light and
shade.

Comparisons of the two palettes are most difficult to make because *La
Baignade* has been recently cleaned (1971) and the present picture has not.
Whereas the predominant background tone of the grass in *La Baignade* is a
brilliant apple green, that of the *Seated Woman* is much more subdued. Certain

1. De Hauke records that the picture was no. 7 in the posthumous inventory. See above cat.
no. 226, for a discussion of this unpublished document. De Hauke is also the source for the
ownership of Gausson, but gives no date of acquisition or sale. It is possible that the painting was a gift from Seurat's mother, Ernestine Faivre Seurat (d. 1898), who gave several of
the small pictures from the atelier as mementos to friends of the artist.

important similarities in the use of color can, however, be pointed out. Fine orange strokes appear throughout the green areas in both paintings; the hair of the boy seated on the edge of the bank, and that of the *Seated Woman,* are painted with the same ranges of dark browns, orange, and blue; the dog in *La Baignade,* though lighter in tone, is painted in the same colors as the coat upon which the *Seated Woman* rests. The bluish garment of the latter is similar to the undershirt of the boy with straw hat, although slightly less violet in tone.

Both Herbert (1968, p. 105) and Homer (1958, pp. 59-60) have rightly discussed Pissarro's influence at this stage in Seurat's development. Evidence for this influence can also be found in a comparison of the *Seated Woman* with Pissarro's *Father Melon in Repose* (Venturi no. 498, ca. 1879), which must have provided the compositional source for the Seurat motif. Seurat's *Young Boy Seated in a Field* (City Art Collections, Glasgow, de Hauke 15) functioned as an intermediate step. In both the Pissarro and the Glasgow Seurat, the figure is placed diagonally against a field that is interrupted in the upper portion of the canvas by a hedge. In the *Seated Woman* the composition has been simplified, and the clear silhouette is seen against an unbroken background. The palette and technique still betray Pissarro's influence, but the composition has become more clearly characteristic of Seurat's own compositional notions at this stage.

EXHIBITIONS:

Paris, Galerie Bernheim-Jeune, *Exposition Georges Seurat,* Dec. 14, 1908-Jan. 9, 1909, no. 8 (dated 1882); Paris, Galerie Bernheim-Jeune, *Exposition Georges Seurat,* Jan. 15-31, 1920, no. 3 (dated 1882); Prague, Cercle Manes, *L'Art français des XIXe et XXe siècles,* 1923, no. 159 (dated 1882; lent by Fénéon); New York, Joseph Brummer Galleries, *Georges Seurat,* Dec. 4-27, 1924, no. 4 (dated ca. 1883); [erroneously recorded in SRGM *Handbook,* 1959 and 1970 as having appeared in 1926 Galerie Bernheim-Jeune exhibition of Seurat drawings];[2] New York, The Museum of Modern Art, *Modern Works of Art; Fifth Anniversary Exhibition,* Nov. 20, 1934-Jan. 20, 1935, no. 26, repr.; Charleston, S.C., SRGM I-T, no. 128; Philadelphia, SRGM 3-T, no. 197; Charleston, S.C., SRGM 4-T, no. 271; New York, M. Knoedler & Co., Inc., *Seurat: Paintings and Drawings,* Apr. 18-May 7, 1949, no. 4 (erroneously identified as a study for the *Baignade*); New York, SRGM 79 (checklist); 83 (no cat.); 84 (checklist); Binghamton, N.Y., Roberson Center, *Treasure House: New York State,* Dec. 5, 1954-Jan. 30, 1955, p. 10; Boston, SRGM 90-T (no cat.); New York, SRGM 95 (checklist); San Francisco Museum of Art, *Art in the 20th Century,* June 17-July 10, 1955, p. 17; New York, SRGM 97 (checklist); London, SRGM 104-T, no. 69; The Art Institute of Chicago, *Seurat: Paintings and Drawings,* Jan. 16-Mar. 7, 1958, traveled to New York, The Museum of Modern Art, Mar. 24-May 11, 1958, no. 18, repr.; New York, SRGM 112, 118, 129 (checklists); Philadelphia, SRGM 134-T, no. 139; New York, SRGM 144, 151, 153 (checklists); 160 (no cat.); 173, no. 2, repr. color; Musée de Bordeaux, *La Peinture française dans les collections américaines,* May 14-Sept. 15, 1966, no. 79, pl. 46; New York, SRGM 199, *Neo-Impressionism,* no. 70, repr. color; New York, SRGM 202, p. 31, repr. color p. 30; 216, 221 (no cats.); 232, 241, p. 402-403, repr. color; 251, 260 (no cats.).

REFERENCES:

D. C. Rich, "Seurat's Paintings," *Seurat: Paintings and Drawings,* exhibition catalogue, Chicago, 1958, p. 12, repr. no. 18 (dated 1881-82); R. L. Herbert, "Seurat in Chicago and New York," *Burlington Magazine,* vol. c, May 1958, pp. 150-151 (dated 1883); W. I. Homer, "Seurat's Formative Period: 1880-84," *Connoisseur,* vol. cxlii, Sept. 1958, pp. 59-60, repr. (dated ca. 1882); H. Dorra and J. Rewald, *Seurat: l'oeuvre peint, biographie et catalogue critique,* Paris, 1959, pp. lxxx, 28, repr. (dated 1882); SRGM *Handbook,* 1959, p. 158, repr. p. 159 (dated 1883); C. M. de Hauke, *Seurat et son oeuvre,* Paris, 1961, vol. 1, no. 59, repr. (dated ca. 1883); R. L. Herbert, *Neo-Impressionism,* exhibition catalogue, New York, 1968, no. 70, repr. color (dated 1883); P. Courthion, *Seurat,* New York, 1968, p. 76, repr. color (dated ca. 1882-83); A. Chastel and F. Minervino, *L'Opera completa di Seurat,* Milan, 1972, no. 24, color pl. V (dated ca. 1882).

2. See above cat. no. 227, fn. 2.

229 Horse. 1884.
(Le Cheval attelé; Cheval dans un champ;
La Charrette attelée).

41.722

Oil on canvas, 13¾ x 16⅛ (32.4 x 40.9)

Not signed or dated.

PROVENANCE:

Percy Moore Turner, Paris-1928?;[1] Félix
Fénéon, Paris, by 1929 (Briant exhibition
catalogue)-1938; purchased from Fénéon
by Solomon R. Guggenheim, 1938; Gift of
Solomon R. Guggenheim, 1941.

CONDITION:

In 1953 the stretcher was replaced and the
surface dirt was removed. A coat of natural
varnish, which was applied at an unknown
date and which has darkened to some
extent, has not been removed.

The overall condition is good, with some
minor paint cracks in the sky areas upper
right and left, and some wear along the
edges. (Apr. 1972.)

See also
color plate
p. 642.

The painting has been variously dated (see below EXHIBITIONS and REFER-
ENCES).

Herbert has made the convincing suggestion (in conversation with the
author, July 1970) that the present picture is contemporary with those studies

1. De Hauke erroneously states that the picture appeared in a sale of the Turner Collection
   at the Hôtel Drouot, Paris, on Apr. 24, 1928, no. 39, and that it was sold for 41,000 fr. to
   Fénéon. No evidence for such a sale on this or any other date has come to light. Dorra and
   Rewald (1959, no. 31) reverse the provenance and state that Fénéon sold the picture to
   Turner, which is certainly incorrect since records at the SRGM show that Guggenheim purchased the picture directly from Fénéon. It is possible that Turner owned the picture at
   some point, but until further evidence comes to light it is impossible to say when this was.

for *La Grande Jatte* that were largely completed in the spring and summer of 1884, as well as with some totally independent works of that period. (See, for example, de Hauke 57, 65, 96, 104, 117, 126.)

Certain elements in the *Horse* distinguish its style clearly from that of *La Baignade* and earlier canvases. The brush strokes are finer and are applied in a denser weave, especially in the foliage where the "chopped straw" texture is evident. A greater number of hues are introduced, in particular a rather intense powdery blue which is characteristic of *La Grande Jatte* and many of its studies but does not appear earlier; contrasted with this blue is a brighter, purer orange than has been found before. A sketch for *La Grande Jatte* (Mellon Collection, Upperville, Virginia, J. Sutter, *Les Néo-impressionistes,* Neuchâtel, 1970, repr. color p. 33; not in de Hauke) provides cogent evidence for Herbert's point. Although the brushwork here is much broader than that of the present picture, the difference is attributable to the fact that the former is a rapid sketch rather than a finished picture. The foreground in the Mellon picture is painted in greens, wine reds, and powder blues that are identical to a similar area in the *Horse*. The use of orange, yellow, and pale green is also similar in both, and the treatment of the tree in the Mellon sketch, with its pink, yellow, and tan, parallels that of the path in the *Horse*.

A sketch in the Collection of Lady Keynes, London (de Hauke 138), represents a slightly later phase in the development of *La Grande Jatte,* when the colors have become even brighter and purer than in the Mellon picture, and it is clear from a comparison between the two that the present painting belongs to the earlier phase.

EXHIBITIONS:

Paris, Galerie Théophile Briant, *L'Adieu au cheval,* Mar. 13-Apr. 5, 1929, no. 34 (lent by Fénéon); Amsterdam, Stedelijk Museum, *Tentoonstelling Vincent van Gogh en zijn Tijdge-nooten,* Sept.-Oct. 1930, no. 271 (dated ca. 1883); Paris, Galerie Paul Rosenberg, *Georges Seurat,* Feb. 3-29, 1936, no. 11 (dated 1882-84); Paris, Palais de la Découverte, *Exposition internationale, la science et l'art,* 1937?;[2] Paris, Le Musée d'Art Vivant, *Oeuvres de la fin du XIXᵉ siècle,* Feb. 3-Apr. 10, 1938, no. 1; Toronto, SRGM 85-T, no. 68; New York, SRGM 87, 129 (checklists); Philadelphia, SRGM 134-T, no. 140; New York, SRGM 144, 151, 153 (checklists); 173, no. 3, repr. color p. 15; 186 (no cat.); 202, p. 75, repr. color; 221 (no cat.); 232, 241, p. 404, repr. p. 405; 251 (no cat.).

REFERENCES:

H. Dorra and J. Rewald, *Seurat: l'oeuvre peint, biographie et catalogue critique,* Paris, 1959, p. 30, repr. (dated ca. 1882); SRGM *Handbook,* 1959, p. 160, repr. (dated 1883?); C. M. de Hauke, *Seurat et son oeuvre,* Paris, 1961, vol. 1, no. 46, repr. (dated ca. 1883); A. Blunt, "Notes on the Plates," in R. Fry, *Seurat,* London, 1965, no. 5, repr. (dated ca. 1882); P. Courthion, *Seurat,* New York, 1968, p. 74, repr. color p. 75 (dated ca. 1883); A. Chastel and F. Minervino, *L'Opera completa di Seurat,* Milan, 1972, no. 52, color pl. IV (dated 1883).

2. This is included by de Hauke, but the picture does not appear in any of the catalogues for this exhibition.

Gino Severini

Born April 1883, Cortona, Italy.
Died February 1966, Paris.

---

230   **Red Cross Train Passing a Village.**
Summer 1915.
(Train de la Croix Rouge traversant un village; Red Cross Train).

44.944

Oil on canvas, 35 x 45¾ (88.9 x 116.2)

Signed l.r.: *G. Severini*; inscribed elsewhere

on surface: $13 / \frac{15}{2317^m} / \frac{15}{122^m} /$

[C]*einture AC 247*; inscribed by the artist
on reverse: *Gino Severini 2 / "Train de la
Croix Rouge / traversant un village,, /
1915.*[1]

PROVENANCE:

Purchased from the artist through Alfred
Stieglitz by John Quinn (1870-1924), New
York, 1917;[2] purchased from the Quinn
Collection (American Art Association, New
York, *The Renowned Collection of Modern
and Ultra-Modern Art formed by the late
John Quinn,* February 9-12, 1927, no. 120)
by J. B. Neumann, New York;[3] purchased
from Neumann, 1944.

CONDITION:

In 1957 a loss in the upper right sky area
was filled and inpainted. In 1966 some
small areas of cleavage were sealed with
wax resin; several small areas of retouching
may date from this time.

Underpainting is visible in the large blue
area at the lower right and the 2 blue signs
adjacent to it. In the case of the former, the
word *"IGNY"* is legible through the grow-
ing transparency of the blue; in the case of
the latter, the left sign originally carried the
formula " $\frac{15}{2317}$," the right sign " $\frac{15}{122}$."
These same numbers were subsequently
dislodged and moved by Severini to the area
below, and the blue color added to oblit-
erate them on the signpost itself. There are
some cracks and losses along the edges, and
several long, widely spaced ground cracks
(visible only in raking light) in the lower
quarter of the painting. Apart from some
minor abrasions, the condition is good.
(Feb. 1972.)

1. Lukach (1971) has convincingly connected this inscription with a handwritten, numbered
   list of works which Severini sent to Stieglitz in Oct. 1916 in preparation for his 1-man
   exhibition to be held at Gallery "291." The list (preserved in the Alfred Stieglitz Archive,
   Yale Collection of American Literature, Yale University, New Haven, and reproduced by
   Lukach, fig. 31) contains under *Toiles* the following entry: "*2 [Train] de la croix rouge
   traversant un village . . . fr. 1000.*" No complete published catalogue has come to light, but
   as Lukach noted (1971, pp. 204-205), there must have been one since quotations from the
   preface are to be found in *The Sun,* Mar. 11, 1917, p. 12; the full text of this preface was
   published in *Critica d'Arte,* anno xvii (xxxv), n.s., May-June 1970, pp. 50-53. A copy of
   the printed checklist for the exhibition is preserved in the library at Yale University.
2. The picture was purchased by Quinn out of the 1917 Severini exhibition at Gallery "291."
   Stieglitz's invoice, dated Mar. 19, 1917, was sent to Quinn on Apr. 11, 1917, and reads in
   part: "No. 2 Train Red Cross Crossing a Village . . . 225" (John Quinn Memorial Collection, Manuscripts and Archives Division, The New York Public Library, Astor, Lenox and
   Tilden Foundations). Further confirmation of this purchase is contained in a printed
   checklist of the works in the Gallery "291" exhibition, annotated with the names of the
   buyers. Quinn is identified as the buyer of No. 2 "Train of the Red Cross Crossing a
   Village" (Lukach, 1971, fig. 32). Lukach has been able to establish that Quinn purchased
   6 oils from the exhibition, 3 pastels, and 1 drawing (1971, p. 199).
3. Neumann is listed as the buyer in "Sale of the Quinn Collection is Completed," *Art News,*
   vol. xxv, Feb. 19, 1927, p. 7.

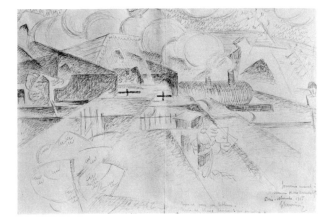

fig. a.
Severini, preparatory sketch (?) for *Red Cross Train
Passing a Village,* pen and ink on paper, 7½ x 11⅜ in.,
19 x 29 cm., Collection Foundation Hannema-de Stuers,
Heino (O), The Netherlands.

A preparatory sketch (fig. a), which differs considerably from the final work
but contains virtually all of the elements subsequently incorporated into it, was
presented by the artist to the Dutch collector H. van Assendelft in November
1915. Although it is conceivable that the drawing was executed after the painting, this is unlikely. The differences between the two works are such as to
suggest stages in the compositional process rather than the relationship between a painting and a later reprise.

Lukach's hypothesis (1971) that the picture dates from the summer of 1915,
when Severini was staying with his family at Igny, is corroborated by the
presence of the word "IGNY" (now overpainted) in the lower right of the
picture. (See above CONDITION; Lukach did not know of the existence of
this word when she wrote her article.) The composition is one of a group of
war pictures which Severini produced during that summer as trains passed by
his window day and night loaded with war materiel, with soldiers, or with the
wounded. He continued the series in the autumn, when he was living on the
rue Tombe-Issoire in Paris, once again overlooking a railway station (G. Severini, *Tutta la vita di un pittore,* Milan, 1946, pp. 236-237; other pictures in
the war series which included trains are *The Armored Train,* Collection Richard S. Zeisler, New York; *The Red Cross Train,* Stedelijk Museum, Amsterdam; there were also a number of drawings).

Marinetti had written to Severini on November 20, 1914, urging him to
develop a new pictorial language for dealing with the challenge presented by

the war: ". . . *immense novità artistiche siano possibili. . . . Cerca di vivere pittoricamente la guerra, studiandola in tutte le sue meravigliose forme meccaniche (treni militari, fortificazioni, feriti, ambulanze, ospedali, cortei ecc.).*" *Archivi del futurismo*, I, Rome, 1958, p. 350, trans. R. Carrieri, *Futurism*, Milan, 1963, p. 158. ("*. . . immense artistic innovations are possible. . . .* Try to live the war pictorially and to study it in all of its marvellous mechanical forms [military trains, fortifications, wounded, ambulances, hospitals, processions, etc.].")

Severini's response to this challenge is fully expressed in the 1915 train pictures, and the artistic and theoretical innovations he made during this period are reflected in his contemporary writings. In a January 1916 lecture on his war paintings, delivered at the Galerie Boutet de Monvel on the occasion of his exhibition and published in *Mercure de France* the following month, Severini explained the nature of his intentions. He was concerned first and foremost to express an idea—in this case the idea of war. The most effective way to achieve this was not through a depiction of the carnage of the battlefield, but rather through a synthesis of elements central to our notion of war. ("*. . . Canon, Usine, Drapeau, Ordre de mobilisation, Aéroplane, Ancre. Selon notre conception de* réalisme idéiste, *aucune description plus ou moins naturaliste de champs de bataille ou de carnage ne pourra nous donner la synthèse de l'idée: guerre, mieux que ces objets, qui en sont le symbole vivant*" ["Symbolisme plastique et symbolisme littéraire," *Mercure de France*, February 1, 1916, p. 475, reprinted in *Témoignages*, Rome, 1963, p. 53].)

As Martin first cogently argued, Severini's concept as here expressed is an almost total reversal of the "plastic analogies" concept which had previously governed his thinking. "Instead of commencing with an object which evoked other objects and ultimately an idea, thus suggesting the continuity of objects through change, he now began with a specific idea and intensified it through a quite literal analogy suggested by relevant objects, thus effecting 'a kind of plastic ideography' " (p. 198).

It is interesting to note that the precedent cited by Severini in his establishment of this aesthetic principle is Mallarmé, the poet who had most fully succeeded in combining words and images to evoke the essence of an idea. ("*Les mots, choisis par Mallarmé, selon leur qualité complémentaire, et employés par groupes ou séparés, constituent une technique pour exprimer une subdivision prismatique de l'idée, une compénétration simultanée d'images*" [*Mercure de France*, Feb. 1, 1916, p. 468, reprinted in *Témoignages*, p. 42].) In 1946, when Severini wrote again about these war paintings and the concept upon which they were based, he once more cited Mallarmé (*La Vita*, p. 236). The theoretical foundation upon which Severini built his concept is Mallarmé's famous essay "Crise de vers," and in particular the final section of it which was originally published as the "Avant-dire au traité du verbe de René Ghil" (*Oeuvres complètes de Stephan Mallarmé*, Paris, Pléiade, 1964, pp. 360-368; I am indebted to Albert Sonnenfeld, Professor of French Literature, Princeton University, for identifying the source of Severini's quotations from Mallarmé).

In the passages actually quoted by Severini, Mallarmé draws attention to the differences between the language of everyday speech and that of poetry and describes the miraculous capacity of poetic language to evoke the purest essence of an object. *"Un désir indéniable à mon temps est de séparer comme en vue d'attributions différentes le double état de la parole, brut ou immédiat ici, là essentiel . . . A quoi bon la merveille de transposer un fait de nature en sa presque disparition vibratoire selon le jeu de la parole, cependant; si ce n'est pour qu'en émane, sans la gêne d'un proche ou concret rappel, la notion pure?"* ("One of the undeniable ideals of our time is to divide words into two different categories: first, for vulgar or immediate, second, for essential purposes. . . . Why should we perform the miracle by which a natural object is almost made to disappear beneath the magic waving wand of the written word, if not to divorce that object from the direct and the palpable, and so conjure up its [idea] in all purity?" [trans. B. Cook, *Mallarmé*, Baltimore, 1956, p. 42; Cook translates *"notion"* as "essence"].) Mallarmé's central concern in this essay, and the one which clearly attracted Severini's attention, is the notion that the poet, conjuring up the idea of an object, does so by using a combination of fragmented words and images which are striking, new, unfamiliar in their combinations, and hence able to convey that same idea of an object in an especially powerful and pure form. *"Les monuments, la mer, la face humaine, dans leur plénitude, natifs, conservant une vertu autrement attrayante que ne les voilera une description, évocation dites,* allusion *je sais,* suggestion." ("It is not description which can unveil the efficacy and beauty of monuments, seas, or the human face in all their maturity and native state, but rather evocation, *allusion, suggestion*" [Cook, p. 40].) *". . . en littérature, cela se contente d'y faire une allusion ou de distraire leur qualité qu'incorporera quelque idée."* ("In literature, allusion is sufficient: essences are distilled and then embodied in Idea" [Cook, p. 40].)

Severini's adoption of Mallarmé's ideas as the basis of his own newly developing style is explicitly acknowledged in the autobiography (*La Vita*, pp. 236-237) and is traceable in many of the theoretical writings of 1914-16. (See, for example, "Idéographie futuriste," ca. 1915, *Témoignages,* 1963, pp. 34-39; "Symbolisme plastique et symbolisme littéraire," *Mercure de France,* Feb. 1, 1916, pp. 466-476, *Témoignages,* pp. 40-54.) His explicit acknowledgement of Mallarmé's importance is in notable contrast to the position taken by various of his Italian contemporaries, such as, for example, Onofri, whose close relationship to Mallarmé has been extensively documented by O. Ragusa (*Mallarmé in Italy; Literary Influence and Critical Response,* New York, 1957). While recognizing Mallarmé's greatness, Onofri insisted that he was "in direct opposition to everything Mallarmé [stood] for" and denied any real relationship between his own ideas and those of the French poet (Ragusa, pp. 136-137). Severini's writings have not been specifically studied from this point of view, but it seems clear that he was among the smaller group of Italian figures who fully acknowledged their debt to Mallarmé's poetics and for whom the French poet provided an immensely important example. (For an illuminating discussion of other aspects of the 1914-16 developments in Severini's writings and paintings, see Lukach, 1974.)

The train paintings of the summer and autumn of 1915 are clearly an expression of these developing theories. As Severini himself said, the earliest examples were based to some extent upon the actual scenes which he observed before him; but gradually they became more "synthetic and symbolic" and the last examples were true "symbols of war" (*La Vita,* p. 236). The *Red Cross Train* almost certainly belongs to the earlier stage, when the landscape still provides a recognizable context; but the symbolic content of the work, the sense in which it expresses an idea of war, is already demonstrably present. The critic Caffin, who saw the picture at the Stieglitz exhibition in 1917, was obviously responding to this element in the painting when he wrote: "The red cross on a white ground is the centre of a shock that radiates from it, rocking the field into wedges and waves, staggering the cottages from their quiet foundations and tossing them sky-high. Some of the roofs appear as red stains on the smoke volumes and the distorted ground shows patches of red and purple. It is as if the horror that is concealed inside the cars had burst out and ravaged and defiled the countryside" (cited by Lukach, 1971, p. 205). The train with its red cross is, in Severini's or in Mallarmé's terms, an allusion to war, a suggestion of it, and an evocation of its essence. Pierre Albert-Birot, writing in the February 1916 issue of *SIC* (and undoubtedly drawing to some extent on Severini's own theories expressed in the Boutet de Monvel lecture), responded, as did Caffin, to the essential meaning of these war paintings when he wrote that they epitomized *"l'image complexe et fugitive qui apparait sur l'écran de votre cerveau lorsque vous appuyez sur le bouton: idée Guerre."* ("the complex and elusive image which appears on the screen of your brain when you press the button: idea of War.")

Lukach has pointed out that Severini's use of road and railroad signals in works such as this is a reflection of his own stated theory that these signs play important roles within the vocabulary of the modern world: they are synthetic expressions of entire actions, just as the painting as a whole is a synthetic expression of a complex idea. (*"Nous avons également des signaux de route, d'automobile ou de chemin de fer, etc., exprimant synthétiquement toute une action"* [*Mercure de France,* 1916, p. 475, *Témoignages,* 1963, p. 53].) The yellow stop sign would have warned cars that the grade crossing was thirteen meters ahead; the folded blue and black sign with its fractions would have probably carried information for the train driver about distances between towns and crossings (Lukach, 1975). The fact that in this instance Severini painted out the numbers on the road and railway signs, deciding rather to let them float freely in the landscape, might have been intended to heighten the sense of confusion and speed conveyed by the whole, or alternatively to convey something of the Futurist sense of time. His decision to paint out the "IGNY" at the lower right might have been motivated by a desire to reduce the literal— and hence potentially anecdotal—nature of the scene in favor of a more generalized, and hence more symbolic, representation.

EXHIBITIONS:

Paris, Galerie Boutet de Monvel, *1re exposition futuriste d'art plastique de la guerre et d'autres oeuvres antérieures,* Jan. 15-Feb. 1, 1916, no. 6 *(Train de la croix rouge traversant un village)*; New York, Gallery "291" of the Photo-Secession, *Severini,* Mar. 6-17, 1917, no. 2 (checklist);[1] Ohio, The Toledo Museum of Art, *Contemporary Movements in European Painting,* Nov. 6-Dec. 11, 1938, no. 99 (lent by Neumann); Del., Wilmington Museum of Art, *Classic and Romantic Tradition in Abstract Art,* Nov. 1-22, 1939 (traveling exhibition organized by The Museum of Modern Art, New York, no cat.), traveled to University of Pittsburgh, Dec. 2-23, 1939, Ill., Springfield Art Association, Jan. 1-22, 1940, Art Association of New Orleans, Mar. 1-31, 1940, Iowa, Des Moines Art Association, Apr. 12-May 3, 1940, Durham, N.C., Duke University, May 14-June 4, 1940; New York, New Art Circle, *Documents of Modern Painting from The Collection of J. B. Neumann,* Sept. 23-Nov. 30, 1941 (dated 1913); Ohio, Cincinnati Modern Art Society, *Expressionism,* Apr. 20-May 20, 1941, p. 11; New York, Buchholz Gallery, *Early Work by Contemporary Artists,* Nov. 16-Dec. 4, 1943, no. 45 (dated 1914); New York, SRGM 79 (checklist, dated 1914; so dated in all subsequent SRGM publications until SRGM 202, 1968); Toronto, SRGM 85-T, no. 70; Vancouver, SRGM 88-T, no. 78 repr.; Boston, SRGM 90-T (no cat.); Montreal, SRGM 93-T, no. 56, repr.; London, SRGM 104-T, no. 71; Pasadena Art Museum, *The New Renaissance in Italy: 20th Century Italian Art,* Oct. 7- Nov. 16, 1958, no. 95, repr.; Boston, SRGM 119-T, no. 52; Milan, Palazzo Reale, *Arte Italiana del XX Secolo da Collezioni Americane,* Apr. 30-June 26, 1960, no. 175, repr.; Paris, Musée National d'Art Moderne, *Les Sources du XXe siècle: les arts en Europe 1884-1914,* Nov. 4, 1960-Jan. 23, 1961, no. 668; Philadelphia, SRGM 134-T, no. 146; New York, SRGM 144, 151, 153 (checklists); 173, no. 39 repr. color; The Baltimore Museum of Art, *Twentieth Century Italian Art,* Oct. 25-Nov. 27, 1966 (checklist); New York, SRGM 196 (checklist); 202, p. 85, repr. color p. 84 (dated 1915, erroneously identified as having been painted at "Vigny"); 227 (no cat.); 232, pp. 413-414, repr. color p. 412 (dated 1915); 236 (no cat.); 241, pp. 413-414, repr. color p. 412; Cleveland, SRGM 258-T, pl. 10.

REFERENCES:

C. H. Caffin, "Severini's Work seen at '291'," *New York American,* Mar. 12, 1917, p. 6; *John Quinn 1870-1925—Collection of Paintings, Water Colours, Drawings and Sculpture,* Huntington, N.Y., 1926, p. 15; M. Martin, *Futurist Art and Theory, 1909-1915,* Oxford, 1968, pl. XV (reverse of present painting visible with inscription, thus making the photograph pre-Oct. 1916); H. H. Arnason, *History of Modern Art,* New York, 1968, p. 214, fig. 371; SRGM *Handbook,* 1970, pp. 412-414, repr. color; J. M. Lukach, "Severini's 1917 Exhibition at Stieglitz's '291'," *Burlington Magazine,* vol. 113, Apr. 1971, pp. 199, 203, 205, fig. 47; J. M. Lukach, "A Study of Gino Severini's Writings and Paintings of 1916-1917, based on his 1917 exhibition in New York City," *Critica d'Arte,* anno xx (xxxix), Nov.-Dec. 1974, pp. 69-70.

231 Dancer. 1915.
(Danseuse; Dancers).

44.943

Oil on canvas, 39½ x 32 (100.3 x 81.2)

Signed l.r.: *G. Severini*; inscribed by the artist on reverse (photographed before lining): *Gino Severini / Danseuse / 4*.[1] Not dated.

PROVENANCE:

Purchased from the artist through Alfred Stieglitz by John Quinn (1870-1924), New York, 1917;[2] purchased from the Quinn Collection (American Art Galleries, New York, *The Renowned Collection of Modern and Ultra-Modern Art formed by the late John Quinn*, February 9-12, 1927, no. 259, repr.) by J. B. Neumann, New York, 1927;[3] purchased from Neumann, 1944.

CONDITION:

In 1953 the work was cleaned with Soilax; a hole at the upper right was patched, and this and some other minor losses were filled and inpainted with PVA. The work was surfaced with PBM. In 1966 it was lined with wax resin.

Apart from some minor losses at the edges, the condition is excellent. (Jan. 1974.)

Severini's autobiography contains the information that while working on his war pictures during the summer and autumn of 1915 he also took up again the theme of the dancer which had so preoccupied him during the years 1911 to 1913 *(Tutta la vita di un pittore,* Milan, 1946, p. 238; for references to the dance, theater, cabaret, and Severini's strong interest in them, see also pp. 52, 58-59, 72, 73, 152-153). Few of the 1915-16 versions of this theme are dated, but Lukach has proposed a convincing chronology for many of them (1971, and in correspondence with the author, June 1974). A review of some of these helps to establish the 1915 date for the Guggenheim painting.

The Metropolitan Museum's 1915 *Dancer-Helix-Sea,* with its clear relationship to the artist's 1913-14 theory of *analogie plastiche,* provides the starting point. The picture is dated 1915 on its reverse, and it was included in the 1917 Stieglitz exhibition in New York; in the introduction to the exhibition catalogue, Severini uses it as his illustration of the theory of plastic analogies, pointing out that in its complex forms "three sensations [are] united by their

1. Lukach (1971) has convincingly connected this inscription with a handwritten, numbered list of works which Severini sent to Stieglitz in Oct. 1916 in preparation for his 1-man exhibition to be held at Gallery "291." The list (preserved in the Alfred Stieglitz Archive, Yale Collection of American Literature, Yale University, New Haven, and reproduced by Lukach, fig. 31) contains under *Toiles* the following entry: "*4 Danseuse . . . fr. 800.*"

2. The picture was purchased by Quinn out of the 1917 Severini exhibition at Gallery "291." Stieglitz's invoice, dated Mar. 19, 1917, was sent to Quinn on Apr. 11, 1917, and reads in part: "No. 4 Dancer . . . 195" (John Quinn Memorial Collection, Manuscripts and Archives Division, The New York Public Library, Astor, Lenox and Tilden Foundations). Further confirmation of this purchase is contained in a printed checklist of the works in the "291" exhibition, annotated with the names of the buyers: Quinn is identified as the buyer of No. 4 "Dancer" (Lukach, 1971, fig. 32). Lukach has been able to establish that Quinn purchased 6 oils from the exhibition, 3 pastels, and 1 drawing (Ibid., p. 199).

3. Neumann is listed as the buyer (misspelled "Newman") in "Sale of the Quinn Collection is Completed," *Art News,* vol. xxv, Feb. 19, 1927, p. 7.

analogies," or a single emotive reality is expressed through three analogous ones (G. Severini, "Préface à l'exposition de New York," *Critica d'Arte,* anno xvii (xxxv), n.s., May-June 1970, p. 50; for an illuminating analysis of some of Severini's *analogie,* see M. Martin, *Futurist Art and Theory: 1909-1915,* Oxford, 1968, pp. 144-146). The Guggenheim *Dancer* is more legible than *Dancer-Helix-Sea,* but as Lukach has pointed out, the two works throw light on one another, and many of the same elements are present in both. When Caffin discussed the present work in his 1917 review of the Stieglitz exhibition, he pointed out some of the similarities: ". . . the composition is constructed in color. The rose and yellow of the costume is prolonged into the surrounding space. The latter is felt as part of the movement of the figure. It is as if one saw the volumes of form, into which the total volume of lighted air had been carved by the sinuous direction of the moving arms and legs." The large triangular planes in both pictures serve partly to define the dancer's skirt, the centrifugal motion of her twirling figure, and the space in which she dances. In an article written in 1934, Severini seems to be describing the interpenetration of planes and figure in the Guggenheim and Metropolitan dancers when he writes: "*. . . une danseuse emporte dans son rythme, dans les plis de sa robe, les tables parmi lesquelles elle danse. . . . C'est ici l'origine de cette idée de la 'compénétration des plans.' . . .*" *L'Amour de l'art,* vol. xi, November 1934, p. 476. ("A dancer carries within her rhythm, within the folds of her dress, the tables among which she dances. . . . Here lies the origin of the idea of the interpenetration of planes.") Here, as in the case of the *Red Cross Train* (see above cat. no. 230), Severini's theory and practice are reminiscent of his 1916 notes on Mallarmé: "*Les mots, choisis par Mallarmé selon leur qualité complémentaire, et employés par groupe ou séparés, constituent une technique pour exprimer une subdivision prismatique de l'idée, une compénétration simultanée d'images*" (*Témoignages,* Rome, 1963, p. 42). In the Metropolitan picture the idea of rippling motion is dominant, and the figure is obscured; in the present painting, where "analogy" is no longer the central issue, the dancer herself emerges as a more legible form.

Very close in style to the Guggenheim picture, and surely completed only shortly afterwards, is the drawing *Spanish Guitarist and Dancer* (The Art Institute of Chicago, Lukach, 1971, fig. 41, dated there ca. 1915). Here the forms are even more readable and the triangular planes have largely disappeared; but the twirling motion of the two figures in the drawing is similar to that of the Guggenheim dancer, and the rippling skirt as well as the definition of the limbs are closely related in conception and form. (The black lace epaulette with fringe worn by both this dancer and the Guggenheim figure has been identified by Lukach, in correspondence with the author, June 1974, as a distinctive part of the Spanish dancer's costume. It is worn by earlier Spanish dancers in Severini's repertoire such as, for example, the *Spanish Dancers at the Monico* of 1913, Maslon Collection.)

Two further paintings of dancers were sent by Severini to the Stieglitz exhibition in New York, and the distinct differences in style between these and the Guggenheim painting help to establish the artist's course of development between the summer of 1915 and the middle of 1916 (when, according to his autobiography, he again gave up the subject of the dance in order to concentrate on static objects; *La Vita,* pp. 251-252). In *Dancer No. 5* (formerly B. C. Holland Gallery, Chicago, Sotheby & Co., sale catalogue, July 7, 1971, repr. color, lot 128) and *Dancer No. 6* (formerly Spingarn Collection, New York, Sotheby Parke Bernet, sale catalogue, Apr. 26-27, 1972, repr. color, lot 92), as well as in two drawings closely related to the Spingarn picture (Lukach, 1971, figs. 42, 43), the fluid circular motion of the Guggenheim painting has given way to a much flatter, decorative, collage-like style—a style which was to be even more fully articulated in the 1916 *Woman Seated in a Square.* Lukach has argued that *Dancer No. 6* in particular seems to be directly illustrative of Severini's theories of geometric composition which he developed late in 1915 and early in 1916 ("A Study of Gino Severini's Writings and Paintings of 1916-1917, based on his 1917 exhibition in New York City," *Critica d'Arte,* anno xx (xxxix), November-December 1974, pp. 59-80). Thus, while the Metropolitan picture is a reflection of his earlier theories of plastic analogies, and the Guggenheim's occupies a middle ground, the Spingarn picture arises out of the newly developing notion of the role of geometry in the construction of a work of art. If, as seems likely, *Dancer No. 5* and *Dancer No. 6* are indeed among the very last examples of Severini's treatment of the theme at this time (he returned to it once again in the 1950's), they would represent the end of a stylistic phase which began about one year earlier with the Metropolitan and Guggenheim pictures, a phase which, as Lukach suggests, took him from a Futurist aesthetic to one which was more nearly Cubist (1975).

EXHIBITIONS:

Paris, Galerie Boutet de Monvel, *1re exposition futuriste d'art plastique de la guerre et d'autres oeuvres antérieures,* Jan. 15-Feb. 1, 1916, no. 14 or 15? (*Danseuse*);[4] New York, Gallery "291" of the Photo-Secession, *Severini,* Mar. 6-17, 1917, no. 4 (checklist);[1] New York, Art Center, *Memorial Exhibition of Representative Works Selected from the John Quinn Collection,* Jan. 7-30, 1926, no. 44?;[5] Rains Galleries, New York, *Modern Paintings, Watercolors and Drawings from the Collection of J. B. Neumann and from the studio of H. Hiler,* Jan. 24, 1936, no. 66 (auction; the picture was not sold); Ohio, The Toledo Museum of Art, *Contemporary Movements in European Painting,* Nov. 6-Dec. 11, 1938, no. 98 (lent by Neumann); Seattle Art Museum, *2500 Years of Italian Art and Civilization,* Nov. 8-Dec. 8, 1957, no. 225, repr.; Tulsa, Okla., SRGM 159-T; Richmond, Va., SRGM 188-T (no cats.); [Paris, Musée National d'Art Moderne, *Severini,* July-Oct. 1967, no. 31, repr.];[6] New York, SRGM 202, p. 83, repr.; Columbus, Ohio, SRGM 207-T, p. 20, repr.

REFERENCES:

C. H. Caffin, "Severini's Work seen at '291'," *New York American,* Mar. 12, 1917, p. 6; *John Quinn 1870-1925 — Collection of Paintings, Water Colours, Drawings and Sculpture,* Huntington, N.Y. 1926, p. 15, repr. p. 81; J. Taylor, "Futurism: The Avant-Garde as a Way of Life," *Art News Annual,* vol. xxxiv, 1968, repr. p. 87; J. M. Lukach, "Severini's 1917 Exhibition at Stieglitz's '291'," *Burlington Magazine,* vol. 113, Apr. 1971, p. 206, fig. 40.

4. Lukach suggests that since neither of these 2 entries can be identified, 1 of them may have been the Guggenheim painting (correspondence with the author, June 1974).

5. Quinn owned several *Dancers* and it is impossible to establish which of them was shown in the present exhibition.

6. The picture was withdrawn from the exhibition at the last moment, but did appear in the catalogue.

Georges Valmier

Born April 1885, Angoulême.
Died 1937, Paris.

232   Figure. 1919.

38.405

Oil on canvas, 45¾ x 28¾ (116.1 x 73.1)

Signed and dated l.r.: *G. Valmier. 1919.*

PROVENANCE:

Galerie l'Effort Moderne (Léonce Rosenberg), Paris (photo archives no. 014-N-1037); purchased from Galerie des Garets, Paris, 1938.

CONDITION:

In 1954 the surface was cleaned and the work placed on a new stretcher. Losses along the lower edge, the lower right edge, and the left half of the top edge were inpainted, and the work surfaced with synthetic varnish.

The edges and corners show slight wear. Scattered drips of white paint are visible in the top quarter of the picture and there are some drying cracks in the dark purple area with red dots. Some minor pentimenti are emerging as the paint film becomes more transparent (N.B., in particular, the large ochre rectangle in the upper right corner which was originally a dotted area). The overall condition is good. (Mar. 1974.)

EXHIBITIONS:

Brussels, Sélection, *Oeuvres cubistes et néo-cubistes,* Sept. 18-Oct. 8, 1920, no. 22?(*"Figure, 1919"*);[1] Paris, Les Expositions de "Beaux Arts" et de "La Gazette des Beaux Arts," *Les Etapes de l'art contemporain V: Les créateurs du cubisme,* Mar.-Apr. 1935, no. 178? (*"Figures, 1919,* 116 x 73, Coll. de M. Léonce Rosenberg").[1]

REFERENCE:

Bulletin de "l'Effort Moderne," no. 40, Dec. 1927, repr. n.p. (*"Figure 1919"*).

1. Several paintings with this title exist and it is not possible to establish which of them appeared in the exhibition.

233   Still-Life. 1925.

37.723

Oil on canvas, 23⅝ x 28¾ (60 x 73.2)

Signed and dated l.r.: *G. Valmier. / 1925.*

PROVENANCE:

Early history unknown;[1] Gift of Solomon R. Guggenheim, 1937. (There is no record of the source or date of purchase.)

CONDITION:

In 1953 the work was cleaned with 1% Soilax, the top margin reinforced with PVA emulsion, and the corners retacked. In 1956 it was removed from the stretcher and impregnated with wax resin from the reverse with heat and pressure. A dent at the bottom, left of center, was flattened; tacking margins were added, and the picture placed on a new stretcher. Some inpainting was done along all edges.

All edges, especially the lower one, are somewhat worn with minor loss of both paint and ground. There is a 6½ in. line of serious crackle (caused by a scratch on the reverse) running vertically 6 in. from the left side and 8 in. from the bottom; also a 1 in. area of circular cracks 9 in. from the left side and 8 in. from the top. Apart from a very few minor abrasions and 3 small areas of transfer material, the condition is good. (Mar. 1974.)

An almost identical *Still-Life,* also of 1925, was reproduced in *Bulletin de "l'Effort Moderne,"* no. 21, January 1926, n.p. (Léonce Rosenberg photo archives, No. 014-N-774).

EXHIBITIONS:

Philadelphia, SRGM 3-T, no. 274; New York, SRGM 195 (no cat.); 196 (checklist).

1. The picture does not appear in the Léonce Rosenberg photographic archives in Paris, but these are incomplete.

Georges Vantongerloo

Born November 1886, Antwerp.
Died October 1965, Paris.

NOTE: Like Kandinsky and Klee, Vantongerloo maintained a record of his work in the form of an Oeuvre Catalogue (hereafter OC). This document is preserved by Max Bill, executor of the artist's estate, and I am indebted to him for granting me permission to consult and quote from it. The entries include number, title, dimensions, date, and in some cases exhibitions or publications in which the work appeared, and the name of the collection to which it was sold; in addition there is usually a small sketch of the work, but these do not always correspond exactly to the finished picture.

The estate also contains a group of preparatory drawings by the artist many of which are, with Bill's permission, reproduced here for the first time.

TECHNIQUE: The polished matte surface of many of Vantongerloo's paintings on wood or Masonite was created in the following manner. Successive layers of paint were carefully rubbed down with very fine carborundum (?) paper as each one dried; the result was an extremely smooth, brushless finish. In a letter to Hilla Rebay (July 10, 1950), Vantongerloo described his method and its carefully calculated aesthetic effect as follows: *"C'est en effet toute simplement de la peinture à l'huile mais appliquée avec le soin nécessaire et en vu de suprimer le côté pittoresque de la peinture naturaliste. Au fond, c'est de la peinture à l'huile ponsée. C'est un travail qui demande beaucoup de soin mais qui est récompensé par le résultat mat-brillant que le ponsage de l'huile donne."* Because of the extreme smoothness of the white surface, bonding between this layer and subsequent applications of color has sometimes been poor, and cracks in the color areas have developed (see, for example, cat. nos. 236, 237 below).

234   Composition in the Cone with Orange Color. 1929.
(Composition dans le cône avec couleur orangé; Composition dans le cône; Composition with Orange Color, No. 58).

OC No. 58, *Composition dans le cône avec couleur orangé,* Paris 1929. The sketch does not correspond to the present picture or to any presently identifiable work by the artist; the identification of the painting with the entry No. 58 is, however, the artist's own, and all other details in the entry are accurate.

51.1298

Oil on canvas, 23⅝ x 23⅝ (60 x 60)

Signed with monogram l.r.: *GV.*

PROVENANCE:
Purchased from the artist, 1951.

CONDITION:
At an unrecorded date, possibly prior to acquisition, the painting was retouched along all edges, up to ¼ in. in width in places, and this repaint has discolored, especially in the gray and white areas. In 1955 the canvas was lined with wax resin and placed on a new stretcher. Fingerprints were removed from the margin areas.

There are 4 fine feather cracks in the white rectangle upper left, and 1 in each of the 2 gray rectangles upper right and lower left. There are also several long thin cracks in the paint film scattered throughout the 2 white rectangles.

Apart from 8 tiny stains (1/16-1/8 in. diameter) in the lower half of the canvas and some slight general soil, the condition is good. (Sept. 1972.)

Two preparatory drawings for the work are in the estate of the artist. Both are ink drawings, and one includes color notations; these correspond exactly to the colors in the final work.

EXHIBITIONS:

Zurich, Kunstsalon Wolfsberg, *Produktion Paris 1930, Malerie u. Plastik,* Oct. 8-Nov. 15, 1930, no. 83; Paris, Galerie de Berri, *Exposition Georges Vantongerloo, 1909-1939, 30 années de recherches,* Feb. 13-27, 1943 *(58—Composition dans le cône)*; Kunsthaus Zürich, *Antoine Pevsner, Georges Vantongerloo, Max Bill,* Oct. 15-Nov. 13, 1949, no. 31; New York, SRGM 67, no. 73; 84, 87 (checklists); 89 (no cat.); Montreal, SRGM 93-T, no. 57; New York, SRGM 95, 151, 153 (checklists); 195 (no cat.); 196 (checklist).

REFERENCES:

G. Vantongerloo, *Paintings, Sculptures, Reflections,* New York, 1948, repr. no. 13; M. Seuphor, *Abstract Painting,* New York, 1961, repr. color p. 66.

235 Composition Derived from the
Equation $y = -ax^2 + bx + 18$
with Green, Orange, Violet (Black).
1930.

(Composition émanante de l'équation y = −ax² + bx + 18 avec accord de vert ... orangé ... violet (noir); No. 62, Accord of Green, Orange, Violet).

OC No. 62, *Composition émanante de l'équation y = −ax² + bx + 18 avec accord de vert ... orangé ... violet (noir). Paris 1930.* The sketch corresponds closely to the painting.

51.1299

Oil on canvas, 47 x 26⅞ (119.4 x 68.2)

Signed with monogram l.r. (extremely faint; the canvas was signed by the artist underneath the final coat of paint): *GV*; on stretcher: *G. Vantongerloo.*

PROVENANCE:

Purchased from the artist, 1951.

CONDITION:

At an unrecorded date the green square in the upper left corner was retouched in places along the top and left edges, along 2⅝ in. of the right edge, and in a small area 1¼ in. from the left 4¾ in. from the top.

There are stress cracks over much of the surface, although these are mostly in the ground rather than the paint layer. There are a few losses at the turn of the canvas on all 4 sides. The condition in general is excellent. (Sept. 1972.)

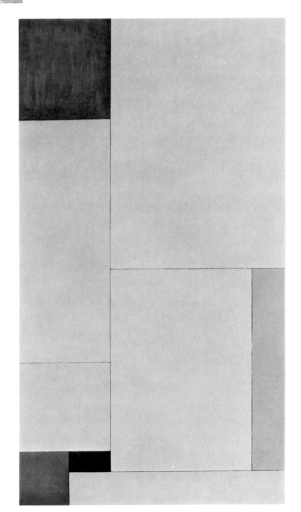

fig. a.
Vantongerloo, *Construction
$y = -ax^2 + bx + 18$,* Paris,
1930, OC 60, 57¼ x 37 x 22½
in., 145.4 x 94 x 57.1 cm.,
Estate of the artist.

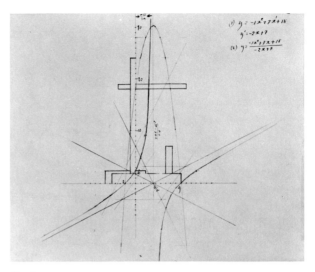

fig. b.
Vantongerloo, study for *Construction $y = -ax^2 + bx
+ 18$,* pencil and ink on paper, 9½ x 13 in., 24.1 x 32.9
cm., Estate of the artist.

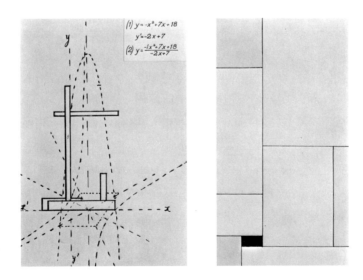

fig. c.
Vantongerloo, study
for *Construction $y =
-ax^2 + bx + 18$,*
1930, ink on paper,
6¼ x 4⅜ in., 15.9 x
11.1 cm., Estate of the
artist.

fig. d.
Vantongerloo, *Composi-
tion émanante d'équation
$y = -ax^2 + bx + 18$ avec
accord d'orangé . . . R . . .
vert . . . violet,* 1930, OC 61,
oil on canvas, 47¼ x 25⅝
in., 120 x 65.1 cm., Collection Silvia Neumann Pizitz,
New York.

Vantongerloo's preoccupation in 1930 with the equation of the present painting led to the creation at this time of two other closely related works. No. 60
in the OC is an ebonite sculpture with the title *Construction $y = -ax^2 + bx
+ 18$* (fig. a). No. 61 in the OC is a painting entitled *Composition émanante
d'équation $y = -ax^2 + bx + 18$ avec accord d'orangé . . . R . . . vert . . .
violet* (fig. d).

Several drawings in the artist's estate record his sophisticated and coherent
mathematical calculations for the sculpture (figs. b, c; I am indebted to Mar-

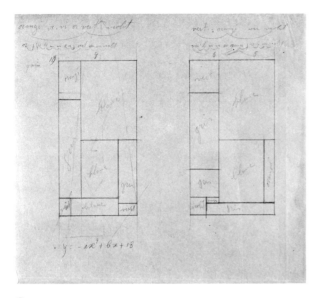

fig. e.
Vantongerloo, studies for OC 62 (left) and 61, pencil on
paper, 4¾ x 2½ in., 12.1 x 6.3 cm., Estate of the artist.

guerite Frank, Princeton, New Jersey, who established the accuracy of Vantongerloo's formulae, and the clear relationship between them and the profile
elevation of the sculpture as represented in these two studies). The precise
relationship of the parobola and hyperbola to the two paintings based on the
same formula has not yet been established, owing to lack of precise mathematical data concerning the dimensions of the sculpture's planes. Several other
drawings in the artist's estate indicate, however, that these paintings too are
susceptible of mathematical explanation (see, for example, fig. e). Further
study of this problem is necessary. Vantongerloo himself stated that the paintings of 1917-36 were characterized by a treatment of space and volume that
was directly dependent upon geometrical analysis (unpublished manuscript,
Conception-Activité, 1950, SRGM archives. The relevant sentence reads: *De
1917 à 1936 (No. 1-93) ma conception de l'espace trouvait sa réalisation dans
l'établissement des rapports des volumes que je vérifiais au moyen de la
géometrie).* The evidence so far provided by the drawings illustrated here
would support this claim.

A small detailed preparatory watercolor for the Guggenheim painting and
one for the Pizitz picture are in the estate of the artist.

EXHIBITIONS:

Paris, Abstraction-Création, 1934, Paris, Galerie Porza, 1936, Paris, Galerie Mache, 1949 (information from OC, but exhibitions not otherwise identified); New York, SRGM 67, no. 79;
78, 95 (checklists); 195 (no cat.); 196 (checklist).

236 Composition $\frac{13478}{15}$. 1936[47].

(Composition 1-34-78 [No. 101]).

OC No. *101 bis,* $\frac{13478}{15}$. *1936. détruite à la guerre de 1939-45. refaite en 1947.* The sketch corresponds closely to the painting.

51.1300

Oil on plywood, 13⅛ x 36½ (33.3 x 92.6); plywood sub-support projecting beyond the edges of the support on all sides: 14 x 37⅜ (35.6 x 94.8)

Inscribed by the artist on reverse: *101 bis /* $\frac{13478}{15}$ */ Paris 1936 / G. Vantongerloo.*

PROVENANCE:

Purchased from the artist, 1951.

CONDITION:

The painting has received no treatment. There are traction cracks in the black squares revealing the white beneath. Poor bonding between the white paint and the wood of the sub-support has resulted in extensive cracking and paint loss along all edges, especially in the right angle where the support meets the sub-support. There are some abrasions with gray transfer material on a vertical line ca. 13 in. from the left edge. Apart from some soil in the white areas, the condition is good. (Sept. 1972.)

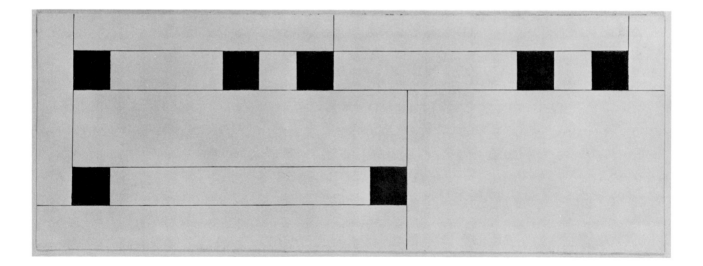

According to the OC, the original composition, which dated from 1936, was destroyed during the war. The present picture is a replacement which Vantongerloo made in 1947.

The formula describes the arrangement of squares in two lines on a module of eight divisions (fig. a). On the upper line the squares appear on the first, third, fourth, seventh, and eighth divisions; on the lower they appear on the first and fifth. A rough pencil sketch for the 1936 version (fig. b) indicates the method of division; an exact small-scale study for the picture followed (fig. c). A later pencil sketch is inscribed on the reverse *"101 bis 1939."* Although the black squares appear in this sketch as rectangles (fig. d), the sketch almost certainly relates to the present picture, rather than to the original, the "1939" being Vantongerloo's mistaken memory of the date of the earlier version.

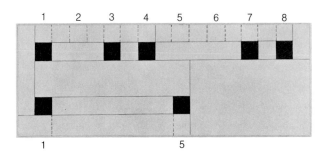

fig. a.
Diagram of Vantongerloo's division of the field into eight parts.

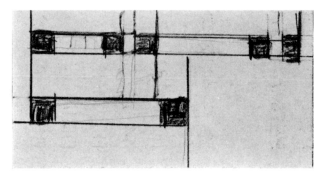

fig. b.
Vantongerloo, study for *Composition* $\frac{13478}{15}$, 1936, pencil on paper, 1⅜ x 2⅝ in., 3.5 x 6.7 cm., Estate of the artist.

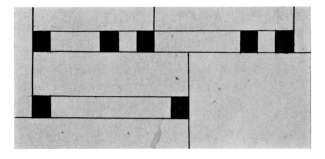

fig. c.
Vantongerloo, study for *Composition* $\frac{13478}{15}$, 1936, ink on paper, 1⅞ x 4 in., 4.8 x 10.2 cm., Estate of the artist.

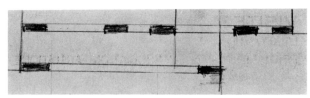
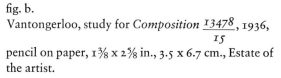

fig. d.
Vantongerloo, study for *Composition* $\frac{13478}{15}$, 1947, pencil on paper, 1⅜ x 4¾ in., 3.5 x 12.1 cm., Estate of the artist.

EXHIBITIONS:[1]
Kunsthaus Zürich, *Antoine Pevsner, Georges Vantongerloo, Max Bill*, Oct. 15-Nov. 13, 1949, no. 36; New York, SRGM 67, no. 74.

1. According to the OC, the original version was exhibited at Galerie Jeanne Bucher in 1937 and in the *Indépendants* of that same year.

237   Function of Lines: Green-Red; Red-
Green-Blue; Blue-Yellow. 1937.
(Fonction de lignes; Verte-Rouge. Rouge-
Verte-Bleu. Bleu-Jaune).

OC No. 103, fonction de lignes; verte-
Rouge, Rouge, verte, Bleu, Bleu, jaune.
1937. The sketch corresponds closely to the
painting.

71.1936R 189

Oil (triplex) on plywood, 28⅜ x 17⅛
(72.1 x 43.4)

Inscribed by the artist on reverse (partially
obscured by diagonal stretcher bar):
Fonction de lignes / . . . rte—rouge. /
. . . ge—verte—bleu / bl . . .—jaune. /
G. Vantongerloo / Pari . . . 937 / N⁰ 103.

PROVENANCE:
Acquired from the artist by Hilla Rebay,

Greens Farms, Connecticut, at an unknown
date; Estate of Hilla Rebay, 1967-71; acquired from the Estate of Hilla Rebay, 1971.

CONDITION:
At an unrecorded date, an area approximately 2¼ x 1½ in. in the lower left corner was built up with gesso and inpainted;
some additional inpainting in the bottom
right corner (ca. ⅜ in.) and the top right
corner (ca. ½ in.) seems also to have been
preceded by work in gesso. The condition
which might have necessitated such restora-
tion is not clear.

Some traction cracks in the colored areas
are clearly visible, especially in the central
red and green forms. Cleavage has developed in 2 small areas: 3⅛ in. from the right
side, 5⅛ in. from the left side; and 2½ in.
from the left, 4½ in. from the bottom.
There is general soil in the white areas. The
condition is fair. (Sept. 1972.)

A small-scale detailed watercolor study, corresponding precisely to the finished
work, is in the estate of the artist.

238 Composition Green-Blue-Violet-
Black. 1937.
(*Composition Vert-Bleu-Violet-Noir*).

OC No. *105, Composition vert bleu violet
noir. Paris, 1937.* The sketch corresponds
closely to the painting. The three bands of
color are inscribed: *vert, bleu, violet,* and
correspond to the colors of the finished
work.

51.1301

Oil (triplex) on plywood, 25¼ x 39¾
(64.2 x 101)

Inscribed by the artist on reverse: *Composition / vert-. . .-bleu-violet-. . .-noire /
G. Vantongerloo / Paris 1937 / Nº 105.*

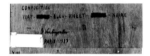

CONDITION:

In 1953 the work was cleaned with petroleum benzine to remove finger marks and
grease stains; inpaint on all edges may have
been done at this time. In 1956 the work
was cleaned again.

There is an overall fine crackle in the
polished surface, and a few cracks have
widened. There are large shrinkage cracks
in the green area, and similar though less
extreme ones in the violet and black areas;
these are due to poor bonding between the
white and colored areas (see above NOTE).
There are some faint yellow stains at the
bottom of the right edge, possibly the result
of an early repair. The edges and corners
are in generally good condition. The condition, apart from some slight soil, is good.
(Dec. 1973.)

An exact watercolor study for this composition is in the estate of the artist.

EXHIBITIONS:

Kunsthaus Zürich, *Antoine Pevsner, Georges Vantongerloo, Max Bill,* Oct. 15-Nov. 13, 1949,
no. 38; New York, SRGM 67, no. 76; 79 (checklist); Philadelphia, SRGM 134-T, no. 154;
New York, SRGM 144, 151, 153 (checklists); 195 (no cat.); 196 (checklist); Dallas Museum of
Fine Arts, *Geometric Abstraction: 1926-1942,* Oct. 7-Nov. 19, 1972, no. 52, repr.

REFERENCE:

D. Robbins, *Painting Between the Wars, 1918-1940,* New York [1966], repr. color slide.

239 Composition $\dfrac{13478}{15}$. 1937.

OC No. *110*, $\dfrac{13478}{15}$, *brun, Beige, verdâtre,*
rouge, vert. triplex. Paris 1937. The sketch
does not correspond exactly to the painting.

51.1302

Oil (triplex) on plywood mounted on plywood sub-support, 23 ⅞ x 39¾
(60.5 x 100.9)

Inscribed by the artist on reverse: *110 com-*
position $\dfrac{13478}{15}$ */ Paris 1937 / G.*
Vantongerloo.

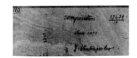

PROVENANCE:

Purchased from the artist, 1951.

CONDITION:

At an unrecorded date, the painting was
retouched along 2¼ in. of the right edge
starting at the lower right corner and extending 3⁄16 of an inch into the painting.

In the lower right section of the painting
extensive traction cracks reveal a yellow
substance underneath, which is probably a
residue from the oil in the white paint. This
residue has been produced by the artist's
technique of sanding successive layers of
paint between applications (see above
NOTE). The oxidized (dried) portion of a
given layer of paint was removed and a successive layer applied before the newly exposed area was able to dry. The cracking
has occurred in the areas where the white is
especially matte—e.g., probably in areas
which were heavily sanded, permitting especially quick drying and hence traction.
The support was attached to the sub-
support with nails hammered through the
support. As the paint film has shrunk, the
ca. ⅛ in. nail heads have become visible
underneath. In several of the areas around
the nail heads cracks in the paint layer have
developed and there is some danger of
cleavage. The surface shows some considerable soil; the condition is fair. (Sept. 1972.)

Three studies for this work are in the estate of the artist: an ink sketch with color notes (fig. a), and two small watercolors.

As in the case of cat. no. 236, the formula describes the division of the canvas into two lines of eight sections each.

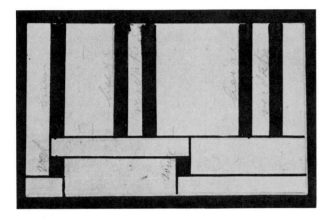

fig. a.

Vantongerloo, study for *Composition* $\frac{13478}{15}$, ink with color notations, Estate of the artist.

EXHIBITIONS:

Paris, Galerie Delcourt, 1937 (information from OC, but exhibition not otherwise identified); Kunsthaus Zürich, *Antoine Pevsner, Georges Vantongerloo, Max Bill,* Oct. 15-Nov. 13, 1949, no. 40; New York, SRGM 67, no. 71.

REFERENCE:

G. Vantongerloo, *Paintings, Sculptures, Reflections,* New York, 1948, repr. no. 22.

240   Function: Red, Green, Beige,
Brown.   1937.
(Fonction: rouge, vert, beige, brun).

OC No. *116, fonction: rouge-vert-beige-brun.-triplex. Paris. 1937.* The sketch corresponds approximately to the painting.

51.1303

Oil (triplex) on plywood mounted on plywood sub-support, 34¼ x 39¾ (86.8 x 100.9)

Inscribed by the artist on reverse: *fonction / Rouge-Vert-beige-brun. / 1937 / G. Vantongerloo. / 116.*

PROVENANCE:

Purchased from the artist, 1951.

CONDITION:

4 small repairs of unrecorded date are visible to the naked eye; 2 of these have a rough finish which contrasts with the smoothly sanded down surface of the painting as a whole.

The support was attached to the sub-support by means of nails hammered through the support. As the paint film has shrunk, the ca. ⅛ in. nail heads have become visible underneath. In several of the areas around the nail heads cracks in the paint layer have developed. A few scattered minor cracks in the paint film are visible, and a few small losses at the edges. Apart from some slight soil along the margins, the condition is good. (Sept. 1972.)

Two watercolor studies for the picture are in the estate of the artist. A closely related work, smaller in size, is in the collection of Marguerite Arp-Hagenbach (OC No. 115, *Fonction-Composition*, 1937, 22 x 30¾ in., 55.9 x 78.1 cm.).

EXHIBITIONS:

Paris, *Salon des Surindépendants,* 1937, Galerie de L'Equipe, 1937, Amsterdam, Stedelijk Museum, 1938, Museum d'Arle[s], 1938 (information from OC, but exhibitions not otherwise identified); Kunsthaus Zürich, *Antoine Pevsner, Georges Vantongerloo, Max Bill,* Oct. 15-Nov. 13, 1949, no. 43; New York, SRGM 67, no. 77.

241   Composition. 1944.

OC *No. 166, Composition. Paris 1944.* The sketch corresponds to the painting, but the format is reversed, making the picture horizontal rather than vertical.

51.1304

Oil on plywood, 36⅜ x 20⅛ (92.4 x 51); plywood sub-support projecting beyond the edges of the support on all sides, 37 x 21 (94.1 x 53.4)

Inscribed by the artist on the reverse: *166 / composition / Paris 1944 / G. Vantongerloo.*

PROVENANCE:
Purchased from the artist, 1951.

CONDITION:
The work has received no treatment.

The support is warped at the upper left and along the entire bottom edge and has lifted from the sub-support in both areas. Apart from some general surface soil the condition is otherwise good. (Sept. 1972.)

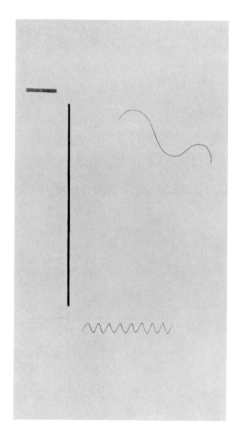

A watercolor for this composition is in the estate of the artist.

EXHIBITIONS:
Kunsthaus Zürich, *Antoine Pevsner, Georges Vantongerloo, Max Bill,* Oct. 15-Nov. 13, 1949, no. 70; New York, SRGM 67, 107 (checklists); Washington, D.C., Corcoran Gallery of Art, *Contemporary Painting in Belgium,* Oct. 3-Dec. 1, 1963, no. 11.

Maria Helena Vieira da Silva

Born June 1908, Lisbon.
Lives in Paris.

242   Composition. January 1936.

37.399

Oil on canvas, 41½ x 63⅝ (105.3 x 161.5)

Signed and dated l.r.: *Vieira da Silva 36.*

PROVENANCE:

Purchased from Galerie Jeanne Bucher, Paris, by Solomon R. Guggenheim, September 1937; Gift of Solomon R. Guggenheim, 1937.

CONDITION:

In 1957 the work was placed on a new stretcher and the margins waxed. It was superficially cleaned with petroleum benzine and surfaced with PBM.

The condition is excellent. (May 1974.)

Vieira da Silva's life-long preoccupation with problems of perspective was first explored in works of the mid 1930's such as the present *Composition* and the slightly earlier *The Studio* of 1935—the artist's first large-scale work (Private Collection, Paris, 45¼ x 57¾ in., 115 x 146.5 cm., repr. *Vieira da Silva,* exhibition catalogue, Galleria d'Arte Moderna, Turin, 1964). In *The Studio* the spatial definition is to a large extent clear, and although subtle ambiguities are already introduced, they play a subordinate role. By the time of *Composition,* however, while many of the same structural elements are used, ambiguity has become dominant. Shortly afterwards, Vieira da Silva embarked on a far more ambitious and complex version of the present composition—*The Weavers,* which she began in 1936 but did not complete until 1948 (Private

fig. a.
Vieira da Silva, *The Weavers,* 1936-48, oil on canvas,
38¼ x 57½ in., 97 x 146 cm., Private Collection, Paris.

Collection, Paris, fig. a). The structural basis of this work is identical, in reverse, to that of the present painting; but the perspectival ambiguities have been multiplied and the disturbing subtleties of interrelationships between planes increased.

The compositional links between these two works and the title of the second inevitably raise the question of their possible mutual source in the iconography of the loom. As G. Weelen, J. Rewald, and many others have noted, however, the titles of Vieira da Silva's works are almost always added long after completion and usually by poets or other friends of the artist. They rarely represent even an *ex post facto* response of the artist to her work. These titles must, therefore, be treated with caution; at best they may serve to introduce an added—if unintended—ingredient to the viewer's perception of the work, but they should not be taken as illumination of the artist's own iconographical sources. She herself has consistently claimed in this connection that titles are incapable of even approximating the "inner dream" which is the subject of her painting. (See, for example, Weelen, *Vieira da Silva,* Paris, 1960 [p. 4].)

EXHIBITIONS:

Lisbon, studio exhibition with Arpad Szenes, Jan. 1936 (no cat.);[1] Paris, Galerie Jeanne Bucher, *Vieira da Silva,* Jan. 1937 (no cat.);[1] Charleston, S.C., SRGM 4-T, no. 183, repr. p. 56; Bennington, Vt., SRGM 24-T (no cat.); New York, SRGM 127 (no cat.).

1. Information from the artist's own records, supplied by G. Weelen, correspondence with the author, May-June 1974.

Jacques Villon

Born July 1875, Dainville.
Died June 1963, Puteaux.

243   Color Perspective. 1921.

53.1356

Oil on canvas, 21¼ x 28⅝ (54 x 72.7)

Signed l.r.: *JV*; on reverse: *Jacques Villon /
21.*

PROVENANCE:

Purchased from the artist by Katherine S.
Dreier (1877-1952), West Redding, Connecticut, probably 1922;[1] Gift of the Estate
of Katherine S. Dreier, 1953.

CONDITION:

In 1953 the surface was cleaned with Soilax
solution, followed by benzine rinse. Minor
losses along much of the right and bottom
edges and scattered along the top and left
edges were inpainted. In 1960 the canvas
was taken off the stretcher, superficially
cleaned, infused with wax resin, and restretched on a new stretcher.

Traction cracks are visible in scattered
locations. There is some cracking and occasional flaking along the edges at the turn
of the canvas. The condition is otherwise
good. (Aug. 1974.)

1. Dreier purchased at least 2 other *Color Perspectives* from Villon in 1922 (Yale University
   Art Gallery, New Haven, Conn., 1941.744 and .745). For a note on the difficulty of establishing her personal ownership, see above cat. no. 68, fn. 2.

Faintly discernable with the naked eye, and rather more clearly visible under ultra-violet or transmitted light, are the traces of one or possibly two earlier painted compositions below the present one. Colors used in these include green and orange, in addition to those colors presently visible. All attempts to decipher these earlier compositions, and to relate them either to the painting now visible or to other works by the artist, have hitherto failed. The canvas is unresponsive to x-ray, and the underpainting remains illegible and largely incoherent.

Villon characterized his ca. 1919 move into abstraction as a "means of producing autonomous creations," but he emphasized that he always felt compelled "to start from observation of nature, a nature perhaps enhanced by intuition" (F. Steegmuller, "Jacques Villon—an Appreciation," *Jacques Villon, Master Printmaker,* exhibition catalogue, New York, 1964, n.p.). R. Massat, writing in 1951, similarly emphasized that the post-1919 abstractions were invariably derived from objective sources. (*"Elles partaient d'une forme figurative pour aller vers la séverité de l'abstraction"* [*Cahiers d'Art,* vol. 26, 1951, p. 66].)

Although no source for the present composition has hitherto come to light, it is clearly possible that this—and other examples of the early 1920's *Color Perspective* series—evolved from a figurative source in a manner similar to that of the 1924 *Jockey* (Collection Société Anonyme, Yale University, New Haven). Rosenblum has described Villon's process of gradual abstraction in the latter case as a "taut distillation of matter and movement into the language of Synthetic Cubism" ("The Duchamp Family," *Arts,* vol. 31, April 1957, p. 23). And indeed the eight surviving preparatory drawings for *Jockey* (Collection Société Anonyme, Yale University, New Haven) document, as G. H. Hamilton has demonstrated, Léonce Rosenberg's 1920 description of Cubist method ("The Dialectic of Later Cubism: Villon's *Jockey,*" *Magazine of Art,* vol. 41, November 1948, p. 269). The highly abstract pattern which constitutes the final painting *Jockey,* though legible in light of the drawings, would probably remain virtually undecipherable without them.

Isolated details of the green and orange underpainting on the present canvas, though illegible in their totality, are suggestive of details subsequently used in the *Jockey* and other compositions. In light of the evidence cited above, further study of the Guggenheim and other *Color Perspective* paintings in relation to pictures such as *Jockey* might help to finally resolve the question of whether these compositions—hitherto considered totally abstract—may in fact have had figurative origins.

EXHIBITIONS:[2]

Brooklyn, N.Y., Brooklyn Museum, *An International Exhibition of Modern Art Assembled by the Société Anonyme,* Nov. 19, 1926-Jan. 1, 1927, no. 59?;[3] New York, The Museum of Modern Art, *Paintings from New York Private Collections,* July 2-Sept. 22, 1946, p. 5; New Haven, Yale University Art Gallery, *In Memory of Katherine S. Dreier,* Dec. 15, 1952-Feb. 1, 1953, no. 68; New York, SRGM 79 (checklist); 81, 83 (no cats.); 84, 87 (checklists); Boston, SRGM 90-T (no cat.); Montreal, SRGM 93-T, no. 58; New York, SRGM 95, 97 (checklists);

101, *Villon, Duchamp-Villon, Duchamp*, repr. n.p.; 118 (checklist); Cleveland Museum of Art, *Paths of Abstract Art*, Oct. 4- Nov. 13, 1960, no. 34, repr.; Paris, Galerie Charpentier, *Cent tableaux de Jacques Villon*, Apr. 26-June 12, 1961 [p. 26], (dated 1929); New York, E. V. Thaw & Co., *Jacques Villon*, Mar. 24-Apr. 18, 1964, no. 4, repr.; New York, SRGM 195 (no cat.); 196 (checklist).

REFERENCE:

R. Rosenblum, *Cubism and Twentieth-Century Art*, New York, 1961, p. 156, repr. no. 109.

2. No catalogue or other record of the 1922 *Société Anonyme* Villon exhibition survives.

3. It is impossible to say whether this, or another of Dreier's *Color Perspectives* was shown. Her own annotated catalogue of the exhibition notes only that no. 59 was not for sale (information supplied by R. L. Herbert, correspondence with the author, June 1973).

---

244   Portrait of the Artist's Father. 1924.

55.1434

Oil on canvas, 21¼ x 18⅛ (54.1 x 46)

Signed and dated l.l.: *Jacques Villon 24.*

PROVENANCE:

Marie Harriman Gallery, New York, by 1934 (exhibition catalogue);[1] purchased from Marie Harriman by Ida Guggenheimer, New York, 1934 (information supplied by Lucien Goldschmidt, 1955); purchased from Mrs. Guggenheimer by Lucien Goldschmidt, New York, 1955; purchased from Goldschmidt, 1955.

CONDITION:

In 1953 the painting was glue lined, placed on a new stretcher, and some minimal inpainting performed by Riportella Studios, New York (information supplied by Clara G. Binswanger, daughter of Ida Guggenheimer, and confirmed by Vincent Riportella, February 1974). The extensive retouching which is clearly revealed under UV (fig. a) is virtually undetectable with the naked eye, was not performed by Riportella, and probably dates from before Mrs. Guggenheimer's acquisition of the work. It is extremely subtle and may have been performed by the artist himself. Analytic tests suggest that this inpainting contains the same natural varnish (probably damar) as was originally used to coat the work, although it has not been possible to establish this with certainty. The fact that some of the inpainting is applied over cracks in the earlier paint layer would suggest that some years elapsed between the 2 applications.

Apart from scattered minor paint cracks, the condition is good. Traces of horizontal and vertical grid lines are visible in some places. (Mar. 1974.)

The artist's father, Justin Isidore Duchamp, was born February 16, 1848, in Massiac, Cantal, and died February 3, 1925, in Rouen. He became a successful and distinguished lawyer and practiced throughout his career in Blainville and Rouen, where he led a quiet and private life, rarely leaving the city and never traveling abroad. He provided encouragement and financial support to all three of his sons, both at the outset of their artistic careers and long after they

1. The records of the Marie Harriman Gallery are presently not available for study and attempts to establish her date of acquisition have hitherto failed.

244

reached maturity. All three remained closely attached to him and paid frequent visits to Rouen up to the time of his death. All three also produced portraits of their father in various media at different stages of his life. The present portrait, painted shortly before the lawyer's death, is reminiscent in particular of a full-length charcoal portrait by Villon dating from 1912 (City Art Museum of Saint Louis, 155:66, *Bulletin,* new series, vol. ii, Sept.-Oct. 1966, repr. p. 9).

EXHIBITIONS:

Paris, Grand Palais, *Trente ans de l'art indépendant,* Feb. 20-Mar. 21, 1926, no. 2629 ("*Portrait*-1924;" a label on the reverse identifies the picture with this exhibition); New York, Brummer Gallery, *Villon,* Oct. 20-Nov. 20, 1930, no. 9? *(Head of a Man);* New York, Marie Harriman Gallery, *Jacques Villon,* Jan. 8-27, 1934, no. 4; New York, Lucien Goldschmidt, *Jacques Villon,* Apr. 1-30, 1955, no. 3; New York, SRGM 97 (checklist); 101, *Villon, Duchamp-Villon, Duchamp,* repr. n.p.; 118 (checklist); Philadelphia, SRGM 134-T, no. 157; New York, SRGM 151, 153 (checklists); 195 (no cat.); 196 (checklist); 207, p. 26, repr. p. 27; 260 (no cat.).

REFERENCES:

J. J. Sweeney, *Villon, Duchamp-Villon, Duchamp,* exhibition catalogue, New York, 1957, n.p.; H. H. Arnason, *A History of Modern Art,* New York, 1968, p. 209, repr. fig. 361.

244, fig. a.
Portrait of the Artist's Father. UV photograph.

---

245   Song. 1926.
(Chanson; The Lovers[1]).

53.1357

Oil (with ink?) on canvas, 23½ x 31¾
(59.7 x 80.7)

Signed and dated l.l.: *Jacques Villon 26.*

PROVENANCE:

Purchased from the artist by Katherine S.
Dreier (1877-1952), West Redding, Connecticut, 1926; Gift of the Estate of Katherine S. Dreier, 1953.

CONDITION:

In 1953 the unvarnished surface was cleaned
with petroleum benzine 265; a small hole in
the center was filled and retouched, and the
work surfaced with PBM. In 1955 the canvas was lined with wax resin on natural
linen, placed on a new stretcher, and
squared, necessitating inpainting approximately ⅛ in. in width along portions of all
edges. In 1957 a 6 in. scratch below and to
the right of center was inpainted.

Apart from some minor crackle in some of
the blue and dark brown areas, and some
minor paint losses at the edges, the condition is excellent. (Apr. 1974.)

TECHNIQUE: The black crosshatching over
much of the surface appears to have been
applied with a quill pen. It has hitherto not
been established whether this is ink or oil
paint, although examination under strong
magnification reveals a crackle in the black
lines similar to that present in other areas of
the paint film. In a 1957 interview with D.
Vallier, the artist alluded to his occasional
practice of adding crosshatching in ink to
an otherwise completed canvas: *"Parfois,
sur les couleurs, je reprends mon tableau à
l'encre. C'est un accompagnement. La toile
est déjà composée et l'accompagnement
peut être libre sans nuire. Là je peux mettre
un peu de mon coeur à moi"* (*Jacques
Villon,* Paris, 1957, p. 31).

1. There is no apparent explanation for the title *The Lovers* which was attached to the painting for the first time in the catalogue of the 1952-53 *Katherine Dreier Memorial Exhibition.*
It is possible that a confusion arose between *Song* and Duchamp-Villon's relief *The Lovers*
of 1913 (Kunstmuseum Basel Öffentliche Kunstsammlung), which inspired a 1924 painting
by Villon.

245

The composition is derived directly from a sculpture by the artist's brother, Raymond Duchamp-Villon, also entitled *Song* (fig. a). The sculpture was first executed in plaster in 1908 (present whereabouts unknown), and the wood version dates from 1909. It has hitherto not been possible to establish whether Villon owned either or both versions in 1926, but he certainly had immediate access to the wood version since he included it in a group of works by Duchamp-Villon that he assembled for the February 1926 *Trente ans de l'art indépendant* (no. 2928).

W. C. Agee first made the convincing suggestion that Duchamp-Villon's fascination with the depiction of complicated human poses had been directly influenced by Muybridge's *The Human Figure in Motion,* published in 1887; Duchamp had confirmed that all three brothers were familiar with and fascinated by Muybridge's work (G. H. Hamilton and W. C. Agee, *Raymond Duchamp-Villon,* exhibition catalogue, New York, 1968, p. 41). Examination of some of the sequences in Muybridge lends cogent support to Agee's hypothesis (see fig. b).

The scale of the sculpture and the painting and the pose of the female figures in each are almost identical. Villon has merely slightly raised the head of the figure on the left and the left shoulder of the one on the right. In conception, however, the two works are dramatically different. Villon's rendering of the human form as a series of angular interlocking planes contrasts with Duchamp-

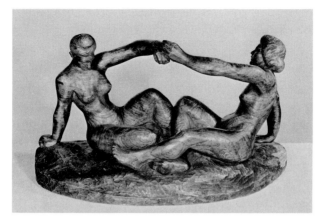

fig. a.
R. Duchamp-Villon, *Song*, 1909, wood, 21 x 38 in.,
53.3 x 96.5 cm., Courtesy The Art Institute of Chicago.
Gift of The Arts Club of Chicago.

Villon's smoothly rounded surfaces; and the clearly defined relationship in the sculpture between the figures and their surrounding space becomes in the painting deliberately ambiguous and complex.

The subject of the painting and of the sculpture that inspired it is obscure. It relates directly to a group of works executed by the three brothers during the years 1907 to 1910, all of which reveal a common preoccupation with apparently ritual subjects placed in outdoor, pastoral settings. (A. d'Harnoncourt first suggested, in correspondence with A. Vondermuhll, 1971, that the 1909 work of the three brothers seemed to be linked by this common subject matter.) In the case of Villon, this subject matter occurs in 1907 in prints such as *The Graceful Helper* (J. Auberty and C. Pérusseaux, *Jacques Villon: catalogue de son oeuvre gravé*, Paris, 1950, 117; hereafter A & P) and *Women of Thrace*

fig. b.
E. Muybridge, *Animal Locomotion,* Philadelphia, 1887, individual frames (left to right)
from: vol. VI, pl. 265; vol. IV, pl. 245; vol. IV, pl. 266.

fig. c.
Villon, *Song*, photographed in original frame by Pierre
Legrain, now lost.

(A & P 119); it may continue in 1908 with *The Little Bathers* (A & P 143) and
in 1909 with *In the Forest* (A & P 162). Duchamp-Villon produced not only
Song, but also the *Young Girl Seated* of 1909 (Hamilton and Agee, op. cit.,
repr. p. 43), which—with its rather more conventional theme—is less explicitly
relatable to a ritual iconography, and *Pastorale* of 1910 (W. Pach, *Raymond
Duchamp-Villon,* Paris, 1924, p. 45). Duchamp is perhaps expressing a similar
preoccupation in his *Two Nudes* of 1910 (W. Schwarz, *Marcel Duchamp,* New
York, 1969, repr. no. 22), in *Baptism* (Ibid., repr. no. 33), *The Bush* (Ibid., repr.
no. 32), and *Young Man and Girl in Spring* (Ibid., repr. no. 37), all of 1911.

Although it is likely that a common iconographic or symbolic thread links
these and other related works of this period, its significance has yet to be fully
explained, and the sources for the iconography are as yet unclear.

Dreier's publication of the picture in 1926 included an appreciation of an
unusual frame especially created for it by the French bookbinder Pierre Legrain
(fig. c): ". . . in its coating of light varnished wood and brilliant reflected silver
blocks, the frame adds a new note to Villon's picture." The frame, which according to Hamilton, still existed at the time of the 1952 exhibition, has since
been lost. (For a note on Legrain's creation of frames for Picabia, see W. Camfield, *Francis Picabia,* exhibition catalogue, New York, 1970, p. 124.)

EXHIBITIONS:

Brooklyn Museum, *An International Exhibition of Modern Art Assembled by the Société
Anonyme,* Nov. 19, 1926-Jan. 1, 1927, no. 61, repr. *(Chanson)*; New Haven, Yale University
Art Gallery, *In Memory of Katherine S. Dreier,* Dec. 15, 1952-Feb. 1, 1953, no. 70, repr.
(The Lovers).[1]

REFERENCE:

K. S. Dreier, *Modern Art,* New York, 1926, pp. 16-17, repr. (published on occasion of
Brooklyn Museum exhibition).

Friedrich Vordemberge-Gildewart

Born November 1899, Osnabrück.
Died December 1962, Ulm.

246   Composition No. 96. 1935.

37.410

Oil on canvas, 31½ x 39⅜ (79.9 x 100.1)

Inscribed by the artist on stretcher:
Vordemberge-Gildewart / K. Nº. 96 / 1935.

PROVENANCE:
Purchased from the artist by Rudolf Bauer
on behalf of The Solomon R. Guggenheim

Foundation, 1937 (information that Bauer
was instructed to buy the work by Solomon
R. Guggenheim supplied by Ilse Vordemberge-Leda, the artist's widow, December
1972); Gift of Solomon R. Guggenheim,
1937.

CONDITION:

The picture was cleaned in 1953.
There is considerable surface dirt, both in
the white background and in the colored
areas, but the condition is otherwise good.
(Oct. 1972.)

The rough textural quality of the stippled areas (designated *"rauh"* by the artist in his unpublished notebook) was first introduced in works of 1933. Vordemberge-Gildewart's earliest experiments with this texture involved the use
of sand, a practice that he employed only occasionally in his later works. In

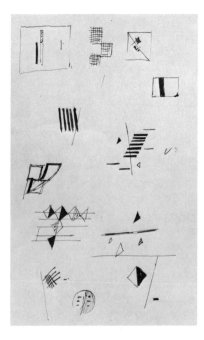

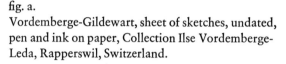

fig. a.
Vordemberge-Gildewart, sheet of sketches, undated, pen and ink on paper, Collection Ilse Vordemberge-Leda, Rapperswil, Switzerland.

general, he came to rely upon a technique that included the use of a tiny brush and concentrated paint that he applied in layers (information supplied by Ilse Vordemberge-Leda in conversation with the author, November 1972; for a description of the artist's practice in this technique, see Jaffe, 1971, pp. 69-70).

An earlier version of *Composition No. 96,* with horizontal rather than vertical bars, is *Composition No. 88,* 1934-35 (23⅝ x 23⅝ in., 60 x 60 cm., *Oeuvrekatalog,* no. 92). In this square version, the design consists of three rather than four separate elements, and the two main bars are identical in length. *Composition No. 111,* 1939, represents a third variation (23⅝ x 23⅝ in., 60 x 60 cm., *Oeuvrekatalog,* no. 116); it is identical in size and format to *No. 88* but has four vertical elements rather than three vertical and one diagonal.

Clearly the artist was intermittently concerned with the compositional problems posed by this configuration. In 1937, during a lengthy visit to Max Bill in Zurich, he produced a whole sheet of sketches with variations on the theme, none of which he ever used for paintings. An undated sheet of sketches in the collection of Ilse Vordemberge-Leda (fig. a) contains in the upper left-hand corner still another version that was never—as far as is known—converted into a painting. (Since this sheet of drawings includes compositional types from as early as 1927 and as late as 1946, as well as some that were never executed at all, its function and date are difficult to establish.)

EXHIBITIONS:

Charleston, S.C., SRGM 4-T, no. 189 (incorrect dimensions listed, dated 1936); New York, SRGM 62, no. 1; Nantucket Island, Mass., SRGM 68-T (no cat.).

REFERENCES:

H. L. C. Jaffe, *Vordemberge-Gildewart, Mensch und Werk,* Cologne, 1971, *Oeuvrekatalog* no. 100; *Art of Tomorrow,* 1939, no. 410, repr. p. 168.

247   Composition No. 97. 1935.

37.411

Oil on canvas, 31½ x 39⅜ (79.9 x 100.1)

Signed and dated on stretcher:
*Vordemberge-Gildewart / K.Nº 97 /
1935.*

PROVENANCE:

Purchased from the artist by Rudolf Bauer
on behalf of The Solomon R. Guggenheim
Foundation, 1937 (information that Bauer

was instructed to buy the work by Solomon
R. Guggenheim supplied by Ilse Vordemberge-Leda, the artist's widow, December
1972); Gift of Solomon R. Guggenheim,
1937.

CONDITION:

Although the picture was cleaned in 1954
and 1956, considerable soil remains in-
grained in the paint, especially in the background, which is extremely thinly painted.
The thinness of paint application poses considerable cleaning problems which have not
been satisfactorily solved. (Oct. 1972.)

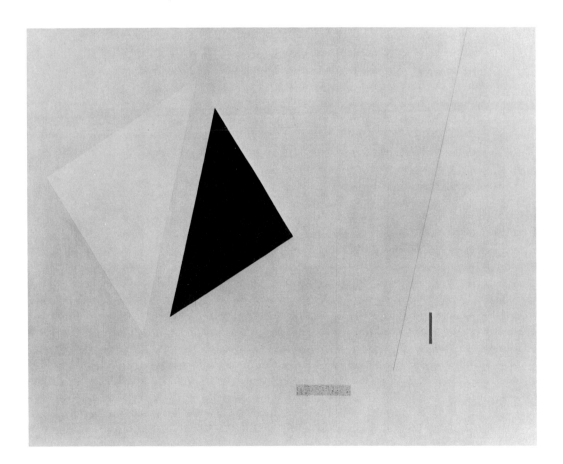

The compositional elements combined in the present picture—two equilateral
but dissimilar triangles in the left of the field, a diagonally placed line with a
small horizontal and a vertical bar on either side of it—are also explored in
Composition No. 112, 1939 (*Oeuvrekatalog* no. 117), and in an undated draw-

ing in the collection of Ilse Vordemberge-Leda (fig. a). Comparison of the two drawings with the painting suggests something of the process by which Vordemberge-Gildewart shifted and altered elements in his design before arriving at an acceptable equilibrium.

Composition No. 108, 1938 (*Oeuvrekatalog* no. 112), is a more symmetrical version of the same composition: the two triangles are now equilateral and identical in size, they are joined together to form a square, and the floating diagonal bar is placed so that its top and bottom are equidistant from the top and bottom edges of the canvas.

fig. a.
Vordemberge-Gildewart, studies related to *Composition No. 97*, pencil on paper, 8¼ x 5¼ in., 21 x 13.3 cm., Collection Ilse Vordemberge-Leda, Rapperswil, Switzerland.

EXHIBITIONS:

Charleston, S. C., SRGM 4-T, no. 190 (incorrect dimensions listed, dated 1936); New York, SRGM 62, no. 2; 78 (checklist); Toronto, SRGM 85-T, no. 71; Vancouver, SRGM 88-T, no. 79, repr.; Montreal, SRGM 93-T, no. 59; London, SRGM 104-T, no. 75; Philadelphia, SRGM 134-T, no. 158; New York, SRGM 144, 151, 153 (checklists); 195 (no cat.); 196 (checklist); 202, p. 35, repr. p. 34; New York, Galerie La Boetie, *Vordemberge-Gildewart: Paintings, Drawings, Collages,* Sept. 14-Oct. 30, 1971 (no cat.); Dallas Museum of Fine Arts, *Geometric Abstraction: 1926-1942,* Oct. 7-Nov. 19, 1972, no. 57, repr.

REFERENCES:

Circle: International Survey of Constructive Art, ed. J. L. Martin, B. Nicholson, N. Gabo, London, 1937, repr. no. 13; M. Bill, "Über Konkrete Kunst," *Das Werk,* 29 Jg., Heft 8, Aug. 1938, repr. p. 250; H.L.C. Jaffe, *Vordemberge-Gildewart, Mensch und Werk,* Cologne, 1971, repr. *Oeuvrekatalog* no. 101.

248   Composition No. 140. 1942.

47.1136

Oil on canvas, 23¾ x 31½ (60.3 x 80)

Signed and dated on stretcher (transcribed but not photographed before replacement of stretcher): *Vordemberge-Gildewart / K. Nᵒ 140 / 1942.*

PROVENANCE:

Purchased from the artist, 1947.

CONDITION:

The picture was restretched on a new stretcher in 1954 and cleaned. In 1956 some cleavage of the paint film had developed and the canvas was impregnated with wax resin from the reverse to arrest it. Some retouching along the left and right margins may date from this time. A traction crack ⅝ in. long in the black triangle striped with green was retouched with watercolor in 1958.

The condition is good. (Oct. 1972.)

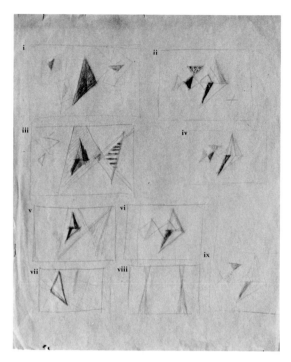

fig. a.
Vordemberge-Gildewart, studies for *Composition No. 140*, pencil on paper, 11⅜ x 9¾ in., 28.9 x 24.8 cm., Collection Ilse Vordemberge-Leda, Rapperswil, Switzerland.

A sheet of sketches in the collection of Ilse Vordemberge-Leda contains three studies for *Composition No. 140* (fig. a, ii, iv, ix). In each the basic configuration is the same and corresponds to that of the painting, but the distribution of textures and designs within the individual triangles varies from sketch to sketch. Each of the three drawings also contains a stippled triangle, an element that was excluded from the final version. A fourth drawing on the same sheet (fig. a, vi) cannot be related definitively to the present painting, for while it contains some of its basic elements it is also sufficiently dissimilar in important details to make a definite connection uncertain.

EXHIBITIONS:

Kunsthalle Basel, *Moderne Holländische Kunst 1885-1945,* May 1946, no. 115 ("*Komposition,* 1942;" the identification of this entry with *Composition No. 140* is derived from the artist's copy of the catalogue, now in the collection of his widow, Ilse Vordemberge-Leda); Lausanne, Musée Cantonal des Beaux-Arts, *Art Hollandais moderne depuis Vincent van Gogh: 1885-1945,* June, 1946, no. 110; Kunsthalle Bern, *Art Hollandais Moderne,* Aug. 3-25, 1946, no. 110; New York, SRGM 59 (checklist); 62, no. 6.

REFERENCES:

A. Roth, "Neue Arbeiten des Malers F. Vordemberge-Gildewart," *Das Werk,* 31 Jg., Heft ii, Nov. 1944, p. ix, repr.; M. Bill, "Pittura Concreta," *Domus,* no. 206, Milan, Feb. 1946, repr. p. 40; J. A. Leerink, "Visie, visioen, visualiteit," *Phoenix, Maandschrift voor beeldende Kunst,* Jg. 1, no. 6, 1946, repr. p. 13; H.L.C. Jaffe, *Vordemberge-Gildewart, Mensch und Werk,* Cologne, 1971, *Oeuvrekatalog* no. 145.

249   Composition No. 150. 1945.

48.1165

Oil on canvas, 29½ x 25⅝ (75 x 65)

Signed and dated on stretcher (transcribed but not photographed before replacement of stretcher): *Vordemberge-Gildewart / Composition Nº. 150 / 1945.*

PROVENANCE:

Purchased from the artist, 1948.

CONDITION:

At an unrecorded date in the 1950's the canvas was lined with wax resin and the stretcher was replaced. At that time some minor inpainting on the right and bottom edges, in the lower right corner, and approximately in the center of the gray area took place.

Apart from some minor scattered abrasions in the paint film and some surface soil, the painting is in good condition. (Oct. 1972.)

This is the only one of Vordemberge-Gildewart's works in which the ground is divided into four major sections. Moreover, a further subdivision of the ground —by means of a thin line cutting from top to bottom across the four sections— occurs in only one other work (*Composition No. 149* of 1945 [*Oeuvrekatalog* no. 154]).

Although no preparatory drawings for *Composition No. 150* exist, several studies have survived in which the artist was clearly experimenting with motifs that were ultimately important for this painting. Two sheets of sketches in the collection of Ilse Vordemberge-Leda (figs. a and b) contain a series of triangles which have been internally subdivided to create smaller triangles, and several pairs of these triangles have been heavily shaded. Two of these paired triangles (fig. a, ii, iii, vi, ix; fig. b, i, v, vi) reappear without their connecting triangular

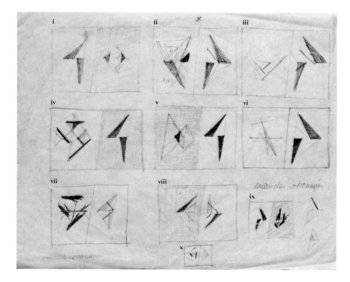

fig. a.
Vordemberge-Gildewart, studies related to *Composition No. 150*, pencil on paper, 8¾ x 11½ in., 22.3 x 29 cm., Collection Ilse Vordemberge-Leda, Rapperswil, Switzerland.

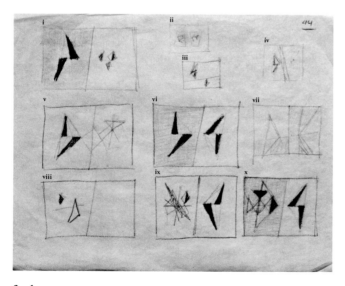

fig. b.
Vordemberge-Gildewart, studies related to *Composition No. 150*, pencil on paper, 8¾ x 11½ in., 22.3 x 29 cm., Collection Ilse Vordemberge-Leda, Rapperswil, Switzerland.

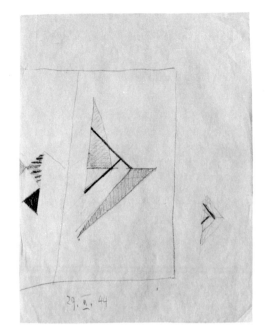

fig. c.
Vordemberge-Gildewart, studies related to
Composition No. 150, pencil on paper,
11½ x 8¾ in., 29 x 22.3 cm., Collection Ilse
Vordemberge-Leda, Rapperswil,
Switzerland.

framework in the right-hand section of *Composition No. 150*. Vordemberge-Gildewart was already exploring the formal possibilities of subdivided triangles as early as 1942, in paintings such as *Composition No. 137*.

The "X" and "Y" motifs in the lower left portion of the present painting derive from patterns in the subdivided triangles of works such as *Composition No. 138*, 1942, and *Composition No. 139*, 1942-43 (*Oeuvrekatalog* nos. 143 and 144). Examples of the "Y" motif are also to be found in the drawing (fig. a, x). A further drawing (fig. c), which relates closely to *Composition No. 140*, also contains a strongly articulated "Y" motif, as well as a pair of juxtaposed triangles nearly identical to those in the upper right-hand section of the present painting.

The drawings reproduced in figs. a, b, and c cannot be specifically identified as studies for the present picture, or for any other existing work by the artist, but they clearly represent the process of experimentation pursued during the years 1943-45, a process that resulted in the execution of *Composition 143, 145, 147-150* (*Oeuvrekatalog* nos. 148, 150, 152-155).

EXHIBITIONS:

New York, SRGM 62, no. 8; New York, Gallery La Boetie, *Vordemberge-Gildewart: Paintings, Drawings, Collages*, Sept. 14-Oct. 30, 1971 (no cat.).

REFERENCES:

Phoenix: Maandschrift voor beeldende Kunst, Jg. 1, no. 4, 1946, repr. p. 21; *Vordemberge-Gildewart: époque néerlandaise*, preface by Jean Arp, Amsterdam, 1949, color pl. 16; H.L.C. Jaffé, *Vordemberge-Gildewart, Mensch und Werk*, Cologne, 1971, *Oeuvrekatalog* no. 155.

Edouard Vuillard

Born November 1868, Cuiseaux.
Died June 1940, La Baule.

250   At the Revue Blanche (Portrait of
Félix Fénéon). 1901.
*(A La Revue blanche [Portrait de Félix
Fénéon]).*

41.725

Oil on board, mounted on gilded board mat
with painted cork overlay. Visible painted
surface, 18¼ x 22⅝ (46.3 x 57.5)

Signed l.l.: *à F. Fénéon bien amicale*[ment]
E. Vuillard; inscribed on reverse, possibly in
Fénéon's hand: *Edouard Vuillard / 1901 /
A La revue blanche (Portrait de M. Félix
Fénéon).*

PROVENANCE:

Félix Fénéon, Paris, 1901-38; purchased
from Fénéon by Solomon R. Guggenheim,
1938; Gift of Solomon R. Guggenheim,
1941.

CONDITION:

The work has received no treatment.

Apart from a 1⅛ in. abrasion with white
transfer material in the lower left corner,
the condition is excellent. (Oct. 1973.)

Félix Fénéon was born in 1861 in Turin. His father was French and his mother
Swiss. In 1881 he moved to Paris where he won a position in the War Ministry.
Within a short time he also embarked upon a distinguished literary career
which he pursued simultaneously with his government responsibilities. In 1884
he founded his first periodical, *La Revue indépendante,* and he later became
one of the principal writers for Gustave Kahn's *La Vogue.* He contributed innumerable articles to the *Revue exotique, Le Symboliste, Le Chat noir, Les
Hommes d'aujourd'hui, La Libre revue, La Cravache, Art et critique, Entretiens
politiques et littéraires,* and *L'Art moderne de Bruxelles.* In addition he wrote
for several anarchist publications (usually under a pseudonym). He published
Mallarmé, Huysmans, Verlaine, Rimbaud, and many other Symbolist writers.
In 1884 he saw and was deeply affected by Seurat's *La Baignade, Asnières;* he
met the artist in 1886 and a close friendship followed. Through Seurat he also
came to know the whole "Neo-Impressionist" group—a term which he himself
invented to differentiate the new generation from the old.

When his friend the poet Jules Laforgue died in 1887 at the age of twenty-
seven, Fénéon became his literary executor and carefully published all of his
remaining writings. When his dear friend Seurat died in 1891 at the age of
thirty-one, Fénéon devotedly shouldered the responsibility for classifying his
works and labored throughout the rest of his life to spread the artist's fame.

In 1888 Gustave Kahn became the editor-in-chief of *La Revue indépendante;*
Fénéon became a major and regular contributor of art, theater, and literary reviews, and he also organized exhibitions on the magazine's premises.

Although Fénéon's identification with the anarchist cause had been limited
to writing art reviews for their periodicals, he was, together with many actual
terrorists, arrested and thrown into prison in April 1894. Later that year he
stood trial in the *Procés des trente* as a member of a terrorist group. The lawyer
Thadée Natanson, who in 1891 had helped to publish the first Paris number of
the *Revue blanche,* arranged for Fénéon to be represented by Demange, the
lawyer who later defended Dreyfus. Natanson had not yet met Fénéon but he
visited him in prison and offered to assist in any way he could. When Fénéon

was finally acquitted and released, he presented himself at the offices of the *Revue blanche* and was hired as editorial secretary. From that time until 1903, when the *Revue blanche* published its last issue, Fénéon was the driving intellectual and literary force behind its success. He was largely responsible for publishing in it every major writer of the day including Verlaine, Apollinaire, Mallarmé, Laforgue, and others. In addition, he organized exhibitions (notably a large Seurat retrospective in 1900) and published books. The enterprise absorbed him totally.

From 1903 to 1906, Fénéon worked for *Le Figaro* and in 1906 for *Le Matin*. That same year he began yet another career—that of art dealer with the Galerie Bernheim-Jeune. By 1908 he was their artistic director, and he promoted the work of Maillol, van Gogh, Matisse, Signac, Cross, Utrillo, Modigliani, Van Dongen, the Futurists, and, of course, Seurat. He retired in 1924, having established the Bernheim-Jeune gallery as one of the most successful in France. Meanwhile from 1919-26, he was the founder and chief inspiration of Bernheim-Jeune's periodical *Bulletin de la vie artistique*.

From 1926-36 he worked on a complete catalogue of Seurat's work, which was to be published by C. M. de Hauke, a French dealer. Fénéon died in February 1944. (The above information on Fénéon is drawn largely from the sensitive and illuminating biographical essay published by Rewald in *Gazette des Beaux-Arts*, sér. 6, vol. 32, July-August 1947, pp. 45-62, and vol. 33, February 1948, pp. 107-126, as well as from the exhaustive chronology published by J. U. Halperin in *Félix Fénéon: les oeuvres plus que complètes*, Geneva, 1970.)

Several other portraits of Fénéon at the *Revue blanche* exist. One, by Vallotton, 1896, shows Fénéon in the identical pose at his desk, absorbed by a manuscript, this time at night (formerly Collection J. Rodrigues-Henriques, Paris, Rewald, 1948, repr. p. 115). A drawing by Bonnard, depicting Regnier, Mirbeau, and the Natanson brothers in the office of the journal, also shows Fénéon at his desk (Ibid., repr. p. 119), as does a pastel by Van Dongen (present whereabouts unknown, Halperin, op. cit., vol. I, pl. VI).

The 1901 date inscribed on the reverse of the present work is stylistically plausible and was probably placed there by Fénéon himself, although the handwriting is difficult to identify with certainty.

EXHIBITIONS:

Paris, Bernheim-Jeune & Cie, *Portraits d'hommes*, Dec. 16, 1907-Jan. 4, 1908, no. 139 (lent by "M.F.F."); Paris, Galerie Les Cadres (chez Bolette Natanson), *Les Peintres de La Revue blanche,* June 12-30, 1936, no. 50; Paris, Galerie Bernheim-Jeune & Cie, *Vuillard: oeuvres de 1890 à 1910,* 1938 (cat. not located, but a label for the exhibition appears on the painting's reverse); New York, SRGM 241 (addenda); 251 (no cat.); Cleveland, SRGM 258-T, pl. 4.

REFERENCE:

J. Rewald, "Félix Fénéon, II," *Gazette des Beaux-Arts,* sér. 6, vol. 33, Feb. 1948, p. 116, repr. p. 117.

Edward Alexander Wadsworth

Born October 1889, Yorkshire.
Died June 1949, London.

251   Composition. 1930.

37.412

Tempera on wood panel, 25 x 30
(63.5 x 76.2)

Signed and dated l.r.: *E Wadsworth 1930*.

PROVENANCE:

Purchased from the artist by Solomon R.
Guggenheim by 1936; Gift of Solomon R.
Guggenheim, 1937.

CONDITION:

The work has received no treatment since
its acquisition.

The edges show rabbet marks from a previous frame and some chips and losses,
especially at the corners. 4 nails embedded
in the stretcher have worked their way
through the paint film and are visible on the
surface, with chipping and loss of the paint
in all 4 areas. Apart from this condition, and
some fine crackle in the vermilion areas, the
condition is good. (May 1974.)

EXHIBITIONS:

Charleston, S.C., SRGM 1-T, no. 107, repr.; Philadelphia, SRGM 3-T, no. 137, repr.;
Charleston, S.C., SRGM 4-T, no. 191, repr.

REFERENCES:

Art of Tomorrow, 1939, no. 412, repr.; J. Rothenstein, *Modern English Painters, Lewis to
Moore*, London, 1956, p. 160.

252   Composition. 1930.

37.413

Tempera on wood panel, 24¾ x 34⅝
(62.7 x 87.9)

Signed and dated l.l.: *E Wadsworth. 1930.*

PROVENANCE:

Purchased from Arthur Tooth & Sons, Ltd.,
London, by Solomon R. Guggenheim,
August 1930; Gift of Solomon R. Guggen-
heim, 1937.

CONDITION:

The picture has received no treatment since
its acquisition, but there is a ½ in. repair
with inpaint 11 in. from the top and 3½ in.
from the left.

The vermilion areas show an overall very
fine crackle pattern with some slight incipient cleavage. This crackle is visible in 1
or 2 other areas. There are some small
blisters in the whites, and a few scattered
minor losses. There is no varnish, and the
work shows moderate surface soil, but the
condition in general is good. (May 1974.)

EXHIBITIONS:

Charleston, S.C., SRGM 1-T, no. 108, repr.; Philadelphia, SRGM 3-T, no. 138, repr.;
Charleston, S.C., SRGM 4-T, no. 192, repr.

REFERENCES:

M. Sevier, "Edward Wadsworth," *Architectural Review,* vol. 72, Sept. 1932, pp. 94-95, repr.;
Sélection chronique de la Vie Artistique XIII, Edward Wadsworth, contributions by W.
George, M. Sevier, O. Zadkine, Antwerp, 1933, repr. p. 62; H. Rebay, "A Definition of Non-
Objective Painting," *Design,* vol. 38, June 1936, repr. p. 5; *Art of Tomorrow,* 1939, no. 413,
repr.

1936 (1-T)   Charleston, S.C., Carolina Art Association, Gibbes Memorial Art Gallery, *Solomon R. Guggenheim Collection of Non-Objective Paintings*, March 1-April 12 (catalogue).

(2-T)   Chicago, Ill., The Arts Club of Chicago, *Paintings by Rudolf Bauer from the Collection of Solomon R. Guggenheim*, May 12-June 6 (checklist).

1937 (3-T)   Philadelphia, Pa., Philadelphia Art Alliance, *Solomon R. Guggenheim Collection of Non-Objective Paintings*, February 8-28 (second enlarged catalogue).

1938 (4-T)   Charleston, S.C., Gibbes Memorial Art Gallery, *Solomon R. Guggenheim Collection of Non-Objective Paintings*, March 12-April 17 (third enlarged catalogue).

1939 (5-T)   Baltimore, Md., The Baltimore Museum of Art, *Solomon R. Guggenheim Collection of Non-Objective Paintings*, January 6-29 (fourth catalogue).

(6-T)   Paris, Galerie Charpentier, *Realités Nouvelles* (including selections from the Solomon R. Guggenheim Foundation): 1re Exposition (1re Série), Oeuvres des artistes français, June 15-28; 1re Exposition (2me Série), Oeuvres des artistes étrangers, June 30-July 15; 2me Exposition, Oeuvres des artistes dont la tendance inobjective s'est volontairement arrêtée avant 1920; Oeuvres des artistes après 1920 (no catalogue; list of participating artists).

1940 (7)   New York, N.Y., Museum of Non-Objective Painting, *Three American Non-Objective Painters: I. Rice Pereira, Balcomb Greene, Gertrude Greene*, January 3-February 14 (no catalogue or checklist).

(8)   New York, N.Y., Museum of Non-Objective Painting, *Eight American Non-Objective Painters: Penrod Centurion, John Ferren, Gerome Kamrowski, Hilla Rebay, Rolph Scarlett, Charles Smith, John von Wicht, Jean Xceron*, February 15-March 30 (no catalogue or checklist).

(9)   New York, N.Y., Museum of Non-Objective Painting, *Charles G. Shaw: Thirteen Recent Paintings*, April 1-May 13 (no catalogue or checklist).

(10)   New York, N.Y., Museum of Non-Objective Painting, *Twelve American Non-Objective Painters: Emil Bisttram, Florence Brillinger, Manuel Essman, Robert Gribboek, Noah Grossman, Lawren Harris, Raymond Jonson, Hanany Meller, Agnes Pelton, Rouben Samberg, Rolph Scarlett, Charles Smith*, May 14-June 27 (no catalogue or checklist).

(11)   New York, N.Y., Museum of Non-Objective Painting, *Three American Non-Objective Painters: Penrod Centurion, Dwinell Grant, Noah Grossman*, June 28-August 5 (no catalogue or checklist).

(12)   New York, N.Y., Museum of Non-Objective Painting, *Six American Non-Objective Painters: Penrod Centurion, Dwinell Grant, Lawren Harris, Raymond Jonson, Rouben Samberg, Stuart Walker,* August 6-September 30 (no catalogue or checklist).

(13)   New York, N.Y., Museum of Non-Objective Painting, *Twelve American Non-Objective Painters: Florence Brillinger, Penrod Centurion, Josette Coeffin, Dwinell Grant, Noah Grossman, Hanany Meller, I. Rice Pereira, Hilla Rebay, Mary Ryan, Rolph Scarlett, Charles Smith, Jean Xceron,* October 1-November 13 (no catalogue or checklist).

(14-T)   Brooklyn, N.Y., Lincoln Gallery, Abraham Lincoln High School, *Non-Objective Art from the Solomon R. Guggenheim Foundation,* October 13-27 (no catalogue or checklist).

(15)   New York, N.Y., Museum of Non-Objective Painting, *Ten American Non-Objective Painters: Penrod Centurion, Josette Coeffin, Manuel Essman, Noah Grossman, Hanany Meller, Marie Menken, I. Rice Pereira, Mary Ryan, Rolph Scarlett, Charles G. Shaw,* November 14-December 31 (no catalogue or checklist).

1941 (16)   New York, N.Y., Museum of Non-Objective Painting, *American Non-Objective Painters,* January 1-February 10 (no catalogue or checklist).

(17)   New York, N.Y., Museum of Non-Objective Painting, *Charles G. Shaw: Twenty-six New Paintings,* February 11-March 9 (no catalogue or checklist).

(18)   New York, N.Y., Museum of Non-Objective Painting, *Ten American Non-Objective Painters: Florence Brillinger, Olga Egeressy, Thomas Eldred, Edward Landon, Lloyd R. Ney, Mary Ryan, Rolph Scarlett, Roland St. John, Edna Tacon, Paul Tacon,* March 11-April 22 (no catalogue or checklist).

(19-T)   Portland, Ore., Pacific Arts Association, Lincoln High School, *Fifteen Non-Objective Paintings from the Solomon R. Guggenheim Foundation,* April 7-23; traveled to Eugene, Ore., University of Oregon, April 28-May 11; Corvallis, Ore., Oregon State College, May 12-30 (held at Corvallis, June, at Foundation's request); Los Angeles, Cal., Chouinard Art Institute, July; San Diego, Cal., Fine Arts Gallery, August; Institute, W. Va., West Virginia State College, September; Massillon, Ohio, The Massillon Museum, October; Normal, Ill., Illinois State Normal University, November (held at Normal, December 1941-January 1942, at Foundation's request); Hazleton, Pa., Hazleton Undergraduate Center, The Pennsylvania State College, February 1942 (no catalogue or checklist).

(20)   New York, N.Y., Museum of Non-Objective Painting, *Paintings and Constructions by Ladislas Moholy-Nagy,* April 24-May 25 (no catalogue or checklist).

(21-T)   Norton, Mass., Wheaton College, *Thirty Non-Objective Paintings from the Solomon R. Guggenheim Foundation,* May-June; traveled to Washington, D.C., The Catholic University of America, July 25-August 10 (paintings returned to New York); South Hadley, Mass., Mount Holyoke Friends of Art, Dwight Art Memorial, Mount Holyoke College, October 3-24; Boise, Idaho, The Boise Art Association, Boise Art Gallery, November; Dallas, Tex., Dallas Museum of Fine Arts, January 4-24, 1942; Pullman, Wash., The State College of Washington, February 22-March 25, 1942; Des Moines, Iowa, Des Moines Association of Fine Arts, April 1942; Detroit, Mich., Women's City Club of Detroit, May 1942 (no catalogue or checklist).

(22)   New York, N.Y., Museum of Non-Objective Painting, *Eight American Non-Objective Painters: Florence Brillinger, Werner Drewes, Dwinell Grant, Maude I. Kerns, Edward Landon, Ted Price, Mary Ryan, Rolph Scarlett,* May 27-June 29 (no catalogue or checklist).

(23)   New York, N.Y., Museum of Non-Objective Painting, *Eight American Non-Objective Painters: Thomas Eldred, Dwinell Grant, Noah Grossman, Marguerite Hohenberg, Ladislas Moholy-Nagy, Otto Nebel, I. Rice Pereira, Rolph Scarlett,* July 25-closing date unknown (no catalogue or checklist).

(24-T)   Bennington, Vt., Bennington College, *Twenty-seven Non-Objective Paintings from the Solomon R. Guggenheim Foundation,* October; traveled to Iowa City, Iowa, The State University of Iowa, January 6-26, 1942; Birmingham, Ala., Birmingham Art Club, Public Library, February 1942; Minneapolis, Minn., The University Gallery, University of Minnesota, March 2-31, 1942 (no catalogue or checklist).

(25)   New York, N.Y., Museum of Non-Objective Painting, *American Non-Objective Painters,* November (no catalogue or checklist).

(26)   New York, N.Y., Museum of Non-Objective Painting, *American Non-Objective Painters,* December (no catalogue or checklist).

1942 (27)   New York, N.Y., Museum of Non-Objective Painting, *Guest Exhibition: Drawings and Woodblock Prints by Mary Ryan, John Sennhauser, Charles Smith,* January 1-February 27 (no catalogue or checklist).

(28)   New York, N.Y., Museum of Non-Objective Painting, *Ten American Non-Objective Painters: Noah Grossman, Marguerite Hohenberg, Charles Johnson, Hyman Koppelman, Hans Kraus, Edward Landon, Grischa Metlay, John Sennhauser, Edna Tacon, Paul Tacon,* March 1-May 10 (no catalogue or checklist).

(29)   New York, N.Y., Museum of Non-Objective Painting, *Twelve American Non-Objective Painters: Lucille Autorino, Penrod Centurion, Noah Grossman, Marguerite Hohenberg, Gerome Kamrowski, H. Felix Kraus, Joseph Manfredi, Ladislas Moholy-Nagy, Michael Schlazer, John Sennhauser, Charles G. Shaw, Edna Tacon,* May 11-June 20 (no catalogue or checklist).

(30)   New York, N.Y., Museum of Non-Objective Painting, *Fifth Anniversary Exhibition,* June 25-October 31 (no catalogue or checklist).

(31-T)   Summit, N.J., Summit Art Association, *Non-Objective Paintings from the Solomon R. Guggenheim Foundation,* November 1-15 (no catalogue or checklist).

(32)   New York, N.Y., Museum of Non-Objective Painting, *American Non-Objectives,* November 1, 1942-January 30, 1943 (checklist).

1943 (33-T)   Cazenovia, N.Y., Cazenovia Junior College, *Nine Non-Objective Paintings from the Solomon R. Guggenheim Foundation,* January 12-February 15 (no catalogue or checklist).

(34)   New York, N.Y., Museum of Non-Objective Painting, *American Non-Objectives, Third Group Show Commemorating the Fifth Anniversary of the Solomon R. Guggenheim Foundation,* February 7-June 13 (checklist).

(35-T)   Savannah, Ga., Telfair Academy of Arts and Sciences, *Non-Objective Art from the Solomon R. Guggenheim Foundation,* March 10-April 10 (no catalogue or checklist).

(36)   New York, N.Y., Museum of Non-Objective Painting, *Loan Exhibition,* June 15-October 14 (checklist).

(37)   New York, N.Y., Museum of Non-Objective Painting, *Loan Exhibition,* October 15-closing date unknown (checklist).

1944 (38-T)   Washington, D.C., Arts Club of Washington, *Forty-five Paintings from the Solomon R. Guggenheim Foundation,* January.

(39)   New York, N.Y., Museum of Non-Objective Painting, *Loan Exhibition,* April 18-closing date unknown (checklist).

(40)   New York, N.Y., Museum of Non-Objective Painting, *Loan Exhibition,* October 15-closing date unknown (checklist).

(41-T)   Cazenovia, N.Y., Cazenovia Junior College, *Selections from the Solomon R. Guggenheim Foundation,* November 11, 1944-January 1945 (no catalogue or checklist).

1945 (42-T)   Fort Worth, Tex., Fort Worth Association, Public Library, *Selections from the Solomon R. Guggenheim Foundation,* January 6-March 21 (no catalogue or checklist).

(43)   New York, N.Y., The Museum of Non-Objective Painting, *In Memory of Wassily Kandinsky,* March 15-April 29 (catalogue).

(44)   New York, N.Y., Museum of Non-Objective Painting, *Loan Exhibition,* June 6-closing date unknown (checklist).

(45-T)   Scranton, Pa., Everhart Museum, *Art of Tomorrow,* June 15-September 15 (checklist).

(46)   New York, N.Y., Museum of Non-Objective Painting, *Alice Mattern Memorial,* October-closing date unknown (checklist).

(47-T)   Chicago, Ill., The Arts Club of Chicago, *Wassily Kandinsky Memorial Exhibition,* November (checklist).

(48)   New York, N.Y., Museum of Non-Objective Painting, *Loan Exhibition,* December 5-closing date unknown (checklist).

(49-T)   Milwaukee, Wisc., Milwaukee Art Institute, *Wassily Kandinsky Memorial Exhibition,* December 1945-January 1946 (no catalogue or checklist).

1946 (50-T)   Savannah, Ga., Telfair Academy of Arts and Sciences, *Selections from the Solomon R. Guggenheim Foundation,* February 9-26; some of which traveled to Augusta, Ga., Augusta Art Club, March; Athens, Ga., Southern Art Association, April (no catalogue or checklist).

(51-T)   Anniston, Ala., United Service Organizations, Inc. (USO), *Seventeen Paintings from the Solomon R. Guggenheim Foundation,* April (no catalogue or checklist).

(52-T)   Utica, N.Y., Munson-Williams-Proctor Institute, *Thirty-five Non-Objective Paintings from the Solomon R. Guggenheim Foundation,* April 7-28 (no catalogue or checklist).

(53-T)   Pittsburgh, Pa., Department of Fine Arts, Carnegie Institute, *Memorial Exhibition of Paintings by Wassily Kandinsky (1866-1944),* April 11-May 12 (catalogue).

(54)   New York, N.Y., Museum of Non-Objective Painting, *Loan Exhibition,* June 5-October 14 (checklist).

(55)   New York, N.Y., Museum of Non-Objective Painting, *Loan Exhibition,* October 15, 1946-February 10, 1947 (checklist).

1947 (56)   New York, N.Y., Museum of Non-Objective Painting, *Loan Exhibition,* February 12-closing date unknown (checklist).

(57)   New York, N.Y., Museum of Non-Objective Painting, *In Memoriam Laszlo Moholy-Nagy,* May 15-July 10 (catalogue).

(58)   New York, N.Y., Museum of Non-Objective Painting, *Loan Exhibition,* July 15-closing date unknown (checklist).

(59)   New York, N.Y., Museum of Non-Objective Painting, *Loan Exhibition,* October 15-closing date unknown (checklist).

(60-T) Kunsthaus Zürich, Solomon R. Guggenheim Foundation: *Zeitgenössische Kunst und Kunstpflege in U.S.A.* (selections shown previously at the *Deuxième Salon des Realités Nouvelles*, Palais des Beaux Arts, Paris, July 18-August 17), October 15-December 15 (catalogue); traveled to Karlsruhe, Kunsthalle, as *Gegendstandlose Malerei in Amerika*, March 18-April 18, 1948 (no catalogue or checklist); Munich, Kunstrunde, May-June 1948 (no catalogue or checklist); Städtische Kunsthalle Mannheim, July 1948 (catalogue); Frankfurt am Main, Kunstkabinett, August-September 1948 (henceforth no catalogue or checklist); Kassel, Staatliche Kunstsammlungen, October 1948; Braunschweig, Galerie Otto Ralfs, November 1948; Hamburg, Kunstrunde, December 1948; Hanover, Landesmuseum, January 1949; Dusseldorf, Kunsthalle, 1949 (specific dates unknown); Essen, 1949 (institution and specific dates unknown); Karlsruhe, Kunsthalle, July 1949; Bremerhaven, Firma Nordkunst, November 19-December 25, 1949; Munich, Amerika-Haus, 1950 (specific dates unknown); Bremerhaven, Amerika-Haus, June-August 1950; Hamburg, Amerika-Haus, September 1950; Bremen, Amerika-Haus, October 1950; Hamburg, Amerika-Haus, November 1950; Braunschweig, Amerika-Haus, December 1950.

1948 (61) New York, N.Y., Museum of Non-Objective Painting, *Hilla Rebay,* November 2, 1948-January 16, 1949 (catalogue).

1949 (62) New York, N.Y., Museum of Non-Objective Painting, *European Painters: Otto Nebel, Friedrich Vordemberge-Gildewart, Lotte Konnerth, Hannes Beckmann,* January 18-February 20 (checklist).

(63) New York, N.Y., Museum of Non-Objective Painting, *New Exhibition, American Non-Objective Painters: Jordan Belson, Ilya Bolotowsky, Kenneth Campbell, Svend Clausen, Hohannesian, Ibram Lassaw, Alice T. Mason, Lloyd Ney, Hilla Rebay, Rolph Scarlett, Zahara Schatz, Charles Smith, Lucia Stern, Robert Wolff, Jean Xceron,* February 22-May 29 (checklist).

(64) New York, N.Y., Museum of Non-Objective Painting, *Tenth Anniversary Exhibition,* May 31-October 10 (no catalogue or checklist).

(65) New York, N.Y., Museum of Non-Objective Painting, *Loan Exhibition,* October 11, 1949-February 15, 1950 (checklist).

1950 (66) New York, N.Y., Museum of Non-Objective Painting, *Loan Exhibition,* February 21-June 11 (checklist).

(67) New York, N.Y., Museum of Non-Objective Painting, *Loan Exhibition,* June 20-October 9 (checklist).

(68-T) Nantucket Island, Mass., Kenneth Taylor Galleries of the Nantucket Foundation, Inc., *Selections from the Solomon R. Guggenheim Foundation,* July (no catalogue or checklist).

(69) New York, N.Y., Museum of Non-Objective Painting, *Loan Exhibition,* November 14, 1950-March 1951 (checklist).

1951 (70) New York, N.Y., Museum of Non-Objective Painting, *Loan Exhibition,* April 3-June 17 (checklist).

(71-T) Avon, Conn., Avon Old Farms School, *Selections from the Solomon R. Guggenheim Foundation,* May (no catalogue or checklist).

(72-T) Cazenovia, N.Y., Cazenovia Junior College, *Selections from the Solomon R. Guggenheim Foundation,* October 1-14; traveled to Ithaca, N.Y., New York State College of Home Economics, Cornell University, October 22-November 9; Delaware, Ohio, Lyon Art Hall, Ohio Wesleyan University, November 15-December 9; Columbia,

Mo., University of Missouri, December 13, 1951-January 21, 1952; Tallahassee, Fla., The University Museum and Art Gallery, Florida State University, January 31-February 22, 1952; Jacksonville, Ala., State Teachers College, March 4-26, 1952; Troy, N.Y., Faculty Club, Rensselaer Polytechnic Institute, April 22-May 15, 1952 (selections shown also at the Emma Willard School and the Troy Public Library); New Paltz, N.Y., State Teachers College, State University of New York, May 22-June 22, 1952 (no catalogue or checklist).

(73) New York, N.Y., Museum of Non-Objective Painting, *Loan Exhibition*, November 27, 1951-closing date unknown (checklist).

1952 (74) New York, N.Y., Museum of Non-Objective Painting, *Evolution to Non-Objectivity*, April 29-closing date unknown (checklist).

(75) New York, N.Y., Museum of Non-Objective Painting, *Group Exhibition: Gianni Dova, Elinor Evans, Ben Joppolo, Alberto Martini, Dale McKinney, J. Jay McVicker, Samuel Olkinetzky, Cesare Peverelli, Mauro Reggiani*, Fall (no catalogue or checklist).

(76-T) New Paltz, N.Y., State Teachers College, State University of New York, *Eighteen Non-Objective Paintings from the Solomon R. Guggenheim Foundation*, October 10-November 3; traveled to Garden City, N.Y., Adelphi College, November 7-December 1; Endicott, N.Y., Harpur College, December 5-23; Summit, N.J., January 16-February 2, 1953 (no catalogue or checklist).

1953 (77-T) Rome, Galleria Origine, *mostra fondazione r. solomon guggenheim* [sic] (selections shown previously Paris, Palais des Beaux Arts de la Ville de Paris, *Septième Salon des Réalités Nouvelles,* July 18-August, 17, 1952), January 24-February 20 (catalogue).

(78) New York, N.Y., The Solomon R. Guggenheim Museum, *A Selection,* February 4-May 3 (checklist).

(79) New York, N.Y., The Solomon R. Guggenheim Museum, *Selection II,* May 13-November 22 (checklist).

(80) New York, N.Y., The Solomon R. Guggenheim Museum, *Sixty Years of Living Architecture: The Work of Frank Lloyd Wright,* October 22-December 13 (catalogue).

(81) New York, N.Y., The Solomon R. Guggenheim Museum, *Interim Exhibition of Museum Collection,* December 2-13 (no catalogue or checklist).

(82) New York, N.Y., The Solomon R. Guggenheim Museum, *Younger European Painters: A Selection,* December 3, 1953-May 2, 1954; traveled to Minneapolis, Minn., Walker Art Center, August 8-September 24, 1954; Portland, Ore., Portland Art Museum, October 8-November 14, 1954; San Francisco, Cal., San Francisco Museum of Art, November 26, 1954-January 23, 1955; Dallas, Tex., Dallas Museum of Fine Arts, February 1-27, 1955; Fayetteville, Ark., University of Arkansas, March 7-April 9, 1955; Dayton, Ohio, The Dayton Art Institute, April 15-May 13, 1955; Andover, Mass., Addison Gallery of American Art, Phillips Academy, October 1-31, 1955; Hanover, N.H., Carpenter Art Galleries, Dartmouth College, November 5-December 18, 1955; South Hadley, Mass., Dwight Art Memorial, Mount Holyoke College, January 3-31, 1956; Middletown, Conn., Davison Art Center, Wesleyan University, February 7-March 31, 1956 (catalogue).

1954 (83) New York, N.Y., The Solomon R. Guggenheim Museum, *Interim Exhibition of Museum Collection,* January 5-March 21 (no catalogue or checklist).

(84) New York, N.Y., The Solomon R. Guggenheim Museum, *Selection III,* March 31-May 5 (checklist).

(85-T)   Toronto, The Art Gallery of Toronto, *A Loan Exhibition from the Solomon R. Guggenheim Museum,* New York, April 2-May 9 (catalogue).

(86)   New York, N.Y., The Solomon R. Guggenheim Museum, *Younger American Painters: A Selection,* May 12-September 26; traveled to Portland, Ore., Portland Art Museum, September 2-October 9, 1955; Seattle, Wash., Henry Gallery, University of Washington, October 16-November 13, 1955; San Francisco, Cal., San Francisco Museum of Art, November 15, 1955-January 22, 1956; Los Angeles, Cal., Los Angeles County Museum, February 1-29, 1956; Fayetteville, Ark., University of Arkansas, March 9-April 10, 1956; New Orleans, La., Isaac Delgado Museum of Art, April 15-May 20, 1956 (catalogue).

(87)   New York, N.Y., The Solomon R. Guggenheim Museum, *Selection IV,* October 6, 1954-February 27, 1955 (checklist).

(88-T)   Vancouver, B.C., Vancouver Art Gallery, *The Solomon R. Guggenheim Museum: A Selection from the Museum Collection,* November 16-December 12 (catalogue).

1955 (89)   New York, N.Y., The Solomon R. Guggenheim Museum, *Interim Exhibition of Museum Collection,* March 1-13 (no catalogue or checklist).

(90-T)   Boston, Mass., Institute of Contemporary Art, *Selected Paintings from the Guggenheim Museum,* March 9-April 17 (no catalogue or checklist).

(91)   New York, N.Y., The Solomon R. Guggenheim Museum, *Robert Delaunay,* March 22-May 22; traveled to Boston, Institute of Contemporary Art, June 2-30 (checklist).

(92-T)   Greensboro, N.C., Woman's College of the University of North Carolina, *Supplementary Exhibition of Drawings,* organized by The Solomon R. Guggenheim Museum, April 1-15; traveled to Atlanta, Ga., Georgia Institute of Technology, April 21-May 5; University, Ala., University of Alabama, May 11-25; Dallas, Tex., The Dallas Museum of Fine Arts, June 1-30; Tulsa, Okla., Philbrook Art Center, July 8-August 5; Long Beach, Cal., Municipal Art Center, August 15-September 15; Reno, Nev., University of Nevada, September 23-October 7; Eugene, Ore., University of Oregon, October 18-November 1; Seattle, Wash., Henry Gallery, University of Washington, November 11-December 30; Missoula, Mont., Montana State University, January 9-21, 1956; remainder of tour cancelled (no catalogue or checklist).

(93-T)   Montreal, Montreal Museum of Fine Arts, *A Selection from the Solomon R. Guggenheim Museum, New York,* June 4-July 3 (catalogue).

(94)   New York, N.Y., The Solomon R. Guggenheim Museum, *Alberto Giacometti,* June 8-July 17 (checklist).

(95)   New York, N.Y., The Solomon R. Guggenheim Museum, *Selection V,* July 27-October 9 (checklist).

(96)   New York, N.Y., The Solomon R. Guggenheim Museum, *Constantin Brancusi,* October 26, 1955-January 8, 1956; traveled to Philadelphia, Pa., Philadelphia Museum of Art, January 27-February 26, 1956 (checklist).

1956 (97)   New York, N.Y., The Solomon R. Guggenheim Museum, *Selection VI,* January 25-May 1 (checklist).

(98-T)   Oberlin, Ohio, Allen Memorial Art Museum, *Supplementary Exhibition of Watercolors,* organized by The Solomon R. Guggenheim Museum, March 1-21; traveled to Cedar Rapids, Iowa, Coe College, March 28-April 19; Albion, Mich., Albion College, April 28-May 12; Hanover, N.H., Carpenter Art Galleries, Dartmouth College, May 21-June 15; Brunswick, Me., Bowdoin College Museum of Fine Arts, June 24-July 22;

University Park, Pa., The Pennsylvania State University, November 1-21; Washington, D.C., Howard University, November 30-December 21; Savannah, Ga., Telfair Academy of Arts and Sciences, January 3-24, 1957; New Orleans, La., Newcomb College, Tulane University, February 2-23, 1957; University, Miss., Fine Arts Center, University of Mississippi, March 3-24, 1957; Lexington, Ky., University of Kentucky, April 2-23, 1957; Collegeville, Minn., St. John's University, May 3-24, 1957; Grand Rapids, Mich., Grand Rapids Art Gallery, June 1-23, 1957 (no catalogue or checklist).

(99-T)   Cornish, N.H., Picture Gallery, Saint-Gaudens Memorial, *Painters of Today*, August 3-September 4 (checklist).

1957 (100-T)   Kalamazoo, Mich., Kalamazoo Institute of Arts, *Supplementary Exhibition of Drawings*, organized by The Solomon R. Guggenheim Museum, February 3-24; traveled to Cedar Rapids, Iowa, Coe College, March 1-31; Beloit, Wisc., Beloit College, April 5-28; Duluth, Minn., College of St. Scholastica, May 5-31; Laramie, Wyo., The University of Wyoming, June 10-August 16; Bozeman, Mont., Montana State College, September 22-October 13; Caldwell, Idaho, The College of Idaho, October 20-November 10; Davis, Cal., University of California, November 17-December 15; Fayetteville, Ark., Arts Center Gallery, University of Arkansas, January 5-26, 1958; Notre Dame, Ind., Art Gallery, University of Notre Dame, February 2-23, 1958; South Hadley, Mass., Dwight Art Memorial, Mount Holyoke College, March 2-23, 1958 (no catalogue or checklist).

(101)   New York, N.Y., The Solomon R. Guggenheim Museum, *Jacques Villon, Raymond Duchamp-Villon, Marcel Duchamp*, February 20-March 10; traveled to Houston, Tex., The Museum of Fine Arts of Houston, March 23-April 21 (catalogue with checklist insert).

(102)   New York, N.Y., The Solomon R. Guggenheim Museum, *Guggenheim International Award, 1956*, March 27-June 7 (checklist). Entries judged in Paris shown at Musée National d'Art Moderne, November 28-December 15, 1956.

(103-T)   Williamstown, Mass., Lawrence Art Museum, Williams College, *Selection of American Paintings from the Solomon R. Guggenheim Museum*, April 8-28; traveled to Middletown, Conn., Davison Art Center, Wesleyan University, May 1-31 (no catalogue or checklist).

(104-T)   London, Tate Gallery, *An exhibition of paintings from the Solomon R. Guggenheim Museum, New York*, April 16-May 26; traveled to The Hague, Gemeentemuseum, June 25-September 1; Helsinki, Ateneumin Taidekokoelmat, September 27-October 20; Rome, Galleria Nazionale d'Arte Moderna, December 5, 1957-January 8, 1958; Cologne, Wallraf-Richartz-Museum, January 26-March 30, 1958; Paris, Musée des Arts Décoratifs, April 23-June 1, 1958 (separate catalogue published by each museum).

(105-T)   Brussels, Palais des Beaux-Arts, *45 Oeuvres de Kandinsky Provenant du Solomon R. Guggenheim Museum, New York*, May 17-June 30; traveled to Paris, Musée National d'Art Moderne, November 15, 1957-January 5, 1958; London, Tate Gallery, January 15-February 28, 1958; Lyon, Musée des Beaux-Arts, March 8-April 6, 1958; Oslo, Kunstnernes Hus, April 18-May 4, 1958; Rome, Galleria Nazionale d'Arte Moderna, May 15-June 30, 1950 (separate catalogue published by each museum).

(106)   New York, N.Y., The Solomon R. Guggenheim Museum, *Recent Acquisitions and Loans*, June 12-August 11 (checklist).

(107) New York, N.Y., The Solomon R. Guggenheim Museum, *Recent Acquisitions and Loans II,* August 21-December 1 (checklist).

(108) New York, N.Y., The Solomon R. Guggenheim Museum, *Piet Mondrian: the earlier years,* December 11, 1957-January 26, 1958; traveled to San Francisco, Cal., San Francisco Museum of Art, February 6-April 14, 1958 (checklist).

1958 (109) New York, N.Y., The Solomon R. Guggenheim Museum, *Sculptures and Drawings from Seven Sculptors,* February 12-April 27 (checklist).

(110-T) Portland, Me., The Portland Museum of Art, *Supplementary Exhibition of Prints, 1958-1959,* organized by The Solomon R. Guggenheim Museum; traveled to Hamilton, N.Y., Colgate University; Cedar Rapids, Iowa, Coe College; Superior, Wisc., State Teachers College; University Park, Pa., The Pennsylvania State University; Scranton, Pa., Marywood College; Charlotte, N.C., Mint Museum of Art; Athens, Ga., The University of Georgia; Talladega, Ala., Talladega College; Ypsilanti, Mich., Eastern Michigan College; Saratoga Springs, N.Y., Skidmore College (no catalogue or checklist).

(111) New York, N.Y., The Solomon R. Guggenheim Museum, *Recent Accessions,* May 14-August 3 (checklist).

(112) New York, N.Y., The Solomon R. Guggenheim Museum, *Selections,* August 13-October 5 (checklist).

(113-T) Baltimore, Md., Baltimore Museum of Art, *Sixteen Paintings by Wassily Kandinsky from The Solomon R. Guggenheim Museum,* September 20-October 31 (no catalogue or checklist).

(114) New York, N.Y., The Solomon R. Guggenheim Museum, *Guggenheim International Award, 1958,* October 22, 1958-February 23, 1959 (catalogue).

1959 (115) New York, N.Y., The Solomon R. Guggenheim Museum, *Twenty Contemporary Painters from the Philippe Dotremont Collection, Brussels,* April 1-May 24 (catalogue).

(116) New York, N.Y., The Solomon R. Guggenheim Museum, *Some Recent Gifts,* April 1-May 24 (checklist).

(117-T) Toronto, The Art Gallery of Toronto, *Paintings by Kandinsky from the Collection of The Solomon R. Guggenheim Museum,* April 24-May 24 (no catalogue or checklist).

(118) New York, N.Y., The Solomon R. Guggenheim Museum, *Inaugural Selection,* October 21, 1959-June 19, 1960 (checklist).

(119-T) Boston, Mass., Museum of Fine Arts, *A Salute to the Guggenheim Museum, Selected Works,* October 30-December 13 (checklist).

1960 (120-T) Ann Arbor, Mich., The University of Michigan Museum of Art, *Images at Mid-Century,* April 13-June 12 (catalogue).

(121-T) Chicago, Ill., The Arts Club of Chicago, *Sculpture and Drawings by Sculptors from The Solomon R. Guggenheim Museum,* April 19-May 19 (checklist with reproductions).

(122-T) Lexington, Ky., University of Kentucky, *European Paintings from The Solomon R. Guggenheim Museum,* May 8-June 19 (catalogue).

(123) New York, N.Y., The Solomon R. Guggenheim Museum, *Before Picasso; After Miró,* June 21-October 20 (checklist).

(124)   New York, N.Y., The Solomon R. Guggenheim Museum, *Guggenheim International Award, 1960,* November 1, 1960-January 29, 1961 (catalogue).

1961 (125)   New York, N.Y., The Solomon R. Guggenheim Museum, *Paintings from the Arensberg and Gallatin Collections of the Philadelphia Museum of Art,* February 7-April 16 (catalogue).

(126)   New York, N.Y., The Solomon R. Guggenheim Museum, *Exhibition of Ceramic Mural by Miró (Untitled,* 1960, lent by Harvard University, Cambridge, Mass., prior to permanent installation), March 30-April 16 (no catalogue or checklist).

(127)   New York, N.Y., The Solomon R. Guggenheim Museum, *Acquisitions, 1953-1961,* April 19-May 21 (no catalogue or checklist).

(128)   New York, N.Y., The Solomon R. Guggenheim Museum, *One Hundred Paintings from the G. David Thompson Collection,* May 26-August 27 (catalogue).

(129)   New York, N.Y., The Solomon R. Guggenheim Museum, *Modern Masters from the Collection of The Solomon R. Guggenheim Museum,* August 30-October 8 (checklist, with some reproductions).

(130)   New York, N.Y., The Solomon R. Guggenheim Museum, *Raymond Parker,* August 30-October 8 (checklist).

(131)   New York, N.Y., The Solomon R. Guggenheim Museum, *Alfred Jensen,* August 30-October 8 (checklist).

(132)   New York, N.Y., The Solomon R. Guggenheim Museum, *Elements of Modern Art,* October 3-November 12; reinstalled January 9-25, 1962 (illustrated commentary, *Elements of Modern Painting,* with checklist insert).

(133)   New York, N.Y., The Solomon R. Guggenheim Museum, *American Abstract Expressionists and Imagists,* October 13-December 31 (catalogue).

(134-T)   Philadelphia, Pa., Philadelphia Museum of Art, *Guggenheim Museum Exhibition: A Loan Collection of Paintings, Drawings, and Prints from The Solomon R. Guggenheim Museum, New York,* November 2, 1961-January 7, 1962 (catalogue).

(135)   New York, N.Y., The Solomon R. Guggenheim Museum, *Chryssa,* November 14-December 17 (checklist).

1962 (136)   New York, N.Y., The Solomon R. Guggenheim Museum, *Sculpture from the Museum Collection,* January 9-February 25 (no catalogue or checklist).

(137)   New York, N.Y., The Solomon R. Guggenheim Museum, *Acquisitions, 1961,* January 9-February 25 (no catalogue or checklist).

(138)   New York, N.Y., The Solomon R. Guggenheim Museum, *Jan Müller, 1922-1958,* January 11-February 25; traveled to Boston, Mass., Institute of Contemporary Art, March 16-April 22 (catalogue).

(139)   New York, N.Y., The Solomon R. Guggenheim Museum, *Fernand Léger: Five Themes and Variations,* February 28-April 29 (catalogue).

(140)   New York, N.Y., The Solomon R. Guggenheim Museum, *Antoni Tàpies,* March 22-May 13 (catalogue).

(141)   Minneapolis, Minn., University Gallery, University of Minnesota, *The Nineteenth Century: One Hundred Twenty-five Master Drawings,* March 26-April 23; traveled to New York, N.Y., The Solomon R. Guggenheim Museum, May 15-June 28 (catalogue).

(142) New York, N.Y., The Solomon R. Guggenheim Museum, *Philip Guston*, May 3-July 1; traveled to Amsterdam, Stedelijk Museum, September 21-October 15; London, Whitechapel Art Gallery, January 1-February 15, 1963; Brussels, Palais des Beaux-Arts, March 1-31, 1963; Los Angeles, Cal., Los Angeles County Museum of Art, May 21-June 30, 1963 (catalogue).

(143-T) Laguna Beach, Cal., Laguna Beach Art Association, *Elements of Modern Art* (selections from The Solomon R. Guggenheim Museum, circulated by the American Federation of Arts), July 1-30; traveled to Salt Lake City, Utah Museum of Fine Arts, August 13-September 3; Washington, D.C., The Phillips Collection, September 17-October 8; Oak Ridge, Tenn., Oak Ridge Community Art Center, October 22-November 12; Durham, N.C., Duke University, November 26-December 17; Oswego, N.Y., State University College Student Union, January 1-22, 1963; Nashville, Tenn., Vanderbilt College, February 5-25, 1963; Greensboro, N.C., Woman's College of the University of North Carolina, March 10-30, 1963; Charleston, Ill., Paul Sargent Gallery, Eastern Illinois University, April 13-May 4, 1963; Clinton, N.Y., Hamilton College, May 18-June 8, 1963; Tampa, Fla., University of Southern Florida, June 22-July 22, 1963; Memphis, Tenn., Brooks Memorial Art Gallery, September 10-30, 1963; Lake Charles, La., Art Association of Lake Charles, October 14-November 4, 1963; Saratoga Springs, N.Y., Hathorn Gallery, Skidmore College, November 18-December 9, 1963; Grand Rapids, Mich., Grand Rapids Art Gallery, January 3-24, 1964; Saginaw, Mich., The Saginaw Museum, February 7-28, 1964 (illustrated commentary, *Elements of Modern Painting*, reprinted November 1962 as *Modern Art: An Introductory Commentary*).

(144) New York, N.Y., The Solomon R. Guggenheim Museum, *Summer Selection, 1962*, July 3-September 30 (checklist).

(145) New York, N.Y., The Solomon R. Guggenheim Museum, *Modern Sculpture from the Joseph H. Hirshhorn Collection*, October 3, 1962-January 20, 1963 (catalogue).

1963 (146-T) Pasadena, Cal., The Pasadena Art Museum, *Vasily Kandinsky, 1866-1944: A Retrospective Exhibition,* organized by The Solomon R. Guggenheim Museum, January 15-February 15; traveled to San Francisco, Cal., San Francisco Museum of Art, March 1-April 1; Portland, Ore., The Portland Art Museum, April 15-May 15; San Antonio, Tex., Marion Koogler McNay Art Institute, June 1-July 1; Colorado Springs, Colo., Colorado Springs Fine Arts Center, July 15-August 25; Baltimore, Md., The Baltimore Museum of Art, September 19-October 20; Columbus, Ohio, The Columbus Gallery of Fine Arts, November 5-December 5; St. Louis, Mo., Washington University Art Gallery, December 22, 1963-January 6, 1964; Montreal, The Montreal Museum of Fine Arts, February 5-March 5, 1964; Worcester, Mass., Worcester Art Museum, March 20-April 20, 1964 (catalogue).

(147) New York, N.Y., The Solomon R. Guggenheim Museum, *Vasily Kandinsky, 1866-1944: A Retrospective Exhibition,* January 25-April 7; traveled to Paris, Musée National d'Art Moderne, April 29-June 24; The Hague, Haags Gemeentemuseum, July 1-August 30; Kunsthalle Basel, September 7-November 7 (catalogue).

(148-T) Worcester, Mass., Worcester Art Museum, *Aspects of Twentieth Century Painting Lent by The Solomon R. Guggenheim Museum, New York*, February 7-April 7 (catalogue).

(149) New York, N.Y., The Solomon R. Guggenheim Museum, *Six Painters and the Object*, March 14-June 2; traveled to Los Angeles, Cal., Los Angeles County Museum of Art,

July 24-August 20; Minneapolis, Minn., Minneapolis Institute of Art, September 3-29; Ann Arbor, Mich., University of Michigan Museum of Art, October 9-November 3; Waltham, Mass., Rose Art Museum, Brandeis University, November 18-December 29; Pittsburgh, Pa., January 17-February 23, 1964; Columbus, Ohio, The Columbus Gallery of Fine Arts, March 8-April 5, 1964; La Jolla, Cal., Art Center in La Jolla, April 20-May 17, 1964 (catalogue).

(150) New York, N.Y., The Solomon R. Guggenheim Museum, *Five Mural Panels Executed for Harvard University by Mark Rothko,* April 9-June 2 (no catalogue or checklist).

(151) New York, N.Y., The Solomon R. Guggenheim Museum, *Museum Collection, Spring, 1963,* April 19-June 2 (checklist).

(152) New York, N.Y., The Solomon R. Guggenheim Museum, *Coins by Sculptors,* May 7-August 26; traveled to Philadelphia, Pa., The Philadelphia National Bank, September 20-27; Waltham, Mass., Brandeis University Library, October 21-November 10; Philadelphia, Pa., Great Eastern Numismatic Society, December (no catalogue or checklist).

(153) New York, N.Y., The Solomon R. Guggenheim Museum, *Cézanne and Structure in Modern Painting,* June 6-October 13 (illustrated commentary with checklist insert).

(154) New York, N.Y., The Solomon R. Guggenheim Museum, *Morris Louis, 1912-1962: Memorial Exhibition,* September 25-October 27 (catalogue).

(155) New York, N.Y., The Solomon R. Guggenheim Museum, *Francis Bacon,* October 18, 1963-January 12, 1964; traveled to Chicago, Ill., The Art Institute of Chicago, January 24-February 23, 1964 (catalogue).

(156) New York, N.Y., The Solomon R. Guggenheim Museum, *20th Century Master Drawings,* November 6, 1963-January 5, 1964; traveled to Minneapolis, Minn., University Gallery, University of Minnesota, February 3-March 15, 1964; Cambridge, Mass., The Fogg Art Museum, Harvard University, April 6-May 24, 1964 (catalogue).

1964 (157) New York, N.Y., The Solomon R. Guggenheim Museum, *Guggenheim International Award, 1964,* January 16-March 9; traveled to Honolulu, Hawaii, Honolulu Academy of Fine Arts, May 14-July 5; Berlin, Haus am Lützowplatz, August 21-September 15; Ottawa, The National Gallery of Canada, October 5-November 9; Sarasota, Fla., John and Mable Ringling Museum of Art, January 16-March 14, 1965; Buenos Aires, Museo Nacional de Bellas Artes, April 20-May 20, 1965 (catalogue).

(158) Washington, D.C., The Washington Gallery of Modern Art, *Vincent van Gogh: Paintings, Watercolors and Drawings,* February 1-March 18; traveled to New York, N.Y., The Solomon R. Guggenheim Museum, April 2-June 28 (catalogue).

(159-T) Tulsa, Okla., Philbrook Art Center, *Elements of Modern Art II* (selections from The Solomon R. Guggenheim Museum, circulated by The American Federation of Arts), March 1-22; traveled to Nashville, Tenn., Vanderbilt University, April 5-26; Charleston, W. Va., Charleston Civic Center, May 10-31; Muskegon, Mich., Hackley Art Gallery, June 14-July 5; Charleston, S.C., Gibbes Art Gallery, September 27-October 18; Saratoga Springs, N.Y., Hathorn Gallery, Skidmore College, November 1-23; Philadelphia, Pa., Tyler School of Fine Art, Temple University, December 6-27; Austin, Tex., Laguna Gloria Art Museum, Inc., January 10-31, 1965; Norfolk, Va., Old Dominion College, February 14-March 7, 1965; East Lansing, Mich., Kresge Art Center, Michigan State University, March 21-April 11, 1965; Montclair, N.J., Montclair Art Museum, May 2-30, 1965 (no catalogue or checklist).

(160) New York, N.Y., The Solomon R. Guggenheim Museum, *Selections from the Museum Collection,* April 2-June 28 (no catalogue or checklist).

(161) New York, N.Y., The Solomon R. Guggenheim Museum, *Frederick Kiesler: Environmental Sculpture,* May 5-June 28 (catalogue).

(162) New York, N.Y., The Solomon R. Guggenheim Museum, *Van Gogh and Expressionism,* July 1-September 13 (illustrated commentary with checklist insert).

(163) New York, N.Y., The Solomon R. Guggenheim Museum, *Albert Gleizes, 1881-1953: A Retrospective Exhibition,* September 15-November 1; traveled to Paris, Musée National d'Art Moderne, December 5, 1964-January 31, 1965; Dortmund, Museum am Ostwall, March 13-April 25, 1965 (catalogue).

(164-T) San Francisco, Cal., San Francisco Museum of Art, *Albert Gleizes, 1881-1953: A Retrospective Exhibition,* organized by The Solomon R. Guggenheim Museum, September 17-November 1; traveled to St. Louis, Mo., City Art Museum of St. Louis, November 19-December 20; Champaign-Urbana, Ill., Krannert Art Museum, University of Illinois, January 9-February 21, 1965; Columbus, Ohio, The Columbus Gallery of Fine Arts, March 11-April 8, 1965; Ottawa, The National Gallery of Canada, April 23-May 23, 1965; Buffalo, N.Y., Albright-Knox Art Gallery, June 1-August 30, 1965; Chicago, Ill., The Arts Club of Chicago, September 20-October 30, 1965 (same catalogue as previous exhibition).

(165) New York, N.Y., The Solomon R. Guggenheim Museum, *American Drawings,* September 17-October 27; traveled to Ann Arbor, Mich., University of Michigan Museum of Art, November 11-December 13; Grand Rapids, Mich., Grand Rapids Art Museum, January 10-February 7, 1965; Minneapolis, Minn., University Gallery, University of Minnesota, February 24-March 21, 1965; Seattle, Wash., Seattle Art Museum, April 8-May 2, 1965; Denver, Colo., The Denver Art Museum, June 6-July 4, 1965; Dallas, Tex., Dallas Museum of Fine Arts, July 25-August 22, 1965; Columbus, Ohio, The Columbus Gallery of Fine Arts, September 12-October 10, 1965; Champaign-Urbana, Ill., Krannert Art Museum, University of Illinois, November 14-December 5, 1965 (catalogue).

(166) New York, N.Y., The Solomon R. Guggenheim Museum, *Alexander Calder: A Retrospective Exhibition,* November 6, 1964-January 31, 1965; half of exhibition traveled to St. Louis, Mo., The Washington University Gallery of Art, February 21-March 26; Toronto, The Art Gallery of Toronto, April 30-May 30; half of exhibition traveled to Milwaukee, Wisc., Milwaukee Art Center, February 25-March 28; Des Moines, Iowa, Des Moines Art Center, April 28-May 30; entire exhibition traveled to Paris, Musée National d'Art Moderne, July 1-October 15 (catalogue with checklist insert).

(167) New York, N.Y., The Solomon R. Guggenheim Museum, *The Shaped Canvas,* December 9-29 (checklist with introductory essay and several reproductions).

1965 (168) New York, N.Y., The Solomon R. Guggenheim Museum, *Eleven from the Reuben Gallery,* January 6-28 (pamphlet with introductory essays and several reproductions; no checklist).

(169-T) Caracas, Ateneo de Caracas, January 10-February 10 and Museo de Bellas Artes, January 10-24, *Evaluación de la Pintura Latinoamericana Años '60,* preliminary version of exhibition, *The Emergent Decade,* organized by The Solomon R. Guggenheim Museum and Cornell University (checklist).

(170) New York, N.Y., The Solomon R. Guggenheim Museum, *Gustav Klimt and Egon Schiele,* February 5-April 25 (catalogue).

1965 (171)   New York, N.Y., The Solomon R. Guggenheim Museum, *William Baziotes: A Memorial Exhibition,* February 5-March 21; traveled to Cincinnati, Ohio, Cincinnati Art Museum, April 9-May 2; Reading, Pa., The Reading Public Museum and Art Gallery, May 23-June 27; Santa Barbara, Cal., Santa Barbara Museum of Art, July 13-August 22; Milwaukee, Wisc., Milwaukee Art Center, September 9-October 10; Waltham, Mass., Rose Art Center, Brandeis University, November 1-30; Utica, N.Y., Munson-Williams-Proctor Institute, December 11, 1965-January 11, 1966; Columbus, Ohio, The Columbus Gallery of Fine Arts, January 27-February 28, 1966; Washington, D.C., The Corcoran Gallery of Art, March 15-April 15, 1966; Minneapolis, Minn., The Minneapolis Institute of Arts, May 15-June 15, 1966; Dallas, Tex., Dallas Museum of Fine Arts, July 4-August 4, 1966; Akron, Ohio, Akron Art Institute, October 10-November 14, 1966 (catalogue).

(172)   New York, N.Y., The Solomon R. Guggenheim Museum, *Illustrations for Opera by Gramatté and Lissitzky,* March 23-April 25 (no catalogue or checklist).

(173)   New York, N.Y., The Solomon R. Guggenheim Museum, *Paintings from the Collection of The Solomon R. Guggenheim Museum,* April 30-October 3 (catalogue).

(174)   New York, N.Y., The Solomon R. Guggenheim Museum, *Masterpieces of Modern Art, by Courtesy of the Thannhauser Foundation,* April 30-October 3 (catalogue with insert of addenda to the exhibition).

(175)   Rotterdam, Museum Boymans-van Beuningen, *de Staël,* May 27-July 11; traveled to Kunsthaus Zürich, July 28-September 5; Boston, Museum of Fine Arts, October 1-November 7; Chicago, Ill., The Art Institute of Chicago, January 7-February 13, 1966; New York, N.Y., The Solomon R. Guggenheim Museum, February 24-April 17, 1966 (catalogue).

(176)   New York, N.Y., The Solomon R. Guggenheim Museum, *Some Recent Gifts,* June (no catalogue or checklist).

(177)   New York, N.Y., The Solomon R. Guggenheim Museum, *Some Recent Gifts II,* July 20-August 29 (no catalogue or checklist).

(178)   New York, N.Y., The Solomon R. Guggenheim Museum, *Jean Xceron,* September 8-October 10; traveled to Providence, R.I., Museum of Art, Rhode Island School of Design, April 7-May 1, 1966; Athens, Zappeion Palace, October 3-30, 1966 (catalogue).

(179)   Ithaca, N.Y., Andrew Dickson White Museum of Art, Cornell University, *The Emergent Decade: Latin American Painters and Painting in the 1960's,* organized by The Solomon R. Guggenheim Museum and Cornell University, October 8-November 8, traveled to Dallas, Tex., Dallas Museum of Fine Arts, December 18, 1965-January 18, 1966; Ottawa, The National Gallery of Canada, April 1-May 1, 1966; New York, N.Y., The Solomon R. Guggenheim Museum, May 20-June 19, 1966; Champaign-Urbana, Ill., Krannert Art Museum, University of Illinois, September 16-October 9, 1966; Lincoln, Mass., DeCordova Museum, November 6- December 4, 1966; Sarasota, Fla., John and Mable Ringling Museum of Art, April 9-May 7, 1967 (monograph; mimeographed checklist).

(180)   New York, N.Y., The Solomon R. Guggenheim Museum, *Edvard Munch,* October 15, 1965-February 20, 1966 (catalogue).

(181)   New York, N.Y., The Solomon R. Guggenheim Museum, *Word and Image,* December 8, 1965-January 2, 1966 (checklist with introductory essay).

1966 (182)   New York, N.Y., The Solomon R. Guggenheim Museum, *The Photographic Image*, January 12-February 13 (checklist with introductory essay).

(183)   New York, N.Y., The Solomon R. Guggenheim Museum, *European Drawings*, February 24-April 17; traveled to Minneapolis, Minn., University Gallery, University of Minnesota, May 10-31; Lincoln, Mass., DeCordova Museum, June 26-September 4; Providence, R.I., Museum of Art, Rhode Island School of Design, September 14-October 8; Ottawa, The National Gallery of Canada, November 28-December 25; Milwaukee, Wisc., Milwaukee Art Center, January 5-February 5, 1967; Atlanta, Ga., The High Museum of Art, March 1-31, 1967; Dallas, Tex., Dallas Museum of Fine Arts, April 15-May 15, 1967; Champaign-Urbana, Ill., Krannert Art Museum, University of Illinois, May 28-June 25, 1967; Raleigh, N.C., The North Carolina Museum of Art, July 15-August 20, 1967 (catalogue).

(184)   New York, N.Y., The Solomon R. Guggenheim Museum, *Vasily Kandinsky, 1901-1914*, Museum Collection and loans, April 19-September 18; loans returned, exhibition reinstalled, November; reinstalled December 4, 1966-February 12, 1967 (no catalogue or checklist).

(185)   New York, N.Y., The Solomon R. Guggenheim Museum, *Barnett Newman, The Stations of the Cross, lama sabachthani*, April 23-June 19 (catalogue).

(186)   New York, N.Y., The Solomon R. Guggenheim Museum, *Museum Collection*, April 23-September 18 (no catalogue or checklist).

(187)   New York, N.Y., The Solomon R. Guggenheim Museum, *Gauguin and the Decorative Style*, June 23-October 23 (illustrated commentary with checklist insert).

(188-T)   Richmond, Va., Virginia Museum of Fine Arts, *Masterpieces from the Collection of The Solomon R. Guggenheim Museum*, circulated in the Virginia Museum's "Artmobile," September 15, 1966-January 15, 1967 (no catalogue or checklist).

(189)   New York, N.Y., The Solomon R. Guggenheim Museum, *Systemic Painting*, September 21-November 27 (catalogue).

(190)   New York, N.Y., The Solomon R. Guggenheim Museum, *Jean Dubuffet 1962-66*, October 27, 1966-February 5, 1967 (catalogue).

(191)   New York, N.Y., The Solomon R. Guggenheim Museum, *Vasily Kandinsky: Painting on Glass (Hinterglasmalerei), Anniversary Exhibition*, December 4, 1966-February 12, 1967 (catalogue).

1967 (192)   New York, N.Y., The Solomon R. Guggenheim Museum, *Paul Klee, 1879-1940: A Retrospective Exhibition*, February 17-April 30; traveled to Kunsthalle Basel, June 3-August 16 (separate catalogue published by each museum).

(193-T)   Pasadena, Cal., The Pasadena Art Museum, *Paul Klee, 1879-1940: A Retrospective Exhibition*, organized by The Solomon R. Guggenheim Museum, February 21-April 2; traveled to San Francisco, Cal., San Francisco Museum of Art, April 13-May 14; Columbus, Ohio, The Columbus Gallery of Fine Arts, May 25-June 25; Cleveland, Ohio, The Cleveland Museum of Art, July 5-August 13; Kansas City, Mo., William Rockhill Nelson Gallery of Art, September 1-30; Baltimore, Md., The Baltimore Museum of Art, October 24-November 19; St. Louis, Mo., Washington University Gallery of Art, December 3, 1967-January 5, 1968; Philadelphia, Pa., Philadelphia Museum of Art, January 15-February 15, 1968 (catalogue).

(194)   New York, N.Y., The Solomon R. Guggenheim Museum, *Joseph Cornell*, May 4-June 25 (catalogue).

(195)   New York, N.Y., The Solomon R. Guggenheim Museum, *Selections from the Museum Collection,* May 4-June 25 (no catalogue or checklist).

(196)   New York, N.Y., The Solomon R. Guggenheim Museum, *Museum Collection, Seven Decades, A Selection,* June 28-October 1 (checklist).

(197)   New York, N.Y., The Solomon R. Guggenheim Museum, *Guggenheim International Exhibition, 1967: Sculpture from Twenty Nations,* October 20, 1967-February 4, 1968; traveled to Toronto, Art Gallery of Ontario, February 24-March 27, 1968; Ottawa, The National Gallery of Canada, April 26-June 9, 1968; Montreal, Montreal Museum of Fine Arts, June 20-August 18, 1968 (catalogue).

(198-T)   New York, N.Y., The Metropolitan Museum of Art, *Selections from The Solomon R. Guggenheim Museum,* November 16, 1967-March 31, 1968 (no catalogue or checklist).

1968 (199)   New York, N.Y., The Solomon R. Guggenheim Museum, *Neo-Impressionism,* February 9-April 7 (catalogue).

(200)   New York, Whitney Museum of American Art, February 14-March 31 and The Solomon R. Guggenheim Museum, February 14-April 7, *Adolph Gottlieb* (joint exhibition); traveled to Washington, D.C., The Corcoran Gallery of Art, April 26-June 2; Waltham, Mass., Rose Art Museum, Brandeis University, September 9-October 20 (catalogue).

(201)   New York, N.Y., The Solomon R. Guggenheim Museum, *Paul Feeley (1910-1966): A Memorial Exhibition,* April 11-May 26 (catalogue).

(202)   New York, N.Y., The Solomon R. Guggenheim Museum, *Acquisitions of the 1930's and 1940's. A Selection of Paintings, Watercolors and Drawings in Tribute to Baroness Hilla von Rebay, 1890-1967,* April 11-May 26 (catalogue).

(203)   New York, N.Y., The Solomon R. Guggenheim Museum, *Harold Tovish,* May 15-June 30 (checklist).

(204)   New York, N.Y., The Solomon R. Guggenheim Museum, *Recent Acquisitions,* May 30-September 8 (no catalogue or checklist).

(205)   New York, N.Y., The Solomon R. Guggenheim Museum, *Rousseau, Redon, and Fantasy,* May 31-September 8 (illustrated commentary with checklist insert).

(206)   San Francisco, Cal., San Francisco Museum of Art, *Julius Bissier, 1893-1965: A Retrospective Exhibition,* September 18-October 27; traveled to Washington, D.C., The Phillips Collection, November 18-December 22; Pittsburgh, Pa., Museum of Art, Carnegie Institute, September 20-February 23, 1969; Dallas, Tex., Dallas Museum of Fine Arts, March 19-April 20, 1969; New York, N.Y., The Solomon R. Guggenheim Museum, May 16-June 29 (catalogue).

(207-T)   Columbus, Ohio, The Columbus Gallery of Fine Arts, *Paintings from The Solomon R. Guggenheim Museum,* October 5, 1968-September 7, 1969 (catalogue).

(208)   New York, N.Y., The Solomon R. Guggenheim Museum, *A Selection of Works by Vasily Kandinsky (1866-1944) from the Museum Collection,* October 8, 1968-January 12, 1969 (no catalogue or checklist).

(209)   New York, N.Y., The Solomon R. Guggenheim Museum, *Mastercraftsmen of Ancient Peru,* October 19, 1968-January 11, 1969; traveled to Los Angeles, Cal., Los Angeles County Museum of Art, March 11-June 1, 1969 (catalogue).

(210)   Los Angeles, Cal., The UCLA Art Galleries, *Jean Arp (1886-1966): A Retrospective Exhibition,* November 10-December 5; traveled to Des Moines, Iowa, Des Moines Art Center, January 11-February 16, 1969; Dallas, Tex., Dallas Museum of Fine Arts, March 12-April 13, 1969; New York, N.Y., The Solomon R. Guggenheim Museum, May 16-June 29, 1969 (monograph by H. Read, *The Art of Jean Arp;* no checklist).

1969 (211)   New York, N.Y., The Solomon R. Guggenheim Museum, *Works from the Peggy Guggenheim Foundation,* January 16-March 23 (catalogue).

(212)   New York, N.Y., The Solomon R. Guggenheim Museum, *Vasily Kandinsky, Selections from The Solomon R. Guggenheim Museum Collection,* February 14-March 9; reinstalled October 12 (no catalogue or checklist).

(213)   New York, N.Y., The Solomon R. Guggenheim Museum, *American Paintings from the Museum Collection,* March 28-May 11 (no catalogue or checklist).

(214)   New York, N.Y., The Solomon R. Guggenheim Museum, *Vasily Kandinsky: Thirteen Paintings from the Museum Collection,* March 28-May 11 (no catalogue or checklist).

(215)   New York, N.Y., The Solomon R. Guggenheim Museum, *David Smith,* March 29-May 11; traveled to Dallas, Tex., Dallas Museum of Fine Arts, June 25-September 1; Washington, D.C., The Corcoran Gallery of Art, October 18-December 7 (catalogue).

(216)   New York, N.Y., The Solomon R. Guggenheim Museum, *European Paintings from the Museum Collection,* April 25-May 11 (no catalogue or checklist).

(217)   New York, N.Y., The Solomon R. Guggenheim Museum, *Nine Young Artists, Theodoron Awards,* May 24-June 29 (catalogue with checklist insert).

(218)   Chicago, Ill., Museum of Contemporary Art, *Laszlo Moholy-Nagy,* May 31-July 12; traveled to Santa Barbara, Cal., Santa Barbara Museum of Art, August 2-September 21; Berkeley, Cal., University Art Museum, University of California, October 2-November 2; Seattle, Wash., Seattle Art Museum, November 20, 1969-January 4, 1970; New York, N.Y., The Solomon R. Guggenheim Museum, February 20-April 19 (catalogue).

(219-T)   New York, N.Y., Art Gallery, Center for Inter-American Relations, *Latin American Paintings From the Collection of The Solomon R. Guggenheim Museum,* July 2-September 14 (catalogue).

(220)   New York, N.Y., The Solomon R. Guggenheim Museum, *Selected Sculpture and Works on Paper,* July 8-September 14 (catalogue).

(221)   New York, N.Y., The Solomon R. Guggenheim Museum, *Collection: From the Turn of the Century to 1914,* September 16-October 12 (no catalogue or checklist).

(222)   New York, N.Y., The Solomon R. Guggenheim Museum, *Larger Paintings from the Museum Collection,* September 18, 1969-January 21, 1970 (no catalogue or checklist).

(223)   New York, N.Y., The Solomon R. Guggenheim Museum, *Roy Lichtenstein,* September 19-November 9 (catalogue).

(224)   Philadelphia, Pa., Philadelphia Museum of Art, *Constantin Brancusi, 1876-1957: A Retrospective Exhibition,* September 25-November 2; traveled to New York, N.Y., The Solomon R. Guggenheim Museum, November 21, 1969-February 15, 1970; Chicago, Ill., The Art Institute of Chicago, March 14-April 26, 1970 (catalogue); Bucharest, Muzeul de Arta R. S. R., June 6-August 20, 1970 (separate catalogue).

(225-T)   Cincinnati, Ohio, Cincinnati Art Museum, *Paintings from the Guggenheim Museum: a loan exhibition of modern paintings covering the period 1949-1965,* October 3, 1969-March 29, 1970 (catalogue).

(226) New York, N.Y., The Solomon R. Guggenheim Museum, *Vasily Kandinsky, 1866-1944: A Selection,* October 14-December 21; reinstalled January 19-February 8, 1970 (no catalogue or checklist).

(227) New York, N.Y., The Solomon R. Guggenheim Museum, *Collection: From the First to the Second World War, 1915-1939,* December 13, 1969-January 18, 1970 (no catalogue or checklist).

1970 (228) New York, N.Y., The Solomon R. Guggenheim Museum, *Kandinsky, Klee, Feininger: 3 Bauhaus Painters,* February 17-April 19 (no catalogue or checklist).

(229) New York, N.Y., The Solomon R. Guggenheim Museum, *Sculpture Selections from the Museum Collection,* February 19-April 5 (no catalogue or checklist).

(230) New York, N.Y., The Solomon R. Guggenheim Museum, *Younger Artists from the Museum Collection,* April 21-September 9 (no catalogue or checklist).

(231) Berkeley, Cal., University Art Museum, University of California, *Pol Bury,* April 28-May 31; traveled to St. Paul, Minn., The College of St. Catherine and Minneapolis, Minn., Walker Art Center, August 2-September 10; Iowa City, Iowa, Museum of Art, University of Iowa, September 20-October 31; Chicago, Ill., The Arts Club of Chicago, November 24, 1970-January 2, 1971; Houston, Tex., Institute for the Arts, Rice University, January 25-March 7, 1971; New York, N.Y., The Solomon R. Guggenheim Museum, April 15-June 6, 1971 (catalogue; Guggenheim Museum published insert listing deletions and additions to the exhibition).

(232) New York, N.Y., The Solomon R. Guggenheim Museum, *Selections from the Guggenheim Museum Collection, 1900-1970,* May 1-September 13 (fully illustrated Handbook, *Selections from the Guggenheim Museum Collection, 1900-1970).*

(233) New York, N.Y., The Solomon R. Guggenheim Museum, *Francis Picabia,* September 18-December 6; traveled to Cincinnati, Ohio, Cincinnati Art Museum, January 6-February 7, 1971; Toronto, The Art Gallery of Ontario, February 26-March 28, 1971; Detroit, Mich., The Detroit Institute of Arts, May 12-June 27, 1971 (catalogue).

(234) New York, N.Y., The Solomon R. Guggenheim Museum, *Carl Andre,* September 29-November 22; traveled to St. Louis, Mo., City Art Museum of St. Louis, May 13-June 27, 1971 (catalogue).

(235) Ottawa, The National Gallery of Canada, *Joaquín Torres-García: 1879-1949,* October 2-November 1; traveled to New York, N.Y., The Solomon R. Guggenheim Museum, December 12, 1970-January 31, 1971; Providence, R.I., Museum of Art, Rhode Island School of Design, February 16-March 31, 1971 (catalogue).

(236) New York, N.Y., The Solomon R. Guggenheim Museum, *The Artist Responds to Crisis: A Sketch for an Exhibition,* October 29-December 3 (no catalogue or checklist).

(237) New York, N.Y., The Solomon R. Guggenheim Museum, *Contemporary Japanese Art: Fifth Japan Art Festival Exhibition,* December 2, 1970-January 24, 1971; traveled to Philadelphia, Pa., Philadelphia Civic Center, February 26-March 28, 1971; Berkeley, Cal., University Museum, University of California, May 25-June 27, 1971 (catalogue).

(238) New York, N.Y., The Solomon R. Guggenheim Museum, *Fangor,* December 18, 1970-February 7, 1971; traveled to Fort Worth, Texas, Fort Worth Art Center Museum, April 4-May 9, 1971; Berkeley, Cal., University Art Museum, University of California, July 6-August 22, 1971 (catalogue).

1971 (239) New York, N.Y., The Solomon R. Guggenheim Museum, *Guggenheim International Exhibition, 1971,* February 12-April 11 (catalogue).

(240) New York, N.Y., The Solomon R. Guggenheim Museum, *Cubist Painters from the Museum Collection,* April 15-June 6 (no catalogue or checklist).

(241) New York, N.Y., The Solomon R. Guggenheim Museum, *Selections from the Museum Collection and Recent Acquisitions, 1971,* June 11-September 12 (Handbook published for SRGM 232, 1970, with printed insert of addenda to the exhibition).

(242) New York, N.Y., The Solomon R. Guggenheim Museum, *A Summer with Children,* exhibition of the Guggenheim Museum's summer program in the arts for inner-city children, September 10-19 (no catalogue or checklist).

(243) New York, N.Y., The Solomon R. Guggenheim Museum, *Ten Young Artists: Theodoron Awards,* September 24-November 7 (catalogue).

(244) New York, N.Y., The Solomon R. Guggenheim Museum, *Piet Mondrian, 1872-1944: Centennial Exhibition,* October 8-December 12; traveled to Kunstmuseum Bern, February 9-April 9, 1972 (catalogue).

(245) New York, N.Y., The Solomon R. Guggenheim Museum, *Robert Mangold,* November 19, 1971-January 2, 1972 (catalogue).

(246) Washington, D.C., National Gallery of Art, *The Drawings of Rodin,* November 20, 1971-January 23, 1972 (catalogue); traveled to N.Y., The Solomon R. Guggenheim Museum, *Rodin Drawings: True and False,* March 10-May 7, 1972 (catalogue with checklist insert).

(247) New York, N.Y., The Solomon R. Guggenheim Museum, *John Chamberlain: A Retrospective Exhibition,* December 22, 1971-February 20, 1972 (catalogue).

(248) New York, N.Y., The Solomon R. Guggenheim Museum, *Museum Collection: Contemporary Prints and Drawings, Selections from the Permanent Collection and New Acquisitions of the 50's and 60's,* December 24, 1971-March 10, 1972 (no catalogue or checklist).

1972 (249) New York, N.Y., The Solomon R. Guggenheim Museum, *Ten Independents: An Artist-Initiated Exhibition,* January 14-February 27 (catalogue with checklist insert).

(250) New York, N.Y., The Solomon R. Guggenheim Museum, *Robert Ryman,* March 3-April 30 (catalogue).

(251) New York, N.Y., The Solomon R. Guggenheim Museum, *Classics in the Collection,* May 9-August 27 (no catalogue or checklist).

(252) New York, N.Y., The Solomon R. Guggenheim Museum, *Kandinsky at the Guggenheim Museum,* May 12-September 5; traveled to Los Angeles, Cal., Los Angeles County Museum of Art, October 3-November 19; Minneapolis, Minn., Walker Art Center, May 5-July 15, 1973 (catalogue).

(253) New York, N.Y., The Solomon R. Guggenheim Museum, *Recent Acquisitions,* May 16-August 27 (no catalogue or checklist).

(254) New York, N.Y., The Solomon R. Guggenheim Museum, *Museum Pieces of the Post-War Era,* September 7-October 15 (checklist).

(255) New York, N.Y., The Solomon R. Guggenheim Museum, *A Year With Children,* September 13-28 (no catalogue or checklist).

(256) New York, N.Y., The Solomon R. Guggenheim Museum, *Amsterdam-Paris-Dusseldorf,* October 6-November 26; traveled to Pasadena, Cal., Pasadena Art Museum, February 20-April 8, 1973; Dallas, Tex., Dallas Museum of Fine Arts, May 2-June 3, 1973 (catalogue).

(257)   New York, N.Y., The Solomon R. Guggenheim Museum, *Joan Miró: Magnetic Fields*, October 26, 1972-January 21, 1973 (catalogue).

(258-T)   Cleveland, Ohio, Cleveland Museum of Art, *Masterpieces from the Solomon R. Guggenheim Museum*, November 15, 1972-February 11, 1973 (catalogue).

(259)   Berkeley, Cal., University Art Museum, *Ferdinand Hodler*, November 22, 1972-January 7, 1973; traveled to New York, N.Y., The Solomon R. Guggenheim Museum, February 2-April 8, 1973; Cambridge, Mass., Busch-Reisinger Museum, Harvard University, May 1-June 22, 1973 (catalogue).

(260)   New York, N.Y., The Solomon R. Guggenheim Museum, *Collection Exhibition*, December 7, 1972-February 22, 1973 (no catalogue or checklist).

(261)   New York, N.Y., The Solomon R. Guggenheim Museum, *Eva Hesse: A Memorial Exhibition*, December 7, 1972-February 11, 1973; traveled to Buffalo, N.Y., Albright-Knox Art Gallery, March 8-April 22, 1973; Chicago, Ill., Museum of Contemporary Art, May 19-July 8, 1973; Pasadena, Cal., Pasadena Art Museum, September 18-November 11, 1973; Berkeley, Cal., University Art Museum, December 12, 1973-February 3, 1974 (catalogue).

1973 (262)   New York, N.Y., The Solomon R. Guggenheim Museum, *American Painters Through Two Decades From the Museum Collection*, February 23-April 1 (no catalogue or checklist).

(263-T)   Rochester, N.Y., Memorial Art Gallery of the University of Rochester, *Works from The Solomon R. Guggenheim Museum Collection*, January 19-July 30 (no catalogue or checklist).

(264-T)   Albany, New York, Albany Institute of History and Art, *Works from The Solomon R. Guggenheim Museum Collection*, February 10-July 29 (no catalogue or checklist).

(265)   New York, N.Y., The Solomon R. Guggenheim Museum, *Jean Dubuffet: A Retrospective*, April 26-July 29 (catalogue); traveled to Paris, Centre National d'Art Contemporain, September 27-December 20 (catalogue).

(266)   New York, N.Y., The Solomon R. Guggenheim Museum *(Selections from the Guggenheim Museum Collection) Recent Acquisitions 1972-73*, August 9-September 3 (no catalogue or checklist).

(267-T)   Danville, Ky., Centre College of Kentucky, *Postwar Painting from The Solomon R. Guggenheim Museum*, September 5-June 2 (no catalogue or checklist).

(268)   New York, N.Y., The Solomon R. Guggenheim Museum, *Richard Hamilton*, September 14-November 4 (catalogue); traveled to Cincinnati, Ohio, The Contemporary Arts Center, January 7-February 14, 1974; Munich, Städtische Galerie im Lenbachhaus, March 15-April 15, 1974; Tübingen, Kunsthalle Tübingen, May 10-June 30, 1974; Berlin, Nationalgalerie, July 16-August 26, 1974 (catalogue).

(269)   New York, N.Y., The Solomon R. Guggenheim Museum, *A Year With Children*, September 21-October 14 (folder with checklist).

(270)   University Park, Pa., Museum of Art, The Pennsylvania State University, *Cuno Amiet, Giovanni Giacometti, Augusto Giacometti: Three Swiss Painters*, September 23-November 4; traveled to Utica, N.Y., Museum of Art, Munson-Williams-Proctor Institute, November 18-December 30; Cambridge, Mass., Busch-Reisinger Museum, Harvard University, February 1-March 9, 1974; New York, N.Y., The Solomon R. Guggenheim Museum, April 5-June 23 (catalogue).

(271) New York, N.Y., The Solomon R. Guggenheim Museum, *Futurism: A Modern Focus: The Lydia and Harry Lewis Winston Collection, Dr. and Mrs. Barnett Malbin,* November 16, 1973-February 3, 1974 (catalogue).

(272) New York, N.Y., The Solomon R. Guggenheim Museum, *Kasimir Malevich,* November 16, 1973-January 13, 1974; traveled to Pasadena, Cal., Pasadena Art Museum, February 4-March 25, 1974 (catalogue).

1974 (273) New York, N.Y., The Solomon R. Guggenheim Museum, *The Graphic Work of Kandinsky,* January 17-February 24; traveled under the auspices of the International Exhibitions Foundation to Cincinnati, Ohio, Cincinnati Art Museum, April 1-30; Little Rock, Ark., Arkansas Arts Center, May 15-June 15; San Antonio, Tex., Marion Koogler McNay Art Institute, July 1-31; Houston, Tex., The Museum of Fine Arts, August 15-September 15; Fort Worth, Tex., Fort Worth Art Center, October 1-31; Kansas City, Mo., William Rockhill Nelson Gallery and Atkins Museum of Fine Arts, November 15-December 15; Davenport, Iowa, Davenport Municipal Art Gallery, January 4-February 2, 1975; Detroit, Mich., The Detroit Institute of Arts, February 15-March 16, 1975; Worcester, Mass., Worcester Art Museum, April 1-30, 1975; Washington, D.C., The Phillips Collection, May 15-June 15, 1975 (catalogue).

(274) New York, N.Y., The Solomon R. Guggenheim Museum, *Within the Decade: Selections from the Guggenheim Museum Permanent Collection,* February 12-March 24 (no catalogue or checklist).

(275) New York, N.Y., The Solomon R. Guggenheim Museum, *Alberto Giacometti: A Retrospective Exhibition,* April 5-June 23 (catalogue); traveled in part to Minneapolis Minn., Walker Art Center, July 13-September 1; Cleveland, Ohio, Cleveland Museum of Art, September 24-October 28; Ottawa, National Gallery of Art, November 15, 1974-January 5, 1975; Des Moines, Iowa, Des Moines Art Center, January 27-March 2, 1975 (catalogue); Montreal, Musée d'Art Contemporain, March 27-May 4, 1975 (catalogue).

(276) New York, N.Y., The Solomon R. Guggenheim Museum, *Concentrations I: Nine Modern Masters from the Guggenheim Museum and Thannhauser Collections,* July 4-September 8 (no catalogue or checklist).

(277) New York, N.Y., The Solomon R. Guggenheim Museum, *Ilya Bolotowsky,* September 20-November 11; traveled to Washington, D.C., The National Collection of Fine Arts, December 21, 1974-February 17, 1975 (catalogue).

(278) New York, N.Y., The Solomon R. Guggenheim Museum, *Jean Dubuffet: Recent Acquisitions and Permanent Collection,* October 1-20 (no catalogue or checklist).

(279) New York, N.Y., The Solomon R. Guggenheim Museum, *Soto: A Retrospective Exhibition,* November 8, 1974-January 26, 1975; traveled to Washington, D.C., The Hirshhorn Museum and Sculpture Garden, September 26-November 9 (catalogue).

(280) New York, N.Y., The Solomon R. Guggenheim Museum, *Masters of Modern Sculpture: The Lydia and Harry Lewis Winston Collection (Dr. and Mrs. Barnett Malbin) and the Guggenheim Museum Collection,* November 19, 1974-February 4, 1975 (no catalogue or checklist).

(281) New York, N.Y., The Solomon R. Guggenheim Museum, *A Year With Children,* November 22, 1974-January 5, 1975 (folder and checklist).

1975 (282) New York, N.Y., The Solomon R. Guggenheim Museum, *Max Ernst: A Retrospective Exhibition,* February 14-April 20 (catalogue); traveled to Paris, Grand Palais, May 15-September 8 (catalogue).

(283)   New York, N.Y., The Solomon R. Guggenheim Museum, *Brice Marden,* March 7-April 27 (catalogue).

(284)   New York, N.Y., The Solomon R. Guggenheim Museum, *Helen Frankenthaler Tiles,* May 2-June 1 (no catalogue or checklist).

(285)   New York, N.Y., The Solomon R. Guggenheim Museum, *Recent Acquisitions,* May 2-June 1 (no catalogue or checklist).

(286)   New York, N.Y., The Solomon R. Guggenheim Museum, *Museum Collection: Recent American Art,* May 11-September 7 (no catalogue or checklist).

(287)   New York, N.Y., The Solomon R. Guggenheim Museum, *Marc Chagall,* June 8-September 28 (catalogue).

(288)   New York, N.Y., The Solomon R. Guggenheim Museum, *Jiří Kolář,* September 12-November 9 (catalogue).

(289)   New York, N.Y., The Solomon R. Guggenheim Museum, *František Kupka, 1871-1957: A Retrospective,* October 10-December 7; traveled to Kunsthaus Zürich, January-March 1976 (catalogue).

APPENDIX

PAINTINGS 1880-1945: WORKS ACQUIRED SINCE 1970*

MAX BECKMANN.

Society (The Party; Gesellschaft). 1931.
Oil on canvas, 43 x 69 (109.2 x 175.2).
Purchased from Catherine Viviano
Gallery, New York, 1970.   70.1927.

MARCEL DUCHAMP.

Apropos of Little Sister
(A Propos de jeune soeur). 1911.
Oil on canvas, 28¾ x 23⅝ (73 x 60).
Purchased from Mary Sisler, New York,
1971.   71.1944.

*These works were acquired when research on the present volumes was too far advanced to
allow for their inclusion. They will be incorporated in subsequent editions of the catalogue.

PAUL KLEE.

Night Feast, No. 176 (Nachtliches Fest, No. 176). 1921.
Oil on board, 19¼ x 23¾ (48.9 x 60.3).
Purchased from Galerie Beyeler, Basel, 1973.   73.2054.

PAUL KLEE.

New Harmony (Neue Harmonie). 1936.
Oil on canvas, 37 x 26 (94 x 66).
Acquired from Galerie Beyeler, Basel, 1971.   71.1960.

MATTA (Robert Matta Echaurren).

Years of Fear. 1942.
Oil on canvas, 44 x 56 (111.8 x 142.2).
Purchased from Harold Diamond, New York, 1972.   72.1991.

JOAN MIRÓ.

The Tilled Field (La Terre labourée).
1923-1924.
Oil on canvas, 26 x 36½ (66 x 92.7).
Purchased from Harold Diamond,
New York, 1972.   72.2020.

PABLO PICASSO.

*The Fourteenth of July
(Le Quatorze juillet).* Montmartre, 1901.
Oil on board mounted on canvas,
19 x 24⅞ (48.3 x 63.2).
Gift of Justin K. Thannhauser, 1964.
64.1707.
Detailed information about this painting
will be included in the forthcoming catalogue of the Thannhauser Foundation
collection.

PHOTOGRAPHIC CREDITS

The photographs of SRGM collection works were made over a period of years by the following:

Hannes Beckmann, Mary Donlon, Paul Katz, Susan Lazarus, and Robert E. Mates, New York.

Works for which no photographers are listed are reproduced by courtesy of their owners.

Courtesy H. Berggruen, Paris: p. 308, fig. a

Courtesy Ida Chagall, Paris: p. 56, fig. a; p. 77, fig. d

Marcel Coen, Marseille: p. 162, figs. a, b; p. 163, fig. e

Robert David: p. 116, figs. a, b

Soňa Divišova, Prague: p. 437, fig. j; p. 439, fig. n

Walter Dreyer, Zurich: pp. 665-666, figs. a-e; p. 668, figs. b-d

Jean Dubout, Paris: p. 235, fig. f; p. 306, fig. a; p. 364, fig. a; p. 438, fig. k; p. 440, fig. r

Tor Eigeland: p. 516, fig. a

Etienne Hubert, Paris: pp. 81-82, figs. a-d

Jacqueline Hyde, Paris: p. 197, fig. a

Courtesy Paul Klee Stiftung, Kunstmuseum Bern, © 1975, Copyright by Cosmopress, Geneva: p. 410, fig. c

Courtesy M. Knoedler & Co., Inc., New York: p. 253, fig. c

Courtesy Galerie Louise Leiris, Paris: p. 463, figs. b-c; fig. b, © S.P.A.D.E.M., Paris, 1976

Ems Magnus: p. 208, fig. a

Courtesy Marlborough Fine Art Ltd., London: p. 395, fig. a; p. 626, fig. a

Robert E. Mates and Mary Donlon, New York, from:

Verzameling Ella Winter, Stedelijk Museum, Amsterdam, Dec. 22, 1961-Jan. 29, 1962, pl. 5: p. 58, fig. a

B. Chagall, *Lumières allumées,* trans. by I. Chagall, illustrations by Marc Chagall, Gallimard, Paris, 1973, p. 256: p. 73, fig. b

G. Schmidt, *Chagall,* Paris, 1952, pl. 4: p. 77, fig. c

Der Sturm, Berlin, Jahrgang IV, Aug. 1913, p. 81: p. 107, fig. i

Ozenfant and Jeanneret, *La Peinture moderne,* Paris, 1924, n.p.: p. 163, fig. g

Grohmann, 1933, pl. 33: p. 233, fig. b

Maîtres français, XIXe et XXe siècles, E. van Wisselingh and Co., Amsterdam, June-Aug. 1958, pl. 25: p. 258, fig. c

Grohmann, New York, 1958, no. 92, p. 265: p. 234, fig. e; no. 82, p. 356: p. 260, fig. h; no. 23, p. 95: p. 267, fig. e; no. 22, p. 94: p. 267, fig. f; p. 130: p. 270, fig. g; p. 176: p. 322, fig. a

XXe Siècle, vol. xxvii, Dec. 1966, p. 121: p. 376, fig. a

INDEX*

---

*References to Solomon R. Guggenheim and to The
Solomon R. Guggenheim Museum are not included
in the Index. The EXHIBITIONS and REFERENCES sections of each catalogue entry and the Chronological
List of Exhibitions have not been indexed. Exhibitions and references have been indexed, however,
when they are discussed in the text or in footnotes.

4000 copies of this catalogue, designed by
Malcolm Grear Designers, typeset by
Dumar Typesetting, Inc., have been printed
by The Meriden Gravure Company in
April 1976 for the Trustees of The Solomon
R. Guggenheim Foundation.